*Imagine
waking up tomorrow,
all music has disappeared.
All musical instruments,
all forms of recorded music,
gone.*

A world without music.

*What is more, you cannot even remember
what music sounded like or how it was made.
You can only remember that it had existed,
that it had been important to you and your civilisation.
And you long to hear it once more.*

*Then imagine
people coming together to make music
with nothing but their voices,
and with no knowledge of
what music should sound like.*

NOTICE

ALL RECORDED MUSIC HAS RUN ITS COURSE.

IT HAS ALL BEEN CONSUMED, TRADED, DOWNLOADED,
UNDERSTOOD, HEARD BEFORE, SAMPLED, LEARNED,
REVIVED, JUDGED AND FOUND WANTING.

DISPENSE WITH ALL PREVIOUS FORMS OF MUSIC AND
MUSIC-MAKING AND START AGAIN.

YEAR ZERO NOW.

The 17 IS A CHOIR.

THEIR MUSIC HAS NO HISTORY, FOLLOWS NO TRADITIONS,
RECOGNISES NO CONTEMPORARIES.

The 17 HAS MANY VOICES.

THEY USE NO LIBRETTO, LYRICS OR WORDS; NO TIME
SIGNATURES, RHYTHM OR BEATS; AND HAVE NO KNOWLEDGE
OF MELODY, COUNTERPOINT OR HARMONY.

The 17 STRUGGLE WITH THE DARK
AND RESPOND TO THE LIGHT.

pb Poster 59   2003

BOOK COMING ON
9 March 2006

I can feel a book coming on. You know, like when you get the first inclinations you might need a shit. I had my suspicions that this book coming on might be happening because this morning before I set out on the long day's drive zigzagging up the land, I went into a WH Smith's to buy a couple of Black n' Red lined A4 notebooks and a six-pack of pencils.

The book will be about a choir ... A choir that has existed inside my head for almost a score of years. About how the voices of this choir torment and inflame my imagination. How they provide my internal soundscapes with some of the most beautiful and terrifying music I have ever heard. And how over these past few months I've been dragging this choir out of my head and into some sort of shared reality, and, with the grace of God, I will continue this dragging out over the coming months and years.

This choir is called The17.

It will also be about standing at the end of an era, where all the recorded music that has ever meant anything to you or me or anybody else is speeding its way to irrelevance. The whole canon of recorded music that has been stockpiled over these past 110 years is going rotten, rapidly losing any meaning for anybody except historians and those who want to exploit our weakness for nostalgia.

The very urge to make recorded music is a redundant and creative dead end, not even an interesting option, fit only for the makers of advertising jingles, ring-tones and motion picture soundtracks. The sheer availability and ubiquity of recorded music will inspire forward-looking music-makers to explore different ways of creating music, away from something that can be captured on a CD, downloaded from the internet, consumed on an MP3 player; and the very making of recorded music will seem an entirely two-dimensional 20th-century aspiration to the creative music-makers of the next few decades. They will want to make music that celebrates time, place, occasion. There may be those that want to keep the craft of recorded music alive but we will think of them in the same way as we now think of those who work with bygone art forms, irrelevant in tomorrow's world.

I can't wait to hear the music that is being made in 100 years from now. These notions keep me awake at night with excitement.

Bill Drummond

It's been one of those early March clear blue days, where all of creation seemed fit for bursting into spring. The Blackthorn blossom already out. The first leg of the journey has taken me from north-east London, up the A11 to my workshop in Norwich, where I met up with work colleague John Hirst and loaded up the Land Rover. We headed west on the A47 across the black soil of the Fens and under its vast skies to Peterborough, then up the Great North Road (A1) to Scotch Corner. All the way, the music of The17 has been soaring and grinding and pumping in my head. Thoughts and ideas were desperate to get down my right arm, through the pencil and onto the open page.

Scotch Corner is a roundabout on the A1 a few miles north of Catterick Garrison and a few miles south of Darlington. As well as a roundabout there is a hotel: Scotch Corner Hotel. When I was a kid and lived in Scotland and we were driving down to our granny's in Norwich, we would drive via Penrith over the Pennines to Scotch Corner, then down the A1. Once, we stopped off at this hotel for my mum and dad to have a pot of tea. I thought it was posh. It isn't, or at least it isn't now. John Hirst and I pulled into the Scotch Corner Hotel about 30 minutes ago; it was gone midnight. We had to hammer on the door for some time before the night porter came. We negotiated a deal on a couple of beds.

I am now in my room, cup of tea on the bedside cabinet, notebook open, pencil in hand, and this feeling that a book is coming on is getting intense. The book will draw in all the strands of thought that have led me to instigating The17. And why we may be about to enter the most exciting time in the history of music in the lifetime of anybody alive on the planet today. In it I will also document my attempts to have performed all 17 of the scores I've written for The17. The vague and untrustworthy discipline of memoir-writing will be used to explore and make plain my arguments. So there may be a lot of reaching back to past years, trying to work out what it is that music means to me and how I've got to this point where I am now, where I seem to have this urge to discard everything that has gone before. The technology to record music that evolved over the 20th century, and liberated it in so many ways, now feels like an entrapment. An entrapment that is preventing it from moving forward. Hence the statement 'All recorded music has run its course' that is there in my head clamouring for attention most mornings when I wake up. I want music to break free of these shackles left over from the 20th century and not just for the *Wire* reading new music elite, but for anybody who cares to take part.

6

Tomorrow morning John Hirst and I will be on a ferry sailing out of the Tyne on to the North Sea. The book-writing proper will start then. I will give myself 12 months to get it done. Not that I will be writing all the time – just when moments make themselves available as I get on with the other things in life. The remit will be left loose, I'll just see what comes out of the pencil, just as long as it somehow defines The17, how I got here and where music might be going.

Another sip of tea, another thought. I will make a pact with myself: I will come back to the Scotch Corner Hotel on this very date in 2007, check myself into a room, read everything I've written over the previous 12 months, toss out anything that seems irrelevant, and put what is left into some sort of order. That will be the book.

And this book will also be a gauntlet flung at your feet. Pick it up and rise to the challenge to make or at least embrace music that supersedes or even makes redundant what I am setting out to do with The17.

WARNING: If you are hoping this book will investigate the more high-profile moments of my progress, DO NOT read any further.

LET ME TAKE YOU DOWN
9 March 2006

On board the *Princess of Scandinavia* as it edges out of the River Tyne and into the North Sea. The sky is grey, the sea is greyer and the *Princess of Scandinavia* is a large modern ferry that I won't bother describing. Twenty-six hours from now we should be docking in Gothenburg. Then there is the six-hour drive across to Stockholm in the Land Rover. Once there I will be spending the next two weeks confronting the contradictions that riddle what I am setting out to do. As well as the performances of The17, I am expected to give a number of lectures on what this is all about. The writing done on this ferry crossing will mainly be me banging down all the ideas one after the other that have got me and The17 to here and form the basis of these lectures. No room for ruminations. There will be time enough to ruminate in the coming months. On the homeward-bound journey more notes will be made, comparing and contrasting the realities of The17 in Stockholm against my current aspirations.

'All recorded music has run its course.' I don't know when this whole thing started but for the sake of my own myth-making, let's say it was at 7.21 on 17 February 1967. The story goes back all that way. My dad had already knocked on the bedroom door twice to get me up. It was a school day and my allotted household chores had to be done before I set off with satchel on back.

This was in Corby, a one-industry town of modest size in the English East Midlands. The one industry was steel. The football team was known as the Steel Men. They languished and continue to do so.

I would have been 13 years old, the transistor radio would have been on and tuned to Radio Caroline. This was in the days before Radio 1 or any of the local radio stations existed. If you wanted to listen to pop music, you had to listen to one of the numerous pirate stations broadcasting from ships outside the three-mile exclusion zone on the North Sea. Although I thought pop music was rather girlie I was beginning to listen to it more and more. What they were playing at 7.21 on this morning and what was stopping me getting up was not laziness but the new single by The Beatles. 'Penny Lane was in my ears and in my eyes,' they sang. And it sounded good. This was the third time I had heard it that week.

Our family had invested recently in a record player, a Dansette Monarch to be precise. I had no records but my big sister had bought a long player (LP) by a jazz singer that one of her teachers knew. My mum had bought the soundtrack to The Sound Of Music and my dad had got an extended player (EP) by Jimmy Shand & His Band. It was a year or so before my younger brother was to buy *The Laughing Gnome* by David Bowie. As I lay there and wondered what a 'fish and finger sky' might be like, I decided to buy a copy of this record. This was going to be the first time I had ever spent my pocket money on anything but fishing tackle and going to the pictures.

After school that day I walked the two miles into town and into the HMV record shop on the market square. I felt inhibited. I was walking into a teenage world, where everyone seemed to know what to say, how to look and where to find it. 'Could I have *Penny Lane*, the new single out this week by The Beatles, please?' I mumbled. Without reply the surly 17-year-old pulled it off the shelf and slipped it into a brown paper bag. 'Eight and sixpence.' I counted out the eight shillings and six pence, handed it over and was handed back the brown paper bag. I walked the two miles home. This small purchase meant nothing in that day's global commerce, meant a little bit to the day's takings in that particular branch of an HMV record shop, but to me it was my first step towards being a teenager, into a world beyond what my parents and teachers knew about. This, for me, was uncharted territory. And uncharted territory is my favourite sort.

At home I plugged in the record player, lifted the lid, switched it on, watched the light grow red and bright as it warmed up. While it was warming I slipped the record from the sleeve. Although the sleeve was only paper, as all the 7" single sleeves of the day were, it was not a generic record company sleeve with a circular hole cut out of the middle so you could see the label and all its details: this was a picture sleeve. On one side were four individual photographs of The Beatles and on the other ... well, I won't describe what that was like as I have since learnt that my memory recalls it differently to what the reality was.

If ever given the choice, I would always choose my fallible memory over the facts, preserved in the cool and indifferent light of day, but I don't expect you to.

Although I had never bought a 7" single before, I knew what they looked like. I knew only EPs with four tracks on them – which cost somewhat more than a single – had a picture sleeve. The fact *Penny Lane* had a picture sleeve made it seem important in my eyes. At that time I would never have heard the word marketing or been aware of its evil ways. This 7" single had a picture sleeve because the record deserved it.

In those days record players had those tall spindles with a ratchet so you could stack up half-a-dozen singles at a time, each one dropping down to be played one after the other. It seemed a complicated but magical thing to watch. But on that afternoon I had yet to learn how they worked. I had trouble getting my one and only record down the spindle, past the ratchet, to sit on the deck.

The record went around and around and around and around and I watched it, not really knowing what to do next. I lifted the arm, felt butterflies in my belly, and my arm, the one that held the record player's arm, tingled with nerves. Records scratched easily, this much I knew. Still it went round and round waiting for me to make the next move. Then I remembered the speeds – 33, 45 or 78 revolutions per minute (rpm). There was a little switch at the side of the spinning deck. It indicated the deck was spinning at 33 rpm. I switched it up to 45. This seemed impossibly fast. It was now or never. Caution thrown to the wind, I lowered the arm down as gently as possible. The needle hit the groove and the music came. And this was magic, a hurdle overcome and the record sounded as good as it had on the radio that morning. But how were you supposed to listen to a record? Should I leap around the room? Should I recline in an armchair holding my chin between thumb and forefinger in deep contemplation? I did neither. I just stayed there on the floor on my knees, hunched over the record player while staring at the vinyl spinning around and around as the needle made its way to the centre.

When the music finished I lifted the arm and put it on at the beginning again. And again I didn't stop watching the record going around and around. It was as if I was hardly listening to the music, I was too transfixed by the knowledge that this was a big deal in my comparatively short life. Then I remembered that records had things called B sides, so when it had played its way through for the second time I lifted the record off, turned it over, put it back on and dropped the needle into the groove as if I had been doing it for at least as long as I had been riding a bike. Once learnt, never forgotten.

My eyes still staring at the revolving record, the music started.

'Let me take you down
'Cause I'm going to ...'
And wherever he was going, I wanted to go too.

'Nothing is real
And nothing to get hung about.'

And a door opened in my brain, a door into a room that I had never been into before.

'Strawberry Fields forever.
Strawberry Fields forever.
Strawberry Fields forever.'

I played it again and again, seven times, until my mum said it was time for tea.

After tea I asked my mum if I could take the record player up to my room. She said I could.

The rest of the evening was spent listening to *Strawberry Fields* over and over again. I had never heard anything like this before. Until then lyrics in pop records had never held my imagination. They had always been trivial – boy meets girl, boy loses girl stuff or trite novelty nonsense like *Puff The Magic Dragon* or something. But the words in this song alluded to something dark and unknowable. And the music? No jangly happy guitars and drum beats to make your toes tap. This music made pictures in my head that hadn't been there before. One of those pictures is the one that for years I imagined was on the sleeve.

And so to bed.

There I lay, holding this record, staring at this *Strawberry Fields Forever*. I wasn't bothered about taking in the train-spotterish information that was printed on the label – the producer's credit, serial number and all that stuff. What I was staring at were the grooves. This one long scratch in the plastic that coiled around and around, getting tighter and tighter. This one scratch that opened doors in my head into rooms that I didn't even know were there and in these rooms strange and weird pictures hung on the walls. I wasn't particularly interested in the mechanics of how all this worked, how the sound was kept on a mere scratch. I wasn't going to be asking my physics teacher at school about the science of the thing. Never been that bothered about having things explained, just give me the magic.

Over the next few years that walk into town to the HMV record shop on the market square became a regular thing. By the time I was 15 it was every

Saturday, pushing the lengthening hair out of my eyes as I flicked through the album racks. Once I made a list of all the LPs that I wanted. There were 47 altogether. If I could have afforded all those, I would have never wanted for another in my life. In all, I only ever got 13 of those LPs before I went to art school at 17 and decided that buying records and reading music papers was for kids. There was a revolution to be had and barricades to be manned. Of course I never manned any barricades and by the time I was in my mid-20s I was buying records and reading music papers again.

CAUSE I'M GOING TO
9 March 2006

Decades passed. In spring 2002 I was in London walking down Oxford Street, passing the massive HMV record shop there. I strolled in, thought I would spend a few minutes innocently flicking through the racks. Buy a couple of CDs maybe. No sooner was I through the doors than I could feel a dread start to grip me. In front of me, aisle after aisle, rack upon rack of CDs, a sea of choice. Every genre of music known to mankind on offer. There was a credit card in my pocket which would allow me to buy at least ten times those 47 long players that I had once thought would make my music-listening life complete. At a conservative guess there must have been 100,000 different CDs waiting to be purchased.

Over the years my taste in music has broadened; I embraced whole continents of music that I never knew existed when I was 17, from Stockhausen to Stock, Aitken and Waterman. I was into genres before they even knew they existed. I walked away from HMV, unable to flick through even one rack, let alone make a purchase. Just got on with the day's affairs. That evening while doing my emails, the dread began to grip me again. I began to feel that every piece of recorded music that had ever existed was behind the screen of the iMac taunting me. Each with the face of an evil little sprite. 'Bill, Bill, we are here, don't you want us? We will make you happy. Just click your mouse a few times and I'll be on your hard drive in no time at all, enriching your life in so many ways.'

The thing is, when Napster first hit the World Wide Web I thought it was the best thing that had happened in the music business for the last 110 years. Suddenly there was going to be no need to have a music business; who would pay for CDs when you could get it all for free? And if recorded music was as free as the air we breathe vast sums would never be spent on recording the bloated crap that the music business has been encouraging musicians to make ever since Sgt. Pepper's Lonely Hearts Club Band hit the racks of the HMV shop in Corby.

But somehow it was the fact that – in theory at least – I could be listening to any piece of music that has ever been recorded within 60 seconds with just a few clicks of the mouse, that is any piece of music from the entire 110 years of recorded music history, left me with an empty feeling. A rational explanation for this hollowness was not what I required. Instead I went up to the attic of our house, found the box that I used to keep my 7" singles in as a youth, and that same family record player that I still had, and brought them downstairs. In the box was *Strawberry Fields Forever* in its original picture sleeve. It was at that moment that I realised that the artwork was not as I had remembered it.

I plugged in the record player, switched it on, and waited for it to warm up and the red light to glow bright. Stroked a finger across the stylus to make sure it was working, it was. Slid the record from the sleeve and placed it on the deck, still having trouble getting it down the spindle past the ratchet. Gently lifted the arm and lowered the needle into the groove. The first thing to confront my eardrums was decades-worth of scratches, clicks and hisses from the uncared-for vinyl. Looking after records was never a forte of mine. Then the music hit.

'Let me take you down
'Cause I'm going to ...'

And the tears welled up. I did not shift my gaze from the revolving Parlophone label. A tear dropped and hit the vinyl. I sneer at nostalgia in others, hate the way nostalgia is exploited by the marketplace. But most of all I loathe it in myself. A weakness I will not forgive. In growing old we have to accept our thinning hair, sagging flesh, failing eyesight, but we don't have to put up with the surges of nostalgia we get when glimpsing a TV programme we once watched or hearing a snatch of record we once listened to. I've never tried to rationalise my hatred for nostalgia – for me, it is too obvious to have to explain. The record came to an end.

If at any time over the previous 35 years someone had asked me what my all-time favourite single was, I would have said *Strawberry Fields Forever*, not a doubt. It had been the one eternally firm fixture on my Desert Island Discs playlist. The urge to play the record again was resisted. Instead I took it off the turntable and picked up a pair of pinking shears that were lying on the table and cut the record up into as many pieces as I could, dropping the bits into the kitchen bin. I took the Dansette Monarch and 45 box back up into the loft, went to bed and slept soundly.

I had a dream, a dream of ridding the world of every copy of *Strawberry Fields Forever* so that it no longer existed anywhere. The dream logic was that once every copy had been destroyed and it was obliterated from the world there might then be room in my head to experience that thing again with another piece of music. Maybe there would be more doors to open, more rooms to enter, more strange and weird paintings to look at. The next morning a plan was there in my head, waiting for me to follow it. I might not be able to stamp out the likes of *Mojo*, I might not be able to stop The Stooges, The Sex Pistols or even The Velvet Underground from doing their re-form gigs and cash-in tours, but ...

The plan was more practical than the dream I'd had in the middle of the night. I wrote the following words on an A0-size sheet of white card using a big black felt tip: 'Only listen to music written, recorded or released in the previous 12 months by composers, soloists or ensembles who have never released music in any format at any time previous to the last 12 months.' I then stuck the card up on my workroom wall.

Following this self-imposed restriction might not deliver a new *Strawberry Fields Forever* moment which like virginity can never be regained, but it is a well-known fact that most artists produce their best work early in their career. They may refine what they do but you usually get the measure of what they are about on their first outing. It's a bit of a generalisation and there may be plenty of exceptions that prove the rule (The Beatles being one) but my life has passed the halfway point so I don't want to be wasting time on people's third albums when their second sounded nothing more than a polished version of their first.

SCORE

319. LISTEN

LIFE IS SHORT.
AT THE AGE OF 50
ONLY LISTEN TO MUSIC
WRITTEN, RECORDED OR RELEASED
IN THE PREVIOUS TWELVE MONTHS
BY COMPOSERS, SOLOISTS OR ENSEMBLES
WHO HAVE NEVER RELEASED MUSIC
IN ANY FORMAT AT ANY TIME
PREVIOUS TO THE LAST TWELVE MONTHS.

pb Poster 162 2007

'THAT MODERN RUBBISH'
9 March 2006

The following Sunday I started to read the record review page in our paper. I wasn't checking how many stars each release had been given, or what subjective thoughts the critic had about this or that; I just wanted to know if it was the first album by the composer, soloist or ensemble and if it was, I made a note of it. The next morning I would order the disks from Record House record shop in Aylesbury.

This went on for almost a year. I was sticking rigidly to the diet but nearly everything I bought sounded like something I had heard 10, 20 or 30 years before. Nothing seemed even marginally new, radical or risk-taking. Everything was safe, tried and tested, even if it was worthy and done from the heart and they meant it. As the months wore on I would at times be sorely tempted to break my vow. In my workshop there were hundreds of CDs that had been bought or sent to me over the last couple of decades, all stacked up against the wall at the end of the bench in no particular order.

Sometime in the following January I was banging nails into wood. Pet Sounds by the Beach Boys kept catching my eye. 'Bill, Bill! What harm would come of it? Just play me one time. Who would know? One time only and you could go back to that modern rubbish.' He had a point. I mean, who the fuck cares what I listen to? But I felt guilt creeping up on me. I locked the door to my workshop from the inside, not that there would be anybody trying to get in or listen. Kids were at school and my partner was out walking the dogs or something. That said, I had never even told them about this listening habit that I had secretly developed.

Pet Sounds was pulled from the pile, slipped into the CD player and the play button was pressed. It was a repackaged version that included the track *Good Vibrations*. By the time it was halfway through *Good Vibrations* the tears were once again streaming down my cheeks. Could music ever be this good again? This new? This risk-taking? This everything? Look, I knew I had let nostalgia slip behind my defences and play havoc with my better judgement but I was helpless before its power. This felt better than riding a bike down a big hill. After the CD came to an end and was shoved back on the pile I couldn't stop myself. My resolve was in tatters. I put on The Byrds' Greatest Hits. I got my 12-string air guitar out of its case and I was chiming along with *The Bells Of Rhymney*, *Turn, Turn, Turn*, *Mr. Tambourine Man* and soddin' *80,000 Miles High*. As the final track faded I started to pull myself together.

Bill Drummond

I had a problem that needed confronting. One that no 12-step programme could solve.

A new plan was hatched. For the rest of that year I would only listen to music made by bands or composers or soloists whose names or surnames began with B, as in The Beach Boys and The Byrds. So for the rest of 2002 it was Bartok, Bach, Beefheart, Bassie, Broonzy, Belle and Sebastian, Black Box Recorder and hundreds of others that I had never listened to before, but who existed in the B racks in the CD section of our local lending library. I assumed I would work my way through the alphabet year by year, finishing off with A in 2028, the year that I would turn 75. It might seem a long time to wait to listen to the album Crossing The Red Sea by The Adverts but I had never heard it and I loved the title, so I was sure that the wait would be worth it.

In some ways this worked very well. I discovered that although I had liked a couple of singles by Bad Finger when I was young, their albums were dreary tosh. But my biggest discovery was that although I had worshipped the Beatles as a teenager in the late 1960s and *Strawberry Fields Forever* still held its place in my heart, listening to them now bored me shitless. I was forced to come to the vastly subjective conclusion that Sgt. Pepper's is probably the worst thing ever to have happened to pop music.

By early December 2003 I was making a long list of C bands and artists that I could start listening to in the coming January. But then on Christmas Day I (again) thought 'Fuck it' and had a change of plan. While the kids were squabbling and the turkey was roasting I wrote:

> Tear up a sheet of paper into 26 pieces.
> Write a different letter of the alphabet on each of them.
> Screw up the pieces of paper.
> Put them in a carrier bag.
> Draw one out.
>
> Over twelve months,
> The music you choose to listen to
> Must have been written or recorded by composers, soloists,
> or ensembles
> Whose name begins with the letter on the piece of paper
> Drawn from the bag.

Twelve months later,
Repeat the process
Minus the letter already used.

Repeat the process every 12 months
Until the alphabet has been used up.

After I had done that I followed my instructions. The letter P came out. I was filled with relief. I was not going to have to listen to the collected works of The Cars. But I was mildly disappointed that I was not going to be able to play one of the other records in the 45 box in the attic – *On The Road Again* by Canned Heat.

SCORE

320. CHOOSE

Life is shorter.
At the age of 51
Tear up a sheet of paper into 26 pieces.
Write a different letter of the alphabet on each of them.
Screw up the pieces of paper.
Put them in a carrier bag.
Draw one out.

Over twelve months,
the music you choose to listen to
must have been written or recorded
by composers, soloists or ensembles
whose name begins with the letter on the piece of paper
drawn from the bag.

Twelve months later,
repeat the process
minus the letter already used.

Repeat the process every 12 months
until the alphabet has been used up.

pb Poster 163   2007

IT'S OVER
9 March 2006

Between the years 1977 and 1992 I had found myself involved in the making of pop music. It happened by accident but had taken over my life. In 1992 I found the strength of will to put a stop to it. Well, almost. I did have a couple of minor lapses. There were a lot of reasons for wanting to stop doing pop. One of the main reasons was there was all this other stuff I wanted to do. Somehow the whole process of making music didn't allow for this, music being a jealous mistress and all that. I needed to create time and space for the other stuff. 'Music is not my first love and it won't be my last,' to misquote a lyric you might have heard once or twice.

But I kept thinking about music. I would find myself thinking about it more than listening to it. Like, what is music for? And why do we listen to it in the way that we do? And what would it be like if ...? But the big questions seemed to be 'Why am I so frustrated with it?' and 'Why do I want it to be something other than it is?' and 'Why do I want it to exist in some other sort of way than it already does?'

So although my new enforced listening regime was cute and vaguely interesting, it didn't solve a much more fundamental problem I was having with music. A vague answer that I was crawling towards was that it was not the fault of the music itself or my loathing of nostalgia or the lack of anything that seemed to my ears to be truly new. It was that it was recorded; the very fact that the technology for recording music had evolved and that we had recorded music and the means to distribute, broadcast and disseminate it in so many different ways into almost every area of modern life. It seemed that all (or should that be 99.99 percent?) of music being written, composed, created was done to be recorded, and once recorded, to be experienced in a very limited way. And, of course, I know, there is plenty of live music going on all over the place but the vast majority of it exists to promote or imitate recorded music.

As for the music that does not fit this definition and thus avoided being turned into two-dimensional recorded music, available to be listened to on your MP3 when and wherever you want, it will by its very nature be irrelevant to our modem lives. The vast majority of pre-20th century music is now consumed and judged in its recorded form. Most of this music was conceived to be heard at certain times, on specific occasions or at preordained sites, be it marching into war, the crowning of a new monarch, creating moments of spiritual uplift, celebrating a wedding or a Saturday night knees-up. Much of its power came from its alignment with time and place. None of it was conceived for repeated performance wherever and whenever the consumer might want. I don't want to go back to old and irrelevant music from a pre-20th-century era. Any form of revivalism is anathema to me. But recorded music has run its course, it has been mined out. It is so 20th century, like paper money and fossil fuels. Maybe we have the internet to partly thank for this, like we have to thank it for so much else. It has helped speed things up, turning recorded music into this dated thing with little value, like what happened to the German mark during the Weimar Republic.

To a small extent we have seen this already begin to happen in the UK over the last few years with the rise and rise in ticket sales for live gigs and concerts and the falling-off of CD sales. Of course I don't expect many music journalists to agree with this statement, I expect them to tell me that the Arctic Monkey's (or whoever it is when you are reading this) debut album is the cultural event of the moment: "Biggest selling debut album of all time, don't you know".

Yeah well, I ain't going to let that get in my way, now that I'm on a roll.

But of course recorded music will carry on. Adverts and films need soundtracks, DJs need something to spin for people to dance to. But the making of recorded music will no longer be the medium of choice that young creative, risk-taking people will use to expose their souls and make their mark. Yes it will carry on but as a creative hobby in a similar way that people do pottery or mosaics or write tunes for brass bands and other irrelevant art forms from bygone eras. You will be able to do evening classes in it. But nobody will ever again consider the course of culture to be changed with the recording and release of a record. In the words of Roy Orbison, 'It's over.'

And on that sunny morning back in spring 2003 when I realised it was over and recorded music was a dead art form, as dead as silent films were within months of the talkies coming in, only fit for the museum, I sat down and wrote the following words:

> All recorded music has run its course.
> It has all been consumed, traded, downloaded,

Understood, heard before, sampled, learned,
Revived, judged and found wanting.
Dispense with all previous forms of music and
Music-making and start again.
Year zero now.

A clarion call to myself, if no one else.

A SPRAWLING KIND OF THING
10 March 2006

A pleasant night slumbering in my cabin bunk has been had. Breakfast is done, the North Sea is still looking grey and there are still some hours before docking at Gothenburg.

Back to writing.

In May 2003 I was involved in making a film with my work comrades John Hirst and Gimpo. The film related to one of the long-term jobs I'm involved in called *How To Be An Artist*.

How To Be An Artist was begun in 1998 and from the time of this book's publication (2008) will probably take a number of years to complete. It is a sprawling job that includes a book, an exhibition, a performance and the cutting up of a work by the artist Richard Long into 20,000 fractions and the selling of these fractions for a dollar a go. To know how and why and when and what for visit penkiln-burn.com and click on *A Smell Of Sulphur In The Wind.*

The film was of the minimal type that you see in art galleries which are not made to entertain or even educate, but just because you can. The film was over two hours long and featured a Land Rover being driven from Hull at one end of the M62 to Liverpool at the other, from the east coast of England to the west. The soundtrack to the film was to be the sound that happened inside the Land Rover's cab as I drove the route: the noise of the engine; the Today Programme on Radio 4; and me singing along to a Belle and Sebastian CD. After all this was done and I was looking at the film I thought, 'But that is not what I was hearing as I did that journey.'

Those might have been the sounds that were going on in the cab but they were not the ones going on in my head. It took some time before I could work out what it was that was going on in my head. And even when I had worked it out, it took some time to tell anybody else about it. It was a massive choral masterpiece, sung by a massive primeval male voice choir.

Now I have to call a halt to this text about the film and soundtrack here, go back a few years and start a new line of thought which, in time, will get back to the problem with the film soundtrack.

After I stopped being involved with the production of music back in 1992 I was asked on numerous occasions whether I missed making music and whether I'd be doing some more music at some time. The answer to both these questions was an emphatic 'No'. But after a while I realised I was lying, or at least sort of lying.

For many years, decades in fact, I have been drawn to choral music. Any sort, from anywhere in the world, from Bach's St Matthew's Passion to those women in Bulgaria; from some tribes people in New Guinea to the Red Army Choir. Before my voice broke I was in the school and church choirs, but what teenage lad wants to sing in a choir? As an adult it never crossed my mind to go back to it. Over the years I would hear bits of choral music and find myself instinctively drawn to it. It touched me in ways that the whole spectrum of pop music could never do. But it never entered my head to buy a record or CD of choral music.

The choral thing began to feature more and more in my thinking about music after I stopped being involved in music in 1992. I started to have fantasies about making choral music. It captured something of the soul of mankind, not just an individual man or woman's. It involved no one ego, no me, me, me but something of the collective spirit. The thing was, I didn't have a clue about how to go about doing this. I also knew it was typical of somebody who'd had a bit of pop success to think they can do whatever takes their fancy: become a racing car driver, compose symphonies, edit newspapers, save the world – anything.

I dealt with this by not letting on to anybody about my choral fantasies and telling myself that I would not attempt to do any of it until I was over 60. I hoped that at 60 I would be wise enough to know better or if not, that everyone would have forgotten I had once been involved with pop music.

This thinking but doing nothing about choral music ran in parallel with my frustrations with all recorded music. Neither thought-process troubled the other much. It was in 2004, when it was the letter P that had come out of the bag and I was listening to lots of Charlie Parker, Portishead and The Proclaimers, that I discovered the Estonian composer Avro Pärt. I fell in love with what he did, especially his choral stuff. Pärt is very much a living composer, had gone through the whole complex avant-garde thing in his younger years. Since the 1970s he has been making a far more stripped-back, less complex, choral music with a serious spiritual vibe to it. I loved it. Avro Pärt's music in some way gave me confidence about doing choral music, or at least fed my fantasies about doing it.

When I started playing guitar at 15 and could only play a couple of chords I started to have my first fantasy band. Maybe if I had had mates who played guitars and drums and stuff I could have formed a band with them but I didn't so I had to make do with fantasy bands. I would make up names for these bands, sketch out logos for them, design album covers, conduct imaginary interviews with *Rolling Stone* magazine, write songs, even write out set lists and imagine what our concerts would be like.

I would usually have two or three of these fantasy bands going on at the same time and they could be vastly different in sound and style. There could be one like The Incredible String Band, and another heavier and louder than Cream live at the Royal Albert Hall. The thing is, I carried on having these fantasy bands even once I was in real bands. We would be having number ones all over the world but when I went to bed at night I would enter into the world of my fantasy bands. They were always so much better than the real ones I was either in or working with.

By the time I was in my 40s I seemed to have put fantasy bands behind me. I had finally become a proper man. But by the late 1990s I had started to have a fantasy choir that would perform choral music that I might one day compose. Right from its inception the choir in my head had a name: The17. I didn't question why it was called The17. It wasn't until I started going public about this and people asked me what significance the name The17 had that I felt the need to come up with a reason.

When I was about 11 I heard that song on the radio, the one that has the line 'She was just 17, you know what I mean'. I stood there looking at the radio thinking, 'I don't know what you mean. What do you mean?' And I remember that years later I knew exactly what he meant. By that time I had started to have this mental tick about the number 17. Nothing to do with numerology or anything superstitious, but any time I heard the number 17 used in a song lyric it would register in my brain and I would think, 'There's another one.' More than often I would hear the lyric wrong and imagine the number 17 was being sung and on a second hearing I would realise it was not.

Then there is the age of 17; 16 is skitty and frivolous. All 'sweet little sixteen'– sexy but not downright dirty. Can stay out late but not all night. Has no hidden depth. 18 is dull, heavy with the dawning of adult responsibilities. Old enough to vote. Old enough to join the army and kill people. Old enough to have a mortgage. Old enough to have a boring job for life. But 17 is this dark and mysterious age in-between. Well it was for me. An age when – if you are a lad anyway – you can get into the most dark and dreary music that is available for your generation. For me it was Van Der Graf Generator. For you it might have been Killing Joke, Sisters of Mercy, Nirvana, Metallica, The Smiths, Korn or even some sort of weird minimal death techno from the Ukraine.

But there may be another reason. There is a choir from Oxford, England, that specialises in singing what is now called early music, which is music from the 18th century or earlier. I'm a big fan of this choir. They are called The Sixteen. So maybe I was just subconsciously wanting to be like The Sixteen but trying to go one better.

I mentioned above how I had discovered the work of Avro Pärt, but I was not wanting to mimic what he had done. As much as I love what Pärt did, he was from the classical tradition, where it was all still about perfect performances, everything being meticulously played and sung. I didn't want any of that in The17.

If I ever tried to nail the sound that The17 made in my imagination, it was a sprawling kind of thing. There were big loud bits and long soft quiet bits. And there didn't seem to be any words, or at least not words that I could hear. No nice melodies or fancy chords and definitely no instruments. There was something uncontrollable about it. With the music of The17 nothing would ever get resolved. There'd be lots of overtones and strange harmonics, at times almost bordering on the out of tune. They would make a sound that came right from the heart of the collective human subconscious. I got that pretentious. But I didn't care.

So, back to the film of the Land Rover on the M62 and its soundtrack and what to do. What I heard when I was driving the Land Rover alone without the radio on was The17. I still do. They sing along with the rumble of the engine, the rattle of the loose bits and the whistle of the wind through the wing mirrors. I wanted The17 to do the film soundtrack but how could I get this fantasy choir into a recording studio? And even if I dragged them out of my imagination into the recording booth, what would be on the music sheets for them to sing? The gap seemed too wide.

I phoned Kev Reverb in Leicester. If in doubt, phone Kev. Not that he has answers but phoning Kev is a good place to start. Kev Reverb has a small studio called Memphis in Leicester, just by the train station. It is a great place to try things out and Reverb is a good man to try things out with.

We went and recorded the physical sounds inside the cab of the Land Rover as I drove it from Hull to Liverpool again. This time the radio was left off and there was nothing of me singing along to anything, not even any talking, just 2 hours and 19 minutes of throbbing engine, rattling bits, wind through the wing mirror and the whoosh of the other motorway traffic. Kev had a couple of plate microphones for the job. Back in the studio I added a basic keyboard part to the 2 hours 19 minutes of the recording. This keyboard was just a drone, roughly in pitch with the engine. Compromises this early on in the game? I know, I know. It would be there as a guide for The17, whoever they may be, to pitch to. Then Kev Reverb, John Hirst, Rob Vom and myself got around a microphone in the booth. In our headphones we could hear the Land Rover and the keyboard. We started and it came without thinking. The sound of The17 started pouring out of our mouths as if it had been there all along, waiting for the moment it could be released. We couldn't do the whole 2 hours and 19 minutes in one take; we needed a few breaks for liquid refreshment, fag breaks and trips to the bog.

What we did was to be a rough guide for whoever these 17 members of The17 might be. Things were getting real.

I phoned the choirmaster for Leicester Cathedral, told him I was a film-maker and that we were putting the soundtrack for a movie together in Leicester and would his choir be up for some session work? He didn't sound too impressed. Instead he started asking questions about score sheets and parts and I told him it didn't work like that and that if his lads came down the studio of an evening, we could work things out. He said that his choir was very busy with their commitments at the cathedral but he would give it some thought and call back to let me know. I never heard from him again. I felt defeated. Four weeks passed and I was for jacking it in. Then Kev Reverb called. He was all excited. It seemed he had been talking about this film and its soundtrack and The17 at some of the recording sessions he had been doing with local bands in his studio, and that most of these bands had wanted to hear what it sounded like. When Kev played them a bit, they had wanted to get involved and add their voices to the soundtrack. Bit by bit, over the month since we had done the original guide, Kev had built up 17 voices doing it over the whole 2 hours 19 minutes. According to Kev, it was sounding brilliant and he wanted us all to get together, all 17 of us, and do it all the way through in one take.

A couple of weeks later we did – all 17 of us; all these blokes from various Leicester bands and myself. We had a couple of beers and bottles of Jacob's Creek were handed around while we were at this epic. The lights were down; it was almost pitch black except for the orange glow of the monitor lights. It was fantastic. One of the best nights I have ever had. The17 sounded better in reality than in any of my fantasies. The music was dark and foreboding, at times almost frightening; not in a Wagnerian camp sort of way – something far more primal than Wagner could ever have dreamed of. It would have put the shits up the Valkyrie. It was as if we had automatically tuned into the deepest part of our being and it was more male than the roar of a football crowd or the bellow of a bull. This was the music that I had longed to hear.

The drive down the M1 that night heading for home was one of joy. I even picked up a further three points for speeding which took my total over 12 so I got a six-month ban. I lay in bed that night making plans for what a performance by The17 would be like; what the choir members should wear, what sort of places we would play. By the next morning I had changed my mind about some things. For a start I didn't want to hear the recording we had made. However good it sounded, it could never compete with what I had experienced the previous evening. The whole notion of this being a soundtrack to a film got ditched. As it happens the film has never been finished. It seemed irrelevant compared to the sound of The17.

Another thing that had changed was who made up The17. The night before, on my drive down the motorway, I had imagined The17 to be the 17 of us in Leicester dressed up in black military fatigues, blasting out what we had been doing through a massive PA, loads of bottom end, to wildly ecstatic audiences around the globe. Pissing all over Finland's Shouting Men or The Polyphonic Spree or any other vocal ensemble that might exist in the modern world.

What I now decided The17 should be was any 17 people who wanted to come together and perform. The17 would be an idea, not a marketable brand made up of a stable line-up of blokes. Anybody around the globe could use the idea of The17 and do it. Then I wrote down the following instructions that could be performed by any of these would-be 17s.

> Choose a journey.
> Record the sounds within your car or cab
> As you drive your journey.
>
> Find 17 men willing to sing.
>
> Gather The17 together in a darkened room.
> Play them the recording of the journey.

Indicate a dominant note in the recording for them to pitch to.
Ask them to open their mouths and bring forth noise.
Ask them to listen and respond to the noises being produced by the
other singers.

Use your initiative.

After this was written I decided it was a musical score. And as a score it should
be published, in the same way as the Penkiln Burn posters that I do are
published.

It was then that I wrote those words that you may have read earlier.

The17 is a choir.
Their music has no history,
Follows no traditions,
Recognises no contemporaries,
The17 has many voices.
They use no libretto, lyrics or words;
No time signatures, rhythms or beats;
And have no knowledge of melody,
Counterpoint or harmony.
The17 struggle with the dark
And respond to the light.

So although The17 was becoming a reality, the fantasy version of it was
getting bigger than ever. Once all previous forms of music and music-making
had been dispensed with, The17 would be there to start music again all fresh
and pure and unsullied, like Pol Pot's new Cambodia was going to be, Year
Zero. When Pol Pot was doing his worst in Cambodia in the 1970s I was
horrified but fascinated by his whole approach. In one sense he was the worst
dictator that had ever existed but there was something shockingly refreshing
about his approach in attempting to destroy all culture and start again. Of
course it was easy for me to indulge in these thoughts on the other side of the
world in a society where every form of safety net exists for me, should I ever
decide to fall.

SCORE

3. DRIVE

Choose a journey.

Record the sounds within your car or cab as you drive your journey.

Find 17 people willing to sing.

Gather The 17 together in a darkened room.

Play them the recording of the journey.
Indicate a dominant note in the recording
for them to pitch to.
Ask them to open their mouths and bring forth noise.
Ask them to listen and respond to the noises
being produced by the other singers.

Use your initiative.

pb Poster 130   2006

Bill Drummond

AN IMPOSSIBILITY MAYBE
10 March 2006

A few weeks after the recording in Leicester in October 2004, I had an exhibition and series of performance lectures at a gallery in north London. It was to be the *How To Be An Artist* show, the one that the film of the Land Rover was to be part of. Instead of showing the film I thought The17 should give a performance at the gallery during one of my talks. The members of this 17 were people who responded to an article in a local paper. I had invited men with voices who wanted to use them in some sort of primitive music-making to get in touch. The first 17 blokes to respond were chosen to be the next incarnation of The17.

Kev Reverb came down and recorded another journey in the Land Rover. This one was only 11 minutes long, from one bit of north London to the Artsdepot, North Finchley, where the exhibition was. We did one rehearsal, 17 men who had never met each other. All sorts: City slickers, dolees, doctors, road diggers. The lot. And it worked, they all got it. I was convinced I was on to a winner and that The17 being any 17 men willing to sing and follow the score would work. Some of these men had been members of local choral societies, some were singers in local bands, others were just up for having a go.

As for it being men, in my head when I'm driving the Land Rover, the choir I hear is all male voices. Maybe when you are driving, you hear a different blend of voices singing to the sound of the engine and the wind in your wing mirror. If so, you must interpret the score in any way that rings true to you.

A week or so later we did it for real in front of the audience at one of the *How To Be An Artist* performances, but this time it definitely didn't work. It was something else altogether. Having an audience changed the dynamic completely. It changed from being a purely communal experience where the joy was in opening our mouths and bringing forth sound to becoming some form of entertainment where audience satisfaction had to be taken into consideration. I was standing there with my mouth open making this noise, looking at members of the audience in front of me, and all I'm thinking is 'What the fuck must they be thinking of this racket?'

On the drive home I got pulled over by the police for having a faulty backlight. They arrested me for driving while banned. The rest of the night was spent in the cells at Hemel Hempstead police station. While lying on the bench in the cell I came to the firm decision that not only should The17 never be recorded for posterity and have no fixed line-up, but also that they should never do any kind of performance for any kind of audience. For The17 to have any relevance and potency it should stand outside of all known recorded music and it should never be a mere entertainment for others to gawp at.

Maybe The17 was evolving into something I could use to explore some of my frustrations with music as a whole. Maybe even the systems I had evolved for listening to music, like getting rid of your favourite piece of music in the world, could all be part of this same thing. They could exist as scores to be performed by would-be members of The17 anywhere.

The job of The17 was not to make great music or even totally original music but to make music as if no other music had ever existed before. An impossibility maybe. But to make music that was not about selling petty rebellion, teenage aspirations to cool, the confessional outpourings of the sensitive, or even the one-time contender still desperately trying to cut it, seemed like a very exciting thing to me. That this music could in some way exist so that other music could follow it in directions as yet unknown would be the ultimate achievement.

Bill Drummond

DIGGING DITCHES
10 March 2006

I was let out at dawn. The next week I went to court. My brief warned me I could get a six-month jail sentence for driving while on a ban so I went to court prepared. In my bag I had a toothbrush, a pair of pyjamas and a copy of *Moby Dick*. I got let off with 60 hours' community service.

We moved house. Christmas came and went. Community service was digging ditches on the Norfolk Broads. It was a bunch of drug dealers, muggers, housebreakers and repeat-offending petty criminals and me. Not quite working on a chain gang like Cool Hand Luke but pretty cool anyway as it was January and the snow fell and the wind blew. The thing is though, I loved it. Good honest hard work. Digging ditches is just what you need to get fit and get your head clear for some serious thinking.

So I thought all these thoughts as I swung my pickaxe. Ideas started to develop about the nature of music; about where it's at and where it's going. I revelled in the romanticism of it all, like I was some Delta bluesman back in the 1920s working on Parchment Farm inventing the blues or something. On scraps of paper I would scribble ideas for other scores I wanted to do. I know that must sound like some desperate attempt at myth-building but hey, these are the facts. Me and Robert Johnson.

Come the middle of February my community service was done. The plan was to turn all those thoughts I had been having into a book, along with the 17 scores I had brewing for The17 to perform.

Gwilly Edmondez, who is a lecturer in composition for MA students at Newcastle University, had got wind of what I was up to. I had met Gwilly once before, when I was doing *How To Be An Artist* at Leeds City Art Gallery. He wanted me to come up and work with his students in Newcastle to explore some of this 17 stuff. From there the idea of it working as a public exhibition at Newcastle University's art gallery, The Hatton, was hatched. I would be able to use the exhibition space as a workshop. Members of the public could come along and take part.

Through the rest of February and March I was spending every weekday in the City Library in Norwich, where we had moved to as a family. The pencil scrawled thousands of words across blank pages. The plan was that I write half a book, then do The17 in Newcastle and write the other half. Then personal shit hit a fan of my own making when my partner and the mother of my three youngest children decided it was over and I felt like Roy Orbison sang those songs for me alone. Devastated and heartbroken, my concerns about where we are with music dwindled to nothing compared to the mountain of self-pity I was lumbering around with. The writing ground to a halt as did nearly everything else. The Newcastle thing had to be postponed.

Bill Drummond

THE ELEMENTS AND ALL THAT
10 March 2006

Months passed, life goes on, my concerns about music started to gather force again. An email arrived from a place called Fylkingen in Stockholm. The people there had heard something of what I was doing. They wanted to invite me over to do The17. I did some Google research and learnt that Fylkingen was a music society that had been going since 1933. Its reason for existing is to promote what we once might have called avant-garde music but are now happier to call new music. It seemed all the big names, including Stockhausen and Cage, had done time there. I was flattered by the invite. If Fylkingen was good enough for them, it was good enough for The17.

The Curfew Tower was bought by Drummond in the mid 1990s. The following text appears on **Knuckle Down** (Penkiln Burn Poster 55) – There is an artist's residency. The residency is in The Curfew Tower, Cushendall, County Antrim, Northern Ireland. The Curfew Tower is a fortified building built in the early years of the nineteenth century. It has five floors, one room on each floor. From the ground floor up: dungeon, bathroom, living room, bedroom, bedroom. There is a kitchen adjoining the back of the tower. The Tower has all modern conveniences. The accommodation allows for no more than two artists in residence at any one time. Successful applicants have to find their own way to the Tower. They will be required to knuckle down, making work that is a response to the Tower, the locality or the people of Cushendall. Some aspect or evidence of the work generated by each artist is to be left behind in the tower. This work will form part of The Curfew Tower Collection. The people of Cushendall will make you feel welcome and the local scenery is beautiful. Warnings: The tower has no curtains. There are no grants to be applied for. Don't go to the Tower if you want to escape.
For further details contact In You We Trust c/o Hearth Housing, 66 Donegall Pass, Belfast, BT7 1BU, Northern Ireland. Email: mp.hearth@vergin.net

The scores started to take shape, constantly being reworked, some getting dropped to be replaced by others. The cut-off point was last week when all 17 had to be printed and sent off to the framers as did the two NOTICE posters that act almost as manifestos for the whole thing. I got the next two paintings done. Or redone – as with most of the text paintings I do, they get painted and repainted numerous times. After some research done by my colleagues John Hirst and John Baker, some specific hardware and software was bought as well as microphones, stands, a small PA, cables, bits and bobs.

After the *DRIVE* score was fully realised, the next to come was the one that I wanted to do in the Curfew Tower in Cushendall, Northern Ireland.

The Curfew Tower has five floors, a room on each floor; the pentatonic scale has five notes in it and is used in all ancient Celtic and Oriental music. It is the natural scale for pathos and longing. The plan is to do this score at the Cushendall Festival this year (2006).

These are the words for this score, entitled *AGE*, as they are at the moment. They will probably evolve with time.

36

Choose a building with five floors.
On the ground floor gather 17 people aged 70 and over.
Ask them to make non-verbal sounds with their mouths on the note of
F sharp for five minutes.
Record The17.
Ensure their performance draws upon their wisdom.

On the first floor gather 17 people aged between 45 and 69.
Ask them to make non-verbal sounds with their mouths on the note of
G sharp for five minutes.
Record The17.
Ensure their performance draws upon their bitterness.

On the second floor gather 17 people aged between 21 and 44.
Ask them to make non-verbal sounds with their mouths on the note of
A sharp for five minutes.
Record The17.
Ensure their performance draws upon their arrogance.

On the third floor gather 17 people aged between 13 and 20.
Ask them to make non-verbal sounds with their mouths on the note of
C sharp for five minutes.
Record The17.
Ensure their performance draws upon their boredom.

On the fourth floor gather 17 people aged 12 and under.
Ask them to make non-verbal sounds with their mouths on the note of
D sharp for five minutes.
Record The17.
Ensure their performance draws upon their innocence.

Gather the above 85 members of The17 in one place.
Play back all five recordings simultaneously.
Do not enhance or mix the recordings.

Delete all recordings.

It was when I was writing this score that I had to start confronting the major flaws in my whole plan. There's me wanting a year zero for music, a chance to wipe the slate clean and start again and here I was writing scores that could be acted upon only by somebody who already had a fundamental knowledge of music and, worse still, somebody who used things like scales that had evolved over thousands of years. I decided to try and ignore these contradictions and just get on with the job in hand. I'm sure Pol Pot had many flaws in his Year Zero plan for Cambodia. 'And he failed.' Yeah, anyway, the people performing the scores need have no musical knowledge; it just requires some knowledge from the person instigating the performance of the score.

The other scores followed. Apart from the ones based on the actions that I had already taken regarding my enforced listening habits they are all pretty theoretical and I am sure that once I put them into practice they will evolve, change or even be dumped, to be replaced by other ones that may work. The one done in a prison, up a mountain, to celebrate a new-born baby, a public declaration of love, a life completed, were all more about the concept than what they might sound like. All forced to fit the theory. It won't be until they have been performed for real that they will really begin to take shape. This is not an apology for their inclusion, just a statement of fact.

What did happen, with the help of Karen Reilly and Jon Baker from the Norwich band Neutrinos, was the putting together of a scratch choir made up of 17 male singers and 17 female singers. We did a couple of sessions using the local Quaker Meeting House to rehearse in. Jon Baker in his other life, when not playing bass with the Neutrinos, is a choral arranger and choirmaster. With his help and guidance we were able to try out a number of the scores to see if they could work in practice. With a bit of tweaking they did.

It's time to stop writing and go up on deck to stare at the North Sea. Inspiration from the elements and all that.

SCORE

4. AGE

Choose a building with five floors.

On the ground floor gather 17 people
aged 70 and over.
Ask them to make non-verbal sounds
with their mouths
on the note of F sharp
for five minutes.
Record The 17.
Ensure their performance draws upon their
wisdom.

On the first floor gather 17 people
aged between 45 and 69.
Ask them to make non-verbal sounds
with their mouths
on the note of G sharp
for five minutes.
Record The 17.
Ensure their performance draws upon their
bitterness.

On the second floor gather 17 people
aged between 21 and 44.
Ask them to make non-verbal sounds
with their mouths
on the note of A sharp
for five minutes.
Record The 17.
Ensure their performance draws upon their
arrogance.

On the third floor gather 17 people
aged between 13 and 20.
Ask them to make non-verbal sounds
with their mouths
on the note of C sharp
for five minutes.
Record The 17.
Ensure their performance draws upon their
boredom.

On the fourth floor gather 17 people
aged 12 and under.
Ask them to make non-verbal sounds
with their mouths
on the note of D sharp
for five minutes.
Record The 17.
Ensure their performance draws upon their
innocence.

Combine and balance all of the recordings so
they can be played simultaneously.

Gather the above 85 members of The 17
in one place.
Play them back the combined and balanced
recordings simultaneously.

Delete all recordings.

pb Poster 131   2006

Bill Drummond

THE MOST BEAUTIFUL EXPERIENCE OF MY LIFE
26 March 2006

'That was the most beautiful experience of my life.' The speaker of this sentence then outstretched her hand for me to shake and went off into the night with her boyfriend. Sod knows what he thought of her being so free and easy with her compliments. She might say this kind of thing all the time, but right now, and for some time to come, I'm going to hold onto what she said to help me through the moments of extreme self-doubt.

She had just been listening to the one and only playback of the recording of the score *AGE* which she had taken part in as a member of The17 before John Hirst clicked apple+delete and it was gone forever. Never to be heard again. Yeah, I know information can theoretically be retrieved from a hard drive but I am not going to let that knowledge spoil things here.

That was the night before last. We are on the ferry back from Gothenburg to Newcastle. The17 is now fully fledged and happening and out there in the real world. The night in question was the last of nine sessions of what could best be titled *An Introduction to The17 with Bill Drummond.*

As I want to keep this text brief I won't go into a full description of Fylkingen and all the bollocks that happened while we were in Stockholm. At 7.10 on each of those nine nights I would walk out of my dressing room into the main auditorium, a room in almost pitch-blackness which could hold 200 but would only have 17 seated punters. On three of the walls hung the 17 scores illuminated in very low light. I would cross from the back of the room and sit on a piano stool in front of the audience. To my right was a top-of-the-range brand-spanking-new Yamaha grand, lid up. The faces of the audience were unseen in the darkness. I could only vaguely make out their silhouettes. I was not lit either.

To my left was a table. Behind the table sat John Hirst, on it his Apple Powerbook would be open and his face up-lit from the screen. Also on the table would be some of the other bits of technology for the job in hand.

I'd peer into the gloom. 'Good evening. My name is Bill Drummond and you are The17 ...' and for the next 40 minutes I would not move from the piano stool while telling my story. Attempting to use all the power at my disposal to explain and illustrate why recorded music is now a dead art form, a relic of the 20th century, and then seduce these 17 strangers in front of me into being committed lifetime members of The17. Equal measures of honesty, deceit, arrogance and effrontery, peppered with assorted self-effacing asides, formed my armoury. The story I told included much of what was written on my outward-bound journey.

There was then a ten-minute break. People could get a drink from the foyer bar, take a piss, buy a pair of badges or go out for a fag. Sweden is already no smoking almost everywhere, which I, of course, appreciate.

Then it was down to the business of performing the score *AGE*. It's the one requiring a building with five floors and five lots of 17 people of varying ages. As there was no five-storey building to hand and only 17 people of whatever ages they were, compromises had to be made and improvisation used to make the score happen. John Hirst and I would get to work, recording The17 taking on the roles of all five groups of 17, one after the other, starting with them being The17 over 70, drawing upon the wisdom of their years, finishing with them imagining being 17 people under the age of 12, drawing upon the innocence of their years.

After the five recordings were done there was another ten-minute break. Then I would summon The17 back into the auditorium to listen to the playback of what they had performed.

Rasmus: I think that Bill really likes the score AGE. It was the one he did with us at the Royal College of Art.

Robert: Perhaps it's the strongest of the scores and the one with the most to talk about.

After the first of the nine nights I thought the whole event was a winner. The performance of the score *AGE* played back to us sounded breathtaking. Over the run of nine nights the performances differed in subtle and less subtle ways, but every time it was very much the same piece and worked as such. I won't try to explain why I think such a seemingly simple musical composition should work so well and be so moving. If I tried, I would be in danger of sounding very pretentious. Some evenings after the playback I found myself telling The17 that what they had just listened to was the collective subconscious soul of the 17 performers in the room. The performance would end with John Hirst calling for silence so we could hear the short whirring sound his laptop makes as the recording was deleted.

Maybe not one of the other 16 people who took part that evening, or any of the other previous eight performances, would express their reaction to it in the same words as the girl at the beginning of this chapter, and maybe those who thought it was shite would leave at the end saying nothing. But the feeling I got was that most were pretty moved. I know I'm in no position to be my own critic but here goes anyway: I think it is the purest and most stimulating musical thing I have ever been involved with. If music were to start all over again, I wouldn't mind it starting out sounding like that. I also know that as a piece of recorded music to be played on your MP3 player or as a CD or even on Late Junction on Radio 3, it would be boring pretentious shite.

As well as these *Introductions to The 17 with Bill Drummond* I visited seven schools in and around Stockholm twice. This was to perform the score *COLLABORATE*. We visited each of the seven schools in the first week to have a bit of chat and to record their parts in the overall score. In the second week we went back to them all to play the finished piece and have a further chat. Although the performance of this score was carried out far more to the letter than *AGE*, it was, in practice, far less successful.

The schoolchildren involved varied in age from eight to 17. The 13-year-old ones were the most difficult. I ended up telling one particularly troublesome 13-year-old lad to 'Shut the fuck up or get out the fucking room before we fucking start.' He left with his posse of mates and I felt pathetic for picking on a 13-year-old.

I don't know what any of them got out of it, if anything. I had the feeling that some of the classes had been told that a pop star was turning up and they were going to be involved in the making of his new record. They must have been disappointed when I shuffled in with my theories about all recorded music being dead, when they are just starting on their voyage into music and were hearing everything for the first time. Some of the pupils who seemed to be the most apathetic on my first visit were the most animated after hearing the outcome on my second visit.

Although all the schools were state schools, the children were quite a mixture: from mainly mixed race and immigrant kids into rap in a school in the suburbs, to a bunch of predominantly white middle-class ones doing dance in an arts academy. The ones doing dance were most at ease with performing. They were also the most critical of what they heard back. To them it did not seem that dissimilar to some of the things they already did in improvisation classes where one of the class stands in the middle while the rest of them sit in a circle around them. Those sitting in the circle have to start improvising oral noise for the one in the middle to dance to.

When I do this score again in the north-east of England come April / May

(2006) I hope to have found ways of making it work better and be more rewarding for those taking part and for the final playing of the track before its deletion to be more stunning.

I asked one bunch of students if they thought it sounded like the first vocal music ever performed many thousands of years ago. A girl among them said 'No. The first music would have been a mother singing her baby to sleep.' She made me think it probably was. Women invented music: it's official. You read it here first, unless some feminist has already claimed it as her profound insight into the cultural evolution of (Wo)Man.

A lad called Eric, not one of the school lads but a lad in his 20s who came along to one of the first performances at Fylkingen, introduced himself to me as a film-maker, or at least a part-time but would be full-time film-maker. He was a teacher of autistic kids in his day job. He wanted to make a film about The17. I said that he could but that he could not use any film or sound recordings of the various 17s performing. He said he already understood this and was keener on filming people's responses to being involved.

Eric sorted out some leave from his teaching job and spent the best part of our stay in Stockholm filming at the various schools as well as at Fylkingen. I have no idea if any of the stuff he has filmed will hang together or will be of interest to anybody but him. He seemed very excited about what he had already when he filmed our departure yesterday. He asked me whom I'd choose if I could have anybody in the world to take part in The17 but not somebody from music. I couldn't think of anybody so I said David Beckham. Eric thought my answer amusing; I thought it lacked imagination. I should have said Eric Cantona. Eric (not Cantona) will have started editing his footage as I write these words out on the North Sea.

Now this chapter is done I have to start rewriting some of the scores, moving their order around and dumping a couple to make way for new ones. Tomorrow after we dock we will be heading into Newcastle for a couple of meetings in the hope that we can reduce the number of places available for each performance – cut from 34 to 17 – and arrange for the room where we are doing it in the Hatton Gallery to be painted black.

I will end this chapter in the same way as I began it, by quoting again the woman who said, 'That was the most beautiful experience of my life.'

SCORE

7. COLLABORATE

Take a map.
Draw a circle on the map.
Ensure that it encircles five schools.

Go to the first school.
Invite 17 people to sing.
Record The 17
making non-verbal sounds with their voices
for seven minutes
on the note of C.
Ensure the performance contains space.

Go to the second school.
Repeat the same process
using the note of D.
Ensure the performance contains light.

Go to the third school.
Repeat the same process
using the note of E.
Ensure the performance contains shade.

Go to the fourth school.
Repeat the same process
using the note of F.
Ensure the performance contains tension.

Go to the fifth school.
Repeat the same process
using the note of G.
Ensure the performance contains release.

Go to the sixth school.
Repeat the same process
using the note of A.
Ensure the performance contains conflict.

Go to the seventh school.
Repeat the same process
using the note of B.
Ensure the performance contains
conclusion.

Combine and balance all seven of the
recordings so they can be played
simultaneously.

Gather the above 119 members of The 17 in
one place, within the circle.
Ensure they all have pencil and paper.

Play back the combined and balanced
recordings simultaneously.

Ask them to document
in no more than one sentence,
the emotions, visions or thoughts they had,
while listening to the music.

Delete all recordings.

pb Poster 134   2006

PISSING IN THE WIND
27 March 2006

John Hirst has just read through what I have written so far. He thought what I wrote on the outward-bound journey was like a series of bullet points and that I should have gone into more detail about how it all went in Stockholm in the homeward-bound bit. He may be right, he may be wrong. I didn't want my writing to sprawl with me going into all the stuff that did and didn't work, about how the school one, *COLLABORATE*, worked out shite and why it was a musical non-starter and how we must try a different tack with it in the north-east of England come April / May.

There was another reason why that section ended up just bullet points. Right now for me writing about that is more interesting and pertinent than writing about how it went in Stockholm. Maybe later I will go back to writing about Stockholm. This is the reason.

I had retired to the ship's bar, got myself a pint and found myself a table and started to write. There were not more than 50 words on the page when I was joined by a handsome, well-built man in his mid-40s. He was a sociable Geordie who started to regale me with stories from his life: his years spent in the Foreign Legion, the SAS, in various African wars as a soldier of fortune; how, although he had killed dozens of black men he was not a racist as he would have killed them even if they had been white; how all the wars he had fought in were just; how he was hired for his skills as a marksman; how to hold two pistols at the same time (he demonstrated) and how they always get that wrong in cowboy films; how he floored this bloke outside a bar in Poland who thought he was harder than him; how his dad was a bare-knuckle champ; how he had fought with Mad Mick (remember Mad Mick, the tabloids' favourite mercenary?); how his dad had forced him to sign up; how he got married at 21 and had his only child, a boy, a year later; how he had the snip at the age of 24; how his wife had left him at the age of 25; how he loved his boy but could never tell him; and how he would love to have another child more than anything in the world.

I told him the snip could be reversed or at least there was a 70 percent chance of it working. He said his partner was ten years older than him and past the menopause; that he traded in Land Rovers; that his partner had chucked him out; that he lived in Malmo; that he was on his way back to Northumberland on Land Rover trading business; that he would floor anybody who touched his neck; and that he had warned his partner that if she ever touched his neck during love-making he could not be held responsible for what happened next. Most of all he talked about fighting in all its manly forms for the best part of two hours. He never asked me what I did or even why I was on the boat. He was of course pissed, although he hardly took more than a sip from his pint in the whole two hours. He told me he'd never let anybody buy him a drink; it's a principle of his. He told me he is a man of principle and his word is his bond.

He was just demonstrating to me how he could kill me with one blow when John Hirst entered the bar. The flow of conversation was interrupted. I made my excuses and headed down to the cabin, wrote up my notes, thought some thoughts, almost fell asleep and then headed back up to the bar. My friendly mercenary was now pissed beyond repair and was up on his feet dancing to the music, lost in his own myth.

The music he was dancing to was provided by Johnny Swank, 'our very own onboard troubadour'. Johnny Swank. What a great name, especially if the S of Swank is said as an apostrophe S after Johnny. Johnny was a man in his middle years too. He had been working the outward-bound journey when we came over two weeks earlier. He sat on his stool, a plugged-in acoustic guitar on his lap, a whole bunch of effects pedals at his feet and a repertoire of songs that seemed unlimited. He could do them all effortlessly: the guitar solos note for note, the intros, the middle eights, the outros, like he was playing all the parts and doing all the harmonies. Jackson Browne, Creedence, Van Morrison, Bob Dylan, Buddy Holly, The Beatles, The Eagles ... in fact anything by a white bloke from the right decade(s). Nothing too new or by a woman.

He was taking requests and our soldier boy wanted one by Dire Straits. He got *Walk Of Life*. His dancing was more of a lurching and swaying to the beat. He tried to grab a couple of teenage girls as they passed. They escaped his clutches. He shouted at whoever might be listening that Mark Knopfler was from the north-east. He then tried to say something about Sting and Bryan Ferry and how Newcastle was the capital of music.

I wondered what the men he had killed in dirty little African wars would think if they could watch him now. What would the unborn son that he longed for think?

John Hirst requested a Tracy Chapman song. Johnny Swank told us that he would feel uncomfortable doing one of her songs but if we were ever in Charleston, South Carolina, we should look him up. His number's in the book. I warmed to Johnny and what he did. There seemed to be an honesty to it, even if his politics were somewhat Southern. Here he was, a native of South Carolina, plying his troubadour trade on the North Sea. His inter-song banter aimed at us lot, 'the lost and the lonely', in this bar out on the sea, informed us that he had 27 more days to go before heading back home, but he would be back come the Fall with his guitar, effects rack and suitcase full of songs.

Johnny was about my age. I knew every song he played almost too well. He must have had dreams when he was a teenager and he got his first guitar. Dreams of writing songs, making records, getting written about in *Rolling Stone*, but here he was singing other people's songs for men like me and our friend who could kill me with just one blow. I wonder when he gave up his dreams and traded them in for whatever this is he is doing now. I wonder what I could get for trading in my dreams. I reckon I would get next to nothing for them and maybe that's why I don't cash them in and just carry on dreaming about The17 and Year Zero Now and all the other stuff. Without dreams there is nothing for me. And I wonder what our mercenary dreamed of when he was 15.

I should try to find some way of tying up what fate has dealt these three men of vaguely similar years – Johnny Swank, the killer and myself – all pissing in the wind. Something life-affirming in a nihilistic way.

Bill Drummond

DEREK HATTON DOES FLUXUS
22 April 2006

The day is Saturday. The place is the offices of the Hatton Gallery on the campus of the University of Newcastle. We drove up from the workshop in Norwich on Thursday, put the show up in the Hatton Gallery yesterday. Today the show opens. It looks good. The next four weeks are going to be spent here and hereabouts, working in schools in County Durham and Sunderland, working with MA Composition (music) students at the university and doing ten *Introductions to The17 with Bill Drummond* performances at the Hatton. The ten introductions are open to the paying public.

I had arranged to use the office to check my email. Logged on, password keyed in, inbox clicked. Met with the usual assortment of emails: penis enlargements, knock-down price Viagra, degrees for the asking and money-for-nothing scams. Then there are the other ones that I will procrastinate about until it's too late to do anything with them. And finally there may be one or two that might make me feel that what I'm up to is worth doing, that somebody somewhere is taking notice.

There was one – I could tell before I even opened it – that fell into that last category. It was somebody sending in a response to Score 17. This is the last score that I have written, and the one that I am still the most pleased with. This score, which also has the title *SCORE*, reads:

> Score your own composition to be performed by The17.
> You need have no previous musical experience.
> The score you produce should be clear and simple, requiring no instrumentation or lyric.
> This score is to be performed by a minimum of 17 people using nothing but their voices.
> Email your score to admin@the17.org
> If it fulfils the above criteria, it will be published and made available to be performed by The17, wherever and whenever applicable.

This was the first response that I had to this invitation; I couldn't wait to read what this score submitted by a member of the public would be like. I clicked the mouse to open it. It looked short and to the point. I knew immediately it would look good once it was designed and printed up as a score poster, in the style of the 17 I had already done. Then I read it.

Subject: The17 Contact
Date: Saturday, April 22, 2006 12:43
From: Paul Ilek blahblah@yablah.co.uk
Conversation: The17 Contact.

Below is the result of your feedback form. It was submitted by Paul Ilek (blahblah@yablah.co.uk) on Saturday, April 22, 2006 at 06:43:58

I've puzzled over your work for years. Various options which I've narrowed down to:
1. Conceptualism lite
2. Smug bastard with money
3. Derek Hatton does Fluxus
4. Suburban radicalism
But all these are preliminaries, the real descriptor is
Raving Narcissism. P.1. xxx

submit: Send

I read it again. Then looked out of the window for some time before I noticed my ageing reflection staring back at me from a window pane. Then I read it for a third and fourth time.

This Paul Ilek was sharp, knew how to put words together, knew the references to make, the buttons to push. 'Derek Hatton does Fluxus' is my favourite. This person must have known exactly what the public perception of Derek Hatton was when he was the deputy chairperson of Liverpool City Council in the first half of the 1980s: 'Scouse barrow boy does Trotsky'. The sharp suits, the smug mug, the media soundbites before the media knew that it could be bitten. The fucking mess he made of it all, the national laughing stock he made of Militant in the eyes of the electorate.

As for Fluxus, I'm sure that I will be getting that again. It is such an obvious comparison to make. But a fair one.

'Conceptualism lite'. Guilty. It's hardly Art and Language at its most hardcore. Those were the days when conceptualism was conceptualism before it went tabloid.

'Smug bastard with money'. Not as good as 'suburban radicalism'. But 'raving narcissism'? Well, I suppose it is all about me.

Bill Drummond

I put Paul Ilek into Google, hoping to get some idea of where this fan-boy was coming from. Nothing came up, so maybe it is not his real name.

'I've puzzled over your work for years.' You might think, 'Why bother, if what I do gets to you so much?' But then I know I could write at least two volumes on why I think U2 are the worst band the world has ever known and why Bono is … There is no point in me even starting because I know it would say far more about my shortcomings than about any that Bono and the boys from County Purgatory might have. And if I was to start, I know where it all began but before I tell you I should say that I have never listened to a U2 album or seen them do any more than a couple of songs live. It started in the Lyceum Ballroom off the Strand in 1979, or was it early 1980? Echo And The Bunnymen, who I used to manage, were the headlining act of the five bands on the poster. The headlining act is the one that is paying for the PA and the lighting rig. This means we were the ones who say what the support bands can use of the mixing desk and the lights.

I knew fuck all about this U2 other than what I'd been told and that was all positive but they had turned up with a whole stage set, a huge big U and 2 made out of what looked like flower pots and they wanted us to move our drum riser to fit it in. We weren't moving our drum riser for any fuckers! Then their sound engineer asked me if they could use some of our channels on the mixing desk, channels that we already had balances on. Balances that we didn't want any jumped-up Paddy arseholes messing with. The answer was a polite 'No'. Their sound engineer told me that I would regret my decision as the day would come when U2 would be the biggest band in the world and the world wouldn't have a clue who Echo And The Bunnymen were.

A couple of years later U2 and The Bunnymen are on the same bill again, but this time it's Top Of The Pops, and we are all backstage. Bono was giving it the big friendship thing. Telling us all how it is our time now and if we all work together we can change things in the world, we can make it more than just a better place, we can sort out the wars and the poverty. And I'm thinking, 'We are doing Top Of The Pops. We already sold out our principles to get this far. Jesus would never have done Top Of The Pops.' I am saying this with the safety of hindsight. If U2 had been dropped by their record company and disappeared back to the banks of the Liffey after their second album, I would never have developed my ideas, that now fill two volumes, on why they are shite and why Bono should be shot for the sake of humanity.

When I first saw someone wearing one of those 'Make Bono History' T-shirts I felt good in an 'I'm not alone' sort of way. I also take great paternal pride in the fact that my 19-year-old son who has vastly different tastes in music to me, thinks U2 are the worst band in the world too. I could go on. I won't. It is enough to say that if this Paul Ilek feels about me as I feel about Bono, then I know where he is coming from. And I also know it's more about your own shortcomings than about any failings the target of your projections may have.

Paul: I think this is psychobabble! He doesn't need to justify his hatred of Bono.

Robert: By making bold statements and then half going back on them, he digs himself out of a hole.

'So what's all this got to do with The17, Bill?'
'It was him who started it. Sending me an email to the17.org under the pretence it was a submitted score.'

UKE 'EM ALL (The return of Tenzing Scott Brown)
23 April 2006

And so to the Cumberland Arms. Our – that is John Hirst, Gimpo and my – digs for the time we are in Newcastle is a house in the Sandyford region of the city. It is a Victorian terrace house. Our landlord, David Fry, is a potter. It was him who took us up to the Cumberland for a drink. The pub was fine, the beer was good, the location fantastic. And it seemed to feature live music of some variety every night of the week.

The Cumberland has two rooms on the ground floor, one for drinking and for debating and the other for music-making. We were drinking and debating. We could hear strains of music from the room next door. After my second pint of Rapper (the guest ale) I went to investigate. The room was no bigger than a moderate-size front room, a bench around two-and-a-half walls and a scatter of tables and stools. The place was comfortably full of drinkers. From a dapper man in his late 70s to a lass in her early 20s with every age, sexual persuasion and physical type in between. What they all had in common was what they held lovingly to their chests: each was holding a small but perfectly formed ukulele.

The ukulele is an instrument that has never troubled my imagination even though *Leaning On The Lamppost* by George Formby was the first song I ever heard on the radio. I was aware of something called the Ukulele Orchestra Of Great Britain but had never heard them. As far as I was concerned the ukulele was a joke. And an old one at that. This lot were singing and playing *Harvest Moon* as written and originally performed by Neil Young.

We found stools, supped our pints and spent the next hour or so listening to what we learnt were the Ukulele Allstars. When the playing finished no one clapped apart from me and my comrades. There was no audience other than us. They then chatted and supped their pints, cups of tea and tumblers of orange and then with not even a nod to each other broke into *King Of The Road*. This too came to an end and more chat about this and that, and then another one of them, a large man with a walrus moustache, broke into a version of *Flowers In The Rain*.

If, like me, you were lying in bed on 30 September 1967 with your radio tuned to 247 on the medium waveband you would know that *Flowers In The Rain*, written by Roy Wood and performed by The Move, was the first record broadcast on Radio 1. On that particular Saturday morning the idea of Radio 1 seemed so incredibly exciting. The radio side of the BBC had finally entered the 1960s.

Hearing this ukulele-driven version of the same song 38 years and 205 days later had an equally powerful emotional impact on me. Back then when it was Tony Blackburn spinning it for the first time as a Radio 1 disc jockey, it was upbeat, sunny, full of promise. London was still swinging and now we had Radio 1 the rest of the country could swing along with it. The version played by this lot and sung by the large man with the walrus moustache was full of pathos and loss reminding the listener of a long-gone golden era.

Walking back up the Ouseburn valley to our digs I was forced to admit that I was smitten with the idea of the ukulele. I wanted to possess one of my very own. I wanted to be in a ukulele orchestra. I wanted to fit in and sing songs and strum along and sup my pint. I wanted to go along every week to rehearsals week in and week out for the rest of my life. By the time we got back to the digs it was all settled in my mind. I could have a parallel life to the one where all this 'All recorded music is rubbish ...' and The17 exists. In this parallel life I could have a ukulele, be a regular down at the local ukulele orchestra practise nights, where they would know me only as Tenzing Scott Brown. Tenzing is a nom de plume that I have used in the past and have been looking for an excuse to use again. Maybe it would be good for me, like porn is supposed to keep a man's wayward and wandering desires sated, thus help him keep faithful to the woman he loves. The ukulele would be my porn, enabling me to stay faithful to the higher aims of what The17 is all about. Nobody need ever know, the ukulele could stay hidden under my bed and once a week I could sneak out and down to the pub where we practise and all my fellow strummers would only ever know me as Tenzing. And if anybody ever asked how I got such a strange name, I would tell them that I was named after the family cat that would climb up the ivy and into a bedroom window every night. The cat in turn was named after the Sherpa who conquered Everest.

COMMUNICATION BREAKDOWN
26 April 2006

A couple of years back I was contacted by a Gráinne Sweeney, who was working for a set-up called Creative Partnerships (CP). She wanted to know if I was interested in getting involved as an artist working with schools in Sunderland and County Durham. She explained that Creative Partnerships is an organisation financed by the Arts Council, that they have numerous regional offices, working independently of each other, each able to approach working artists and commission them to create work with young people in schools. They sent me a train ticket so I could come up and have a meeting with them and find out more about the way they worked. So I took the train north. I have always been a sucker for that East Coast Line. They – Gráinne and colleague Lorna Fulton – met me at Newcastle station and took me for lunch in a café in a former pit village that was now embracing the arts. I liked the soup and I liked the space they had upstairs above the café which was now a small theatre. I wondered what Arthur Scargill would think of all this.

I have gone on record on more than one occasion stating how suspicious I am of any art that is state-sponsored. However independent the artist claims to be, I have always felt the work they produce is in some way compromised if they accept money from any government. This is naive thinking on my part: all art down through the centuries has been sponsored by someone or something, whether it is the church, wealthy patrons or a government; even Vincent had his brother sending him handouts down to Arles. I also know I have been able to hold on to such lofty, if misguided, ideals because the loot that I made from pop music has given me a temporary safety net.

They asked me if I had any new projects that might work with school children. The only thing that was brewing away in my head at the time, that I thought might work in this context, was The17. I told them about it. They seemed to be open to whatever I wanted to do.

'How long might you want me up here?'
'As long as you think you need to get the work done.'
'I could only be up here for a month at the most. I have family commitments.'
'That's fine.'
'When do you want me to start'?'
'Whenever is convenient.'
'What is the budget like?'
'Put one together. Email it to us and we will let you know if it can be done.'

I did, and it could, well almost. And that felt good. Was I compromising myself? Was this the beginning of a slippery slope? Will I spend my days from now on filling out forms to apply for grants from government bodies to make government-friendly art? Last month I applied to the British Council for a grant to cover my travel costs to Moscow. I was turned down.

It was after the meeting with Gráinne and Lorna that I put together the score that is now named *COLLABORATE*.

Dates were agreed so that doing this work with a bunch of schools would tie in with the whole 17 exhibition and public introductions that I had been planning to do at the Hatton Gallery at Newcastle University. They sent me a schedule with times, dates, addresses, contact names and numbers. I had no excuses for being at the wrong place at the right time or ... well, you know. The first school on the list was Broadway Juniors in Sunderland. We were to be there at 10.00 in the morning last Wednesday (26 April 2007). The contact name was John McCabe.

John Hirst and I set off from our digs in Newcastle at about 9.00. Although on our schedule it reckoned we would only need 25 minutes, it took us the full hour.

Just walking past a school still makes me uncomfortable; I hated every aspect of my education and have yet to take on board that things have changed. For 15 years I have done my duty and have regularly attended parents' evenings at the various schools my children have attended. On every one of these occasions, however friendly and warm the teacher I may be talking about one of my children, I cannot help but think of them as the enemy.

I will now shift into the present tense for literary effect.

It's a sunny day. We find the school; it's on a 1960s council estate. We drive through the gates. Cherry trees are in full blossom. We park up and ring the bell. An attractive woman with a friendly face and a decidedly local accent opens the door for us. We explain who we are. She offers to make us a cup of tea. I assume she is the school secretary. She is the head teacher. She tells us how good it is to be working with Creative Partnerships. And about all the interesting and inspiring artists they have had in the school and the work they have done. And she tells me how honoured they are to have me and how John McCabe, the teacher we are going to be working with, is very excited about it all. I have to remind myself that she is the enemy – doubly so as she is a head teacher. Her friendliness is obviously a front.

We are taken down to the school hall where we are supposed to be doing our stuff. John McCabe turns up. A pleasant and eager-looking man in his mid-30s with a neatly pressed shirt. He tells us how the kids are so excited about working with me and he tells us about the musical he has written with the children based on *The Lion, The Witch And The Wardrobe*. He tells us he plays in a band himself and he used to be into the Bunnymen. He tells us he has no idea what we are going to be doing but is sure it will be great.

I don't tell him I haven't got a clue and I'm sure that the children would rather be putting together a musical that they could perform for the rest of the school and their families. At least with the musical they will get cheers and claps and shouts for more at the end of their performance on the big night and then be told by everybody for the next few weeks how great it was. What they don't need is some bloke turning up and telling them that all recorded music has been done, it's rubbish and by the way I want you to stand around and make a noise with your mouth for the next seven minutes.

The kids start to turn up. John McCabe gets them to give us a hand bringing our stuff in from the back of the Land Rover. The children, all 29 of them, are sat in two rows in front of me looking up at my face expectantly. My head is empty. There is nothing up there that is of any use for them to know about. They have got all their lives in front of them. Pop music must seem like this incredibly exciting thing. Something from another universe where everything sparkles and if you lived there, you'd have enough money to buy whatever you want and to go on holiday wherever you want. And you don't have to go to school or even work and nobody bullies you and everybody likes you.

'Good morning. My name is Bill Drummond and his name is John Hirst and we are artists. But we are not the sort of artists who paint pictures. Although sometimes I do. Sometimes the art I do involves going

Robert: I wonder what he thinks the kids are going to take from this experience. For most children it's not until they're teenagers that pop music becomes a really important thing for them. Bill has reached the stage where he's fed up with pop music. While we, as adults, might empathise strongly with that concept, I wonder if it goes over the heads of children.

Rasmus: I was thinking the same thing. I understand why it works well in the schools for Bill, but it is not clear to me what the kids get from it.

Paul: When I was at school, I was in a choir. It's quite amazing to experience your singing voice in harmony with others. Whether or not they understand Bill's intentions, they could still be enjoying it.

Robert: But what differentiates this situation from taking part in a normal school choir then? It seems obvious for us to differentiate between a normal

on a journey. And sometimes it involves me asking people questions. And sometimes it involves me writing books. And sometimes it involves me making music or at least thinking about how music is made and why.'

I'm losing my way already and I can see their minds beginning to wander. I tell them how they, along with six other schools, are going to be taking part in the making of a piece of music with me. That the music has no words and no tune and no beat. Their minds are wandering further. I wonder where their minds are wandering and I remember how my mind used to wander further and further and further at school. That was the only thing that was good about school when I was a kid. It was a place where you could be where your mind could wander further than anywhere else. Maybe in my version of the perfect school you would have mind-wandering lessons where you could just sit at your desk with your arms folded on it and your head resting on them and for a full 40 minutes you could let your mind wander. I was going to say then that you would be marked by how far you let your mind wander in that 40 minutes but maybe bringing competition into mind-wandering would undermine its special qualities.

'… So when we've been to all seven schools you will all come into Newcastle to the gallery where I've got this exhibition on, and you will hear it played back – what you have done.'

This mention of a trip to Newcastle seems to bring their wandering minds back.
'Do any of you have any questions before we start recording?'
Some hands go up.
'Yes, you.'
I'm pointing at the kid with the specs.
'Do we get to make a video?'
'No, I'm afraid not. Next? Yes, you.'

choir and this very specific choir. With The17 we are asked to consider what we are doing as performers, and to put this into the context of music history.

Rasmus: What you're saying is that the children are not ready to have those considerations.

Robert: But I think that perhaps in later life the value of this experience will come back to them, and mean a lot more.

Paul: Obviously you can appreciate things in different and unexpected ways to the way they are supposed to be appreciated. I think at whatever age you can get a lot out of this, whether or not you want to contextualise and critique what is going on.

Rasmus: I wonder if it would be more interesting for the kids to sing a song that they like. A song of their choice.
Bill seems to avoid talking about his own role in the 'The17 choir'. This choir has a choir leader, and that leader is Bill Drummond. He makes the scores. He chooses which score to perform. This is very much his project.
For most parts, the performances of The17 consists of two sections. The first section is when Bill is speaking, and the second section is when the choir sings. When we were in the choir, I felt that the first section was just as important as the second. If you remove Bill Drummond and Bill Drummond's story from the equation, then The17 becomes something very different.

I'm pointing at the girl with the frizzy ginger hair.

'Do we get to go on Top Of The Pops?'

I am beginning to be aware that there has been a bit of a breakdown in communication going on. In my head I can hear that riff from Led Zeppelin One, that track that goes 'Communication breakdown, it's always the same, I'm having a nervous breakdown, drive me insane!'

What do they think I'm doing with them here? What have they been told? I'd better try and explain before the mind-wandering begins again.

'We are not making pop music today. This has nothing to do with pop music. In fact, it is as far from any kind of pop music as you can get.'

'But, sir, we were told you used to be a pop star and that you wanted to make a song with us.'

Now, nobody actually spoke that last sentence, it's just what I thought might be going on in their minds.

We then get down to the business of recording them for seven minutes going 'Aaaaaaaaahhhh' on the note of C. There is one of those school pianos on hand for me to get them to pitch to. We have a few short trial runs for them to get the idea and we are off. It must be the longest seven minutes of their lives. It's certainly one of the longest of mine. But they get there and most of them hold the note pretty well all the way through.

When I tried out the same score in Sweden I encouraged the kids to express themselves by using their voices. I took on the role of the conductor, getting them to build things up and then take it down to a whisper. But in the end it was just a racket and there was no note being held. And with each school that I went to, although I had been indicating a note for them to pitch to, it had just ended up with us layering track upon track of racket. When we did the final playback over there, there was no way, even for the most trained of ears, that you could hear anything of the seven individual notes in the scale of C. It had qualities, it had a wildness, but there was nothing there to hold it together.

This time I wanted to get something of the harmonic structure coming through. Not that I wanted to suppress whatever individuality each child has. But – and maybe this is one of the areas where what I am trying to do is flawed – choral music, by definition, is about voices working together, not competing with each other. In Stockholm we ended up getting all the classroom show-offs trying to make the most stupid sounds they could, trying to make the others laugh.

Most artists brought in to work with school children are, I assume, there with projects that will encourage the kids to explore their own ideas and to express them with confidence. Was I just using them as pawns, each one a mere semi-quaver on my giant stave?

After we had done the seven minutes we discuss things a bit further and then we get packed. You could tell some of them are getting more out of helping us take things back out to the Land Rover than they had from what we had been doing in the hall. The plan is that we will come back in a couple of weeks to try something else with them.

We drive back into Newcastle to the Hatton Gallery and back to the various problems we were having there. I will leave out of this story what those problems were and let them appear elsewhere.

Bill Drummond

HOW TO BE A FAMOUS ARTIST
27 April 2006

To be a famous artist is a very easy thing: all you have to do is make work about fame, violence, sex and death. It is a cliché to say it, but nonetheless true – the media will never tire of covering work that touches these topics. We all know this, even if our knowledge of it is not conscious. This has led me to a position where my reading of most work that uses fame, violence, sex and death as a central theme is not first and foremost about those topics but about the artists themselves looking for the fastest shortcut to their own fame. And again, they might not be conscious of this either but just be instinctively drawn to subject matter that will deliver them fame in the shortest time possible.

This knowledge has led me to write off most work that uses any of these topics as its subject matter. Fame, violence, sex and death are as likely to grab my attention as they are anyone's. These are undeniably the big topics in life, but once the imagination has been grabbed what does the artist tell us, what do we learn? So often work seems to be no more than grabbing attention. All headline and no content. For many of us that is all we want or expect from art. We just want our attention grabbed. We like the sensation of it being grabbed. Another route to being a famous artist is to make big art. If you make big art, it will, by its very obvious nature, get noticed. If Christo were to wrap up the ashtray in front of me it might make better art than the iconic buildings he chooses, let alone the coastlines he attempts to wrap up, but it would not deliver the fame he seems to crave.

I have written before about my unease with big art and the compromises I have made in my own work to accommodate this unease. There are numerous reasons why the statue David by Michelangelo is rubbish, but first and foremost the reason is its size. The story of David and Goliath works on our imagination because David is a boy, the youngest son, the most unlikely. But he settles the war. We all know that in later life David goes on to be an arsehole and a cunt, or you do if you had the education that I had. The David that Michelangelo is supposed to be celebrating is the young David moments before he is about to do battle with Goliath, yet Michelangelo resorts to using size and sex to grab our attention and in so doing the statue is unable to deliver any other meaning. If he had made a life-size statue of a 12-year-old Middle Eastern boy, its power would have resonated meaning beyond his excuse for a celebration of male beauty.

To offer a little balance here, his statue of Pièta is one of the most potent and throbbing with meaning in the Western canon. The dead Jesus draped over his mother's lap. Jesus with the perfect figure of a young man cut down in his prime. Mary, who must have been 50 by then, is portrayed as the young virgin, no older than the night her baby was born and she held him in her arms for the very first time. Actually I don't know if I agree with myself. Maybe it would be far stronger if she was portrayed as a middle-aged woman worn down with the struggles of life, her virginity a distant memory. A completely different Mary to the innocent mother who has been rammed down the throats of Roman Catholic women for hundreds of years, as the woman they should all judge themselves against (and fail).

As for the fame bit of my equation, time and time again artists have made work that attacks, ridicules or even just comments upon the famous or iconic. It may not be great art, or even good art, but it works every time. For a start you are using subject matter the public will already have an emotional connection with. Add something negative or disturbing into that emotional connection and you are onto a winner. Make work attacking McDonald's and you will find plenty willing to leap on your bandwagon; make work about something as iconic as one million pounds and your fame will last the full 15 minutes; make work with somebody who is already famous and others will take notice.

I know for certain that some of the examples I give work as they, as you may already know, are works that I have been associated with in the past. Admittedly it has only been with the luxury of hindsight that I have put these theories together. Over the past few years I have found myself wanting to evolve ways of working that do not use these methods. This has in part been conscious and in part instinctive, wanting to make work that does not seek to shock, or feign to attack the powerful. Some of the work that I initiated some time ago which is still in process does fail by these standards: the *How To Be An Artist* piggy-backed on the reputation of Richard Long; youwhores.com obviously appeals to an appetite for the sordid; *Is God A Cunt* seeks notoriety by association with the most powerful force in creation.

However hard I try the one I always seem to fail at and am failing at right now is the fame-by-association one. In the past it might have been ABBA, Doctor Who, Tammy Wynette, the Turner Prize or the already mentioned Richard Long. But now it is me, Bill Drummond. I know I am not famous in a celebrity stakes sort of way but for certain people my name is a brand of sorts. They read my name and it triggers things off in their head, whether I like what it triggers or not. With what I've been doing over the past few years, I've tried to keep my name away from the actual job being done. My thinking is that if people come across the websites that I have set up, like openmanifesto.com or mydeath.net or youwhores.com, they will respond to it in a far more natural and I hope true way. This is compared to if they came across them knowing them to be associated with whatever the Bill Drummond brand means in their head.

So on to The17 and the lack of ticket sales for the ten performances at the Hatton Gallery. At Fylkingen in Stockholm and at the Hatton Gallery in Newcastle I tried to insist that the poster and advertising did not use my name. I wanted people to come along, shell out good money and take part because they knew it would be a good thing. I suppose I thought the name alone, The17, resonated something powerful and unmissable. It did in my head, so why not in others'? 'The17, a choir that is going to change our relationship with music? That sounds great. I'd better not miss it then.'

Ben from Amino, the promoters of the performances in Newcastle, made it clear to me this morning. 'Bill, whatever you think The17 is, it is not that. What it is, is the latest work by the artist known as Bill Drummond. Doing what you wanted us to do – and we have been trying – has been like trying to sell tickets for a name band without putting the name of the band on the poster, just the name of their new album that nobody has heard of yet. No one would buy the tickets.* Or an exhibition by Andy Warhol without his name, just what the curator of the show dreamt up as a title. You have to accept your name is now a brand name out in the public domain. As a brand name, Bill Drummond resonates in the imaginations of a section of the population. They might not like what you do but there are a lot of people out there who have an interest in having an opinion about it. If we had put flyers and posters out there across the north-east with your name big and bold on them, we would have sold out immediately.'

What Ben was saying made sense. I understood what he was telling me, even if I didn't want to accept it. In my head it still meant that whatever I did in future would be condemned to suffer the fate of seeking fame by association with that bloke who used to manage Echo And The Bunnymen, was a one-hit wonder with The Timelords and who tore up a 20-quid note or something.

Originally this story was going to be called Fame By Association; it got changed as soon as I started writing it to How To Be A Famous Artist but somehow the theme of the chapter seems to be split between the two titles.

Maybe to resolve this difference I should accept that The17 should seek fame by association, but find someone or something far more famous and iconic than Bill Drummond to achieve fame with. Any suggestions?

Reality time. I have to come up with a way of using my name in conjunction with the name The17 which works before I take this 17 thing any further and piss off people trying to sell tickets down the line. Just as long as they don't use those three letters K, L and F anywhere.

Post Script
Me going on about Michelangelo, as if I knew what I was talking about. Trying to big myself up, by making light of one of the giants. It is so easy to be the armchair critic. If you don't like something, go and do something better. Does this mean I have to go and do my version of David? I bet at least I could get him in proportion.

Contradictions, contradictions, contradictions.

* John Hirst has just pointed out that it was him who first made the analogy about a poster for a concert without the band's name on it.

STAMPEDING FOR THE DOOR
27 April 2007

This morning we were back in the loaded Land Rover crossing the Tyne and heading south towards Belmont, on the outskirts of the city of Durham. The conversation went something like this:

'Bill, I think you need to try to engage the kids more right away,' said John Hirst

'What do you mean?' said me, in a rather defensive voice.

'Well, there is no way they will be able to relate to all your theories about recorded music being over and done with. For them it is only beginning. For them music, especially recorded music, is opening up a whole new world. A world away from what they might perceive to be the narrow confines of their life up here. In the same way as you are always banging on about *Strawberry Fields Forever* opening up things for you.'

'So what are you saying?'

'As far as they are concerned, who are you to be telling them that all music that is being recorded now, and that they might like, is pointless, finished and probably rubbish?'

'What do you think I should do then? Pack it in?'

'No. I just think it would be a good idea when you start with these kids this morning if you ask them what kind of music they are into, what bands they like. Everybody likes talking about their favourite records.'

Thirty-odd minutes later.

'Good morning. My name is Bill and his is John. We are artists but ...' etc, etc.

'... But first I want to know what music you are into.'

A good few hands go up.

'You.'

I point to the lass with the ponytail.

'Rave, sir.'

'And what about rave do you like?'

'It's great to dance to.'

'And you.'

Pointing to the lad with the white trainers on.

'Rave, sir.'

These kids are around the 13 age group. All sullen with spots and fringes to hide their faces, and attitude to hide their insecurities. I ask a coven of likely lasses at the back who don't, as yet, seem to have taken my bait of getting them to talk about what music they are into. I level my gaze at the one who seems to possess the most attitude.

'So what are you into?'

'Mumble.'

'What did you say? I'm a bit deaf.'

'Rave, sir.'

And I'm thinking, what the fuck's going on here? How come these kids are into a genre of music that in my head was over by 1989?

'Who else is into rave?'

Most of the hands in the class go up.

'Who is not into rave?'

Some spotty lads put their hands up.

'What're you into?'

'Green Day, sir.'

'Great. I love *American Idiot*. Do you know the album Dookie? As far as I'm concerned that is their best one.'

Now if truth be told I would not have a clue if it is their best one. In fact I could not name one track, but it is the Green Day album that my now 19-year-old son used to insist playing at full volume in the Land Rover anytime he got in it during the summer of 1999. And now I'm thinking that I've got to be careful that I don't start coming on like one of those teachers who are desperately trying to be down with the kids.

After spending some more time getting them talking about what music they were into I steer the conversation to how it was when I was their age that I first got properly into music, but then at some point over the last few years I had started becoming disillusioned with music. All music. And how I started to imagine what it would be like if we woke up one morning and all music had disappeared. It was about then that I started to notice that their minds were beginning to wander. And I wished mine could wander too. But I stopped it and somehow explained what I wanted to do, the score *COLLABORATE* and them going 'Aaaaaaahhhh' for seven minutes on the note of D.

This seven minutes was definitely the longest to date in my life; some of the kids started to giggle halfway through. I tried to look at them severely, which made them giggle even more. But all in all, the note was held for seven minutes without too many problems.

What I haven't mentioned was that this was all happening in a proper music lesson in the music block of the school. Their teacher, whose name was Laura Boyle, sat there for the whole duration of the lesson, watching me struggle my way through the ordeal. At the end she thanked me, not for the quality of my effort or ideas but for being able to keep them under control for an hour. Is this a depressing fact that I have to acknowledge that teaching secondary-school kids in these modern times is more about struggling to keep them contained and under control for the period you have them than about any sparks of inspiration you can ignite in them or wisdom you can impart to them?

'I will be back in a couple of weeks to do something else with you that ...' But by the time I had got halfway through whatever that line was about, the bell was going and they were all stampeding for the door.

NAME A STAR
3 May 2006

Got an email from the artist Paul McDevitt yesterday. He is asking some artists and some scientists to name some stars for a luminous star chart he is making. The star chart is to be part of a larger project called Strategic Questions curated by Gavin Wade (strategicquestions.org). Naming stars has never been an ambition of mine and I didn't really know what the project was about but it seemed easier to say yes than to say no. Hey! Why not? It's not every day you get asked to name stars. Last night I found myself lying in bed awake, 2.45 according to my mobile. The curtain was open and from where I was lying I could stare up at the sky. Maybe by staring up into the heavens I would get some star naming inspiration. All that was visible was the orange glow from the streetlights reflected on the clouded sky. No millions of twinkling stars to fill me with awe at the wonder of creation. Then an idea hit. An idea for a score. This was it:

When in a pub
And the night sky is starry
Get 17 drinkers out
Ask them to stare at the stars
Ask them to hum in unison
While humming
Ask them each to focus on
A faint, distant star
And give it a name
Once their star is named
They can stop humming
Once all the humming has stopped
Return to the pub
And continue drinking.

Rasmus: These written instructions reminds me of Yoko Ono's instructions in Grapefruit. The funny thing with Grapefruit is that you don't have to perform the instructions, you carry them out in your head while you read them.

Robert: And that's where they're strongest.

Paul: Do these scores work in the same way? I play the instructions out in my head but there's only so much I get from it. I can't hear the sound.

Robert: There's a different strength to these instructions. They ask you, the reader, to do part of the work.

Rasmus: I really enjoy Yoko Ono's instructions but I've never done a single one of them outside of my head.

Now this didn't stop the problem of how I was going to approach the naming of the stars for Paul McDevitt but I was able to get back to sleep.

When I awoke this morning and read through the above score another idea presented itself. Each of these lines in the score could be a name for a star. I hope Paul McDevitt goes for it.

COLLABORATE
5 May 2006

The next school we visited was on this past Tuesday (2 May 2006). In-between the one where they did the stampeding and the one on Tuesday I had my 53rd birthday so I had been having all these thoughts about time running out and settling down and cottages in the country and anyway ... So Tuesday morning John Hirst and I were back in the Land Rover crossing the Tyne, heading south. We had to be at Easington Colliery Primary by 9.30. I remember when I was at school learning about these coal mines in the north-east that were right on the edge of the sea, that the mineshafts were hundreds of feet down and then they went miles out under the North Sea. Somehow the idea of going down a mineshaft has never filled me with fear but going down one that then goes out a few miles under the sea is about as scary as it gets.

Anyway that is what Easington Colliery was before Maggie put a stop to it. You know, Maggie as in Margaret Thatcher, our prime minister back in the 1980s who decided to do battle with the miners and close all the coal mines down. Now it is just the name of a village. It took some time for us to find the school. We did.

'Good morning. My name is Bill, his is John and we are *blah blah blah* ...' and off I went. They were a good bunch but yet again even though this lot were aged nine to ten their tastes in music were split between rave and rock. When pushed to name rave tracks they liked, they named tunes I had never heard of. And when pushed to name rock bands they liked, it was always Green Day. No one name-checked any of the current pop bands like Kaiser Chiefs or Franz Ferdinand or even the Sugababes or Girls Aloud that you might expect the girls to go for.

This lot did the note of E and it worked and John and I were getting slicker at what we were doing.

Over the next three days we visited the other four schools that we were supposed to be doing. One was called Wearhead. It was a tiny village junior school up in the hills. It took us almost two hours to get to. There was Bexhill and Southwick, both urban schools and what some might term rough areas. These were also junior schools.

When all this was still in the planning stages with Creative Partnerships I had been asking for all the schools to be secondary. My thinking was that the pupils in junior schools would be too young to understand any of what I was trying to get over. But as we have worked our way through the list of schools that we were scheduled to visit, things started to click in. I don't know if it was just that I was learning how to communicate to them or what, but they have been responding, taking on board the idea of music disappearing or how it first started. Every one that we visited did the full seven minutes. Sadly I've been learning how to keep mind-wandering to a minimum. Mind you, I've just remembered, at one of the schools, John Hirst called a stop to the proceedings because of kids chattering and giggling while they were supposed to be aaaahhh-ing for seven minutes.

This afternoon we visited the last of the seven schools, a secondary school called Shotton Hall. It is a massive comprehensive on a huge council estate. We were in the arts block. These kids are 15 or 16. They are all doing music and drama for GCSE. They were totally up for it and delivered the goods perfectly.

As I said I had been booked into each of these schools for another session in a couple of weeks. This was because if I had followed the original draft of *COLLABORATE*, I would have had to visit each school twice. On the second visit I was to have done a mix of all the tracks from the seven schools. I would have had seven different versions of the combined performance. One was to be selected at random. Then all the school children from all seven schools were to be brought together and a randomly selected mix would be used as a template, to base a performance by all 119 (17 x 7) children. At some point over the couple of weeks leading up to me coming to the north-east, I thought this whole score, as it then stood, would be too unwieldy. No sodding way was I going to be able to keep 119 kids under control, let alone conduct them through a performance of a choral masterpiece. And anyway there was going to be a lot more than the 119, as I had agreed to work with as many kids as there were in each of the classes and not just a selected 17. Even so, my ambitions had run away with themselves. So I simplified the score of *COLLABORATE* to the way it now is without the different mixes from each of the seven schools. In fact there is no real mixing done at all. The plan is just to get all the children at the Hatton and play them back the recording of the seven schools at the same time. All the notes from the scale of C major, playing at the same time with no tampering whatsoever.

But here lies a problem. I've got it arranged with all seven schools that I'm to be coming back in a couple of weeks' time and now there is nothing I need to be doing with them. John Hirst thinks I should just cancel them. He doesn't like getting up early in the morning after he has been down the pub the night before and then spending the afternoon working in the gallery space and then us doing a performance in the evening.

SCORE

17. SCORE

Score your own composition to be performed by The 17.

You need have no previous musical experience.

The score you produce should be clear and simple requiring no instrumentation or lyric.

Email your score to admin@The17.org

If it fulfils the above criteria,
it will be published
and made available
to be performed by The 17,
wherever and whenever applicable.

pb Poster 144   2006

Bill Drummond

ON A ROLL
11 May 2006

I've just reread what I have written to date about the schools visited and there are some things I should come clean about. That thing about the teachers being the enemy was maybe a bit of a pose. I did hate school; there was not one teacher in the 11 years that I spent going to school who ever made me feel inspired. They always made me feel stupid. The teachers were the enemy. But there have been numerous teachers that I have met as an adult who I have thought truly inspirational and wished that they had been my teachers when I was a kid. Which would have been impossible on many counts but mainly because most of them have been younger than me. John McCabe at the first school I went to was one of these truly inspirational teachers – you could tell by the way his pupils so readily engaged with what I was trying to do with them. And the kids at his school, Broadway Juniors, were not from a more privileged background than the others. It was just another school on another estate in a part of England where shipbuilding and coal once provided the employment but now nobody is quite sure how long the next job is going to last. That's if there is one.

Now I know I'm in dangerous water, singling out one of the teachers for what might be seen as praise. There is a good possibility that all the teachers who were involved may read this so I had better add the following. I got total support from all the teachers in the seven schools. They seemed to appreciate and value, if not me in particular, artists coming in and working with their pupils. It made me appreciate the hard work and stress that these teachers have to go through on a daily basis. I would be ground down within a few weeks and end up screaming and shouting at the kids. And then there are the SATS and all that stuff and the pressure of fulfilling everything in the national curriculum.

So now that I have got the grovelling out of the way I can get on with writing about what I was going to do on our return sessions at each of the schools.

We weren't going to be visiting them in the same order as we had the first time around. This morning we revisited Belmont, the one with the sullen and attitude-laden 13-year-olds. I wasn't looking forward to it. We took with us three or four of the framed scores from the gallery including the one about listening to skylarks and the last one about encouraging people to write their own scores for The17 to perform.

'Good morning. Remember how last time I was here I got you to go "Aaaaaaahhh" for seven minutes? Well I'm not going to ask you to do that again.' A sigh of relief goes around the classroom. 'Or even try to imagine what it would be like if music had disappeared. What I want you to do is write a score for other future members of The17 to perform. Now the score that you write does not have to be one that involves people making sounds at all, even with their mouths. It could be just asking The17 – remember The17 can be any 17 people – so asking The17 to go somewhere and listen to something. Maybe there is a sound that you have liked hearing. Maybe it's when you are lying in bed in the morning and you can hear the milk float coming down the street, stopping at all the houses and picking up the empties and putting down the new ones.'
'Sir, we don't get a milkman coming round our way anymore.'
'Yeah, OK. I remember when I was about your age we had this classroom that was in a prefab built in the playground. When we had lessons in there and it began to rain I loved the drumming sound of the rain on the roof. My mind would always drift off from what the teacher was going on about and get lost in this drumming of the rain. That was a very special sound for me. Do any of you know what skylarks sound like?'
Not a hand went up. Maybe some of them did know what skylarks sound like, maybe they even love the sound of them but felt it would not be cool to let on they knew. I used to love listening to skylarks as a kid. Where we used to live in Scotland when I was about ten there were these fields up the road at the back of our house. I would go up there by myself around June time and lie on the grass and wait for a skylark to start ascending.

'Skylarks are little brown birds, a bit bigger than a sparrow, about the size of a starling. And what they do is start flying up into the sky from the grass, not a tree or a bush, and they climb higher and higher and higher into the sky until they are just a tiny spec against the blue, or most probably grey. And all the time they are flying higher they are singing this song of theirs. It's not a particularly musical song like a robin's or a blackbird's but it just keeps going and going. Now I don't know why I liked listening to it back then when I was ten. Nowadays when I listen to one it sounds to me like it is saying "Isn't it great to be alive in this world today, right now, up here, just me and the sky." Now I also know that this is just me anthropomorphising the situation, and that in fact he – 'cause it's always a he that is doing this thing – is just up there strutting his stuff for the female skylarks to check out.'

I could see their attention beginning to drift; I curtailed my soliloquy to the skylark. 'So I wrote this score here called *TAKE* about taking 17 people out to listen to skylarks.

> In June
> Take 17 people to a place
> Where skylarks climb
> High into the sky.
> Request the 17 to lie on their backs
> On the grass and listen
> To the skylarks as they climb
> High into the sky.

'But if you do a score about getting The17 to listen to something, you don't have to limit it to something you have already heard yourself. You could give them an instruction to go anywhere you want in the world. There are no cost restrictions or time restrictions, anywhere your imagination wants to take people to listen to something or to make sounds with their mouths. Or it could be just down the road to the bus shelter.

'So just write it out like a short list of instructions, sort of like I have done it, put your name on it and we will have it designed and printed up so it looks like one of these that I have done. Not that I'm going to be paying to have one of these frames made to put them in, but we will put them up on The17 website so everyone can see it and download it and perform it, if they want.'

I was on a roll with these kids, they were actually listening to what I was saying. 'What I want you to do is to get into groups of no more than four, but you can do it by yourselves if you want, and put together your own scores.'

I realised that getting them into small groups might cause all sorts of problems about classroom politics and pecking orders. My two younger girls report back to me or their mum daily about all the politics that go on between girls in their classes. All the falling out and the new best friends until next week. I remember none of this going on between my mates when I was at school and I must have been oblivious to it among

Rasmus: I would like The17 to go and listen to the sound of a Draken fighter jet fly over the small town of Karup in Denmark. The air base outside Karup used to be the largest in northern Europe. In the 1980s it was the home of all the Danish Draken jets. The runway was not very far from Karup, so the jets were always flying low over the town.

The delayed roar of a jet breaking through the sound barrier is truly amazing. My teachers at the local school would pause mid sentence whenever a jet passed over us and continue as if nothing had happened once the noise had disappeared. It was a part of the daily life. It happened every hour. We never even thought about it.

the girls. Mind you, I have always been oblivious to what's going on with girls or women, could never understand why they found stories about relationships so interesting. Relationships to me always seem to get in the way of the action, the real life where things happen.

When they decided to retire the Draken jets and move all other jets away from Karup, there was a local outcry. There was demonstrations. The locals had become used to the sound of the jets. They loved it and did not want it to disappear.

I put that bit in so you can go, 'I wonder what he is trying to tell us here about himself.'

Back to the action in the classroom. We hand out unlined sheets of A4. In fact, they were taken from the same block of A4 paper that I am writing on at the moment as I have filled my Black n' Red notebook and have not got round to getting a new one yet. They get down to work with a gusto that I found surprising. Even those three girls that had been so full of attitude on our first visit are embracing the idea of writing their own scores. John Hirst and I spend the rest of the session with them flitting from group to group to answer questions and give encouragement. The time flashes by and the bell announces the lunch break. They rush for the door leaving us to collect the sheets of A4 with their scores.

SCORE

42. REV

TAKE 17 PEOPLE TO THE GARAGE

ASK THE17 TO LISTEN TO THE CAR AND MOTORBIKE NOISES.

ASK PAUL AND HIS FRIENDS TO REV THE ENGINES.

Daniel, Dylan, Jake, Luke and Steven Broadway Jnr School 2006

pb Poster 145   2006

'SO WHAT INFLUNCE HAS CORNELIUS CARDEW HAD ON WHAT YOU ARE DOING?'
12 May 2006

I'm in a café just on the edge of the University of Newcastle campus. Not a café you would choose to spend much time in, but it is the closest to the Hatton Gallery and so handy for the interview I am doing with Neil Cooper for the Scottish art magazine *MAP*. *MAP* is a comparatively new magazine. I got a copy of the first issue in early 2005 and liked the look of it and my sometime colleague Duncan McLaren seems to have an outlet in it for his creative musings, which is a good thing by me.

The question posed in the title has just been put to me and this is the way I am answering it. Well, maybe not quite 'cause I'm writing these words early the following morning and maybe I'm not remembering everything I said and maybe I'm writing more than I said to make myself sound more articulate.

If I had been asked this question six months ago, I could have gone hand-on-my-heart and said I'd never heard of him. But this is now the third time I have been asked this in the past few months so I can't deny ever having heard of him. As for him having an influence on me, that is a more complicated matter.

The first two people to ask me were Gwilly Edmondez and James Saunders, both involved academically with new music. They know their history of 20th-century serious music. They both thought there were parallels between what I am attempting to do and what this Cornelius Cardew had done in the 1960s. Both Gwilly and James emailed me blurb on Cardew, which I read. And I thought it was more than interesting, but it did make me wonder what the point is in doing The17. It has all been done before, 40 years ago. This Cardew bloke turns out to be a giant of postwar serious contemporary music; everybody who's anybody knows his stuff and what he was about. It's like me having never heard of the Sex Pistols but wanting to form a fast and furious rock band in 2006, screeching songs about anarchy, destruction, getting pissed and swearing on TV. Pointless.

Then I reread what they had sent me and went on Google and decided that what I am trying to do is different but yes, there are some parallels with the Scratch Orchestra work he was doing between 1968 and 1972. I learnt that Cornelius Cardew was born in 1936 and died in 1981, was British, studied with Stockhausen in the late 1950s and had started something called the Scratch Orchestra. The more I read about him the more I became aware of the influence he had on me. As with so many influences, they happen in roundabout and unbeknown ways. The rest of this chapter details an example of a roundabout and unbeknown way.

In May 1973 I was in my last throes of being an art student at Liverpool School of Art. Whatever was going on in the art school was losing any meaning for me. But one day in May I did amble into one of the art school buildings that has long since been flattened. It was called the Deaf School and had, in a previous life, been a school for the deaf. On this particular day in the main studio a space had been cleared and there was a man there, a visiting lecturer I assumed, and he had with him boxes of violins, cellos and an assortment of other classical instruments. As I may have pointed out earlier, I hated anything to do with classical music then, but I wondered what he was going to be doing with these violins and things. I thought if I hung around and listened it seemed like a valid reason for not getting on with whatever else I was supposed to be doing.

Rasmus: This book is full of jumps back and forth in time. There are so many stories within a story within a story. The problem is that Bill has this timeline within the book, so he can't just talk about when he was 12. He has to say 'I am sitting out on a ledge and thinking about when I was 12' and then he can tell us the story. Most of the time it works really well, but am I the only one who gets a little bit confused sometimes?

Within five minutes I had a viola under my chin and a bow in my right hand. There were about half a dozen of us in similar positions with these instruments and he was beginning to show us where to put our fingers so that we could play the opening bars to *The Blue Danube* waltz by Strauss. He was also telling us you didn't have to spend years learning to play classical music, you could do it in a day, and that by the end of the afternoon we would all be playing a whole chunk of *The Blue Danube* waltz.

And he was right. By the end of that afternoon we were and it sounded brilliant in an out-of-tune cacophonous sort of way. He told us that we could be part of the Portsmouth Sinfonia and that they were going to be doing a concert at the Royal Albert Hall. He told us he was serious about what he was doing; that we had to try hard; that this was not a piss-take; that if we wanted to take part, we would have to commit; and that it didn't matter if we were unmusical or had no ambition to be professional musicians.

If you can call it a lecture, that was the last one I ever went to in my life. Within a month I was no longer at art school. I was off into the big wide world.

The Portsmouth Sinfonia went on to reach some sort of infamy, releasing a couple of albums that I never heard, playing the Royal Albert Hall that I never went to. But that day trying to learn to play *The Blue Danube* waltz in the Deaf School had a profound and long-lasting influence on me. This influence was two-fold. The first is one that never a day (or a week) goes past without me thinking about it. Whoever the visiting lecturer was, he said stuff on that day that has stuck with me ever since. Of course I can't remember any of the actual words he said but the overall message was that the classical music world is all about keeping people out by making it harder and harder for people to take part. It is a place where the cult of the virtuoso reigns supreme, where they want the audience to sit quietly, know their place and appreciate genius. This, he told us, has brought about stagnation in music and music-making.

Now I didn't know anything about the world of classical music but what he seemed to be saying fit perfectly with what I had been feeling about the rock music being made in Britain over the previous couple of years. It had become all about musicianship: the more of a virtuoso you were, the better. The distance between being a 17-year-old lad with a guitar and those on stage was so vast it was like there was no point in having a go yourself.

What this bloke seemed to be saying to us was that if you want to do something, don't wait to be asked or given permission by anyone, be it your mother, teacher, peer group, music press, record companies or art establishments. The fact that you may lack confidence and don't know what the fuck you are trying to do should not be reasons for not doing whatever it is. There will be a million people out there who will want to let you know that you are shit. Ignore them. There will be others who will think that without their validation what you are doing is worthless. Ignore them. This, if anything, has been the guiding principle in everything that I have tried to do ever since. I am a person riddled with insecurities but that one day in the Deaf School made me think 'Fuck 'em!'

The following week at art school we were meant to be putting on our end-of-year show. I had literally nothing to show, as I had already burnt all my paintings and most of my days were spent wandering around Liverpool, in the thrall of this broken-down and fucked-up city. I believed there was nothing I could do within the confines of the art school which could compete with the reality on offer at every turn of the corner in this city.

Bill Drummond

There was an old piece of packing case in the yard of the house where I was living. It measured about 2 x 3 ft. I painted it white. Then I stencilled on it in black paint 'Is Clapton still God?' This bit of tat was the only thing I put in the show. I gave no explanation. I had none to give. They sent me a letter asking me to consider my future at art school. I'm still considering it. With hindsight, an explanation could have been:

'In the late 1960s a graffiti started to appear on walls around the country. It read "Clapton is God". The Clapton referred to was Eric Clapton, the former guitarist with Cream. This was in the days before graffiti was a ubiquitous part of the urban landscape. It was also not part of a cynical record company marketing ploy. Lads of my generation had been moved in various quarters of the country to go out, pot and brush in hand, and paint on walls "Clapton is God" for no good reason.

'Although I had never done this myself, in early 1969 I would have gone along with the sentiments and did go so far as to scrawl it on the cover of my geography jotter.

'My generation thought of Eric Clapton as the greatest guitarist in the world; we knew that Hendrix was maybe better but he was too exotic for us to identify with in any way. But by elevating Clapton to the pantheon of the gods we distanced ourselves from ever even dreaming we could do anything as worthy. It wasn't long before his feet of clay became all too obvious. It was something in that day spent with a viola under my chin trying to play *The Blue Danube* waltz and listening to what this bloke had to say that prompted me to stencil those words on the side of a packing case.

'By June 1973 it must have been almost four years since anybody had bothered to graffiti the original proclamation. What I had done in no way connected with anything in the outside there-and-then world but it connected with everything going on in my head. The more you put an artist, musician or anybody, however talented, on a pedestal, the more you take away something from yourself.'

After being asked for the second time if Cornelius Cardew and his Scratch Orchestra had been an influence on me, I did some minor research. I discovered that Gavin Bryars, an English experimental composer of now major repute, was a member of Cardew's Scratch Orchestra. In 1970, inspired by the Scratch Orchestra, Bryars went on to set up the Portsmouth Sinfonia while teaching at the Portsmouth School of Art. It must have been Gavin

Bryars who spent a day working with a bunch of us in the Deaf School buildings in 1973.

Once you start reading what the Scratch Orchestra was about and then about the Portsmouth Sinfonia, it becomes very obvious what influence Cornelius Cardew has had on not only The17 but on everything I have done since that late spring day in 1973.

As l said, the influence was two-fold. The following term Gavin Bryars returned for a few more sessions in the Deaf School building at Liverpool Art School. The nucleus of students which I had been part of was joined by some fresh recruits from the new intake. Gavin Bryars was as good as his word. They all took part in the infamous performance of the Portsmouth Sinfonia at the Royal Albert Hall. The bunch of students, or at least a chunk of them, were inspired by Bryars to go on and form their own band. This band carried on rehearsing in the same space. They called themselves Deaf School. Deaf School's music was everything but classical.

By this time I had escaped the clutches of the city and I was out in the world trying to be Jack Kerouac or Jack London or somebody, searching for that beckoning peak or at least a road to be on. It didn't last long. By autumn 1975 I was back in Liverpool, building stage sets at the Everyman Theatre.

Deaf School – the band not the building – had evolved from a concept to a real thing. Music papers put them on front covers; Warner Brother Records signed them. They recorded and released three albums, but the hits did not come so they split up. Deaf School are now cited as Liverpool's most influential band after The Beatles.

One of the fresh intake of students who got involved with the Gavin Bryars stuff was Clive Langer. He was the musical driving force of Deaf School. Clive and I met and became friends sometime after my return to Liverpool. At 7.35 on 5 May 1977, on the eve of Deaf School's first US tour, Clive Langer, Phil Allen, Kev (James) Ward and myself were in The Grapes pub on Mathew Street. Later that evening we were going to be seeing The Clash. Kev had been in the year above me at art school; he designed much of Deaf School's artwork. Phil was the brother of Enrico Cadillac, Deaf School's frontman, and roadie for the band. Clive was holding forth. Punk was happening. Deaf School were not. Clive had an idea. On this tour of the US the band were not taking their own equipment with them but hiring everything out there. Clive's idea was that Phil, Kev and me should form a band while they were in the

States, and seeing as we didn't have any gear we could use some of Deaf School's. Phil would be the drummer, Kev the bass player and me the guitarist.

None of us had ever played in a band before. I don't think Kev had ever picked up a guitar, let alone played one. By the time Clive came back from America we had played our first gig as a three piece at Bretton Hall College near Leeds; got ourselves a name – Big In Japan; recruited Jayne Casey to be our front person; headlined the Hope Street Festival; we got our first press cutting, the opening line of which read 'Sadly, they saved the worst for last.'

So the slightly strained logic goes – no Cornelius Cardew and the Scratch Orchestra, no Gavin Bryars and The Portsmouth Sinfonia; no Gavin Bryars and The Portsmouth Sinfonia, no Clive Langer and Deaf School, no me and Big In Japan and no me doing The17 and everything I have done in the meantime. So without Cornelius Cardew – different life-path, different everything.

So back to me in the café in Newcastle and being interviewed by Neil Cooper from this *MAP* magazine. When he asked me if I had been influenced by Cornelius Cardew, I don't think he was expecting the full-on and in-detail times-dates-places answer that he got. Although I did miss out the Eric Clapton thing with him. I also forgot to mention Bob Wooler's input into the conversation we had with Clive Langer in The Grapes.

I got another cup of tea and Neil asked his next question.

'HAS FLUXUS HAD AN INFLUENCE ON YOU?'
12 May 2006

I took a sip from the cup of tea. Looked out the window at some students walking by all dressed up as doctors and nurses. Then took another sip from my cup and started. What I said went something like this:

'Ten years ago I had never heard of Fluxus. All right, maybe 15 years ago but it would have been years before I had any idea what they were about. Added to that it was only four years ago that I bought a book about them and then got that big Codex Fluxus book. It was after I started doing the Penkiln Burn and people started to ask me if I had been influenced by Fluxus that I thought I had better find out what this Fluxus was all about.

'It was only after I started to read up about Fluxus that I began to realise how influenced by it I had been over the years. And as with Cornelius Cardew, I had no idea how influenced I had been by this bunch of New York-based artists and composers from the early 1960s.

'When I was six years old, back in 1959, my sister had already been having piano lessons for a couple of years. In our house we had what was rather pretentiously called an upright grand. It had belonged to my paternal grandmother. But before that it had belonged to someone else in the family. It had a date of manufacture on it: 1874. It was a very ornate piano with candelabra to help the pianist read music in the evenings. I had no idea if it was any good. Other than a wind-up record player and some 1920s 78s that had belonged to my great uncle, this piano was the only access to music we had in the house. There was no television and my parents never listened to music on the radio, but on Sunday evenings my mother would occasionally try to get us around the piano to sing while either she or my big sister played. What these songs were I can't remember; all I know is they must have been dull to leave no impression on me. What I do remember is that I wished I could play the piano and if I had been able to, I'm sure the music I would have made would have been far better than the dull fare on offer on those far-off Sunday evenings.

'I asked my mother if I could have piano lessons. She told me I couldn't have any until I had learned to read properly. At the time, I was in the backward class at school. My reading was way behind. It never caught up, so I never got the piano lessons.

'It must have been around that time when I was refused the opportunity to have piano lessons that my complicated relationship with this piano began. Left on my own I would spend hours tinkling on it, making up random tunes. And other things like how high I had to drop a marble to hit one of its keys to make a sound. I don't remember ever trying to work out proper tunes that other people knew. It was always just these odd random ones. Some days I would take out my frustrations on this piano; I would bang the keys as hard as I could with open hands, all over the keyboard. Then I would do it as quietly as I could. Then build it up again louder and louder. As much as I may have been tempted, I never used my actual fists. At that stage I doubt I had ever heard a piano concerto or seen one of the great pianists like Rubinstein on TV so I don't know what I might have been mimicking.

'Then some time in the early 1960s I discovered that I could remove a board above the foot pedals and below the keyboard. Once this was removed I could stick my head inside the sound box of the piano. Once my head was in I would stay there for up to an hour at a time while I scratched, tapped, plucked or did anything else that would get sounds out of the piano wires. It always helped if I had one of my knees on the sustain pedal of the piano. This would enable the sounds that I was making while my head was stuck in the sound box to reverberate on and on and on.

'I'm not saying I was doing this every day or even every week, and I would only ever do it if there were no family members about, but I carried on doing it for the next 25 or so years until I was 33 $\frac{1}{3}$.

'There was nothing like it. It was an escape into this world where endless sound was all around. Sound as big as the universe. Sound not tied down to hummable tunes or corny rhythms.

'Some time in the mid-1960s, by which time I'd been doing my head in the piano exercises for a few years, I saw a feature on telly about people smashing up a piano with sledgehammers. It not only looked fantastic, it also sounded like nothing I had ever heard before. What I wanted to do was get a sledgehammer and smash up our piano just to hear those sounds at close quarters for myself.

'At that time the country was full of old pianos that nobody could play anymore. They were all left over from a time before radios and record players, when people had to make their own music. To be able to play the piano was a social skill that many a young man aspired to. Every pub had one. But you know that – you've seen enough old films. There was another problem for these old pianos. Central heating. When it came in for the masses in the 1960s, central heating completely fucked these pianos. Buckled their frames, made them impossible to keep in tune.

'After this one showing of a piano being smashed on telly, piano-smashing swept the country. No village fete was complete without a piano-smashing contest. Soon all the pianos available for smashing in the country had been smashed. So piano-smashing faded from the place it held for a few years in the public imagination and popular culture. Except I kept dreaming of smashing our piano. By the time I reached my teens neither my sister nor mum ever played it. I was the only one in the family who used it for anything other than stacking things on top.'

Piano-smashing, and this piano in particular, will be brought back into this text at a later stage. But for the time being they are being sidelined in favour of Yoko Ono. I first became aware of Yoko Ono as the girlfriend of John Lennon and when they started doing those things together in the late 1960s. I had no idea who she was or where she came from. I also had no context in which to place what they were doing. I just took it for granted and thought ... I was going to say brilliant, but I am aware that whenever I think something is pretty good I either use the word brilliant or the word fantastic. There was an article by a journalist, in *The Guardian* I think, who was telling us how the words brilliant and fantastic were banned by their reviews editor, as these words tell you nothing about what is being described and only inform the reader of how bland and unoriginal the journalist is. I agree with this reviews editor but find myself time and again drawn to using the words brilliant and fantastic. I will endeavour to get through the rest of this book without using either.

Well, back to John and Yoko. Not only did I love the ramshackle nature of The Plastic Ono Band singles they made *Cold Turkey*, *Give Peace A Chance* and *War Is Over* one, but all their activities too: like spending a week in a bed as a protest against the Vietnam war; sending an acorn to all the world leaders; placing a billboard advertisement up in Times Square that read 'War Is Over If You Want It'; releasing an album with a picture of yourselves naked in a completely asexual way on the cover and calling the album Two Virgins. The fact that the album was completely unlistenable seemed to make it even better. Every soddin' act in the world could make a listenable album; it took something else to make one that nobody could ever listen to all the way through, even one side let alone the whole thing.

'Sometime around then I read about how this Yoko Ono had got a pair of step ladders and when you climbed to the top of them there was a small mirror facing you and on the mirror was the word YES. In all the acres of sneering press coverage that surrounded the antics of John and Yoko I must have read that Yoko Ono was an artist. I presumed that her being an artist meant she painted pictures or something, I had no idea at this time that all this, what John and Yoko were doing together, was art. Her art. Their art. Even great art. All I knew was that I thought it was both brilliant and fantastic.

'Everything that John Lennon did after The Plastic Ono Band I found immensely dull. As for the *Imagine* song and even worse the promotional film that went with it, I could not believe how pompously trite a record could be. This was vanity writ large. It almost excuses Bono.'

Between the years 1983 and 1986, when I was working as an A&R consultant for WEA Records (Warner, Elektra, Atlantic) I was given an office in Soho, off Broadwick Street. In the office I had the roll-top desk that my father had used all his life and the family piano. There was no record or cassette player. I never listened to any cassettes that anybody sent in. If anybody came by and wanted me to listen to their stuff, I asked them to play it on the piano. By this time, after years of damage caused by central heating, this piano was beyond being tuned. My reckoning was that if a song were any good, it would still sound good on an old, broken and out-of-tune piano. I don't think any of them ever did. Jimmy Ruffin once came in looking for a deal. I told him I'd buy him lunch if he played *What Becomes Of The Broken Hearted*. He sat down at the piano and sang it for me while playing it. This seemed to prove my rule. It sounded like an eternally great pop tune should. Pete Townsend also came in one day. It was when he was a part-time editor at Faber & Faber; he was interested in me doing text for a book about Liverpool. I wanted to ask him to play *My Generation* on the piano, but I didn't have the nerve.

During these three years of prostitution I would still find myself removing the panel under the keyboard, sticking my head inside the sound box and scratching, plucking and banging the wires. I would be there exploring a world of sound weirder and more exciting than anything I was supposed to be listening to with a view to signing and turning it into an international platinum-selling act. On my last day at Warners I planned to go out and buy a sledgehammer and smash up the piano then and there in my office. It was to be my parting shot to music. Other things happened. I never bought the sledgehammer and I don't know what happened to the piano.

It was not until some point in the 1990s that I got to hear about Fluxus; that they were an art movement of sorts, based in New York although the individuals involved were drawn from all around the world; that Yoko Ono, although Japanese, had been part of this movement. I also started to learn that what she had been doing in the late 1960s and very early 1970s with John Lennon was as much part of her practice as an artist as anything she might have done that was put into a gallery with white walls and a catalogue essay and everything.

'When I was learning about the history of art in the early 1970s there was no mention of Fluxus. New York in the 1960s was Pop Art and colour-field painting. As I said, it was only after numerous people had asked me about Fluxus that I got around to reading a book about them. Up until then I had never heard of George Maciunas. I had no idea they were as much about music as visual arts. Their thinking about music had nothing to do with what had evolved in the US over the previous 100 years. A big part of me had been thinking for over a decade that if ever there was to be a music to engage me again, it would have to have evolved from some source other than the American tradition. As for what was now being called World Music, it so often came over as Easy Listening for the hip and liberal. It was never listened to by us Western whites in the same way or for the same reasons as those for whom it was being made originally.

'But I digress; back to Fluxus. What I discovered, and you probably already guessed, was that this piano-smashing thing that I saw on telly in the 1960s was a Fluxus concert. I have no idea which of the composers or artists associated with Fluxus came up with the score that required the performer to smash up a piano but I am sure whoever it was had no idea that it would have such an influence on grass-roots popular culture in Britain. And on me in particular.'

Yet again, I didn't say all this to Neil Cooper from *MAP* magazine. After I took that last sip of tea a few pages back I rounded it off by saying something about how the actions of Yoko Ono with John Lennon in tow had a huge influence in the whole way that I approach many of the things that I've attempted to do: the power of the symbolic act has had a great hold on my imagination ever since. Whether those symbolic acts have had any influence, positive or otherwise, on the world at large, I have no idea.

Without Fluxus I don't think Yoko Ono would have developed as an artist in the way she did. Without the inspiration of Yoko Ono I don't think my mind would have developed in the way that it did. And then there is the destruction thing. The need to destroy what has gone before to enable one to move on has been a recurring theme in what I do, even if I wish it wasn't. So, yes, Fluxus has had a powerful influence on me. Even if it has been roundabout and unseen from where I was standing.

Before I get on with responding in full to Neil Cooper's next question I have one last thing I want to say about Yoko Ono.

Some years ago I was asked by a BBC Radio producer to write and front a radio series about the influence of art on pop and pop on art. It was obviously a rich seam to be mined. I was not only flattered to be asked, I was up for the challenge. The trouble was, I had a ton of work things of my own to be getting on with so I put the BBC off for a year. When the year was up they contacted me again. I told them I was still busy but went in for meetings with them. They were people I got on well with. The remit seemed pretty broad but the last thing I was interested in doing was interviewing ex-members of all those British bands that had started their lives in British art schools. I no longer had any interest in the music they had produced, and I couldn't fake it.

By the end of the meeting I had agreed that if some once-in-a-decade chance of an interview came up, then I would make myself available. Two months later I got the call. Yoko Ono was going to be in the country promoting some remix of one of her 1970s records. Obviously I had no interest in whatever this music record was, but I duly came into the BBC to interview her.

Now I want you to know that I had never thought of Yoko Ono as a physically attractive woman. I liked the fact that she had never felt the need to try and present herself in an obviously sexualised way. Mind you, I hated the way she presented herself in that subservient role of opening the shutters on the promotional film for *Imagine* while John Lennon sat at the piano playing the genius.

The men from the BBC wanted to know if I had done my homework on Yoko Ono. I felt I didn't need to, as I knew more than enough already. And what I really wanted to achieve was an interview with her that didn't mention John Lennon.

And so to Broadcasting House. I turned up and so did Yoko. We were put in a studio together, a small table between us. Behind her was the studio window, behind which I could see the engineer and the two producers and Yoko Ono's PR people all staring back at me.

I've been interviewed hundreds of times. I know the mistakes that interviewers make. I have learnt how to help them out when they seem to lose their way. I also know that if there is something particular I want to say, I will be able to shoehorn it into the interview whatever the questions that are being asked.

Yoko Ono was not what I was expecting at all. She was a woman who had just turned 70. I had done that much research. And as I have already stated, she had never figured as a sexual being in my imagination. An interesting and, at times, great artist but not 'Yeah, Yoko Ono, I'd give her one.' But sitting in front of me was this diminutive 70-year-old woman who oozed sexuality. And then there was the cleavage. What is a poor man supposed to do?

The green light goes on and I make the classic journalistic mistake. I ask long convoluted questions that she is then able to answer in one word, 'Yes'. Then another long, convoluted question, another one-word answer, 'No'. There I was, wanting to show her that I knew and respected a lot about her work but I failed to just ask something simple like 'What do you consider in your long career as an artist is your most important work?' Corny I know but at least it might have got her going. When she did move off the one-word answer it was to try and bring John Lennon into it. We spoke for about 30 minutes. At no time did it feel like a conversation. And that was that.

So maybe this last bit about me and Yoko Ono has nothing to do with the question 'Has Fluxus had an influence on you?' but there again: no Fluxus, no Yoko (well, in the way that we know her and her work); no Yoko, no me interviewing her; no me interviewing her, no me coming to the realisation I should never have thought I could front a radio programme.

I take the last sip of tea from my cup, order another one and ready myself for the next question.

'HAVE THE SITUATIONISTS BEEN AN INFLUENCE ON YOU?'
12 May 2006

I took a sip from my fresh and very hot cup of tea. Looked out of the window. The students dressed up as doctors and nurses have disappeared to be replaced by the Newcastle University Women's Rugby Team, dressed in full match kit and posing for a team photo. The cup of tea required another sip from it and then I began my answer. It's not a one-worder, or even a one-liner.

When punk happened, certain British music journalists who took their craft seriously took to mentioning this thing called the Situationists, in particular when discussing the Sex Pistols and Malcolm McLaren. I had no idea what the Situationists were or where they came from but after a while I became aware that they were from Paris circa 1950s. To quote my now-dated version of the history of art again, as far as I understood it the epicentre of Western art had moved from Paris to New York at some point in the late 1940s. Yes, there was Sartre and his existentialism and yes, I was a big fan of Sartre's books although I didn't hold with all that 'a universe without God' bit. As far as I was concerned belief in a god was irrelevant. God was as real as the chair I am sitting in and the table I am writing on. God did not need my belief to exist. I would have found the question, 'Does God believe in me?' more interesting. But anyway, Jean-Paul Sartre was not part of the history of art, not part of the canon as it has been constructed for us to consume.

It was not until about 1995, after Jimmy Cauty and I had done our work as the K Foundation, when I got to sort of know this bloke who knew all about the Situationists that I became aware of how they could be seen to relate to us. But as far as he was concerned it was the Letteristes – who came just before and evolved into the Situationists – who were the more important. Like Joy Division before New Order or Dada before surrealism or something. He went on about a thing called the *dérive*, where you just get up in the morning and wander about the city and explore a thing called the city's psychogeography. This all sounded like an intellectual justification for what I had been doing most of my life. And if I had been doing it, then most of mankind had been doing it for as long as we have had cities to wander around and lose ourselves in and get in touch with something else.

Then he was telling us about Red Indians burning their wigwams in a war of competitive gift-giving with a rival tribe. He told us this was called potlatch and somehow potlatch was a big part of the Letteriste / Situationist thinking. He somehow thought our money-burning was a huge example of potlatch, writ large across the imagination of the British public.

He also went on about something called the spectacle: in this was all that was wrong with modem society. But I didn't understand what he was on about. The only reason why I keep referring to him as 'he' is because I can't remember his name and as I am writing this a couple of hundred miles from my workshop I don't have access to my old diaries to check it.

Then around 2002 a biography of Guy Debord came out. Debord was perceived as the main mover and shaker in the Situationists. After reading that and attempting to read Guy Debord's masterwork *Society of the Spectacle*, I sort of understood what it was all about and understood why this bloke thought Jimmy Cauty and myself had been influenced by the Situationists. The biography of Debord explained how the students who took part in the Paris riots of 1968 were very much influenced by Debord and *Society of the Spectacle* in particular, that they would take phrases from the book and daub them on to the walls of Paris as slogans.

In Liverpool there is a wide tree-lined avenue called Princess Avenue. Well, one side is called Princess Avenue, the other is called Princess Road, but everybody calls it Prinny Ave. It cuts through Liverpool 8, a grand and fine boulevard worthy of a great Victorian city like Liverpool. The large town houses lining both sides of the avenue have long been split up into bedsits and student flats. At either end of Princess Avenue are a pair of statues mounted high on plinths. Who this particular pair of the great and good were, I have no idea.

In the mid-1970s I used to get the 82c bus into town every morning and back again every evening. I must have passed these statues a few hundred times without even noticing them. That is until one day somebody had sprayed a graffiti on the statue the bus passed on the way into town. It read 'Never Work'. On the way back home I noticed that on the plinth for the other statue, in the same spray hand, were the words 'Drift Around'.

Day after day I would notice these two examples of graffiti. They went round and round in my head like a mantra. There was a strange poetry to it. It seemed so incongruous compared to all the other graffiti around the city by young lads wanting to make their mark. Twenty years after first seeing these two statues graffitied in Liverpool, I came across a photo in this biog of Debord. The photograph was of some graffiti on a Parisian wall; underneath the photo was a translation – 'Never Work – Drift Around'.

I still do not know exactly what Guy Debord was on about. From the biography he came over as a somewhat unpleasant and egocentric man and I do not agree with what seems to be the sentiment of the graffitied statement. But I cannot deny that it still has an ongoing and powerful pull on my imagination.

THOUGHTS, FEELINGS AND IMAGINED PICTURES
19 May 2006

With each of the remaining seven schools that I have been to the pupils seemed to respond very positively to what I was inviting them to do. One of the recurring problems has been that if I gave them any sort of example of something I might think of as a sound that would have a special place for me, they would seem to latch onto it and use a very similar theme themselves. At every school I would read out the skylarks one that I did. Maybe this is the reason there has been a number of scores asking The17 to listen to birds or animals.

Some of the classes seemed more lateral in their thinking as a whole group. I don't know if this is because they had a particularly inspiring teacher or because there was something in the ethos of the school. There were a couple of schools where I got a slight sense of cynicism from the teacher about what I was doing on my first visit, but this has been non-existent on my second visit. This may be because getting the pupils to come up with their own scores was more inclusive, but from the off they were all up for it.

I spent months contemplating the 17 scores that I wrote to try and kick this thing off before I wrote any of them down. Those words that got written down and printed will continue to be tampered with and knocked about at various times over the coming months and years. Always refining, trying to get closer to something, but maybe never getting any better. Even some of those original 17 scores will get kicked out, dropped from the side to make way for others that have already been brewing away for some time. There was the one about making up a chant and the one about taking all The17 abroad to perform: they are for the dumper. Mind you, they may have been long since dumped by the time you read this and there will be no record of them in this book or anywhere else.

But these 50 or so scores done by the kids in Sunderland and County Durham have been done with no contemplation, no thoughts about the state of music, no half an eye on their own place in the history of art and music-thinking in the early years of the 21st century. They just did them 'cause some bloke turned up in their class and asked them to do it and probably by the time they were at home having their tea that day they had completely forgotten what they had written. Maybe it is the fact that very little thought had gone into them that gives them, at the very least, charm and in some cases a real potency and charge.

Bill Drummond

The one school that has been markedly different from the others was Wearhead Primary. All the others were urban schools. Wearhead is a little village and as you may guess is up near the source of the Wear. The Wear flows on down through Durham and heads out into the sea at Sunderland. By the time it gets to Sunderland it is a large deep river where ships have been built for centuries. Up in Wearhead it is a babbling brook.

The village school has no more than 48 pupils and only two teachers. It took us a couple of hours to drive from Newcastle up to Wearhead; high up on the Pennines among the fields of spring lambs and primroses and dry-stone walls. And the kids were different: not posh or anything, but aware of things in different ways. When asked what kind of music they were into, there still seemed to be this taste for rave on one side and Green Day on the other.

The lot we were working with at Wearhead were drawn from school years 4, 5 and 6. At the other schools they were all from one class in one year. When we got there the second time the teacher, Liz Gill, had already done work with them over the previous few days that related to The17. She had downloaded a number of the scores and had been using them with her pupils. Kathryn, one of the girls in her class, had taken it upon herself to write a score at home for The17 to perform. She had brought it in and the teacher had got the class to do it. Liz Gill got the class to perform it for us. It is the score that is now called *PLACE*.

Liz Gill asked the kids to stand in a circle and invited John Hirst and me to join in with them. She asked us to think of a place, close our eyes and think of a picture of our place; this picture was to represent an atmosphere, and we had to think of a sound that was in the picture or atmosphere. Think about all of this for 17 seconds. She indicated when the 17 seconds were up and she asked us to keep our eyes closed and sing the sound for a further 17 seconds.

I was not only moved that this girl had taken it upon herself to write this score and that the teacher had taken it seriously enough to get the children to perform it, but also that it worked. It worked brilliantly – all the children joined in, or it sounded like it to me as I stood there with my eyes closed, joining in and making my sound. It also sounded great. If you are a junior school teacher, I recommend you try this score with them. If you do, let us know how it went (via admin@the17.org).

In each of the schools that we visited this second time, there was always one kid who seemed to really get what I was going on about, in a way that was well beyond how I am implying that all of the children sort of instantly got it. This one kid in each class of these seven classes would never be the classroom comedian or from the clique of cool girls or smart-arsed lads. They were always the slight outsiders, maybe not the ones with the obvious good looks that you think might mark them out for success.

I used to have a theory that in every class in the country there is somebody with the potential to be a pop star. And I don't mean an also-ran in some faceless boy or girl band. I mean somebody with something real to put over whether it be a Robbie Williams, Bono, Bowie or that lad out of The Streets (those four were not chosen for any particular reason; they were just the first four that leapt out of my pencil). Now I've said that, I noticed I didn't include any girls so to make up for that I will put Poly Styrene, Madonna, Joni Mitchell and Lily Allen. The difference between those in the class who make it as a pop star (also read actor, artist or whatever) and all those thousands of others in those classes who don't, is not because they didn't lack talent or even motivation. It is because they didn't have the opportunity, they weren't in the right time, right place; the Zeitgeist wasn't knocking about. Maybe I have already said this, but now I want to say it in a more straightforward way. Plenty of pop stars who had their 15 minutes or more whose talents, however slim, only made any sense at a particular point in the history of pop. John Lydon (Johnny Rotten) could never have happened either a few years earlier or a few years later; he would have just ended up doing some dead-end job and would have been remembered by classmates as the odd kid. The same goes for John Lennon, Bob Marley. Even Elvis Presley.

This theory of mine is not based on any extensive research. It's more of a firmly held hunch based on some things I experienced. In the late 1970s I was part of a peer group that had drifted together in Liverpool. My guess is we were all the odd kid in the class in our various schools. This must happen in every cosmopolitan city in the world, this drifting together of like, even if the like is only based on unlike, on not fitting into the usual groups. The spotlight fell on this peer group in Liverpool, the Zeitgeist came a-calling and nearly every sodding one of us who could string a few chords together, warble a tune or had something to say, got their 15 minutes.

There was at least one kid in each of the classes in each of the seven schools I'd been working with who had that take on things from a different angle, something that was coming from somewhere else. Now I know the world has too many would-be pop stars as it is. But maybe those kids had what it takes to be a great architect, engineer or entrepreneur. All of these and other disciplines have a common need, which is for their successful practitioners to be able to see things from a different angle and a willingness not to be afraid to make an arsehole of themselves in front of other people.

I'm not trying to convince you that there is a Shakespeare in every class but there are lot more could-be Bards or whatever knocking about than you could ever imagine, just doing the dead-end jobs that Johnny Rotten didn't get to do. But maybe one Shakespeare is all we need.

Football is completely different though; the talents that are needed are so specific. There is only one Wayne Rooney. Every lad who shows any sort of promise kicking a ball about the playground in this country has the opportunity to rise to the top. There is such a solid infrastructure in place for finding the next Wayne Rooney, Ronaldinho or even George Best, not a single one will be missed.

Anyway, enough of my theories. That bit about football at the end I just made up now; is based on the fact that my youngest son's best mate – they are both six – has just been approached by both Arsenal and Chelsea.

Back to the classroom at Wearhead primary. All the children did their scores. We got each group to read them out. In fact this was something we had done at a couple of the other schools but it was only when we got to Wearhead that this idea clicked in my head.

Paul: I'm convinced by this footy analogy.

Robert: As a kid you still have to find the right relationship with a coach who can nurture your talent.

This is it. I may be against making permanent recordings of performances of The17 but I would love recordings to exist of these pupils from the seven schools reading out their scores. Hearing their voices gives them a different context than reading them on the page. I'm not trying to imply one is better than the other, just ... well, I suppose it's an accent thing. We all have an idea in our head about what a Geordie accent sounds like or at least we do if the 'we' I'm referring to is folk living in the British Isles. But although all of these seven schools were in the north-east and so have an accent that on a surface level is similar to the Geordie accent of Newcastle, they were all markedly different from it. They also had accents that were subtly different from each other. It is those subtle

Rasmus: Part of being a successful pop musician is having the skills for making connections, going to the parties, meeting the right people, being in the right places, having the right attitude. You don't become a pop star by staying at home, practising on your acoustic guitar. I think if you have those skills, if you're good at being in the spotlight, then you'll be picked up.

differences that I would like to capture.

I would like to revisit the schools at a later stage when I could record each of them reading out their scores and then at the17.org you would be able to listen to them, to read them as well as download a PDF of each of the scores. This may be sentimentality on my part but right now it seems like a good idea.

SCORE

71. PLACE

Take 17 people.
Think of a place.
Close your eyes.
Think of a picture of your place.
Each picture must represent atmosphere.
Think of a sound heard in the picture.
Think together for 17 seconds.
Then imediately sing the sound
for 17 seconds.
Do not record the sound.

Kathryn (and class 2) Wearhead Primary School 2006

pb Poster 167   2008

THE PLAN
19 May 2006

The plan was that all the pupils from the seven schools were going to be bussed to the Hatton Gallery for the playback of *COLLABORATE* that they had taken part in performing. Because of the time and costs of getting the Wearhead kids to and from Newcastle, the plan was to do a playback for the Wearhead children in their school. It was a lot easier and cheaper for John and I to get out to them.

We did this yesterday. After we had collected in the scores they had written for us, we drew the curtains to block out as much light as possible. John Hirst suggested they all lie on the floor and close their eyes. We then played them back the full version of *COLLABORATE*. I lay on the floor and closed my eyes as well. It sounded so much better than the version of *COLLABORATE* we had done in Stockholm before Easter.

After it came to an end we asked them what pictures, thoughts, feelings it brought up in them. They seemed to respond to this very well, each telling us what they thought and why. But after a while it seemed they were trying to out-extreme each other with who could come up with the scariest description of what they felt and thought.

And that was that. We could hear the dinner ladies getting the school dinners ready behind the pull-down shutters. The curtains were opened. Sunlight poured in. Lambs were bleating in the fields. We packed up the gear and loaded the Land Rover.

Liz Gill took us aside before we left. She asked us if we had noticed how one of the lads in particular had responded to the playback. I hadn't because I was lying on the floor with my eyes shut and John said he hadn't because he had been keeping his eyes on the recording levels. It seemed that they suspected one of the lads had a mild form of Asperger's. And children with Asperger's syndrome have more than a tendency to hear sounds louder and more intensely than other people. According to Liz Gill this lad had been freaked out by the playback; he had kept his hands over his ears for the full seven minutes and needed comforting by the teacher. She felt we should be aware of this and suggested that before we did any other playbacks we should check with the teachers in case of any pupils with similar conditions.

We said our farewells one last time, climbed into the Land Rover and headed down the valley for the drive back to Newcastle. Just as I was thinking how it's weird that we all hear the same sound in different ways, John Hirst chips in with 'Bill, I told you it was too loud. Just 'cause you are getting deaf you think everybody is hearing it the same as you.' If I am getting deaf, I am in denial.

THIS MORNING
19 May 2006

This morning was our last school visit. It was our second visit to Shotton Hall. These were lads and lasses in years 10 and 11, so were all about 15 and 16 years old. They were kids who did drama and had no problem standing in front of each other and expressing themselves, using words, sounds, movement or whatever.

As we had more time at this school's second visit than we had with the other schools we did a complete version of *AGE* with them. Remember *AGE*, the score that we did in Stockholm that should have a building with five floors and people of all ages if done properly? They loved it. Could not believe it was just their voices, that nothing had been added. When John hit the delete button and got rid of the lot they were almost incensed that something they had created that they considered to be beautiful had been consigned to the trash bin of eternity.

Robert: When we took part in The17 it felt like everyone had come together and formed one large organism. All moving in the same direction at the same speed.

I explained to them that if they were to follow the score for *AGE* they could recreate it whenever they wanted with the few bits of recording gear that the school had and that that was the point. And it was definitely not about cluttering up the world with more recorded music that no one will ever get around to listening to. The teacher wanted to know if it could be used as a soundtrack to a play that they had been putting together. 'No way! The sound of The17 is never, can never, will never be used as a soundtrack to anything. Whoever's asking. Whatever they are offering.' I think I laboured the point with them so much they must have thought I was some sort of nutter.

Paul: If someone next to you sings a note close to the one you are singing, then it's really difficult not to drift into that same note. I remember when we were kids, the music teacher would keep the three kids who were the best singers back at the end of the lesson. As a test she'd ask them to sing a note and then she'd sing a note really close to theirs to try and throw them off.

Rasmus: It is so difficult to sing with a person standing next to you who can't sing. It's like 'Mum, shut up, you are ruining the song for all of us'.

After that was settled they got down to the business of performing score number 17, *SCORE*. And strangely, this bunch of 16-year-olds who, as I said, were very confident at expressing themselves verbally and physically, when it came to writing their own scores did not have the unconstrained magic of some of the junior school kids.

Job done. We packed up and headed back to the Hatton Gallery in Newcastle.

THIS AFTERNOON
19 May 2007

This afternoon was the climax of this whole job of working with the seven schools. Even without Wearhead there were going to be more than 180 children being bussed in. Because of the numbers and fears about having this many school kids in the building at once we had to split them. Three schools at 1.30, the other three at 2.15.

At 1.25 the first lot started to troop in. I took control. Or at least tried to. I felt like a head teacher taking assembly. We handed each of them a blank sheet of paper and pencil. Asked them to lie down on the gallery floor, dimmed the lights right down and then played the track back to them. I again lay down and closed my eyes. The sound enveloped me. My head teemed with visions, thoughts danced in and out of my consciousness and one particular lad annoyed the crap out of me with his incessant sniggering. But that did not spoil the overall affect.

When the track ended I stood up and asked them all to write on the piece of paper, in no more than one line, the thoughts or feelings they had while listening to the music, or to describe the pictures that it had brought up in their imaginations. They did. We collected them in. We all clapped each other and then they all filed out to get on the coaches to take them back to wherever their lives were happening.

After a few minutes' break the other three classes trooped in and we went through the same process again. The only difference was that after this playback the track was deleted.

Working in these schools has been mentally, and at times physically, draining. If nothing else, I have ended up having so much more respect for what teachers have to do. But there is a lot more besides. This has been one of the most rewarding creative experiences I have ever been involved in. It has reconfirmed my belief in what I'm trying to do with The17.

The best way I can think of ending this text is by adding the thoughts, feelings and imagined pictures that these young people had written down on their pieces of paper:

> An aeroplane spiralling on fire out of control with people all around worried and scared. Then crashed.

A loud group of bees.
The seaside because it was calm.
Running through a jungle.
A train coming.
It felt like thunder and lightning and people screaming.
Like I was in a tunnel.
A whirlwind/hurricane.
War.
A deep sea choir.
It felt like I was standing on the edge of a cliff and all the sound was the wind and noises that you would hear.
A huge grey mass.
I felt scared.
It was like a storm in my head.
I felt like I was stood on the shoreline of an ocean of dead peoples souls.
I felt as though I was stuck in a really dark prison and all I could see was the stars as I looked up.
A big army coming to get you or attack you.
Angels singing.
Scary.
People dying and coming back alive making noise like snakes.
A space ship flying around at night.
A ballerina dancing.
A boat sinking.
I thought it was a rabbit but it wasn't it was a baby elephant.
At first I thought it sounded like a ghost train then I heard just the ghosts and they were trying to communicate.
In the jungle at night and lots of animals making a loud noise.
A red and black shadow.
It felt good.
Like lava chasing me through a tunnel.
Underwater, people struggling for breath as they are caught in seaweed and can't escape.
War.
Thunder.
Rain.
An owl at night.
People sad.
It sounds like a car crash.
A horse getting knocked down.
Lots of animals making the same noise.

Mostly birds and animals.
People getting thunder.
Dark and loud.
Thunder.
It sounded like wind blowing strong.
Trees.
A storm.
Scary ghosts coming out of graves.
A relaxed feeling.
It was spooky.
I thought it sounded good.
A rocket taking off.
Like the music from an African charity advert.
A train coming towards me.
Stormy night. Thunder storm. Scary.
A scary sensation.
Like I was in a dark tunnel.
A scary movie because it got louder and louder.
I thought it sounded good.
Tiring and deep.
Scary, frustrating, hearing voices in the mind.
An owl at midnight.
People racing.
Nightmare.
Scary.
Horrible.
People screaming.
Loud and scary.
An orchestra warming up before a concert.
A storm.
Like a person stomping up the stairs.

CHEAP AND EASY SHORTCUTS
10 JUNE 2006

'Can you fucking shut up? I'm trying to talk here.'
'Well you're talking bollocks.'
'Just fuck off, I'm on stage now. You wait your turn'.

I'm on stage at the Lynton and Lynmouth festival. It's a free and voluntarily run small-scale music festival held on the village green of the beautiful twin villages of Lynton and Lynmouth on the north Devon coast. The audience is made up of a few hundred folk, sitting around in family groups enjoying the sunshine, eating ice creams and accepting, even enjoying, whatever music has been put on for them. All is good vibes; my two youngest children are running around and having fun.

A friend of mine, Tom Hodgkinson, who lives locally and is now on the festival committee asked me to come down and do The17 at the festival. His offer was accepted. The17 would be performing in the village youth club hall that evening at 7.00. Tom Hodgkinson introduced me to some of the committee members, all men of my age or thereabouts. Men into their music. Men who wanted to bring some of it down here. Not big names but people who meant what they did. Bert Jansch was going to be the headlining act this afternoon but the two bands that I had already seen had driven me up the wall. Both were playing a form of British jazz that was totally irrelevant by the time that Ian Carr's Nucleus had formed sometime in the early 1970s. Jazz is a dead art form and no amount of learning your scales and blowing your horn is going to change that. As soon as any art form has stopped being done by those who do it for real and becomes something done in academia, it is dead. That is why Wynton Marsalis is shit, no matter how good he is at playing or how worthy his activities. Black kids in the States with something to say use hip hop, not jazz. As for these white middle-aged, middle-class jazzers this afternoon, they are as meaningless as a brass band on a bandstand, even if some of them are women, even if I secretly still love listening to free jazz in the privacy of my own home. And I have tickets to see John Zorn at the Barbican later in the month. What, you don't know who John Zorn is?

Anyway, one of the committee members was also the MC for the festival; he was going to make an announcement from the stage about The17 in the youth club hall that evening. I suggested that I make my own announcement from the stage. They agreed. They wanted to know if I would do it before or after the next band soundchecked. I said before. So I went on stage with one of my framed posters. The one about all recorded music having run its course, been consumed, traded and found wanting, time to dispense with all previous music-making etc. I read this as aggressively as I could. Then I started to tell the crowd about the *Introduction To The17* that evening, that there would be 17 tickets available and if they wanted one, I would be over at the festival office tent in a couple of minutes. But I didn't get all this out of my mouth before the next band on the bill were up on stage banging drums and twanging guitars and attempting to soundcheck.

That's when I told the leader of this band to shut the fuck up. Our onstage spat was being picked up by the stage microphones and broadcast to the audience. Then my microphone got pulled. So I used another one to finish my message off. Some sections of the audience booed me. Others cheered. When I came off, the committee, who only a couple minutes earlier were all smiles and handshakes, were trying to ignore me. Over at the festival office tent a large throng of people were gathering around, wanting to enlist and know more about The17.

On stage the offending band were now playing the worst sort of 'white men singing the blues' that you can imagine. It was all fake 1950s Chicago black bluesmen vocals. Tight slick arrangements with more attention to detail than Muddy Waters or Howlin' Wolf would ever have done, but ultimately completely pointless.

I don't think that the way I behaved is particularly big, brave or clever, but if I mean what I say, I have to be able to stand up in public and say my stuff and maybe in confrontational circumstances like this. The trouble is, I know and you know and even your mother knows that there is nothing like a bit of public confrontation to get the media interested. It is the cheapest and easiest shortcut to infamy. And that is one very good reason why I don't want to be using it.

IN THE MIST
1 July 2006

In Moscow for the launch of MyDeath.net, the Russian language version.

The following text appears on **What You Want** (Penkiln Burn Poster 56) – *My Death is a register. This register is kept at MyDeath.net. It exists as a place for you to document what you want said, sung, played, read or done at your funeral. This service is free and it has nothing to sell. You are encouraged to be as creative, demanding or sensitive as you want. It is your funeral and you only get one go at it. You can update, embroider or delete any of your instructions as often or whenever you like. You can browse through all other entries. In turn, your entry can be read by anyone else visiting the site. Thus it is ensured that your friends and family will know exactly what you wanted.*
WARNING: *My Death takes no responsibility for making sure that those you leave behind follow your instructions. Visit MyDeath.net and prepare to die.*

This site was set up by Drummond in 2003 because a friend of his died of cancer in his 40s and had a crap funeral. It did not reflect him or his life in any way. People deserve better funerals.

Got in late last night. Woke early this morning and started writing a chapter for this book. It is a habit I have, writing in my head while lying in bed. The trouble is, once I have done the writing in my head, at some level I think I have done it for real and then I find it difficult to draw upon the thoughts and emotions to get it done properly on paper like this.

The launch of mydeath.net in Russian is part of a joint exhibition with the artist Tracey Moberly. The exhibition is called Death & Desire. My half is obviously the Death bit, hers is the Desire.

Over breakfast I'm telling Tracey Moberly about the problem of writing in my head in bed and she wanted to know what the story was so I told her and how it ended up with me stood on the edge of the Pacific Ocean in 1986 and how that was my earliest memory of hearing The17 in my head. And she said, 'What about the pylon?'
'What pylon?'
'The one in Corby in your back garden. The one you showed me.'
'Oh yeah.'
'You know I took a photo of it. It never came out.'
So now she has reminded me about this pylon maybe I should tell you about it. It may be relevant to The17.

We, the Drummonds, moved to England in 1964 and were living in a council house on the Beanfield estate in Corby. I was 11 at the time. At the bottom of the garden was a pylon. When I lay in bed awake in the early morning I would always know if it was a misty day because there would be this humming. The first few times I heard this humming I had no idea where it was coming from. On more than one occasion I went outside in my pyjamas to try and find the source of this humming but it didn't seem to have any source. It seemed to be omnipresent.

Bill Drummond

Over a period of time I deduced that it came from the pylon, up where the power cables were strung. This was decades before the scare about living near pylons being carcinogenic. Once I learned where the sound came from I would long for misty mornings so I could lie in my bed in the early mornings listening to this deep humming. I would lie there humming along with it, trying out strange harmonies. Seeing how long I could keep the note without taking a breath before seeking another stranger and more distant harmony.

If asked at the time, I would never have recognised this as a form of music-making. I would probably have denied that I even did this humming in harmony along with a pylon in the mist in the early morning.

Paul: I used to do the same thing with the noises from the fridge and the sound of my mum hoovering on a Sunday.

Ever since then I have felt an attachment for pylons. I have written about this attachment on numerous occasions but never had the chance to hum along in harmony with one again.

'SO HAVE YOU BEEN INFLUENCED BY STOCKHAUSEN?'
2 July 2006

This chapter was going to be the story I had written in my head in bed on the first morning in Moscow. But on sitting down to write on a Sunday morning in a Moscow café – a themed Spanish tapas bar one, one with MTV Base pumping out all this aspirational American R&B (the VJ is an English Afro-Caribbean) – I realised that there was another story that I had to tell first.

A few weeks back an email arrived from a Robert Barry, a student at Goldsmith's College in London. Goldsmith's is considered a bit of a prestigious college for the arts in the UK. This student was doing an MA in Music Philosophy or something. He had stumbled upon the The17 on the internet and had some questions to ask me for his dissertation. His questions had barbs, or I perceived them to have barbs. His questions made me feel defensive. He was asking me about my influences and there was a list of names, most of whom I had never heard of. One was the now-ubiquitous Cornelius Cardew. What if all the other people he was name-checking had been doing the same thing as I had but 40 odd years earlier? I put off responding to the email. Then I did. After a couple more emails between us we agreed to meet and for me to try and answer some of his questions. We met last week. I told him the story. A condensed version of what you have read in this book so far. My defensive guard lowered. I didn't feel I was being attacked for being some novice jumping on a new music train that had come and gone decades ago.

Then he asked me, 'So do you think you have been influenced by Stockhausen?'

I know very little about Stockhausen other than he is German, still alive and in the 1950s and 1960s had developed electronic contemporary classical music and that without him the whole Krautrock thing would never have happened in the 1970s. Nothing that I understood Stockhausen to be about has had any direct influence on what I am trying to do now in any way. Then I remembered a number of consecutive incidents that I told this Robert Barry about. What I told him sort of goes like this, with a couple of bits added that I forgot to tell him.

Corby is twinned with a German town called Velbert. Velbert is an industrial town in the Ruhr Valley, of a similar size to Corby. Our school was doing an exchange programme with pupils from a school in Velbert. Early summer

1967 this German lad came to stay with us. His name was Hans. Sgt. Pepper's Lonely Hearts Club Band by The Beatles had just come out. It was the first record released by The Beatles since *Penny Lane / Strawberry Fields Forever* in March. I bought it on the day of release. On first play I thought it was shit. It opened no doors in my head in the way that *Strawberry Fields Forever* had done. I persisted and within a week grew to love it, especially *Day In A Life*. This was obviously years before I realised that Sgt. Pepper's was the worst thing that happened to music in the 20th century. Anyway, Hans came to stay. He was a couple of years older than me, was arrogant and wore a blonde wig. The wig was never mentioned.

Hans fell in love with Sgt. Pepper's. He played it over and over again. On the morning that he was leaving to go back to Krautland my mother suggested that I give him my copy of Sgt. Pepper's. I didn't like her idea. Then she said that if I gave it to him, she would buy me the next LP to be released by The Beatles.

I had a long wait by the standards of the day. The next one didn't come out until near the end of November the following year (1968). It was the white one. My mother felt cheated on the deal as it was a double album and cost twice as much as Sgt. Pepper's had. It too was shit on the first hearing. On repeated listening some of the tracks grew on me, but *Revolution Number 9* stayed in my ears as completely rubbish. It wasn't even sodding music, just a load of noise and people talking, but over the years what that track represented has grown in my head and taken on significance.

In the summer of 1968 a bunch of us from my school went over to spend a week in Velbert, to do the return visit. For some reason I didn't spend the time staying at Hans' house; I was put with another lad's family. He was the same age as me and we got on fine. But one evening I was asked over to Hans' for supper. His folks seemed rich by our standards, with a large detached house in a wooded garden. In the house there was a large living room. In that living room stood a massive pair of cabinet speakers.
'What are those?'
'Stereo speakers.' (You have to imagine his German accent).
Up until then I had never heard stereo. I sort of knew what it was in theory but I didn't know anybody who had stereo.
'Oh. They are big.'
'Yes. My father invented stereo. He made these speakers.'
Now I don't know if his father invented stereo or not, but that's what he told me.

'Oh, that's good.'
'You like electronic music?'
'I don't know what electronic music is.'
'You never heard of Stockhausen? He is the best'
'But I thought you thought The Beatles were the best.'
'No. The Beatles are pop rubbish. Stockhausen is the best.'
I still resented the fact that my mother had pushed me into giving him my copy of Sgt. Pepper's and as The Beatles were as yet to have a new LP, I felt like I was down on the deal.
'Oh. So what does Stockhausen sound like?'
'You listen. It will blow your mind.'
He put on the record. Nothing could have prepared me for the swirling monstrous unfathomable noise that came from this pair of huge speaker cabinets. My mind wasn't blown but my eardrums almost were. He played it for about ten minutes.
'It's great, yes?'
I didn't know what to say. I had never heard anything like it before. Didn't know if I wanted to again.
Then he asked, 'Do you like Little Richard?'
'I don't know. Does he make electronic music as well?'
'No, don't be stupid. Little Richard is a rock 'n' roller. Here, look at this.'
He hands me an LP. On the cover was a close-up portrait of a strange-looking black man with make-up on and a ludicrous bouffant hair do. I think the title was Little Richard Live in Berlin. The subtitle was 'All the hits by the most beautiful man in show business'.
'You stand here between the speakers and listen.'
Hans put the record on: there was some muffled crowd noise, and then, from nowhere, the loudest, craziest, darkest, all-encompassing voice I had ever heard in my life: 'A-wop-bop-a-loo-bop-a-wop-boom-bang' – or something.
Hans let the rest of what I later learned was called *Tutti Frutti* come to an end before he lifted the needle off. 'What do you think? Isn't he the best?'

I can't recall my reply. Or what I thought. Or if what I thought could be put into words, but definitely in my head another door had been opened. Hans didn't tell me anything more about Little Richard. It was over the next year or so that I learnt where Little Richard stood in the pantheon of rock 'n' roll greats. Up there with Elvis, Buddy, Chuck, Fats, Eddie and Jerry Lee.

I never went and bought any Little Richard records. Maybe I instinctively knew nothing could ever touch the effect on me of hearing those first two opening bars of *Tutti Frutti*. Hans's mother then came into the room. Supper was ready. They had a thing where we had to stick bits of meat on thin metal rods and cook them in a pot in the middle of the table. It seemed pretty crap to me that you ask somebody round for a meal and then expect them to cook it for themselves.

To get back to Robert Barry, the student from Goldsmith's – I told him about hearing Stockhausen this time in 1968, but I didn't tell him about Little Richard or my first and only brush with fondue cooking. I told him I didn't think Stockhausen had any direct influence on me and The17. I did acknowledge that I knew he was a huge influence on early Kraftwerk before they cut their hair and went all showroom dummies on us, and that when that happened and they became the godfathers of electro-pop they had a huge influence on me. So indirectly, yes, he had. But in that sense he had an influence on everybody who has been involved in making pop music in the last 30 years.

'I didn't mean an influence in that sense. I meant like this.' He produced from his bag a small slim volume. It was a paperback, cheaply produced, badly bound and falling to bits. The cover was a dull blue with some black print. In the bottom right-hand corner of the cover in pencil was the price, 7/6d. That is seven shillings and sixpence in pre-1970s sterling. The text on the front cover read, and I know this because I wrote it down in my diary that I am now copying it from:

> Stockhausen NR 26
> From *The Seven Days*
> Composed in May 1968
> Universal Edition UE 14790 E

I was running late for picking up my children from school so I only had a chance for a quick flick through. What I saw was a number of scores all written using words as opposed to being notated on staves. From this flick through I could see at a glance that they were closely related in style and attitude to what I had been attempting to do with the scores for The17.

That evening I went on to Google to try and track down these scores so I could read them in full, take them in and let them have their impact on me. Although I found numerous mentions of them within biographical blurbs on Stockhausen, I didn't find the actual scores.

Not mentioning the Little Richard thing to Robert Barry meant I also failed to mention something else. What I wrote about my experience of hearing Stockhausen for the first time was almost dismissive but what I did experience listening to both Little Richard and Stockhausen was nothing to do with the surface of the noise on offer or their separate and vastly different iconic positions that I was later to learn they held. It was to do with something somewhere in the heart of the noise being made. Something beyond rhythm and words, melody or harmony. Something beyond intellectual theory or show-business craft; something I am unable to hear in the R&B tracks being pumped out of the TV on the wall in this fake Spanish tapas bar down a side street in Moscow. Why does modern R&B sound so sterile to my ears when for 30-odd years the music of black America was the music that I could always rely on to have what I needed? It is undeniably the most technically advanced pop music in the world and I understand it to be the biggest grossing, but to my ears it sounds like the most boring music to be making. I know I am missing something. Even when I see Beyoncé shake her arse on her latest video, it leaves me cold.

But before I get too carried away on this topic and start to give you my thoughts on the collected works of the Neptune production team I will stop and tell you that the window by my table is open and outside is a tree and this tree is full of chirping and squabbling sparrows. Contained within the sounds made by these sparrows is what I need. They have what was in both Stockhausen and Little Richard when I first heard them back in 1968. There are numerous other times when I have heard this and, yes, it is what I am after in The17. And yes, I do believe it is there each and every time The17 have performed the score *AGE*.

Certain themes in this story have been touched on before and will be revisited over the months before this book is done. But enough has been said now for me to try and start writing the story I was writing in my head in bed this morning.

Bill Drummond

THE BOY FROM THE RECORD COMPANY
2 July 2006

Ya Ya were a band from Essex. They existed in the mid-1980s and they aspired to a style perfected by American bands like Journey. Do you know any bands like Journey? No? Well, anyway, like that, whatever that is. For a band from Essex they did it very well. To my ears they sounded like the real thing.

They were signed to WEA Records in the UK. In my capacity as an A&R consultant for WEA Records I was given the job of A&R-ing Ya Ya. It wasn't my type of music but I respected their talent and I got on with them. Nothing pretentious or arsey about them. Mike Chapman had agreed to produce their debut album. Mike Chapman was a sort of hero of mine. He, with Nick Chinn, had written and produced lots of trashy British glam hits in the first half of the 1970s, all The Sweet's big ones, the Suzi Quatro smashes and whatever got Mud into the top ten – all grade-one trash, only to be outdone by the king himself, Gary Glitter.

Mike Chapman then moved to the States and went on to have major worldwide success and critical acclaim by producing the big hits for Blondie and a couple of other platinum-selling crap American acts. Then he went AWOL. Had enough of it all and, in his own words, 'I went and sat on a mountain and smoked a sack of weed.'

Anyway, it's spring 1986, Mike Chapman is on the comeback trail and he thinks Ya Ya are just the band for him to work with to put him back where he belonged – in the US Top 10. Contracts were sorted. Ya Ya and I flew out to LA to start working with Mike Chapman. My job was to oversee things, make sure LA doesn't go to the heads of this bunch of lads from Essex and that Mike Chapman keeps focused. From a music business point of view Mike Chapman was a bit of a risk even with his track record. It had been a few years since the Blondie triumphs.

We checked into the Mondrian Hotel. The band was provided with some big old black Buick to get themselves to the studio and back. I was provided with some convertible sports car. As well as keeping an eye on Ya Ya there was another job I was supposed to be doing. Some months earlier WEA had signed Little Richard who had recently had a freak hit with a song on the soundtrack of Down And Out In Beverly Hills. Little Richard hadn't had a hit in decades; even when I first heard the man back in Germany in 1968 he hadn't had a hit for some years. Over the decades the myth of Little Richard had grown in my head. He was the ultimate complicated rock 'n' roller, his life oscillating wildly from debauched drug-fuelled sex binges to born-again Southern Baptist preacher and back again, with little temperate climate between the extremes.

There have been hundreds of thousands of words written about the greatness of Little Richard's early recordings, his voice and piano-playing. I have nothing new to add to them here. For this bit of the story all you need to know is that when he got signed to WEA Records he got flown over to London to work with a British producer, Stuart Coleman. On his first night in London he went out on a binge and ended up breaking his neck in a car accident or something. All recording had to be postponed, for almost a year. He was starting again this week with the same British producer, but in LA. I was somehow responsible for making sure he didn't go on another wild whatever, that the cocaine was kept at bay and his sexual odyssey was curtailed and he got the job done. Or that was what was expected.

All this rather dull backstory is to give you an insight into one of the strangest 24 hours of my life. In that 24 hours I took no drugs and had no sex but the whole history of rock 'n' roll seemed to be condensed into one day and I came out the other end never wanting anything to do with any of it again, not out of disgust but with the feeling that it was done with.

I will lay out the facts and in doing so hope to gain some understanding and maybe learn why this day led me to hear The17 in my head for the very first time.

This 24 hours started early on the Saturday afternoon with me driving from the Mondrian over to the studio complex where Ya Ya were working with Mike Chapman. Melrose Avenue looked like it did in the movies from the driver's seat of the sports car with the top down. The LA chicks were what you would want and expect. At the studio complex I got lost and found myself in this large studio. There was no one in it but music was booming out of the speakers. It was pumped-up LA soft rock with a female voice, a voice I recognised. As my eyes got accustomed to the dark I became aware of a figure in the middle of the recording room in the place where the band would be, if there was one. The figure belonged to a rather bloated woman dressed in flowing latter-day Californian hippy chick garb. She was twirling around, arms in the air, eyes closed, lost in the music. I stood there for no more than a couple of minutes watching her. She obviously had no idea that anybody was watching her. Although something about her was familiar it took some 30 seconds or so before I realised it was Stevie Nicks from Fleetwood Mac.

Drummond has written about sitting on a plane across from his teenage hero, Peter Green, also ex-Fleetwood Mac, in the story *The Autograph Hunted* which was included in his book *45*, published by Little Brown in 2000.

In the late 1960s Fleetwood Mac were this English underground blues band. In the 1970s, minus Peter Green and plus some Americans, they made Rumours, then the biggest-selling album of all time, and Stevie Nicks became the most desirable singing rock chick in history and the inspiration behind the infamous song *Sit On My Face, Stevie Nicks* by The Rotters. Before the track ended I let myself out of the studio. There is no reason to think that she was aware that she was being watched.

Next, I found the room where Ya Ya were working. Mike Chapman was midway through rehearsing one of their songs with them. The band was giving everything they'd got, hitting all the harmonies, blistering all the solos. Not my sort of music but they meant it and played it incredibly well. For them it was not corporate rock, it was the real thing.

Mike Chapman was lounging on a chair staring at them as they played. He was wearing a pale blue shirt open to halfway down his chest, a pair of pale yellow slacks and a pair of expensive-looking deck shoes. He was also sporting a pair of sunglasses. By his side was a young woman in her mid-20s with long blonde hair. On her lap was a notebook open to a blank page, in her right hand a pen was at the ready. She was Mike Chapman's personal assistant.

The song came to an end. The four members of Ya Ya plus their hired keyboard player, Nick Coler, looked towards Mike Chapman for his comments, his suggestions: what he is paid to do. He says nothing. He says nothing for quite some time. His PA waits to take notes. Then Mike speaks and what he says is 'Rock 'n' Roll. That is Rock 'n' Roll.' The PA notes this down. There is another long silence. Then he speaks again. 'Yes. Rock 'n' Roll. Pure Rock 'n' Roll. Just play it one more time.' The PA writes these words down as well.

So the band plays the song again and for whatever reason it sounds better than it did the first time.

I decide to leave the studio and go for a bit of a drive around LA. At some point in some anonymous suburb I decide to get out and walk. The sun is beating down. No one is about. That line by Joni Mitchell, 'The hissing of summer lawns', is making sense. I'm walking along lost in thought wondering what it is like to be Stevie Nicks and what Mike Chapman meant by saying 'Rock 'n' roll', and what is rock 'n' roll anyway, when I notice somebody walking towards me. Like I said, there was nobody else about. No one walks anywhere in LA. The first thing I notice about this person walking towards me, when he's about 30 yards off, is that he is wearing a pair of baggy khaki shorts. The sort that would be worn by British soldiers when fighting with Monty in the desert in the Second World War. As he gets closer I notice the brown leather sandals. The traditional ones, the ones that we all wore as kids before what we used to call Jesus sandals came in during the early 1970s. This man and I were getting closer, and just as we are about to pass he looks into my face and says 'Good afternoon'. I had to stop myself saying the words that had been going round in my head. These words being 'Rock 'n' roll'. Instead I am able to say 'Good afternoon'. We both carry on walking; neither of us slows our pace.

The face that had said 'Good afternoon' to me and I had said 'Good afternoon' back to belongs to Morrissey, the then lead singer of the Manchester band The Smiths. I had never been a particular fan of The Smiths but some months earlier I had read an interview with Morrissey where he proclaimed that The Smiths would never play in the United States and that he had no interest in ever visiting the place. But here he was walking along a sidewalk in a LA suburb. I said out loud, but at a volume that even the hissing summer lawns couldn't hear, 'Rock 'n' roll', and I wondered if Morrissey walking along this pavement and saying 'Good afternoon' to me was rock 'n' roll. And if he was, did he think he was?

I got back into the sports car and found my way back to the studio where Ya Ya were working. When I walked in the band were halfway through a song. It sounded fucking brilliant. Ten times better than I had ever heard them playing before. And I'm thinking that this album they are making with Mike Chapman is going to be massive. I'd better make sure I've got a couple of points on it before it comes out. Mike Chapman is in the same position as he was a couple of hours earlier, as is his PA. The song comes to an end.

Silence. Then Mike speaks. 'Rock 'n' roll. That, boys, is rock 'n' roll.'

Mike Chapman keeps office hours. No late into the night recording sessions with him. Back at the hotel I'm having a cool beer by the pool with a couple of the band members.

'So how do you think things are going with Mike?'

'He doesn't do a fucking thing, Bill. Givin' us no ideas, no pointers. Nothin'. After every run-through of every song he just says "Rock 'n' roll".'

'Is that it? Nothing else?'

'Sometimes he tells us we are the best band he has ever worked with. But nothing constructive.'

'Well, whatever. You are sounding brilliant. The amount you have improved since you started working with him this morning is astounding.'

'Bill, at the end of the day, it is costing us 50 grand to have Mike Chapman producing us. I know we ain't paying for it now but his fee, us being over here staying in a posh hotel and expensive studios is all recoupable against our royalties. We are going to have to sell millions before we see a penny. When I get back to England I've got to go back on the building site with my brother for months just so I can afford to take my missus on holiday.'

I want to say 'Rock 'n' Roll' but I don't. I just get the next round in. Later that evening I walk up the road with some of the band to a club. The place is almost empty. A band is on stage. A three-piece: guitar, bass and drums. They are doing a version of *Purple Haze*, a pub-band version of the Hendrix classic. It sounds shit. But this band is the reason I had wanted to come to this club. The band – if they had a name, I can't recall it – in truth is not what I have come to hear; I've come to watch and listen to the drummer. It's Mitch Mitchell, the drummer from the Jimi Hendrix Experience. When I was 16 I thought he was the second-best drummer in the world, just below Ginger Baker but above Jon Heisman. But now, 17 years later, he is in a pub band playing covers of what he was once doing for real.

I make my excuses to the Ya Ya's drummer and bassist who had come with me. I dragged the pair of them to this dive and here I am splitting without even getting the drinks in. We agree to meet up later at the Rainbow Rooms. The Rainbow was an infamous LA rock club that certain members of Ya Ya were desperate to visit. I get in the sports car and drive to another club. As I drive I could hear myself say 'Rock 'n' roll' over and over again. Sometimes in my head, sometimes just under my breath but sometimes out loud. I find the street, then the club. This was a totally different affair. It was a supper club, the clientele mainly black, middle-aged couples. I get myself a drink.

On stage is a band, all in those suits favoured by the likes of The Temptations in the early 1970s with big velvet bow ties and flairs. The six-piece band are laying down a half-arsed groove. A bit of wah-wah guitar, a bit of 1950s rhythm and blues and a bit of disco drumming all mixed in together at a volume mother would be pleased with. Up front is a five-piece vocal act. Four of them look young but are still sporting Afros that surely were out ten years earlier. The lead singer of these five, shorter than the rest, a man in his middle years, definitely does not look like he wants to be there. This was Hank Ballard and the Midnighters, or at least Hank's latest line-up of Midnighters. They had their first hit back in 1953, the year I was born. I guess none of these Midnighters are from the original line-up. Most of them, I guess, were not even born then.

Hank Ballard had numerous American R&B hits through the 1950s. One, *Work With Me Annie*, even made the *Rock 'n' Roll Hall Of Fame's 500 Songs That Shaped Rock 'n' Roll* list. It was the song he did as a B-side in 1959 that became a number one hit giving birth to the greatest dance craze of the second half of the 20th century. The thing is, it wasn't his version. Chubby Checker recorded the hit version. The song was *The Twist*.

I didn't know this information about Hank Ballard because I was a follower of him in my pre-school years but because I have made it my business to read the books that give me this sort of information.

The last song in this lacklustre set is Hank's original version of *The Twist*. The poor man is down there on the stage in his tight, ill-fitting velvet tuxedo suit trying to twist while singing the song that never made him famous. Hank's dead now, died a couple of years ago of cancer.

Got back in the car and headed for the Rainbow Rooms up on Sunset Strip. In my head I can hear a voice, but it's not my voice and not Mike Chapman's voice or even Stevie Nicks'. The voice keeps saying 'Rock 'n' roll! Rock 'n' roll, Bill. You want some rock 'n' roll, Bill? This is rock 'n' roll.' And the voice keeps changing as it morphs into other people's voices.

I get to Sunset Strip and find the Rainbow Rooms. This is an infamous rock hangout. Although I've been to LA a number of times before on Bunnymen business, I've never been to the Rainbow Rooms. The Bunnymen wouldn't be seen dead in this sort of place. I go in. The place is packed. Members of Ya Ya are not to be found anywhere. I check the toilets in case they are in there. Just queues of blokes chopping out lines of coke. I use the term 'bloke' loosely here; I don't think there is a bloke in the whole club who would choose to be called one. It's early summer 1986 in the US, poodle rock is at its zenith. There seemed to be dozens of interchangeable Spandex-panted, hair-metal bands around then and Mötley Crüe were both the kings and queens of them all.

Not that I could name a Mötley Crüe song, let alone sing a hook-line from one. At the time I would have thought it to be the most despicable genre of music ever.

This club must have been the epicentre of the genre. Every male is done up as if they were the lead singer of Mötley Crüe or at least the drummer, but caught on a day when he is making a special effort to be even more poodle-like than the singer. Spandex pants to a man, hair backcombed to the ceiling and more make-up than even the most diligent of make-up-counter girls. But not a member of Ya Ya is to be found.

I left without passing judgement. Got back in the sports car and drove back down Sunset Strip, heading for another address across town. It was another recording studio. I was supposed to get there at around midnight. Stuart Coleman, the English producer who has been contracted to produce Little Richard, had told me The Real King of Rock 'n' Roll does not start hitting the groove until after midnight. I find the studio. I'm nervous. Real nervous. I was not only going to be meeting one of the absolute-and-no-contest rock 'n' roll gods, one of the very few about whom you can say if they had not existed, the world – or at least Western culture of the last few decades – would be a very different place. No Little Richard, no Beatles; no Beatles, no nothing. But ... well, we will never know. And I was going to meet him. Stuart Coleman had tried to put me at ease on the phone earlier in the day. He said Richard was a very sweet man, if somewhat erratic; that he was desperate to prove that he could still cut it. Stuart Coleman had also told me that Little Richard was still in a neck brace because of his accident. Because of this they had evolved a way of Little Richard doing his vocals. It was done in the mixing room with him sat on a stool facing Stuart and the engineer across the mixing desk. I had asked Stuart what to call him. 'You just call him "Sir".' I didn't know if this was irony.

I rang the buzzer. I was let in. The lights were dimmed in the mixing room. I could see Stuart and the engineer behind the desk and the back of a hunched figure on a stool. The figure turned around. The face was covered in foundation, the eyes heavily lined with mascara. The bouffant wig was in place.
'Are you the boy from the record company?'
'Yes, sir.'
'And who am I?'
'Little Richard.'
'And what is Little Richard?'

I thought fast: 'The Real King of Rock 'n' Roll.'
'That is correct. And what else am I?'
'It depends.'
'It depends? I'll tell you what I am. I am the most beautiful man in show business.'
And he said that with a bit of a shriek and then giggled afterwards as if to let me know that he is OK and quite approachable really.
Then he says, 'Come closer. I want to see your face properly.' I move closer.
'Closer still, boy.'
I move closer again.
'Real close.'

My face is now about 18 inches from his. He stares into my eyes and then lets out the loudest non-amplified vocal sound I have ever heard in my life.
'A WOMP-BOMP-A-LOO-BOP, A WOMP-BAM-BOOM'.

Those opening two bars of *Tutti Frutti* alerted the world to Little Richard and everything that was to come. Maybe this was his party piece. Maybe he did it for everybody who came into the studio or every new person he met just to let them know he was the real Little Richard and not some lookalike, some impostor, that in case you'd forgotten, he still was and will always be the real king of rock 'n' roll.

What happened next has paled into insignificance. They probably played me back a couple of tracks and I handed out some bland encouragement. I never heard whatever tracks were recorded in these sessions. An album did come out called Lifetime Friend but I have no idea how it fared in the brutal world of the marketplace where being the real king of anything does not count for much.

I drove back down to the Mondrian. Went to bed. Fell into a deep and dreamless sleep. Woke early the next morning at around 6.00. Got up. Got dressed. Went out to the sports car and started driving. I had no idea where I was going or what I was hoping to find.

As I drove I became aware there was no voice in my head going 'Rock 'n' Roll'. Just silence. But after driving along almost empty freeways for a while I could hear something else. It was like a distant choir. But not singing any words or even a tune. I remember thinking at the time it sounded like space music. I kept driving. After an hour or so I found myself on the coast road north of LA. I pulled the car up in a lay-by, climbed over the crash barriers and down some rocks to the edge of the sea, the Pacific Ocean, the biggest bit of water in the world. It's something us humans have to do from time to time: stand at the edge of the ocean by ourselves and listen. And what I could hear in my head is this choir getting bigger and louder until it is all around me and there is nothing else but it and the sea.

And then I got back into the car, drove back to the hotel, had a breakfast of pancakes and maple syrup with members of Ya Ya. I didn't tell them anything about the choir in my head or even the voices going 'Rock 'n' roll'.

After I returned to the UK to let the band get on with working on their album with Mike Chapman, fully expecting it to be a triple platinum one, they had musical differences. The singer got kicked out halfway through the sessions. The band then got dropped from the label and that was that. I chucked working with WEA soon after, before they had a chance to sack me.

If you have read some of the stuff I have written before, you will know that this is not the first time that I have driven about aimlessly and ended up standing at the edge of a lake or a river or a sea and I'm sure it won't be the last. But this was the first time I did it while listening to The17 in full flow in my head.

As for the various voices that say 'Rock 'n' roll', they do return from time to time. Sometimes I welcome them like an old friend. Sometimes I resent it.

As for Little Richard screaming 'A womp-bomp-a-loo-bop, a womp-bam-boom' straight at me, inches from my face, the effect of that will never leave me. It was like I could see right into the heart of the beast that was rock 'n' roll. Nothing will ever compete with it. I knew that rock 'n' roll was over for me, but in another sense it will live forever.

THE LEDGE
9 July 2006

London is a place I never wanted to live in. I've held fast to a theory over the last 30 years that all the best bands / artists / writers have come out of the provinces. The thinking is that young people in the provinces who are drawn to creativity have less to distract their imaginations. In London there is too much on offer; in the provinces they have more time and space to evolve whatever it is they are doing before the spotlight of the media finds them and uses them up and spits them out. This holds true whether it is Shakespeare, The Beatles or the band being championed for the particular month you are reading this.

I have always been proud of the fact that I've never felt the need to live in London. So it was with reluctance and even shame that I gave in and moved to London. The reasons I won't go into here.

A flat was found that suited my needs. It's in the Stoke Newington area, moved in on 1 April. I had been living in the flat for a couple of months before I wondered if the large frosted window halfway up the stairs could be opened. It could. I opened it as wide as it would go. What I found outside the window was a ledge about two by three metres. I climbed out. This ledge is two and a half floors above back-garden level.

It has been a warm evening. I went and got a deck chair and a bottle of beer and I have been sitting out here for the last three hours. Well, not all the time. I climbed back in a few times to get another and another and maybe another bottle of beer from the fridge.

While sitting out here I have done sod all but listen to the distant sounds of the city, watched the sky darken and the lights of the planes cross it and take in my new surroundings. I feel like a tomcat perched up on some high wall surveying his kingdom. The view is not panoramic and is in no way picturesque, even in an urban sense. From up here I can see no more than four unkempt back gardens (not being in a ground-floor flat, I don't have one); the roof of a small factory; the back of a street of three-storey Victorian town houses and one distant tower block. What I can't see are any cars or buses because I can't even see a road. I can't see any people because nobody is out in the unkempt gardens.

Maybe it is the gentle fug brought on by the bottles of beer but I get the feeling I'm going to be spending many an evening out here by myself, just sitting, looking and listening. Although I am in a city of some 7 million people, out and up here I feel distant from it. Not part of it. Free from it. Like when I climbed a tree as a kid and would sit up there in the branches, hiding from the world and at the same time watching it all go by. With this comes a sense of freedom, which we can only ever experience when we are on our own. Do we ever tire of watching a plane cross a night sky wondering where those people, 30,000 feet above us, are off to, about the lives they are leading, the mistakes they have made, or how their futures unfold?

I'm listening to the sounds of the city again, the distant sirens, children playing out late a few streets away, the bus pulling up at the other side of my flat, the far-off hum of traffic. But for some reason up here tonight I don't feel hemmed in and trapped by the sounds of the city. There are days when I'm in the middle of London, when I can sense I am about to have some sort of claustrophobic panic attack. I get overcome with this desperate need for the open space of the countryside or the woodland glade, the bank of a brook. I know it sounds like I am coming on all Wordsworth in the Lakes, but that is the way I feel.

Right now, up here on this ledge, I am getting what I need. This is now my favourite place in all of London. Official.

SCREAMING SWIFTS
10 July 2006

Back up on the ledge escaping the world, or maybe returning to it. Listening. Listening. Listening. Wondering why reality sounds so much better up here than anywhere else.

When I first went to art school at the age of 17 in September 1970 I was plunged into a world of seeing. Being made to think about, and focus on, what everything – I was going to say looks like, but it is far more than just what something looked like – more like everything's complete and utter being in relationship to every other physical object around you. I suppose this is what art schools were traditionally supposed to instil into students – a total awareness of the visual presence of everything around them and what signals those things were giving off, and what those signals meant.

Robert: Is Bill suggesting that art schools don't do that anymore? I think they do, and you could say that art in itself should be doing that too. When you engage with an artwork it should provoke wider thought and alter the way you see things.

Come the following March and spring was beginning to break its way through. I had never experienced anything like it before. As a kid I had been a total nature boy. The changing seasons had always been very much part of my life, defining all the activities and games that I was interested in: fishing, collecting bird's eggs, swimming in the Penkiln Burn, scrumping apples, playing conkers, sledging. But nothing could have prepared me for the spring of 1971. Now I am sure that spring of 1971 was no different in any major way from any spring that had come before or since the last ice age at least, but to my senses it was like the first one that had ever been.

Paul: It's about being turned on. It's about being alive to things that are going on around you. It can happen when you first go to art school for example. In the first years you do lots of projects based on observations, photographs of surroundings or collections of things – ordinary stuff. It's about looking at the world with new eyes.

When the buds on the trees burst open to reveal their new young and tender leaves I couldn't believe there were so many shades of green. When the wild flowers started to blossom on the verges the strength of colour almost hurt my eyes. Colours in nature were more intense than I had ever experienced. It was almost shocking, as if it had been turned up way past 11. No drug has ever been able to replicate what I experienced that spring. Although this had a lasting effect on me and upped my appreciation of spring ever

Rasmus: 'Being turned on' is a perfect phrase for describing it. Perhaps that is what happens when you begin to study anything in a serious and engaged way. If you are tuned into the world of mathematics, then you see it everywhere, you discover connections and it changes your view of the world.

Robert: How you receive information is a fundamental part of the creative process.

since, nothing could ever compete with that spring in 1971.

But something similar has been happening this year to do with sound. Yesterday evening I spent almost three hours out here on the ledge just losing myself in the sounds of the city. A film-maker using this scene would probably want to smother / enhance these sounds with some subtle soundtrack or at the very least have the sounds of somebody practising jazz trumpet coming out of one of the open windows.

Tonight, like last night, every sound, distant or near, muffled or clear, seems ridiculously perfect and I want it to go on and on. I want to spend all night here, just listening. Now I'm not going to make any case for what I'm listening to being music, and there is no way I would want to record it for anybody else to hear. I'm not interested in using 'found sound' in the making of new music. I got all of that out of my system in the late 1980s.

Something has happened to my hearing over the past few months to make sound seem richer, more heavy with abstract meaning. Of course it is not. It is all in my head. Weirdly, I know grudgingly that my hearing is not as good as it was some years ago, down to the ageing process I guess. It is also different from when I was making pop music, when I could deconstruct every record that I heard on a passing car stereo. That used to drive me up the wall: it meant I couldn't enjoy hearing the record for what it was.

The way that I am hearing sounds right now is in some sense the way I experienced the colours in the spring of 1971. Has this come about because of what I have been doing over the past few months with The17? Have I been subconsciously upping my awareness of the sounds around me? Or would it have happened anyway? What I do know is that it will not last in the same way, just as the spring of 1972 was nothing compared to the previous one.

Back to the here and now. I've just heard some swifts screaming as they tear across the evening sky. One of the major things I knew I was going to miss living in London was the comings and goings of migratory birds. Swifts are about the only migratory bird that you can easily be aware of in London. Screaming is maybe not the best word to describe the sound they make but the next time you hear them tear across the sky above your head maybe you can come up with one. Time to turn in, unlike the swifts that will keep flying all night.

THE THIRD EVENING
11 July 2006

The third evening in a row spent on the ledge, and I've got myself a pot of tea and a bag of chips for company. The swifts are back, wheeling and tearing across the sky. I've got my pencil and notebook out here as well, not so I can come on all Wordsworth again but because I got an email from a woman in Austria.

We are off to Vienna in a couple of days time to do The17 there and the woman who is coordinating the practical details of the event needs to know exactly what I am going to be doing. So I hope to put down as succinctly as I can what it is I do and how it works before it gets too dark to write anymore out here. Here goes ...

In a small room I will be sitting
Worrying that tonight it may not work
Even though I know every other night
That I have done this it has worked.

In a big room, a room with dimmed lighting,
There will be a piano;
A piano stool;
A table with some equipment on it;
17 chairs arced around the piano, stool and table.
Behind the table will be a man called John Hirst.
John Hirst is in charge of the equipment.
On the walls of the room will be 17 framed text works.
These text works are A0 in size
They are also scores to be performed.

In a third room there will be 17 people
Wondering what they have come to.
If there is no third room available
The street outside will suffice.
These 17 people will be offered a glass of wine
Then ushered into the big room.
They will sit down and wait.

I will leave the small room.
Come into the big room.

Bill Drummond

Sit down on a stool in front of them and say
'Good evening. My name is Bill Drummond
And you are The17.'

I will then spend the next 40 minutes talking.
Talking about why we are at this point in the history of music
And what The17 is and why
They are now all members of The17
For life.
Me talking will both entertain them
And enlighten them.

There will then be a short break of about ten minutes.
In the break they can leave the big room
Have a fag, take a piss,
Drink another glass of wine
And worry about what will happen next.

What will happen next is
They will come back into the big room
Sit on their seats
And I will explain to them about
how we, as in they, John Hirst and me,
Are now going to do a version of
One of the scores specifically composed for The 17.
The one called *AGE*.

We will then spend the next 40 minutes
Putting together this version of *AGE*.

Then there will be another short break
After which the lights in the room will be switched off
And we will play back to them what they have just recorded.
This will take five minutes.
One member of the audience will think it was:
The most beautiful thing they have ever experienced.
Another will think:
They have heard it all before.
The rest will be glad they made the effort to take part,
I hope.
I will then chat for another couple of minutes.

Then John Hirst will delete the recording.
There will be a gasp.
And maybe some applause.

And that will be that.
Some people may try and ask me some questions.
I may answer some.

I will return to my small room.
They will go home.
The history of music will have changed.

And now that is done I will pour myself another mug of tea, watch the moon
as it lifts itself above the skyline, and listen.

Bill Drummond

SYD IS DEAD
12 July 2006

Driving up England. Doing the dad thing. Kate, my eldest daughter, has just finished university. Got her degree in philosophy and I'm driving back up the A1 to pick her up and all her three years of student accumulations, and take them back down to her mum's in Aylesbury.

The sun is shining, the corn is golden, the window on the driver's side is down and I have this great big loving feeling inside me. I also feel like crying. This has got nothing to do with me wallowing in thoughts of being a good, average or bad dad, and everything to do with the copy of a newspaper that is lying open on the empty passenger seat.

I keep glancing from the road in front to the newspaper. Syd Barrett is staring back at me. Syd died yesterday. He had cancer. He was 60. Lots of people die of cancer when they get to be 60 or thereabouts. Also on the front page of this newspaper is a report that at least 60 people have been killed on packed commuter trains in Mumbai: 'A synchronised series of bombs ripped through packed commuter trains and stations in the evening rush hour ...' Mothers, children, young men in the prime of their lives with so much to offer, are dead, not some wasted old rocker in his 60s who only ever made a few good tracks. But it is because of Syd that the tears are welling up. How fucked-up is that?

When Jimi Hendrix died in September 1970, I felt nothing. Saw him on Top Of The Pops in 1967 playing *Purple Haze*. It was the wildest thing I had ever seen. Bought the Axis Bold As Love LP in 1968. *Little Wing* was the most beautiful guitar-playing that had ever been done. Saw him on Lulu's TV show in 1969 playing a version of *Sunshine Of Your Love*; as far as I was concerned it was revolution live on Saturday night TV. Saw him play live at the Isle of Wight pop festival in 1970. He was shit. Washed-up and pointless. He died 17 days later. I'm not saying he deserved to die but if he had lived any longer he would not have done anything else of merit. His load was shot.

When Lennon got shot in 1980 I thought, well he had to go. Everything he had done since The Plastic Ono Band album was shite, but the most crap was his comeback Double Fantasy album. John Lennon no longer served any purpose for me.

Why now as the fields of Lincolnshire speed by and my elbow rests on the open window, am I having to hold back tears? I look over at the angelic face of Syd again. He must have been the same age as Kate is now when the picture was taken. Fuck it. I'm letting those tears flow. There is no point in trying to stop them. Everybody who knows anything about the history of rock 'n' roll knows that Syd Barrett has done fuck-all since 1971, and even if he had, we would have wished that he hadn't.

So why am I crying for Syd? Well obviously I'm not. You can't mourn somebody you have never met or hardly know anything about. I'm sure someone who knows about these things could explain it all, how I'm mourning my own lost youth, bemoaning my own mortality. It's not like I was even a huge Syd Barrett fan. When the *Arnold Lane* and *See Emily Play* singles came out in 1967 I thought they were great but I also thought *Rainbow Chaser* by Nirvana (the original ones) was just as great. But I haven't got a clue who was in that Nirvana or if they are alive or dead now.

Paul: I think Arnold Layne is spelt with a 'y', and I always thought it somehow relates to Syd using y in his name. It became kind of an identity, a running theme to create links between works, like a branding device used in a slightly ironic way.

The LP Atom Heart Mother came out in 1971. It was the first all-new studio post-Syd LP by Pink Floyd and at that time I thought it was the best thing they had ever done. I played it and played it. In comparison, the first Syd solo album, The Mad Cap Laughs, was twaddle. But as the years went by, Pink Floyd became more bombastic and Nick Mason's collection of cars grew, and Roger Waters' ego grew even bigger and Dave Gilmore spent years making a solo album and Rick Wright ... what did Rick Wright do? Syd kept his counsel and, as all us white rock boys knew, he lived with his mum, lost his hair, got fat and did nothing but occasionally get photographed when popping out to the shops. But for us his iconic status grew and grew. And I'm not going to try and explain that. I'm sure there are plenty of rock journalists at this very moment tapping away on their keyboards explaining the impact of Syd's silence and what his burgeoning cult fame was all about.

What I will tell you is that sunny summer days like this always make me think of the sunny summer days in the English countryside in the late 1960s. But, more importantly for me and my life and what I'm doing now and what I may have been doing for sod knows how long is that it was on a day like today, a day when the corn was already golden and house martins fluttered around the eaves and it was 1968, when I was in my bedroom listening to a second-hand LP that I had just bought at a jumble sale that morning. The LP was The Piper At The Gates Of Dawn, the first album by Pink Floyd. This, according to one of the rock critics writing in this morning's paper, was Syd's masterpiece.

Maybe it was, but I remember being disappointed with it at the time. I mean, it had cost me five shillings and I was hoping it was all going to sound like *Arnold Lane* and *See Emily Play*, but it didn't. I persevered and listened to it all again and then again. Then when I was listening to the last track on side two for the fourth time, *Interstellar Overdrive*, I had an idea. My sister had this Spanish guitar; she'd had it for two or three years. She'd had a few lessons at school but never really bothered with it. Her room was next to mine. She was out somewhere. I went in and got it. Up until then it had never really crossed my mind to learn to play the guitar. The rest of the Saturday afternoon was spent trying to learn and play the riff to *Interstellar Overdrive*. Now I'm not saying that if it were not for Syd I would never have picked up a guitar, but even these days it is still that riff that my fingers automatically drift towards playing any time I absentmindedly pick up a guitar. After all, it was Peter Green who went on to be the guitar hero of my mid-teen years. There was never another Pink Floyd song that I consciously learned to play.

But on this sunny summer morning as the golden fields of Lincolnshire still flash past and my elbow still rests on the open window of the Land Rover I can hear The17 in my head. What they are singing is this huge and sprawling version of *Interstellar Overdrive*. No guitars or drums or keyboards, no lead singer and no words. Just the massed ranks of The17 as they sing that most foreboding of riffs. The sound gets bigger and louder and wilder like an untamed mountain and then they take it down to almost a whisper and the tears keep rolling down my cheeks.

'Syd is dead. Syd is sodding dead.'

PUBLIC SPACES
14 July 2006

Standing on a patch of mown grass on the edge of a small rundown playground. There is some dog shit inches from my left foot and I have just realised my right foot is standing on a patch of dried puke. A posse of teenagers is playing football in a caged basketball court. There is also a small park café with a few tables and chairs. The café is closed but a bunch of mothers are sitting at one of the tables and their toddlers and brats are messing about. The air is hot and sticky; a thunderstorm threatens. Surrounding this public space are blocks of pre-Corbusier flats. Windows are wide open, washing is hanging out of some of them, people out of others.

I'm in district 20 of Vienna where most of the 'guest workers' live. I was going to call it the immigrant quarter but that seems too loaded with pretentious, romanticised, patronising crap. 'Hey, we're hanging out in the immigrant quarter.' Somewhere else in this city The Rolling Stones are soundchecking for their concert in the national stadium this evening. I wonder if they will play *Paint It Black*? Mick Jagger is the sort of person who would – so his lyrics suggest anyway – like you to think he hangs out in the immigrant quarter.

It's late Friday afternoon. The working week is done and I'm digging the vibe. Then this ugly noise fills the air, like when a pneumatic drill kicks in and whatever vibe I thought I was digging instantly evaporates. The lads stop playing football, the toddlers and brats cover their ears and run to their mums, the folk hanging out of the windows want to know where the racket is coming from and my nostrils suddenly pick up the scent of the dried puke on the grass under my right foot.

The reason I am in Vienna is because I have been invited over by Robert Jelinek. He is an Austrian-cum-Czech artist and founder of the State Of Sabotage (SoS). I may write more about SoS later, if I can in some way squeeze it into the rather loose remit of this book. Robert Jelinek is curating a series of events for the community radio station Orange 94FM. I only have a vague idea of what these events are about.

A woman from Orange told me they were doing the project with a number of other non-commercial radio stations across Europe, including Resonance FM in London. Robert told me it was something to do with artists being commissioned to use radio in a very non-radio sort of way. Robert Jelinek thinks The17 – a music thing that cannot be broadcast by any radio station, even this Orange one, but can be discussed on air – fits the project perfectly. Tomorrow evening I am doing *An Introduction To The17* and performance of the score *AGE* in one of the station's studios. Listeners to Orange were invited to take part. The first 17 people to apply got tickets. Afterwards I will be talking about the performance and The17 in general on air.

The scent of the puke is invading my nostrils even more and for some reason I am unwilling to move from where I am standing. Robert Jelinek's other invited artists are performing this evening. The artists are Claudia Marzendorfer and Nik Hummer. I understand they are a couple. In her work she often uses ice. He is also a musician. When working together they make records out of ice. This is how I understand it's done. They start by recording some music, grow a metal stamper from acetate. So far this is the traditional way of making a record. I won't go into all the technical process of how this is done, it would take pages. If the traditional process were to be followed, the metal stamper would be taken to a record-pressing plant and used to press records out of hot vinyl. Then you could buy the records and play them at home until you got bored with it or it wore out. But with Claudia Marzendorfer and Nik Hummer that doesn't happen. They take the metal stamper and put it in a circular tin box the same size as the disc, fill the box with water and then put it in the deep freeze. At any time after the water has been frozen it can be taken out of the tin, very carefully of course, and this perfect record can be played on a record player. It being ice, it starts to melt immediately and has a playing life of no more than ten minutes before its grooves have melted away.

Now I know this idea of records made out of ice serves no practical purpose. It's definitely not the format that the global music industry is looking for to entice the buying public away from free downloads, but I love it. It ticks so many of the boxes that I enjoy ticking at the moment. For a start it is impermanent. It is of the moment. There is nothing left but water that you can either drink or, more symbolically, wash your hands with. Or, with the water shortage, you could use the water again to make another record.

A few weeks ago when Robert Jelinek was telling me about Claudia Marzendorfer and Nik Hummer and their ice records (*Eisplatten*), I thought he was suggesting they make a record of The17 performance and that this recording is played the next evening to those who had taken part. This sounded like a very good idea to me, very much in keeping with what I like to think The17 are about. But it seems that due to my hectic and somewhat out-of-control lifestyle communication had broken down between us. He had not had confirmation from me that I was up for having The17's performance being committed to ice. Thus Robert followed a different path.

Some years ago I was sent in the post what looked like a CD of the album Chill Out that Jimmy Cauty and I had recorded as The KLF in late 1988. The cover of the original record was a photo of some sheep in an English field. In our heads the cover was, among other things, a nod of respect to the cover of Atom Heart Mother by Pink Floyd. The cover of Atom Heart Mother featured a cow in an English field. I won't bother trying to describe the music on Chill Out. It seemed to become a blueprint for a whole genre of music that might have been best left uninvented. It also took on iconic status and benchmark qualities. It took us an afternoon to record in Jimmy's front room. It may be the piece of music that we did together that I am most proud of.

There have been times when I have even indulged in the idea that at some point in our later years Jimmy and I could cash in on our legacy by going out and performing the complete and extended version of Chill Out live, or as live as these things can be. In the same way that Brian Wilson goes out and performs the Beach Boys' Pet Sounds. It would not be a KLF-reformation, just as Brian Wilson is not reforming The Beach Boys to play Pet Sounds. It would be billed as Jimmy Cauty and Bill Drummond perform The KLF's Chill Out. Now you have to understand this will never happen, but there are times when I think about it and all the practicalities of us putting it on.

So this CD came through the post some five or six years ago that looked like Chill Out. It wasn't. The sheep had been Photoshopped out and replaced by wolves. A play on wolf in sheep's clothing I guess (or is it sheep in wolves' clothing?).

The music on the CD was nothing like the spacey comedown music that we had made back in late 1988. It was unlistenable-noise music. Each track by a different act. I liked it. I liked the cover. Having one CD cover based on our original did not quite put Chill Out in the same league as Sgt Pepper's. The sleeve to Sgt Pepper's has been parodied, homaged and ripped off almost every year by someone ever since it came out in 1967.

This album with the wolves on the cover had been put together by Robert Jelinek in Vienna. He had not been a KLF fan nor was music particularly part of his own practice as an artist; it was just one of the numerous things he had done along the way. Sending it to me had established a line of sporadic communication between us and I have become a keen follower and soon to be citizen of State Of Sabotage.

Remember how I was telling you about the excruciating noise starting and kids running to their mothers with their hands over their ears? Well I'm picking up from where I left off there. This music that is hardly music is being pumped out of a pair of speakers that are stood either side of the open doors to Radio Orange. (Just in case you are worried, and I was, Radio Orange is not sponsored by Orange the mobile phone people.) What is being played is the *Eisplatten* made especially by Claudia Marzendorfer and Nik Hummer for the occasion. What you hear first is the eardrum-spiking crackles and crunches. It's as if the stylus on the record player that is following the groove on the *Eisplatten* is like one of those ice-breaker ships crunching their way through the pack ice. And, to stretch this analogy even further, the bits of dark water that are revealed in the wake of the ship is the actual music that I am now hearing beneath all the crackles and crunches. This music, and it takes me some time to realise this, is Chill Out by The KLF.

Whatever artistic qualities Claudia Marzendorfer and Nik Hummer's work may possess are not being appreciated by the local residents. Rock 'n' Roll may not be noise pollution, to almost quote AC/DC, but this certainly is. I feel somehow responsible for their Friday evening's good vibe being so rudely shattered in the name of contemporary art. Radio Orange is a community radio station. I don't think this community is appreciating it that much right now.

I stay rooted to the spot. Dog turd still to the left of my left foot, puke under my right. Then I feel guilt from another quarter. Most of the 30 or so people who had been hanging about with cans of free beer in hand, guests of Radio Orange, have gone back through the open doors into the radio station to where Claudia Marzendorfer and Nik Hummer are spinning their *Eisplatten* – I guess, to fully appreciate what they are doing.

Hearing a KLF record always makes me feel acutely embarrassed. Not that I think they were all bad, but they just do. Now I am thinking that they will be thinking that I am being very rude by not going in and physically demonstrating my appreciation of what they are doing by nodding my head or tapping my toe to the music. Not that Chill Out contains any beats to tap your toe or nod your head to. So the spot still has my feet rooted to it while my mind does all sorts of whizzing about. And now an idea has entered my head. The best one that's arrived all day.

I'm wearing a turquoise blue T–shirt with some orange writing on the front and the back. On the front it says 'MyDeath.net' and on the back 'Prepare To

Die'. The thing is, even though the MyDeath site has been up since 2000, I've never got around to thinking about my own funeral. But now there is this idea in my head. I want Claudia Marzendorfer and Nik Hummer to make an *Eisplatten* of a performance of *AGE* and as my coffin goes through the curtains to whatever lies at the other side, this *Eisplatten* can be played. The melted water from the disc is to be collected and kept in a jam jar to be poured later into the Penkiln Burn from the rock where some of my children know I want my ashes scattered.

Thoughts of my funeral are now being broken by the sounds of people clapping. The Chill Out *Eisplatten* has come to an end. The normal sounds of a summer evening return to fill the air. Children take their hands off their ears, teenagers return to playing football and I pull up my roots from a spot beneath my feet and move away from the stench of the stale sick.

I SEE A RED DOOR
14 JULY 2006

Sitting in a bar some time around midnight. The bar is named the Hermi and it's in a back street in Vienna. The Hermi is empty save for two men drinking on their own who look like they have been drinking all night on their own and did last night and will be doing so tomorrow night. There is also my colleague John Hirst and me. The barman is bringing in the tables from outside. It's a place for the lost and the lonely but the music being played is not Elkie Brooks, it's Eric Clapton.

Somewhere else in this city that is celebrating the 250th anniversary of Mozart's death (I wonder what he would have liked to have had played at his funeral) the Rolling Stones will have done their show by now. I wonder what percentage of the audience thought they were still the greatest rock 'n' roll band in the world. I wonder if Mick Jagger is as knackered as me. And I wonder if he sang *Paint It Black*.

The reason why l wonder about *Paint It Black* in this story and in the story I wrote earlier this evening is that my 11-year-old daughter Bluebell asked me on Thursday evening if I knew how to sing *Paint It Black*, and since then it has been going round in my head, When I was in Big in Japan in 1977/78, *Paint It Black* was the only cover version we played regularly. I used to love playing it. It was always my favourite Rolling Stones single.

Bluebell has just started getting into music. A few weeks ago she discovered Limewire and has now downloaded more than 1000 songs on to her hard drive. She never listens to pop radio or goes into record shops; the way she discovers music is via her peer group and MySpace and also from the adverts on TV. Three weeks back she got into the Scottish band Pilot who had a couple of hits back in the early to mid-1970s. It seems they had a song she liked that was used on an advert. She put what she thought was the title of the song into Google and found out it was Pilot. Now she seems to have every song that Pilot ever recorded on the hard drive. Last week she was asking me about the Beach Boys. I wanted to know how she knew about the Beach Boys. She said everybody knew about the Beach Boys.
'But how?'
'Because there is this advert on TV that uses the song that goes "We are going to have fun fun fun 'til her daddy takes the T Bird away." I love it and now I've got loads of Beach Boys songs and so do my friends.'
'Wow'.

'What do the Beach Boys look like?'
I don't think I answered that one.

As for *Paint It Black* by the Stones, Bluebell has just got this computer game or something that is like a home karaoke. It seems there are hundreds of songs on it. All sorts of genres. 'It's got one section for all those old rock songs you like. Some of them are great.'

Now I didn't know how to take this. Do I tell her I hate all old-fashioned rock songs and so should she? Or do I take pride in my daughter's wide-ranging tastes in music and her capacity to appreciate some of the all-time greats from the pantheon of rock classics? Or should I try to explain to her why recorded music is a dead medium, redundant for expressing anything relevant to modern times? Or should I buy her a copy of Blonde On Blonde?
'Dad, do you know the song *Paint It Black*?'
'Yes.'
'That is my favourite. I love singing that one.'
'It is my favourite by the Rolling Stones.'
'When you come back from Vienna you must have a game with me and see who can sing *Paint It Black* best.'
'What do you mean sing it best?'
'On the game they have this thing at the bottom of the screen while the song is playing that shows you how well you are singing, how in time you are, how in tune you are and then it gives you points at the end.'
'Points?'
'Yeah, points. A score. I bet I can beat you.'

Do I buy her a copy of Let It Bleed? Warn her of the evils of U2 or throw away her karaoke games and empty her hard drive of any song older than last Tuesday? Or maybe I should go and find Mick Jagger now, wherever he is in Vienna, and invite him round to have a go as well. I wonder how many points he'd get.
'Ok. I'm back Sunday afternoon. I will play you then.'
'Great.'

Now back to this bar for the lost and the lonely. When I got my notebook and pencil out ten minutes ago it wasn't to tell you all that stuff about my daughter. It was thinking about the Stones that set me on that path. What I wanted to tell you was how much I loathe the music of Eric Clapton. On one wall of the bar is a huge projected page from the barman's iTunes. We can see about 20 tracks all by Eric Clapton, each one more dreary than the one before. I'm sitting here sipping my watery beer, wondering if I'm dreading the unplugged version of *Layla* that is coming up the song after next more than the one about some slag looking shaggable tonight. At least we have missed the one about his dead kid. I mean, how can someone with so much professed guitar talent be so bereft of an original idea?

But it's when he is singing a blues song that he gets my goat well and truly tethered (anyone for a game of mixed metaphors?). How can anybody allow him to record a blues classic when they know all he can ever do is make a mockery of it? How can he allow himself? He should be done under the Race Relations Act or something. What makes all my prejudices against Eric Clapton a bit weird is that I used to love Cream, the short-lived supergroup he was in during the 1960s.

Last week me and two of my sons, James (19) and Flint (6), sat down on the sofa together to watch School Of Rock starring Jack Black. James said, 'Everybody should be made to watch this film. It is the only film that has ever got right what rock 'n' roll is about.'

Flint wanted James to start teaching him how to pay the guitar immediately. I don't think he knows I can play. I will keep that quiet. The reason I am mentioning School Of Rock is that there is one bit where there are a few bars of *Sunshine Of Your Love* by Cream. It leapt right out at me screaming, 'Bill! This is what music should sound like!' I tried to ignore it so it screamed even louder at me, 'You know I'm better than any piece of rock music that has been recorded in the last ten years!' I succeed in ignoring it and just got on with watching the film, laughing at Jack Black's body movements and cheering at the bits we are meant to cheer at.

But now in this late-night Vienna bar, I am wondering how Eric Clapton can be responsible, if only partly, for some of the greatest rock recordings ever made and then be content to spend the next 30 years churning out drivel. And just as we are about to hear the unplugged version of *Layla* the barman clicks his mouse and Eric is no more. He is replaced by the unmistakable intro to *Boom Boom Boom* by John Lee Hooker. The relief washes over me. If only all music could be this good. *Boom Boom Boom* is followed by other Hooker classics from the 1950s. How could Clapton as a grown man ever consider recording blues songs when he knew this sort of perfection had already been reached 30 years earlier? 'Because I can' is never a good enough answer.

A conversation of sorts starts to develop between John Hirst and myself. The central theme to this conversation seems to be 'Can only young men make truly innovative music?' I try to argue the case that there are plenty of men (and I'm afraid it's men and not women that we are discussing) making innovative music well into their later years. Beethoven for one. His late string quartets were like no other music ever made. Miles Davis was well into his 40s when he did Bitches Brew, where he single-handedly announced the end of modern jazz. And this was from a man who had had a big part in inventing it in his early 20s in the late 1940s.

Wouldn't it have been great if Eric Clapton, or, even better, the Rolling Stones, had made a record in their late 40s that had suddenly rendered the making of rock music a completely redundant thing? Is this making any sense outside the confines of this bar some time after midnight? I mean, there is no way that Miles Davis in his late 40s would have been playing tunes from his Birth Of Cool phase from the late 1940s or even the Kinda Blue phase from the late 1950s. The man moved on. Burnt bridges. Tried things out, made mistakes and fucked up but was still always searching for that door in his head which had not been opened before.

Why has rock music always been so willingly stuck in a rut of peddling its own past? You know if you had been stupid enough to have bought a ticket to see the Rolling Stones tonight, you would have seen a bunch of pensioners still trying to pretend to be in the first flush of manhood, singing songs that in no way reflect the lives they are leading or even the thoughts that are going through their heads.

It is too late and maybe I have drunk too much to make any more sense out of these thoughts. At a later stage in this book I want to return to the subject of the rock band. Maybe dedicate a whole chapter to exploring why the rock band was potentially the greatest art form of the 20th century, one that was squandered.

Tonight I will try and find my way back to the hotel while singing 'I see a red door and I want to paint it black. No colours anymore I want them to turn back.'

Bill Drummond

BACON SANDWICHES
16 JULY 2006

On a plane high above the Alps, on our way back from Vienna and heading for somewhere that is my current home. The notebook is on my lap, the pencil is out and the trolley is yet to arrive with refreshments. I'm trying to tie some thoughts together. I'm not going to bother you with any more of that whole rock business or whether older men can have fresh ideas. I will leave that for another time. What is concerning me is what did and didn't work on this visit to Vienna and what can be learnt for the future and what opportunities it has opened up.

First, what didn't work. The heat. The performance started at 5.00. It was not late enough in the day for the heat wave we are experiencing across Europe to subside. To do the *Introduction to The17* you need all air-conditioning switched off. If left on, the sound is always picked up and interferes with the recording. For the same reason, all windows and doors must be kept closed to prevent sounds from the street coming in. The room was too small, or too small considering we had to have 19 people crammed in there with no air conditioning, no windows and no doors open for nearly two hours in the middle of a heatwave. It took its toll: my concentration kept wandering when I was doing the talking bit. During the singing I think all anybody could think of was 'When is all this going to be over so we can get some fresh air and a long cool beer?'

Next there was the light problem. Light could not be sealed out of the room. For this to work fully we need to have almost total darkness so people can feel more at ease with the singing and to create the right atmosphere for the playback.

John Hirst reckons that in future we should stipulate the room dimensions we need and that the room should be 'light-tight'. 'Light-tight' were his words, a phrase I had not heard before but which he assures me is not some affected turn of phrase but industry-standard terminology used by photographers. He also reckons I shouldn't do any promotion on the same day as doing a performance, which to me would sound a bit diva-ish on my part.

The promotion I did was a one-and-a-half-hour interview for a programme on Austrian state radio that specialises in new music, from the classical, jazz or any other tradition, that is interested in breaking with form. The other interview was with Radio Orange itself. It was an hour long and went out live.

It was done almost immediately after the performance of The17. It was through this interview that the listeners of Radio Orange, other than the 17 of them who had been able to get tickets for the performance, would have any idea of what had been going on and why it could not be broadcast.

I've it said before but I love the twist that this musical performance was being done for a radio station and could not be broadcast, only discussed.

I got a lot out of doing both these interviews, not because of any promotional influence they might have but because I found myself having to challenge my own thoughts on what The17 is about. I was forced to try and articulate thoughts that might have been left vague and unfocused in my head. Not quite Prime Minister's Question Time in the House Of Commons but still a good thing. Trying to explain why I think recorded music is in the process of becoming as dated as mosaic or pottery is pretty difficult when for most of us recorded music is the form of artistic communication that has had the most emotional impact on our lives.

The two TV interviews that I did were both trivial soundbite based and with any luck were only seen by a handful of people watching a late-night cable channel.

The good things to come out of the visit were the possibilities of coming back at a later stage and doing a full-scale exhibition and series of performances, maybe once this book is out.

Eva Kuntschner was the woman at Orange responsible for putting the logistics of it together. She also had to do menial jobs like pick us up from the airport on Friday morning and take us back there this morning. Today she had her partner with her who was also called Eva. (Thought this was great, a lesbian couple both named after the first woman, the mother of us all.) I bet they would inspire much Adam and Steve-type laughter and bigoted debate in the heartlands of the US Christian Right. But that's enough sexual politics for this book. Maybe another book one day will sort all that out for everyone. Right now I still have to sort out music.

Eva is a smart woman, with plenty of ideas and seemingly the wherewithal to make them happen. This whole Radio Territories: Interventions In Urban Space event that is linking up seven community radio stations across Europe has been instigated by Radio Orange and she is coordinating it. I ask her which cities and she tells me Berlin, Prague, Bratislava, Sofia, Budapest,

London and Vienna. I ask her which station in London. She tells me Resonance FM. I tell her how I bumped into Ed Baxter, who is in some way at the helm of Resonance FM, in a pub in London a few weeks back. And how we discussed Resonance observing No Music Day on 21 November this year. I explain what No Music Day is to Eva and about nomusicday.com. How it started from the personal and how I want to broaden it out. And then I suggested that maybe Orange 94.0 would like to observe it. She thought this could be a good idea but thought the individual producers at the station might think it a difficult concept to take on board. But she was up for the challenge of trying to convince them.

Way above the clouds and whatever nation lies 30,000 feet below us, my ideas are getting a bit carried away. But before I tell you them I want to quote from some of the blurb about Radio Territories: Interventions In Urban Space. There's a difficulty because most of it is in German and what isn't is in art-speak that has been translated from German into English. But here goes:

> Addressing broad audiences the electronic medium radio establishes part of the public sphere. Considering the heterogeneous constitution of European societies, there is a need to develop new forms of diverse communication – also reflected in contemporary art. The project 'radio.territories' intends to link artistic production with the means of media and ongoing discussions on participation of citizens in pluralistic public space.

And even if you can't read German you might get the gist of this.

> radio.territories umfasst:
> :: 14 experimentelle multimedia-interventionen in 7 europalschen
>   Stadten (London, Berlin, Wien, Prag, Bratislava, Sofia und Budapest)
> :: Kooperationen und Arbeitsaufenthalte von Kunstlerinnen
> :: die Entwicklung von technischen Losungen fur die transnationale
>   Verbreitung von Live-Veranstaltungen uber das internet.

So what I'm thinking is, wouldn't it be good if I could get all of these seven radio stations to observe No Music Day? If not this year, next, and have it all coordinated from Orange 94.0 Das Freie Radio in Wien.

OK. No more German.

I will email Eva tomorrow and start a dialogue with her about this. The trolley is now here. They had promised us bacon sandwiches, which sounded good. It is in fact ham made from chicken meat [sic] with some sliced gherkins. That sounds as far from a bacon buttie as you can get. I settle for a cheese and lettuce sandwich and a cup of tea. Then I fall asleep before eating or drinking them.

SCORE

13. CELEBRATE

Two meet, fall in love, make a commitment.
Celebrate this by asking 17 females, willing to sing, to stand on one side
facing 17 males, willing to sing, standing on the other side.
Both groups staring into each other's eyes.

Indicate the notes A and B to The 17 (males).
Indicate the notes F and E to The 17 (females).

The 17 (males) start by bringing forth sounds from their throats and mouths in unison.
The sounds must constantly shift from the note A to the note B and back again,
over and over.
They must draw upon and express all the emotions they have ever felt in relationships.
They must never shift their gaze from those of the females opposite them.

At a suitable point
The 17 (females) start by bringing forth sounds from their throats and mouths in unison.
The sounds must constantly shift from the note F to the note E and back again,
over and over.
They too must draw upon and express all the emotions they have ever felt in relationships.
They must never shift their gaze from those of the males opposite them.

At times The 17 (males) should allow The 17 (females') singing to take precedence over theirs.
At other times The 17 (females) allow The 17 (males') singing to take precedence over theirs.

Let the performance last as long as the group dynamic see fit, allowing it to fade leaving
nothing but the buzzing in their ears.

Applaud.

pb Poster 140   2006

MANHOLE COVERS
18 July 2006

Back from Vienna, back on the ledge, a distant siren is getting closer. I got the deckchair I am sitting on from Ikea. I wanted a traditional stripy one but they didn't have any so I got this.

When did you first start noticing manhole covers? Did the idea of these portals into the underworld fascinate you as a kid? How many films feature a man or a woman escaping from or into a manhole?

I didn't become aware of my interest in them until about 2001 when for a short but very intensive period I found myself photographing hundreds of them. Wherever I went – and especially if that wherever was abroad – I would constantly have my head down as I walked along, camera in hand, in case I missed any manhole covers I had not seen before.

Paul: I believe that there already is a book about manhole covers published in Britain. They used to sell it in Zwemmers books on Charing Cross Road.

This need to photograph them only went on for a few months and then it was over. I have even been able to throw away all the photos I took.

Earlier this month when I was in Moscow with Tracey Moberly I noticed she was doing the same thing – taking photographs of manhole covers wherever she went. At least she was only using her mobile phone to take the pictures; for some reason using a mobile makes it seem less questionable. We got into discussion about how wonderful manhole covers can be, how aesthetically interesting they are. How ... once you start on a subject like this, it's hard to stop and you know it's going to lead to some train-spottery nether world. All you need to know for the purpose of this text is that although I no longer need to go around taking photographs of manhole covers everywhere I go, I still love them. They enrich my life as I plod along, wherever I am.

On Saturday, a couple of days ago, when I was in Vienna, the artist Robert Jelinek took us to his studio. It was on the top floor of an old factory on the outskirts of the city. It was an incredibly impressive place, everything any film director would want for a scene set in a contemporary artist's studio. It pressed all the right buttons. I was jealous. And the rent was dirt cheap. On leaving I noticed five brand-new manhole covers he had sitting on the floor. They were obviously ones that had never yet been used to cover a hole that a man had gone down. So I asked why, where and what, and he told me he had been in love with manhole covers for years and that he had been looking for an excuse to have some made himself. Various people asked him to contribute a work of art to such and such an exhibition in such and such a country. He decided he would get a set of manhole covers cast with the coat of arms of his State of Sabotage on it. The plan was to send one of these out whenever he was asked to contribute a piece of work to an exhibition. He told me there was now a standard size for manhole covers worldwide and that with a lifting key they were quite easy to remove and replace.

He also said that during a recent visit to Vienna by George Bush all the manhole covers in the city were sealed, in case any of those Islamist terrorists might be hiding down the holes.

Since I got back from Austria I have been thinking about manhole covers far more than is healthy. There is no way round it. I have to admit it, I wish I had decided to do manhole covers before I saw Robert Jelinek's. Right now in my head, they are the most perfect things to use to make art. There they are in our midst every day. I mean, how many manhole covers do you pass on an average day? But we hardly notice them. Wouldn't it be great if when you did, it informed you about something other than who the local council was?

Sod it. I can't stop myself. I know it will look like I am ripping off Robert Jelinek but I've got to get a manhole cover cast for The17. I've just climbed back through the window, got on Google and found a place that can cast manhole covers. Nowhere near as expensive as I had feared.

Pour myself a mug of tea from the pot. Climb back through the window with the mug. Settle into the deck chair and calm my mind by listening to the near and distant sounds. The swifts have packed it in for the night. Get my pen out and write the following score:

CAST (after R. Jelinek)

Choose a manhole cover.
Stand on it, close your eyes and listen.
Warning: Do not get run down.

Design and cast a new manhole cover
with the same proportions that
incorporates the words:
STAND ON THIS MANHOLE COVER.

CLOSE YOUR EYES AND LISTEN.
WARNING: DO NOT GET RUN DOWN.

Replace the old manhole cover
with the new one.

SCORE

12. CAST (after R. Jelinek)

Choose a manhole cover

Stand on it, close your eyes and listen.

WARNING: Do not get run down.

Design and cast a new manhole cover
with the same dimensions that
incorporates the words:

STAND ON THIS MANHOLE COVER.
CLOSE YOUR EYES AND LISTEN.
WARNING: DO NOT GET RUN DOWN.

Replace the old manhole cover
with the new one.

pb Poster 139   2006

CHOIRS ARE BORING
19 July 2006

'They look brilliant.'
'Maybe you should do a book of them.'
'What, like a music manuscript-size book?'
'No, I was thinking of a small A5- or even A6-size one.'
'I could put in the text that I wrote about working at the schools.'
'I thought that they were going to be chapters in The17 book?'
'Yeah, but I could have them in here too. The17 book is not out until 2008; we could have this little one out by the time The17 do Huddersfield in November this year.'
'Maybe you should also write a short introduction to the book that gives it some sort of context.'

This conversation took place last Monday up in Norwich. John Hirst had just shown me the rough layouts he had done of the 59 scores written by pupils in the seven schools we had been working with in Sunderland and County Durham. Yesterday I wrote the introduction. It may seem irrelevant appearing here in this book or if it was to appear, it should have done so much earlier, but it didn't. This is it:

> This small book contains 59 scores daydreamed, made up and composed by pupils from seven schools in Sunderland and County Durham in the northeast of England in May 2006. Five of the schools were primary, the other two secondary.
> The scores were realised as a response to me visiting the schools and working with the pupils.
> We explored their ideas about music
> And I introduced to them my ideas about The17.
> They told me what music they liked and what they hated and why.
> I told them that The17 was an imaginary choir that I had made up.
>
> Some of them thought this silly.
> Then I read them the words on this poster that I had made.
>
> All recorded music has run its course.
> It has all been consumed, traded, downloaded,
> Understood, heard before, sampled, learned,
> Revived, judged and found wanting.
> Dispense with all previous forms of music and

Bill Drummond

Music-making and start again.
Year zero now.

The17 is a choir.
Their music has no history, follows no traditions,
Recognises no contemporaries.
The17 has many voices.
They use no libretto, lyrics or words; no time
Signatures, rhythm or beats; and have no knowledge
Of melody, counterpoint or harmony.
The17 struggle with the dark
And respond to the light.

This may have gone over their heads but I did not want to patronise them by explaining it further or asking them if they understood what it was about.

Then I asked them to imagine waking up one day and all music had disappeared.
Nothing on their CDs, nothing on the radio and all instruments had vanished.
One boy asked, 'What about downloads?'
I said, 'Them as well, everything, all gone.
And we can't even remember what music sounded like.
All we know is that we liked it and it had been important to us.'
I tried to tell them that The17 was becoming a real choir but not one that sang songs with words and tunes.
One of them said, 'Choirs are boring.'
I told them that they were now all members of The17.
A teacher looked askance.
I said that the music that The17 would make should sound like music would if it was starting all over again, or at least that is what I hoped.
A girl said this would be impossible.
'I know, but that should not stop us trying.'
I showed them some of the scores that had already been written for The17 to perform.
These scores were just lists of instructions to be followed.
They did not use musical notation.

All of the schools took part in the performance of one of these scores, it was called *COLLABORATE*.
I then read a short score out to them about taking 17 people out into the countryside in June and asking them to lie on their backs and listen to skylarks as they climb high into the sky and sing.
When asked, none of the children said they knew what skylarks sounded like.
One boy said he liked the sound that lapwings make when they tumble.
I asked them about sounds they like to hear that are not considered musical.
One girl said she liked the sound of a flock of sheep running.
I told them I had loved the sound of rain on the roof of a prefab classroom where I used to sit and be bored when I was at school.

The last of the scores that I wrote for The17 to perform was called *SCORE*.
This is how it goes:

Score your own composition to be performed by The17.
You need have no previous musical experience. The score you produce should be clear and simple requiring no instrumentation or lyric.
This score is to be performed by a minimum of 17 people using nothing but their voices.
Email your score to admin@the17.org
If it fulfils the above criteria, it will be published and made available to be performed by The17, wherever and whenever applicable.

I asked them to respond to this score.
They did.
Some in small groups, some in pairs and some as individuals.
All the scores they produced appear in this book unedited, although the odd spelling has been corrected.
The order is random.

Robert: What's great about The17 is that it's doomed to failure. You can pretend that music has never existed but you can never shed all of your preconceived ideas about music, even just for an afternoon. The17 will never produce something as accomplished musically as say Good Vibrations, but let's not let it stop us trying. Anyway, it is not the point of The17 to produce something; an object. It is an experience.

Rasmus: You learn something by trying. By failing. I think that there is a lot of that in Bill. Doing something very idealistic that is doomed to fail, to see what will happen. He uses his own naive idealism as an engine to create work.

Robert: And he uses a similar technique when he expresses ideas, not always taking time to justify extreme comments. Because he is being naive and brash, we are forced to really think about the statements he makes. This reminds me of a great Samuel Beckett quote: 'Ever tried. Ever failed. No matter. Try again. Fail again. Fail better.'

They are also available at the17.org to download as PDFs.

The rest of the text in this book tells the story of the time I spent
working with these pupils and explores the ideas that working with
them threw up. It will also form a chapter in a more comprehensive
book about The17 to be published in 2008.
If you want to know why 'all recorded music has run its course' and why
The17 might exist, visit the17.org.

So that was the introduction for a small book that at the time of writing is yet
to come out, but by the time you are reading this will have come and gone. I
doubt we will do a run of more than 500 of them. They will be mainly for
sending to the children who took part and for other interested parties. The
scores done by the students will be up on the website, if you are interested in
looking at them.

SCORE

8. TAKE

IN JUNE,
TAKE 17 PEOPLE TO A PLACE
WHERE SKYLARKS CLIMB
HIGH INTO THE SKY.

REQUEST The17 TO LIE ON THEIR BACKS
ON THE GRASS AND LISTEN
TO THE SKYLARKS AS THEY CLIMB
HIGH INTO THE SKY.

pb Poster 135   2006

CONFRONT YOUR MAKER
31 July 2006

A few minutes ago the sky was almost all blue but now the small fluffy white clouds are gathering together, linking arms, closing down on shrinking patches of blue. A lone crow flies from left to right across my field of vision. The phrase 'field of vision' is one I have never used before and I feel somewhat uncomfortable using it now. The crow has now left my field of vision and I hope that is the last time I ever use that phrase.

In the distance can be heard the low hum of early morning cars taking their drivers to jobs somewhere. Also in the distance I can hear some rooks in a rookery. I'm lying on my back in a Norfolk field. It is 6.38. I've been lying here for almost 17 minutes listening and staring at the sky. I'm listening for and hoping to hear a skylark.

In May / June last year, when I was living near Norwich, I used to walk through this field three mornings a week. There were always skylarks climbing high into the sky, singing their unbroken and unchained melody. Then, as now, I would lie on my back, heavy dew notwithstanding, and look and listen.

I planned to return to this spot in June this year and do the same thing, but it didn't happen. Although skylarks are known to sing through the year, May and June is when they do it most frequently.

I'm sure it was this concentrated bout of skylark-watching and listening last year that prompted me to write the score *TAKE*. But lying on my back in a field staring up at the sky and waiting for a skylark to start rising is something I've done since boyhood.

I acknowledge that our love of the skylark is almost clichéd. Every half-baked romantic has fallen under its spell and tried to express something about it. And that *Lark Ascending* by Vaughan Williams has been rammed down the nation's collective throat, by the nation's guardians of middle-brow values, ever since he wrote it back in the 1920s. But as I'm lying here in this Norfolk field and I can feel something scratching at the back of my neck and I'm wondering if it's an insect that is going to take a bite of my flesh or if it's just a bit of a twig, I start to evolve a theory. This is sort of it:

All of us who in the past few thousand years (or maybe even hundreds of thousands of years) have lain on our backs watching a skylark climb higher and higher into the sky until he is just a tiny little dot against the vast sky, while he continues to sing his song without even stopping to take a breath, have wanted to identify with him. This small brown nondescript bird takes on the universe without fear, rising above all the petty squabbles and trials of our daily lives to confront his Maker. And we all need to confront our Maker from time to time, however existential you think you are. Not by shaking your fist at the heavens but with song and the derring-do, to climb higher than any other living creature of comparable size.

So, back to Score 8, *TAKE*, that I was saying I wrote last year. Don't bother waiting until you have 17 other people to take out with you to listen to these wee brown birds. Get out yourself as soon as a May or June is at hand and your busy life allows. I promise you – 17 minutes of lying on your back listening to this tiny speck hundreds of feet above you will be one of the musical highs of your year.

My 17 minutes are up. I retrieve the twig from the back of my collar, pull myself up and trudge back across the fields to where the Land Rover is parked and a busy day awaits.

Bill Drummond

THE SYCAMORE TREE
3 August 2006

Been sitting here for over an hour now. Just doing nothing but emptying my mind. Moving so little I might become part of the deckchair. The air is still. Nothing is moving. Can't see a soul. Not even aware of the pigeons, and the swifts seem to be elsewhere. The only other thing I can see is a ginger tomcat in his usual place perched high up on the gable end of the factory. No idea what goes on in there. The evening is warm, the sky a dark turquoise. I suppose the sunset must be visible at the other side of the building but from my vantage up here on the ledge it is the eastern half of the sky that I can see.

Even the sounds of the city seem more distant. Not one siren, no cries of children playing in the streets.

Just realised I was wrong about something. It is not just the ginger tom and me. There is a great big huge sycamore tree that stands some 20 yards away from me. It grows in the neighbours' garden but its intense presence fills almost half the space in front of me. So it's the tomcat, the tree and me. All three of us motionless, taking in the evening. Man, cat, tree: masters of all we survey. Or at least for the moment.

I have a complicated relationship with sycamores. If this were an oak or a beech in front of me, I would have nothing but respect for it: oaks for all the obvious reasons – it's the ultimate male tree, strong and tough and lasts for hundreds of years; beeches because there is nothing like their elegant feminine trunk, the smooth grain of its timber and its sweet green leaves in spring. But sycamores are feral. You can't trust them. They get everywhere. Always growing where you don't want them. Make a crack in a pavement and you will have a sycamore seedling coming up through it by next spring. On every rail embankment or bit of wasteland you'll get sycamore sneaking in with the brambles and nettles like so much unwanted second-rate graffiti. And the timber is no good for anything that I rate. It's also a Johnny-come-lately: only been on these islands for the last couple of thousand years and now it's everywhere. But I can't deny this particular one is a fine handsome specimen of a tree.

And while I'm thinking all these thoughts and wishing I didn't anthropomorphise anything and everything so easily, and worrying that people might read a sort of racist subtext to what I've just written, something starts to happen. The leaves on the sycamore start to rustle. The rustle starts to grow and grow. But from where I am sitting I have no sense of there being even a gentle breeze. Within 30 seconds the rustle has grown into what can only be described as a roar. But still I am unaware of any wind.

The logic of what is happening is this: where I am sitting is completely sheltered from the wind. Nothing is stirring on the ledge. But the sycamore is completely exposed to this sudden wind. Usually when there is a wind the loudest thing you can hear is the wind rushing past your ears. The sound of that masks – or at least goes some way to deaden – all other sounds. But that is not happening right now. All I can hear is this sycamore roaring at me and the world. And I can't stop myself from doing the anthropomorphising thing again. The intensity of the effect that the sound of the tree is having on my senses is overpowering. It's as if I'm some Old Testament prophet witnessing the presence of God, right here, right now. I cannot move. I refuse to give whatever this is any symbolic meaning, although I sense there are dozens of symbolic meanings clamouring to get in. After a minute or so the roar starts to fade and within seconds we are back to the still calm evening of only a couple of minutes earlier. And so far I've steadfastly resisted giving shape to any of those clamouring symbolic meanings.

I know I will never hear anything like that again in my life. Well, I may hear it but it will not have the effect on me that it had this evening. It's like that spring in 1971 when I can pinpoint a particular moment on the top deck of the 254 bus going into Kettering, looking out at the trees and the hedgerows, as the moment in my life when colour had its most potent effect on my senses. In the past few minutes a sound from the natural world collided with my heightened senses in a way that will never happen again. There may be birdsong that affects me, but that triggers a different part of my emotions. This was something else altogether.

Time to climb back through the window and put the kettle on. As I do, I notice the big ginger tom is no longer at his post. The sycamore keeps its counsel.

FOR BIG DOUGIE KING
15 August 2006

Kos is a Greek island off the Turkish coast. The Aegean View is a holiday complex on Kos. Most of the clients are Dutch. Lastminute.com sold us a two-week package here. I'm lying on a sun lounger by the pool. Members of my family are in the pool; others are gorging themselves on the 'free' cola (not Coke) served at the poolside bar. From somewhere I can hear the distant strains of *We Are The Cheeky Girls* as sung by those Cheeky Girls. In my head I am trying to marshal thoughts about the vast and sprawling subject of the rock band and why it is now a dead form.

I have carried some of these thoughts around in my head, unmarshalled, for decades. They may have gradually evolved, percolated, even imbued the subtle flavour of the sherry barrels they have been lying in for 33 ⅓ years. That last one could be an analogy too far.

In April 1973, 33 ⅓ years ago, when I was just about to turn 20, I first started to think about the rock band as a cultural force in our society, and why it was the only art form worth considering in modern Britain at the time. The trouble was, I was already thinking of the rock band in a historical sense. Something whose moment as a living form had already come and gone: I was already feeling a sense of nostalgia for it and there was still a part of me that hoped for a new lease of life for this played-out form. Maybe not a new messiah but at least a band that showed that there was a different way to do things.

I was in my first year at Liverpool Art School doing a Diploma in Art and Design (Dip AD) in painting. It was the Easter break of what turned out to be my last year. As part of the course we were supposed to deliver an essay on a general studies topic and another on a history of art topic. The titles of the two essays I felt driven to write were *Liverpool As A Mythical Place* and *The Rock Band As A Cultural Force And Artistic Form*. I also had this other title, *Why Andy Warhol Is Shite*: I loved this one as a title but didn't know which of these two proposed essays it suited most, or maybe it was a title that could be used to cover both of these subjects and a load more shit that I wanted to tie in. As a title for a book, *Why Andy Warhol Is Shite* has stayed with me over the years. I hope to use it one day for a book that has the subtitle *Liverpool Versus The Rest Of The World*, and when the book is done and published I will hand it in to Liverpool School Of Art as my belated essay.

Although I thought long and hard over this Easter break in 1973 about the subject matter, I don't think I got more than a page of notes down on paper. Other things had been happening in my life in Liverpool that seemed to prevent any concerted bouts of essay writing. In this chapter I hope to get some of those unmarshalled thoughts on paper.

By the time of this particular Easter, I had long since stopped buying or even listening to records by rock bands (long, in the terms of a 19-year-old being two years). It had been about three years since I had bought a music paper. In those days it would have been *Melody Maker* – the *NME* was yet to have its renaissance as the thinking young man's rock paper. Maybe it was the distance between being a consuming fan of rock at 16 and a mature 19-year-old who by then had read some books that enabled me to at least think about rock with some sort of an overview. This still-unfocused thinking has informed me, in part, ever since, whether as manager of Echo And The Bunnymen, a member of The Justified Ancients Of Mu Mu or instigator of The17.

As I reported when I was on the ferry heading for Sweden, *Strawberry Fields Forever* by The Beatles was the first record I ever bought and subsequently it was bestowed the mantle of being my all-time favourite record. This first-time purchase was followed up by me being totally consumed by The Beatles. I bought everything. Even the four-track EP that you could only get if you sent off for it with four wrappers of Wall's ice cream, and the EP wasn't even by The Beatles, but four acts they had signed to their Apple label.

I wasn't bothered about what The Beatles had for breakfast or what their middle names were, or even what they thought about. It is what The Beatles did as a collective unit which captivated my imagination. Now what I am going to tell you may have been documented in hundreds of books already but the only book I've ever read about The Beatles is the Hunter Davis one that came out in 1968. I read it the week it came out and then promptly forgot everything I read.

Before *Strawberry Fields* I was not particularly interested. Although they were this worldwide phenomenon, to me they were just another form of light entertainment for the masses. I would have far rather gone fishing than listen to The Beatles. After *Strawberry Fields* they embodied a new medium or art form through which everything that seemed vital in the modern world of Britain in the latter part of the 1960s could be expressed. This new medium was the rock band. Although by 1972 I was no longer a record-buying rock fan, the 19- and soon to be 20-year-old wise and thinking me thought this (now not so new) medium, the rock band, pissed all over painting, sculpture, film, photography and whatever else was on offer in art schools at the time, as a way for young people to express their reactions to the world as it was. But enough of me at 19, almost 20, and the overview and back to The Beatles and 13-year-old me.

Back then in 1967 my father was the minister of a Scottish Presbyterian church in Corby, a new town in the English East Midlands. Eighty-five percent of the population of Corby was Scottish. I won't go into the historical reasons why, it just was. My father was minister of St Ninian's, a brand new church that had ten years to pay off something like 50 percent of the building costs. The other 50 percent, I guess, had been met by the Church of Scotland headquarters back in Edinburgh. Raising cash to pay off the debt was the main focus of fundraising activities in the church.

I had an idea. I got it while sitting in the art room at Kingswood Comprehensive on a Friday afternoon in May 1967. There was this park near the middle of Corby. We called it the Glebe. I reckoned you could get 20,000 people on the Glebe. That figure was based on me going to see Leicester City play at Filbert Street and if they could get 20,000 in there, we could easily get 20,000 on to the Glebe. If we booked The Beatles to play outdoors on the Glebe, we could sell 20,000 tickets even at the extortionate price of ten shillings (50p, $1, €1) each. People would buy them to see The Beatles. Twenty thousand at ten bob a time would be ten thousand quid, which to me sounded like a king's ransom. We would pay The Beatles £1,000 which I guessed must be more than they usually got for a night's work. So that would be £9,000 profit. Enough to clear what was left of St Ninian's building debt.

It all seemed so obvious and simple as I sat in the art room painting a picture of a pirate ship being strafed by the sort of helicopters the Americans were using in the Vietnam war we saw on the TV news.

OK, so I don't actually remember what I was painting in the art class that particular Friday afternoon and I've just made that up. But what is worse is I've had to cross out a whole page of writing where I had started making up a story about when I got home and tried to phone Brian Epstein, The Beatles' manager, to book the band. That is the trouble with this sort of writing, this myth-making of your own life. The temptation to embroider the facts is always there. I am usually able to resist that temptation but of course I am selective with the facts, only choosing the ones to use that somehow in my head bolster the case for The17 and me looking good. Or at least interesting.

When I started writing the bit about me ringing Brian Epstein's office all this dialogue started streaming from the end of my pencil. It suddenly became so easy. There was no longer any struggle trying to remember the facts; I could just make it all up. Maybe I should jack in The17, forget about thinking about music and where it should be going, and become a novelist instead. My fear is that if you catch me out making up one tiny bit, then you won't believe any of it and the whole construct will fall apart.

So what happened is this. I spent the weekend thinking about booking The Beatles and decided I should ask Big Dougie King. Dougie was the biggest lad in the class by what seemed about a foot. Once he got the ball on the rugby field nobody else had a chance. Big Dougie also knew everything there was to know about pop music. At the age of 14 he was running a mobile disco; at 17 he was running his own record shop. When local radio started up in the early 70s Dougie was in regular employment playing the hits and chatting the chat.

Paul: I wondered if all those amazing details in Bob Dylan's Chronicles were also fabrications. They must be, but I'm happy to believe that the high definition image he presents really is fixed in his mind.

Here we have a detailed image of what happened 30 years ago that Bill can't possibly remember. In Dylan's chronicles the same thing happens. We get an incredibly rich picture of a flat in Greenwich Village that he can't possibly remember that well.

Robert: Is it important whether it's true or false?

Paul: No, It's not.

Robert: He's only ever going to give his version of events ... mediated through his memory.

Rasmus: Someone once told me to 'never let the truth get in the way of a good story'.

That Monday morning I went into our class, 3T, and said to him, 'Dougie, I am going to put a concert on in the Glebe with The Beatles. Do you want to be the DJ?'

I was then going to ask him if he had any ideas how I could contact The Beatles to book them. But before I could ask, Big Dougie came back with 'What are you talking about, Bill? The Beatles no longer play concerts. They played their last one last year.'
'What? Why?'
'So they can concentrate on making records.'
Not for a moment was I disappointed that I could no longer stage the proposed concert by The Beatles and cancel the church debt. What happened was that I was overcome with this powerful sensation about The Beatles. For some reason this seemed like one of the most exciting things I had ever heard. The Beatles had not only made a record that sounded like nothing I had ever heard

before, but they had turned on its head the whole reason musical ensembles of any sort, as far as I knew, had for existing: to play music live, for people to hear. There is no way I could have explained at the time why this was such a massive shift in the ground rules – I just found it extremely exciting.

I know you must be thinking this is ridiculous – a 13-year-old boy gets excited like this if his team wins the cup maybe or even gets his first snog, but not on learning that a band was not playing live. Just one sentence from Dougie King and the idea of a band that played concerts seem so passé. Through that day – or maybe not that day but over the next few weeks and months – I started to think that if ever I had a band, they would not play concerts. It would free the band up for being so much more than mere purveyors of light entertainment.

From that time in May 1967 through to the summer of 1969 everything The Beatles did seemed to be something that to my knowledge had never been done before, like releasing singles that were not on albums, releasing albums with no singles, or even without anything on them which sounded like singles. They went to India and played sitars, celebrated and absorbed its culture when in the past Britons had only gone there to exploit it. They grew moustaches when having a moustache had not been in fashion since the 1920s. They made records that started with the French national anthem. They released a double album. A double fucking album, with just a white cover and no name. Every song they wrote sounded different in every way to every song that had ever been written. They released a double EP with a booklet and it tied in with a film they had made themselves and it went out on telly on Boxing Day. They made a single that was seven minutes' long. They wore stupid clothes and did not care. They were going to open a shop that only sold white things. They employed an inventor. Their manager died. They told the world all you need is love. And all you need *is* love, nothing could be truer. Then they played live. The Beatles live again for the first time in four years, but on top of a building where no one could see them but me because it was filmed so we all got to see it. And when they finished playing this song on the top of the building one of them said 'Did we pass the audition?' and this was one of the funniest things ever.

And then they became boring. They released Abbey Road and it sounded good, polished and there were some great songs but they released a dreary single from it. I wanted The Beatles to announce to the world on 31 December 1969 that they were going to end. Not split acrimoniously but reveal their job was done. But they didn't. Instead they went on and released Let It Be. To me it sounded like a record by an ordinary band that wanted to do ordinary things like go and tour and release singles to promote the album. And the cover looked like it could have been by any band from anywhere. And they split up and it was dull and tawdry and they were a used-up, spent force.

There were plenty of other bands that I was into for an album or so, but their careers seemed so dull. Their ambitions seemed no wider than sex, drugs, and rock 'n' roll and breaking America. None of them seemed to want to expand the horizons of what a band could be. In interviews they just talked about progressing musically or about how big an influence Muddy Waters was. Then there was decadence. I hated decadence. Decadence is what I thought we were all against. Snorting cocaine and swilling champagne was what old-school lovey actors did and not what young revolutionaries should be doing. Getting wasted seemed so boring compared to getting up early in the morning and doing something that had never been done before.

As I wrote earlier about Fluxus, I thought some of what John Lennon did with Yoko Ono was exciting but that did not last. I gave up on rock bands then as a force for change or even as something of interest. They all seemed so dull, so willingly toeing the party line even when they put on make-up and played with sexual stereotypes. It was all the same but with different costumes.

If I needed music to listen to or tap my toe to, American rhythm 'n' blues or country and western singers provided it for me, but I wasn't looking to them to stimulate my imagination, only to provide a soundtrack to whatever else I was up to.

Which takes me up to the Easter Break in 1973, when I was supposed to be writing those essays. The art history that I was learning about in the extensive library at the Liverpool School of Art seemed irrelevant to the world as I experienced it. Even the pop art, not much more than a decade old, seemed irrelevant. I had been to see this huge Andy Warhol retrospective at the Tate the previous summer. Although spectacular, images of Marilyn Monroe, Liz Taylor and a young Elvis seemed to be from a different age, not just the previous decade. The work also seemed to be designed to appeal to the frivolous and rich. Hence my title: *Why Andy Warhol is Shite.*

The art that me and my art school colleagues were trying to make seemed as irrelevant as what Andy Warhol had been doing, but in a different way. We were all so earnest about our goals. As soon as you stepped outside of the front doors of the art school and into the real world, our art made no sense. It connected with nothing. Not that I was for some modem equivalent to what

Stalin thought that art for the masses should be like, but I wanted art that connected with real life rather than just the history of art that existed in the Art School library.

Also, being a young idealist of some vague sort, the idea of making one-off art in the future for some rich patron was a no-no. As far as I was concerned my now well-worn copy of *Strawberry Fields* was the greatest work of art of the 20th century. And it had cost me less than ten bob (50p, €1, $1). The fact that there may be a few million of these around the world no better, no worse and no different to mine made it a better work of art. As did the fact it didn't need to be signed by an artist to make appreciation of it any more complete. And it was made by four blokes who had no proper further education, may have known little of the history of art or had any thoughts about their place in it.

You didn't need to have detailed knowledge of its history or a refined sense of aesthetics to get it; you just needed to live in modern Britain and be vaguely aware of the world around you. And it wasn't only about what was on the record, the actual music, it was the whole way the band placed themselves within society: the record sleeves, the TV appearances, the things they didn't do.

I was not advocating that The Beatles should be worshipped or even copied; what I wanted to advocate in this unwritten essay was that the rock band was the perfect medium to express the things that needed to be expressed, to explore the modern world; to reach an audience way beyond the confines of the audience that existed then for modern art. Remember this was decades before the whole Brit Art / Tate Modern explosion of appetite for contemporary art.

I planned to argue a case that on every housing estate, in every village across Britain, bunches of lads were forming bands, or at least planning on forming bands, each and every one totally different from any bands that had gone before. I was going to argue that never before in our history had bunches of young men from any background been able to do this. They needed no class structure giving them the nod; no City and Guilds qualifications, let alone a degree; no academy to hand out the validation. Whatever validation was necessary would come from the people. Complete and total democracy.

But to reuse the vague analogy I made at the beginning of this chapter, I never marshalled the thoughts. Maybe if I had done, I would have been forced to come to the conclusion that it was a dream that did not reflect the reality. The only reason why The Beatles could do any of the things that they did was because they had already become so commercially successful that there was nobody in a position at that stage in their career to stop them following their whims.

The vast majority of rock bands that got anywhere were more than happy to fit the predictable formula of wanting to shag loads of girls, take drugs, conquer America, be better musicians and release albums that sounded almost like the last one they did but took longer to record. To me this was as uninteresting and narrow-minded as the career of any successful postwar British artist like Graham Sutherland or Henry Moore or Jacob Epstein. Even the long hair and flared satin trousers that most of these bands sported seemed conservative in some perverse way – none of it was ever surprising.

There are a couple of other things that I have just thought of that I should slip in here. Like musicianship. When The Beatles were at their creative zenith, their musicianship was not the point. It was not the thing that was being measured. It was their ideas that made things work. Their willingness to take risks, not being one thing all the time – in fact they seemed to be a hundred things all at the same time.

My family are now telling me that it is time for lunch and asking me why I have to keep writing in my notebook. Most of the other dads are in the pool having fun. My lunch is the same every day: tomatoes, cucumber, olives, feta cheese and stuffed vine leaves. It's an all-in deal. Suits me fine.

After lunch I read through what I have written so far. I'm worried that I may be about to lose the thread, if I haven't already lost it. The kids are back in the pool, my neighbour on the sun bed next to me is reading a Dan Brown book in Dutch and now I'm thinking about The Rolling Stones again.

There was always that cliché: you had to be either into The Stones or into The Beatles. If you were a bad girl, you were into The Stones and all that. Obviously The Stones were sexier, had the threatening vibe. I also have to admit that, given the choice, I would rather listen to a Stones compilation of 1960s hits than a

Robert: I like it when Bill talks about writing this novel in his notebook, it takes you outside of the book; it makes you consider the act of writing a story.

Rasmus: As we read this book to make comments and discuss our opinions, we notice all of the tricks that the writer uses to tell us the story. Especially the one where he drops us in the middle of a story and we have to work out where we are; the one where he takes you back to his notebook – all of those things.

Robert: It's just like us dropping our comments in here – the reader will read this text and our words, and they realise that we are reading the book as well.

Beatles one. To take it further, I would not recommend listening to Beatles records to anyone. Bands that take their musical influence from The Beatles have a tendency to be the most boring of any particular era, like ELO or Oasis. To get what The Beatles had to offer the world, you had to experience it as it unfolded at the time. And that is the way it should be. All art and all music should be of the moment and experienced in the moment.

Paul: Like someone reading it with them.

Rasmus: Sometimes I get annoyed by the tricks though. Occasionally I think 'Just get on with the story. You don't always have to remind me what situation you are in while writing.'

There is something else I want to get down on paper about The Beatles before one of my children insists I get in the pool with them to play water polo or something. This something is maybe the most documented fact about the phenomenon that was The Beatles and it was something I didn't appreciate when I was between the ages of 13 and 16, when they were everything to me. Before The Beatles there was nothing like them. Yes, before The Beatles there were rock 'n' roll bands, beat combos and pop groups but they seemed to exist primarily as backing bands for a singer or play songs made popular by somebody else. They relied on novelty. Solo singers or individual bandleaders had always been the major stars, the serious players, the ones who went platinum. The Beatles were the first group that seemed to be from somewhere, and that somewhere was not a cosmopolitan or capital city. They seemed to be about something. They wrote their own songs, even if their songs were not that good in the beginning. They sang in their own voices; they did not pretend to sound like black American singers. They definitely were not a backing band for some pretty boy pop singer. They didn't even rely on having an obvious front man in the band. That last point gave them an internal dynamic that we all related to. It wasn't Paul McCartney and his backing band or even John Lennon and his band. Ringo was as important to the dynamic as any of them, or he was as far as we were concerned.

The Beatles were the first rock band. They presented a new form to our world, a new way of expressing ourselves creatively to the world. Without The Beatles The Stones would have just been another band that had a couple of hits with R&B covers. They would never have attempted to write their own songs.

Before the 20th century the working and peasant classes in Britain had their own culture, their own music, their own stories, their own heroes and their own myths. Once the mass media started to grow and flourish in the 20th century, with cinema, radio, magazines, popular songs and, lastly, TV, the working and peasant classes were supposed to consume the new media. Their own culture was left to wither and die or, if they were lucky, tamed, tidied up and sold back to them. It was a one-way transaction in the sense we had to consume what was fed to us in exchange for handing over our hard-earned wages. The working and peasant classes had little or no input into what was available, although they were used at times as puppets to front whatever the media was doling out to give the masses something to identify with.

The Beatles were the first, in Britain anyway, to take control of their own creativity. Maybe not quite the means of production, but there was no denying they were for real. As I have said before and I will say again, they sang their own songs, talked in a way we related to and were soon making their own decisions.

Is what I am saying making sense or am I just on one and going up my arsehole with it all? I mean it's not as if The Beatles were leading some people's revolution: they wanted the wealth, the big houses in the country; the private education for their kids (except McCartney). The Beatles were a perfect example of the whole being far more than the sum of their parts. As individuals they were weak, flawed and dull.

Being bigger than the sum of their parts was another big lesson I learnt from The Beatles, or at least in theory. Back in 1973 the history of art as I had learnt it, from the renaissance down to the present day, was all about the individual and the struggle with the inner vision (of course the patron's wishes had to be taken into account but …). The same was true of serious music: it was always the story of the great composer forging the new music of their day. Even in opera where librettists were used, they were just considered to be employees of Verdi or whoever. It wasn't until the rise of the American popular song and the musical that you get any sort of equal billing and recognised collaborative partnership going on.

'Yeah? What about Gilbert and Sullivan?'

I will ignore that question and get on with my polemic.

The Beatles taught me that the rock band as an art form could work in a different way. To work properly the rock band had to be collaborative. That was one of its main strengths. That is what it had over the artist-as-individual at his easel or lump of marble. The trouble was – and maybe it is why I never got the essay written – this was all theory. I hadn't got a fucking clue in reality. The only people I knew who had ever been in bands were some of my school mates who played in a covers band back in Corby, one of whom went on to be the drummer in the band St Cecilia who had a hit with *Leap Up And Down (Wave Your Knickers in The Air)*.

I could play guitar a bit but I was going to be turning 20 in less than two weeks, too old to even consider trying to start one. And anyway, I didn't have the confidence. As much as my theory went against the whole virtuoso thing that had taken over rock music, my lack of any sort of guitar-shop-assistant-virtuosity would have inhibited me from trying to form one. So that was that. The essay did not get written, rock music was dead and I had a new vocation to be the next Jack Kerouac. But that's a whole other story.

If it was not for the unfocused thinking that fuelled an unwritten essay about the rock band as a medium back in 1973, I would not be doing The17 now.

Later. It is now a month or so since I wrote this last chapter and I have been going through it correcting spelling, checking facts and editing. In doing this I decided to put Dougie King's name into Google to see if I could find out what he was now up to. The last time that we spoke was some time in the 1980s when I did a phone interview with him. He was working on a local radio station somewhere – Peterborough I think. I found hundreds of entries for him, but then found one that told me Dougie had died of a heart attack back in 2004. I can see now how Dougie was a great inspiration to me at the time. He was the only person in our class who seemed to have the courage to do things beyond what you would expect of teenage lads living where we did. That memory has stayed an inspiration for me. At some other time and place I would like to think that I would write more about what that inspiration was and how it continues to work.

THE BIRTH OF ROCK & ROLL
20 December 1958 – 18 August 2006

There is a man with thimbles on the ends of his fingers. I liked putting my mother's thimbles from her sewing box on my fingers. This man is sitting on a chair. On his lap is a washboard. We have a washboard at home but we never use it now because my mum has a Bendix washing machine. The man is not washing clothes or even darning socks. He is rubbing the washboard up and down with the thimbles on the ends of his fingers. This makes a loud noise.

There is another man. He is standing up. In front of him is a tea chest. I have a tea chest in my bedroom to keep things in. I like tea chests. I like the smell inside them, the smell of tea leaves. The smell of tea leaves is my favourite smell. A stick as tall as the man is fixed to one of the corners of the tea chest. The man is using one hand to hold this stick. There is a string that goes from the top of the stick, where his hand is, all the way down into the tea chest. The man is using his other hand to hit the string. This makes a sort of sound but I can't hear it properly because another man who is standing closer to me is making a lot of noise.

The other man standing closer to me has a wooden box on his chest. This is a type of wooden box I have never seen before. It has one bit that sticks out and he holds in one hand. The main bit is a sort of a box with a hole in the front of it. But it is the sort of box you couldn't put anything in. It doesn't have corners but it does have curves. There are wires that go from the end of the bit that sticks out to past the point where the round hole is. This man is using his other hand to hit the wires. This makes a noise. He is also shouting. I don't know what he is shouting about but sometimes the words sound like 'The Rock Island Line is a mighty fine line'.

The noise these three men are making is very loud. I don't know if it is music but it might be. There is no tune, only shouting. But the noise they are making is making me want to jump up and down. I am jumping up and down and I am shouting too. I try to shout 'The Rock Island Line is a mighty fine line', like the man.

My name is Bill and I am five. I am at a Christmas party. I am in primary one. Mrs Gilchrist is our teacher. It is 1958. In five days it will be Christmas. I hate parties. I hate having to play party games. I hate the pink and yellow dresses that girls wear at parties. I hate the tie and stiff collar that I have to wear.

Bill Drummond

I love party food.

This Christmas party is in a prison. The three men are prisoners. They have done something very bad. That is why they are prisoners. If I do something very bad, I will be a prisoner too. I want to be a prisoner and make a loud noise and shout 'The Rock Island Line is a mighty fine line'.

Nineteen years and five months later there is a man with sticks in his hand. He is sitting on a chair. In front of him is a drum kit. He is banging the drum kit with the sticks as hard and as fast as he can. His name is Phil Allen. There is another man. He is standing with a bass guitar around his neck. He is playing one of the four strings on the bass as hard and as fast as he can. He doesn't play any of the other strings. His name is Kev Ward. If you met him today, you would call him James. There is a third man. He has a Gibson ES-330 hanging around his neck. He bought it second-hand in 1970 from a shop in Denmark Street in London for £120. It is tuned to an open E. He is banging out a very basic riff and shouting into the microphone 'Big in Japan, we are big in Japan'. In front of this man people are jumping up and down and shouting back. This man is me.

My father was a missionary in the Transkei in South Africa between 1950 and 1955. I was born out there on 29 April 1953. They headed back to Scotland in time for Christmas 1954. He became the minister of a church in Newton Stewart, Galloway, in the south-west of Scotland. Part of his duty as the minister of this church was to be the chaplain for the local prison. It was an open prison called Penningham. Each year they had a Christmas party for the children of the staff.

As I said, I hated parties. I used to try and run away from them. But I had to go. I still hate parties. I still find myself running away from them. The memory of this particular party has stuck with me. In some way I knew it was important. Nothing is made up. I had never seen a guitar before or even heard one. We didn't have a TV. Scottish folk music back then never used the guitar; it was all fiddles and accordions. The only other instruments I knew about were those in the pipe band, the organ at church and the piano at home. What I heard at this party sounded so loud. So exciting. Even louder and more exciting than when in August 1969 I saw Pete Townsend smash his guitar up, Keith Moon kick his drums over while Roger Daltry sang *My Generation* and Roger Entwistle stood stock-still as he plucked his bass. The thing is, these prisoners would have had no amplification. Nothing more than the natural sounds their improvised instruments made. The singer would not even have

172

had a microphone. The Who would have had the loudest amplification then known to mankind.

Sitting in the back of my dad's car as we drove back from Penningham Prison to our house in Newton Stewart that night after the party was the first time I started to think about music, what it does and how and why and how else and where else it could be done. And why not in my bedroom?

Screaming 'Big in Japan, we're big in Japan' into a microphone in front of people jumping up and down was happening less than a fortnight after Clive Langer had told Phil Allen, Kev Ward and me to form a band. We were in Bretton Hall College, somewhere outside Leeds, playing to a bunch of students. We were supporting some friends whose band had just changed their name from Albert Dock & The Cod Fish Warriors to The Yachts. We had written three songs: *Clive's in America*, the one called *Big In Japan* and another one. When we finished, the students that had been jumping up and down wanted more so we played what was then a punk standard, *Louie Louie*, and then the *Big in Japan* one again. This time all these jumping up and down people were shouting 'Big in Japan, we're big in Japan' along with us.

We had driven from Liverpool to Bretton Hall together in one van. Both bands. Three in the cab in the front and the rest in the windowless box in the back. On the two-hour drive back, Henry Priestman and J.J.J. Campbell of the Yachts kept us amused in the pitch-black claustrophobia of the back of the van. They are both very funny men, too funny to be in a serious power-pop combo that had ambitions to go places. But however amused they kept us it couldn't stop my mind from thinking about music and what was music for and how and why and what was a band and what it could do and when. And why not now?

I had tried to stop thinking about music since I had failed to write my essay about *Why Andy Warhol Is Shite* and had given up my chances of being a future member of the Portsmouth Sinfonia in 1973. Of course stopping had not been completely successful. I had thought about Stravinsky's *Rite Of Spring* quite a bit. I had wondered why, although I hated classical musical on principle, this particular piece of classical music affected me in such a strange way and I thought about its structure and how atonal music affected the senses in different ways. I thought about the records of Hamilton Bohannon and why they worked and how he made them. And what made the interlocking guitar parts on *Clean Up Woman* by Betty Wright work so well. And why labels with strange names and cheap graphics from towns and cities in the southern states of the USA released the best records. But mostly I thought about how the whole concept of the rock band as the people's art form had shrivelled and died and that all the bands that existed seemed so unambitious that they thought being a pub rock band was a radical alternative.

Then I saw a picture of Johnny Rotten and thought 'That looks different.' I heard The Damned sing *New Rose*. And everything changed. Suddenly everything seemed possible, as it should have been all along. Anybody could form a band. Everyone has something to say, everyone could play two chords. Poly Styrene of X-Ray Spex was my female icon for a new age. I believed.

Kev Ward was a year older than me. He had been at the art school. In some ways we were similar. We both naturally thought of bands as concepts through which a lot of ideas could be expressed. He definitely did not think of bands as merely a source of employment for musicians.

Our band became known as Big in Japan. It evolved, it changed; people joined and people left. We wrote dozens of songs, played scores of gigs. We became proficient. We became almost famous. But the better we got, the more like an ordinary band we became, like any other OK band hoping that a major record company would sign us and turn us into pop stars of sorts. I had stopped thinking about what a band could be and how everything could be different every month, if not every day.

I had traded in my ideals to be just a member of a band and I wasn't even very good at being a member of a band. I was the one who ended up writing the most conservative songs, the songs that sounded most like average power-pop, the most retro ones. The decision to knock it on the head was a great relief. It freed my head up to think of a way forward to explore the possibilities of music and music-making and what music could mean for me and the different ways that it existed in our heads. Being in a real band meant I had no overview. I found myself thinking more about getting the van booked and how tight we were and trying to please the audience than making the world a different place or at least make things happen so that others could see the world in a different way. But before I wind this chapter up there are a couple more thoughts I want to get down.

In August 1977 I went off to spend ten days in Brittany with my then wife. In that time Elvis died. I've written about Elvis's death and what it meant to me elsewhere so I won't here.

Bad Wisdom by Mark Manning and Bill Drummond, first published by Penguin in 1996, is an account of the pair's attempted journey to the North Pole with an icon of Elvis Presley. They believed that if they were to succeed and leave this icon of 'The King' at the pole it would leak good vibes down the longitudes and out across the latitudes causing an outbreak of world peace. In *Bad Wisdom* Drummond goes into great detail about his ongoing relationship with Elvis Presley in general and his identification with the record *Hound Dog* in particular.

The other thing that happened while I was out of the country was that Roger Eagle, who ran the club Eric's in Liverpool and who was to become our manager, asked the band to go into a local studio and record the song *Big In Japan*, the one that had proved such a hit with the students at Bretton Hall and our subsequent gigs. They did, using Clive Langer as a stand-in for me. When I got back and heard about this and that it was to be our first single I was … I was going to say devastated but that would be too strong a word, but disappointed isn't the right one either. I thought it sounded shit but I was in no position to say so seeing as I was the one who had gone AWOL to France. This record sounded weedy and small. I had all sorts of ideas that I wanted to try out when we got to record it. It was to be an epic, not quite *Born To Run* or *Bohemian Rhapsody* but something that took liberties with the rigid form that punk had already become.

Not a month has gone by in the past 29 years that I have not spent some hours imagining what the re-recorded version of *Big In Japan* by Big In Japan would sound like. Some months it is sounding like a Giorgio Moroder classic, other times like Led Zeppelin, or it is purely orchestral. Usually the fantasy involves sampling parts of the original recording. I know in reality this would be a pointless exercise and only serve my own vanity. It would also go against all the ideals that I want to explore with The17.

The other thing I wanted to get into this chapter is about Frankie Goes To Hollywood. Holly Johnson, who replaced Kev Ward as our bass player in Big In Japan, went on to front Frankie Goes To Hollywood. During those few months in 1984 when Frankie Goes To Hollywood, in all their glory, had three consecutive global number ones, they presented to the world a radically different type of band. They seemed to tick every conceivable box for a band existing in that era. Then Holly bailed out at just the right moment as the seconds were closing on their 15th minute.

And then I wonder what happened to those three skifflers doing time at Penningham Prison. Did they go on to become repeat offenders or future members of The Sensational Alex Harvey Band? Penningham Prison closed down in 1999. If it was still open, I would be wanting to do the prison score for The17 there.

Bill Drummond

PUSHING THE BUTTON
19 August 2006

The taxi driver has the radio on – Greek music. I'm sitting in the front seat waiting for other members of my family to get here from the apartment. Does he have the radio station with Greek music on because he thinks that's what we want to hear as tourists in his country? When he goes home does he listen to Celine Dion? Or maybe Bruce Springsteen is his favourite. He puts out his hand to change the station to what I guess will be one playing hits from the 1980s because he thinks that is what middle-aged Western European would rather be listening to. I imagine in that slither of a second we have to imagine these things that it is going to be *Gold* by Spandau Ballet playing when he hits the preset button. It's not. It's more Greek music: a girl singing a ballad with the bouzouki trilling in the background. Maybe she is the Greek Celine Dion. He listens for a few seconds and then hits another preset button. More Greek music. A male singer, more up-tempo, the sort you could imagine Greeks smashing plates to. Remember when I was going on about Red Indians burning their wigwams and tepees? Well, after I'd learnt about that, the next time I saw that Greek plate-smashing performance I guessed it must be an example of potlatch. I imagined the rival families at a Greek wedding competing with each other to see who could smash the most prized dinner service, handed down through the generations.

So this taxi driver does not give a shit what I would prefer to be listening to. He wants to listen to Greek music and he has discerning tastes – any old Greek music will not do. It might sound the same to us, as in 'It's all Greek to me', but to him it all sounds different.

The children turn up and we are off. No more station-hopping during the ten-minute taxi ride from where we are staying down to the harbour in Kos where we are to get a ferry across to Bodrum in Turkey.

Back in the 1960s my mum used to like watching the Nana Mouskouri Show on the telly. I used to like watching it with her. If I was with my mates, we would be listening to Disraeli Gears by Cream, but with my mum it was Nana Mouskouri. Both seemed right. Both fitted.

On this ten-minute taxi ride these are my thoughts. In the summer of 1973, after working for a couple of months in the steel works, I went and bought a Young Persons Euro Railcard for £26. This allowed unlimited train travel across non-Soviet Pact Europe. I ended up in Greece. It was while I was there that I decided to knock art school on the head and become a writer instead. I would set out to experience as much as I could in life so I would have lots of material to draw upon. I might have been too old to start making pop music of any kind, but you're never too old to write. My second favourite writer at the time, Henry Miller, was still writing and he was very old. In fact, it was his book about Rhodes that had made me want to go to Greece.

In Greece I was pleased to discover that the new Roxy Music or David Bowie albums were not being played everywhere. All every sodding art student was playing was Bowie or Roxy. Every bar, café or tavern that I found myself in as I wandered and hitched my way around Greece played only Greek music. That is except for one bar in the port of Piraeus that had *You're My Venus* by Shocking Blue on the jukebox. Back then I thought this only natural. If I had been in Italy, I would have expected only Italian music; in Poland, Polish and so on. That is the way things should be, the natural order. As far as I was concerned it was only Britons and people in the English-speaking world who would have been into the pop and rock that we consumed.

Thirty-three years later back in Greece and I am surprised that Greeks are still listening to Greek music. The globalisation of what the American corporations promote to us has not worked here. I find this heartening, but here lies the contradiction. If I follow the logic of what I am proposing with The17, then surely the Greeks should dump all this listening to Greek music. Within my experience alone they have been listening to it for a minimum of 33 years. As a form it must have been completely explored by now. There is nothing new that it can do, nowhere left for it to go. But I want to pat the Greeks on the back for still listening to the same sodding music that all sounds the sodding same. What does this say about me? Whatever it is, I don't like it.

Me going on about Greeks and Greek music is an example of thinking about music too much. Why can't I just enjoy it for what it is? The Greeks seem to. They have obviously hit on a music that expresses everything in life that needs to be expressed through music in a form that never runs dry for them.

Yesterday I wrote the chapter about the prison skiffle band and me at the age of five, cutting in with me at 24 and the first Big In Japan gig. I thought it was a really clever bit of writing but nothing could really follow it up. The piece lost focus. This morning I wanted to write about the contradictions we can have in our thinking about music. I thought the taxi driver and his changing channels and Greek music would only take the opening paragraph of this chapter.

Between the 'never runs dry' line above and the 'yesterday I wrote' line we have taken the ferry from Kos in Greece to Bodrum in Turkey. The difference between these two civilisations has fascinated me since I first read the Trojan War stories as a kid. As a young man I used to read the Nikos Kazantzakis books, all set in a time when so many Greeks were under the thumb of the Ottoman Empire. I love the choral music of the Greek Orthodox Church but I would rather eat at a Turkish restaurant. Last night I went for a haircut in a Greek barber's. On the TV was a Saturday night family variety show. It was all Greek music. Right now I am sat in a Turkish barber's waiting to be given a shave. You may already know that I have a big thing about going to different barbers, which forms a whole strand in what I do.

What I will say is having a shave in a Turkish barber's is one of the best things you will ever experience. I am not one for decadence, a point I have laboured on numerous occasions, but a shave in a Turkish barber's is a decadence I can't turn down. If you are a woman, I would stretch the recommendation to you as well, just for the sensation, even though you would have little for his cutthroat razor to shave.

Bodrum is a tourist hellhole. The family members are seeking shade and solace in an ice-cream parlour. I clocked this rather rundown barber's squashed between the shops selling tourist tat and fake designer gear. Balanced on top of the mirror is a tiny transistor. Blaring from it, at full volume, is distorted Turkish music. My relationship with Turkish music does not stretch back over the decades like Greek music but nevertheless over the past few months it has been quite intense.

Stoke Newington, in north-east London, has a big Turkish / Kurdish community. All the grocers' and most other shops of any kind are run by Turks and Kurds. Everywhere you go in Stoke Newington Turkish music is blaring out, unless they have got Turkish football matches on. Turkish music differs from Greek music in many ways; the most obvious difference is that it is more Arabic in sound. What is similar is that they are both driven by a plucked string instrument: for the Greeks the aforementioned bouzouki, for the Turks the saz.

For a few weeks in Stoke Newington I was unable to get myself online so I used to go out and use a Turkish internet café to do my emails. This internet café also doubles as a music shop. They sell Turkish music. They have stacks to choose from. They also sell Turkish instruments and give music lessons in the basement. Young Turkish boys and girls would come in clutching cases containing their saz. There were a few times in there when I would pick up a saz from the display rack and have a go. I even had thoughts about signing up for the lessons but every time I picked one up I got looks of serious disapproval from the boss; I imagined I was being caught stepping over some cultural divide and that it was more than impolite to even think about doing so.

As for the CDs and cassettes on sale, I have on a number of occasions found myself flicking through the C rack and choosing one to purchase based on the cover. Every time I get one home I discover it is shit. So, the question is, how come Turkish music sounds so brilliant coming out of a tiny radio, all distorted, but shit when coming out of my system at home? The answer may be obvious but I needed to pose it anyway. But the question I really wanted to ask in this chapter, after I had done my opening paragraph in the taxi was, why do I love the record *Push The Button* by the Sugababes so much?

Bill Drummond

ONE MORE TIME
20 August 2006

Push The Button by The Sugababes is my favourite pop record so far this decade. I would be quite happy to never hear another record by The Sugababes in my life. Does my devotion to this record undermine everything that I have written in this book so far?

In the summer of 1966 I was at a scout camp. Pop music was being discussed around the campfire. As I have said before, *Strawberry Fields*, released in February 1967, was my great awakening and before that I had never felt that passionately about pop music. It was what the girls in my class were into. With hindsight I would say that 1966 was the greatest year for pop music. I have also said often that every year is the greatest year for pop music; it just depends on your age. Nowadays I don't know if any of these statements holds any truth.

One of the other scouts around the campfire asked me if I had heard The Supremes' new record, *The Happening*; I said 'Yes' and he then asked me 'Don't you think it is the best record ever?' 'No,' I said, 'it is not even the best record by The Supremes.' He didn't answer me, just poked the fire and started to sing *The Happening*. I got up and walked away to climb a tree in the certain knowledge that *Baby Love* was the best record by The Supremes and there was no need to ever hear another record by them.

I don't know if I ever thought through the theory of what I imagine was an obvious truth. If I had done, it would have gone something like this: why bother listening to another record by an artist if they have already made a great one when it is obvious that any other will only ever be a pale imitation of the great one and if you were to hear too much of that singer's voice or the sound of the band or the production, it would put you off them. In turn this would diminish your appreciation and love of the first one.

In this chapter, and it might be a long one, I want to try to bring a number of strands of thought together. These relate to girl pop, the one-hit wonder, the indescribable sound and the vision of the producer and how this all relates to The17.

From the top of the tree I climbed I could see for miles and nobody could see me. I kept singing that opening refrain to *Baby Love* over and over again: 'Ooooh ooooh baby love, my baby love', especially the repeated descending 'ooooh' bit.

Over the years there have been dozens of girl-pop records I have loved with an intense passion. Not one have I bought or even wanted to buy. It is enough for me to carry the sound and memory of them around in my head.

Lyrics have never been a big thing for me; it has always been the sound of the record I go for. But if I was to do a little research, I would find that in the vast majority of these records the girl is singing from a position of weakness. She has either been dumped or she has the boyfriend up on a pedestal. In at least two cases the boy has died.

Now this must say some pretty negative things about me and what I want from women but in real life l have always been drawn to strong women: women who appear to know what they want. *Baby Love* was not the first of these records and I am sure that *Push The Button* will not be the last. *Terry* by Twinkle is one of the greats. Everything about it: Twinkle's flat singing voice, the way she stood stock still on her TV performance, the fact she never had a follow-up hit to tarnish the beauty of *Terry*. And to list a few more for no other reason than I like making lists: *Will You Still Love Me Tomorrow?* by the Shirelles; *Past, Present And Future* by The Shangri-Las; *As Tears Go By* by Marianne Faithfull; *White Horses* by Jackie; *Single Girl* by Sandy Posey; *Identify* by X Ray Spex; *Like A Virgin* by Madonna; *Man In The Moon* by Voice of The Beehive; *I Wanna Dance With Somebody* by Whitney Houston; *Bang Bang (You Shot Me Down)* by Cher; *Since Yesterday* by Strawberry Switchblade; *It Should Have Been Me* by Yvonne Fair; *Clean Up Woman* by Betty Wright; *Band Of Gold* by Freda Payne. I could carry on – there are dozens more – but I won't.

Obviously some of the singers of some of these records went on to have massive careers, building themselves up diva or women-of-strength-and-substance images, and so selling millions of albums. But only one of them has made more than a couple of good records. Some of them took it upon themselves to try to learn to be good singers. But for me it was when they sounded at their most vulnerable or innocent that it worked.

Diana Ross, Whitney Houston and Madonna are the biggest examples of singers building up those huge and ridiculous careers, none of whom could now make a record in a century of Sundays that would make you want to cry. *Terry* by Twinkle pisses all over their careers after they sang on those records that touched my heart. Maybe if I was a woman it would be different – I could then view the likes of Madonna as a positive role model, a woman succeeding in a man's world on her own terms – but I'm not.

Now to sidestep the girl-pop thing for a while – its thread will get woven back in later – and move on to the one-hit wonder. There should have been far more one-hit wonders in pop music in whatever epoch they reached the charts. Give me one – *Something In The Air* by Thunderclap Newman – rather than the whole of U2's career. If Dire Straits had only recorded and had a hit with *Sultans Of Swing*, I would have remembered them fondly, but they had to go and spoil it all by recording a whole raft of platinum-selling albums followed by what's-his-face struggling on with a solo career.

More one-hit wonders would have brought more joy to our lives, more art and creativity to the world. All the best records have been made by artists who had very short careers. Yeah, yeah, I know about the exceptions. The trouble is the record companies hate them. They see a one-hit wonder as a wasted opportunity. What is the point of a hit being had, if a career cannot be built from it? A one-off hit is just taking up space that could have been occupied by an artist with a serious career.

Record companies now have to spend hundreds of thousands to get a career off the ground. It is no longer trial and error, no longer throwing mud at the wall to see which one sticks and then backing it. And once the record company can see sales figures looking good, and a career seems to be blossoming, the last thing it wants is that act straying too far from the brand sound and image they have already established. And this goes across the board for all types of acts, not just the genres you don't like.

OK, that's enough about the one-hit wonder for the moment.

It was 1962, we had driven up from Newton Stewart to Ayr, the seaside town on the west coast of Scotland. We visited the skating rink. What I remember is standing on the balcony looking down on the skaters going round and round. The sound of the blades slashing across the ice and the big kids and teenagers screaming and laughing. Then this massive room, the biggest I had ever been in, was filled with an even bigger sound. It took a few seconds to realise the sound was music. Since the incident with the skiffle group in Penningham Prison I had become accustomed to pop music. Mainly through the picture house, Elvis Presley films and of course when the fair came to town. The fairground may be the best place to experience pop music still. All the lights and the movement and the throbbing generators and people screaming. It was at a funfair in Victoria Park, Hackney, that I first heard *Push The Button* by The Sugababes, while driving a dodgem.

But back to the skating rink in Ayr and this sound that was music of some kind that was bigger than the building itself. It made all the skaters going around and around go around even faster and scream even louder. At first I thought there must be a band playing the music, but there wasn't. It was an even bigger sound than when a bagpipe band marches past you only inches away from where you are standing on the pavement. I tried to work out where the music was coming from. Even at the fair you could see the music was coming out of the Tannoy speakers. But here in the skating rink the music seemed to be coming from everywhere, all at the same time. It was like it was inside my body as well as in everybody's bodies.

Then the record came to an end and it was followed by some drivel by Tommy Steel or something. I don't know when I next heard that record or when I learnt it had been *Telstar* by The Tornados; it could have been years later. Flipping back to what I was on about a few pages ago, who in their right mind would ever want to hear another track by The Tornados after they have heard *Telstar*, let alone a whole album? Telstar was a total and complete statement, nothing needed to be added.

Now I want to fast-forward to 1966. I'm sitting in our front room on my own, watching Top Of The Pops, a weekly pop show on at 7.30 every Thursday evening. It featured bands miming to their current hits. Some weeks they would feature a film clip of an American act having a hit in the UK but were not over here touring, and so unavailable to perform on Top Of The Pops. This particular Thursday evening they introduced a film clip of a band that I had never heard of before. It was a black American act, but not like The Four Tops or The Temptations with their shiny suits and their corny dance routines. It featured a full band led by a man who looked like he would slit your throat for sixpence. There were three girl backing singers shaking their collective ass – to make a contemporary comparison, they made Beyoncé, at her most ass-shaking, look like she was still in junior school. And out front was a woman who was the most terrifying thing I had ever seen. Everything about her was total sex. Every part of her body shuddered and shook. Her lips and mouth were so big she could have swallowed me whole as I sat there on the sofa.

But all of this was nothing compared to the sound they made. It was a bigger sound than even *Telstar* by The Tornados in the Ayr skating rink. But how could this be? We had a black and white Bush TV with one little speaker in it and I hadn't even turned the sound up to full. The song came to an end and then Jimmy Saville informed me it was Ike and Tina Turner performing *River Deep, Mountain High*. Although I never bought the record and was never bothered about hearing anything else by Ike and Tina Turner, this, in my reckoning, is the third greatest record ever made.

It wasn't until the early 1970s that I started to become aware of what a record producer was. If I'd heard of them when I was younger, I guess I would have thought of them as some very boring, straight, even posh types who were there to keep the band in order. Photos of George Martin, the Beatles' producer, were often in the papers and he looked like some boring square whose job description was to stop people having fun and just get on with work, a traditional authority figure.

It was in my late teens, when I had tired of rock bands and all their boring pompous antics, that I became aware of, and drawn to, these mysterious people who worked under the job title of record producer. The most famous being Phil Spector, who had produced *River Deep, Mountain High* by Ike and Tina Turner. Billions of words have been written about Phil Spector. I have no interest in reading those words or knowing anything about his life. All I need to know is there were a handful of records by artists in the 1960s – artists who never went on to have meaningful and lasting careers – who each in their own way touched pop nirvana. This handful of records were all produced by Phil Spector. I learnt that *Telstar* by The Tornados was produced by a man called Joe Meek. And then I learnt that out there somewhere in the twilight zone was a force known as Shadow Morton who was responsible for producing *Leader Of The Pack, Remember (Walking In The Sand)* and *Past, Present And Future* by the Shangri-Las!

As with Phil Spector, I wasn't interested in learning anything about the lives of Joe Meek or Shadow Morton. It was all there in the records they produced. These records had massive vision. They took what was seemingly a trite form and turned it into the highest art form that then existed in the world. Cinema, painting, photography, 'serious' music, jazz, poetry, novels, theatre – none of them could touch what these pop records achieved. Or that's the way it seemed to me on certain days when I stood by the side of the road with my thumb out, attempting to hitch a ride to some vague destination. And especially if it was raining.

Through the first half of the 1970s I gradually learned there were dozens more of these producers who had been working across the cities and states of the US. Joe Meek seemed to be the only British one with a similar breadth of vision. I have no idea what motivated these men. Whether it was the regular fame and fortune that people usually think of as the great motivators, or if it was some indefinable higher goal.

Before Phil Spector, the recording studio was just a place where what musicians played was recorded. Everything had been arranged, musically speaking, before the recording session began. Spector changed all that. He used the musicians and singers as his tools, his paints. The studio was his instrument. The musicians and singers were always exploited, maybe not financially, but for whatever could be squeezed out of them to make the producer's vision a reality. But after Sgt. Pepper's most of what these producers could do was redundant. The music industry wanted bands that could sell vast amounts of albums. The industry didn't want visionary producers with their epic singles. The marketplace wanted bands and singer-song writers with artistic integrity, not pop-singing puppets.

These visionaries could only work with bands and singers they could dominate and mould. Rock bands had their own visions – they weren't going to be putting up with some wanker telling them how they should be playing guitar, or even worse that the recording didn't require a guitar part in it at all.

Sexual politics came into it as well. These visionary producers worked best with the solo girl singers, ideally those who had no aspirations to write their own songs, girl singers who they could control in almost every sense. According to the few accounts that have strayed my way, Joe Meek was so sexually fucked-up he worked best when there was no singer, let alone a real band. Being a producer of hit singles as a form of creating great art existed across the then-dominant genres in popular music, from R&B to country and western, taking in folk and pop along the way. Because the big bucks in the record industry by the 1970s were to be made out of real bands and singer-songwriters, this whole producer-with-vision way of making records was pushed to the margins and was only to find international commercial favour in the disco boom of the mid-1970s. Once again records by artists we had never heard of before came hurtling from nowhere onto the dancefloors and into our hearts and the charts. Three months later their careers were back to where they had been before the hurtling. The greatest of these disco records is the exception that proved the rule as the artist in question had more of a career than the visionary producer might have thought she deserved. The record was *I Feel Love* by Donna Summer, produced by Giorgio Moroder, the greatest disco record of all time.

By the time *I Feel Love* had been a number one hit in the UK in 1977 I was already in Big In Japan. And sadly it was becoming a real band. When we knocked it on the head I was fuelled with enough punk attitude of 'I don't need to ask anybody's permission to do whatever I want' to decide to form my own record label. There were numerous small American labels that I was a fan of, most producing local R&B and country acts. Most of the visionary producers seemed to have their own labels. This was done in partnership with Dave Balfe the bass player in Big In Japan towards the end, who also seemed to have a thing about the visionary producer and disco. We settled on the name Zoo Records. Before Balfe had decided to come in with me it was to be called Bill's Records.

Other than sticking out some old Big In Japan recordings, the first record I wanted to make was with Pete Burns. Pete and I had talked about it and I had half a song written that was a bit like *You Make Me Feel (Mighty Real)* by Sylvester. Pete Burns worked in Probe record shop round the back of Mathew Street in Liverpool. He used to come on a lot of the Big In Japan away gigs with us. He also seemed to have star potential although I never heard him sing. The recording never happened. Pete decided I was persona non grata for some reason I don't know and he went on to be the face and voice of one of the best records of the 1980s.

There was another half-conceived song that I had. It was one that I originally thought could be done with Big In Japan but it was definitely something that could never be done as a live song at a gig. I told Balfe about it and we worked on it together. I wanted it to be like one of those sad 1960s girl-pop records that I loved but with a sort of disco beat. There was no singer we had in mind. Then we saw this girl in the street who looked weird and pretty and vulnerable with big sad eyes. We asked her if she wanted to be on a record. She said she had never sung. We said that didn't matter because all she had to do was talk the lyrics, so she said yes.

We booked ourselves into Amazon Studios in Kirkby on the outskirts of Liverpool for two days. It was the first time I had been into a 24-track studio. It was going to cost us a fortune. We didn't have a penny or any idea about how a disco record was made. We knew we wanted to have a bass drum that hit fours to the floor all the way through and we knew we wanted syn drums on it making that sound syn drums do on crap disco records. The girl was called Lori Lartey and she was on the Foundation course at Liverpool Art School, or I think she was. Balfe and I had already decided to call ourselves The Chameleons as a production team. (Should add here that we were nothing to do with the rock band The Chameleons that came out of Manchester some years later.)

The record was to be credited to Lori And The Chameleons. The song was called *Touch*. The lyrics told the tale of romance across the cultural divide between the singer and a Japanese boy in Tokyo. We recorded it with the help of Tim Whittaker, the drummer from Deaf School, doing the drum parts, Balfe doing the keyboards and me doing the guitar bits. I revelled in my cod-oriental guitar hook.

Balfe and I thought it sounded brilliant. Even revolutionary. We thought it sounded exactly how pop music should sound. Fragile, mysterious, beautiful, sexy. I haven't heard it for 25 years now and if I did, I am sure I would think it sounded quaint at best.

We released it on Zoo Records. It got 'single of the week' reviews in the music papers. WEA Records wanted to license it from us and give it a major push. We agreed and signed a deal. Dave Lee Travis made it his single of the week on BBC Radio 1. That means he played it every day for a week on his afternoon shows. This, in our eyes, was major exposure. It got to number 70 in the official UK singles chart. But the next week it dropped out, but then WEA picked up the option on us recording a follow-up single. Balfe and I wrote the song together – *The Lonely Spy*. This time the lyrics placed Lori on the edge of Red Square in Moscow. She watched her boyfriend gunned down in a hail of bullets as he tried to escape into her loving arms from the clutches of the KGB. *The Lonely Spy* required Lori to sing. We had no idea if she could. We booked ourselves into Rockfield Studios in Wales. It took us three days. We thought we had made the greatest pop record ever. It didn't even dent the top 100 and never troubled a Radio 1 playlist.

I had wanted Lori and the Chameleons to be a one-hit wonder. After two failures we gave up. A one-hit wonder should appear to have happened by accident; it's not something to be worked at. This also meant my first stab at girl-pop had failed. I was never to be responsible for something with the shimmering beauty of *Terry* by Twinkle or *Past, Present And Future* by The Shangri-Las or even *White Horses* by Jacky.

At the same time as our attempts to be the Shadow Mortons of the late 1970s we were putting out records on Zoo by our Liverpool peers Echo And The Bunnymen and The Teardrop Explodes. The Bunnymen got signed to a major with us in tow as their managers and producers. Nobody wanted The

Teardrop Explodes so Balfe and I used the £4,000 we got for doing *The Lonely Spy* as down-payment on recording the first Teardrop Explodes album.

It was another ten years before I would have a go at the one-hit wonder again. This time it was with Jimmy Cauty as The Timelords. Our one and only record under this name did get to number one in the official UK charts. Sadly, it was not girl–pop of any persuasion but it mined another tradition of British popular music. It was a great stomping turd of a record that gatecrashed the national and international charts in a way only the rudest and crudest of novelty records can. For some it was one of the worst records ever made. For Jimmy Cauty and myself it was one of those fabulous pop moments, when stupidity and genius seem to be the same. That said, it was no *Telstar* by The Tornados and should not be mentioned in the same book as the shimmering glory that is *River Deep, Mountain High* by Ike and Tina Turner.

On two or three of the pop singles that Jimmy Cauty and I were later to make we attempted to touch those heights that Phil Spector once reached. Not by trying to mimic his over-mimicked sound, but by throwing everything we had and plenty of things we had no right to have at the canvas while we worshipped at the altar of pop one last time. Even roping in Tammy Wynette was a nod to one of the great visionaries of record production, Billy Sherrill, who produced the greatest country record of all time, *Stand By Your Man*.

I will celebrate getting this chapter written by diving in the pool then getting a beer and playing in my head *Push The Button* by The Sugababes one more time.

Tomorrow I will read it through to see if it can be tightened up; cut out the flab, find the focus.

UP ON CLEEVE HILL
27 August 2006

Sitting up on Cleeve Hill facing west, down below and some way beyond Cheltenham, the River Severn glinting in the late afternoon sunshine. In the distance is the Forest of Dean and even further off in the far haze, the Black Mountains of Wales.

Up here on the Cotswold escarpment is a good place to be thinking about YouTube, a recurring pastime of mine these last few months. I'm sure many of us around the world are doing the same thing. Maybe this time next year we will not be thinking about YouTube at all; it will be so much part of the cultural landscape it won't inspire a flicker of thought. Last year those who think about the marketing of pop music were spending their time thinking about how MySpace was going to change things. Now I guess they have it all worked out and everyone knows how to make it work for them.

But YouTube, that is something else altogether. It doesn't just shift the goal posts like MySpace did; it is creating a whole new game. And I like the game and only wish it had existed in the mid-1980s when I was working with a band called Ellery Bop, from Liverpool. I was responsible for signing them to WEA Records. I signed them because of the force of personality of Jamie Farrell, their main man. Jamie was a complex man with much anger directed in many directions. The music of Ellery Bop was rock with a swagger; what it lacked in colour it made up for in its direct approach. Although they made one good single, the music they produced was the least interesting thing about them.

Paul: Do you remember there was a point when YouTube blew up just like MySpace did?

Rasmus: But MySpace is gone; now it's all about Facebook; tomorrow it will be about something else.

Paul: Exactly.

Robert: Its nice that he uses the word 'flicker'. It should be Flickr.

Jamie played guitar and wrote and sang the songs. He also looked like a rock star, with his quiff and mean good looks. There was a bass player and drummer too. They were good but they were there to do what they were told to do. There was another member of the band, Kevin Connelly, who didn't play in the band or help write the songs or manage them or even drive the van. Kevin just had to be Kevin. His presence was enough.

Jamie and Kevin were Ellery Bop. It was their vision; the band was their vehicle to make their mark on the world. They were both from a Liverpool Irish background. Jamie had a fierce intelligence. Did well at school. His great aunt was the legendary Liverpool Member of Parliament, Bessie Braddock. It had been decided by his family that he would follow in her footsteps and become a Labour MP for a Liverpool constituency. The way that I heard it, it almost seemed like it was Jamie's birthright. He went to Liverpool University to study politics and philosophy. But he rebelled and signed up for officer training in the Guards. He rebelled again and formed Ellery Bop with his friend Kevin Connelly. He was the first non-Muslim person I had ever met who had read the Koran and the youngest person I knew to have an ulcer. He had a violent streak that was beyond justification. Kevin and Jamie together did a lot of bad things and I don't mean in the trivial sex, drugs and rock 'n' roll way that the music papers like to glorify. But Jamie contained genius and it was pretty obvious to anybody who heard Ellery Bop that rock music was not going to be the outlet for his genius.

Portable video cameras were just becoming affordable at that time. It was self-evident to me that Jamie and Kev should get a video camera and knock on the head any attempt at making music as a band and instead just make short films of what they got up to or what they had to say about whatever needed to be said. These short films could be released and put out there on VHS. But WEA was a record company and Ellery Bop were managed by traditional rock 'n' roll management who knew about touring and albums and all that old-fashioned shit.

I don't think I ever even had the conversation with Jamie and Kevin about their future as film-makers. Jamie 'retired' from the music game some time in the late 1980s. His career took a darker path. Too many bridges were burnt for him to ever consider a career in politics. I have often thought about the films that Ellery Bop never made.

It is cheaper now to get the gear to make and edit your own films than it is to get the gear to form a band. I love the fact that up and down the land there are gangs of youths making films and showing them on YouTube. And if their stuff is any good, they will have an audience for it within days.

Robert: I'm really interested in the way that a thing like YouTube accelerates the nature of pop. Pop becomes more pronounced because things become popular so quickly and are discarded immediately. Things become popular overnight then disappear. Viewers too are becoming really impatient: as you look at clips on YouTube you are already being tempted away by the list on the right-hand side of other clips you could be watching. It's this culture of always wanting something else and never being happy or not able to appreciate what you have because there is so much on offer. It worries me that we look for quick entertainment. It discourages people to invest time into something of quality.

Paul: But you can't argue that because of YouTube there won't be brilliant films made. There is always a way to make money from good things that are popular. Like in the music industry – record sales may be dropping, but they can make shitloads of money by going on tour.

Robert: It's great that the physical experience has become more valued as a by-product of the digital reproduction of recorded music.

WHAT IS REAL?
13 September 2006

A couple of weeks back I got an email from an Irish artist named Dennis McNulty. He had read something about The17 in a Dublin magazine, which had prompted his email. He reckoned there were similarities in our approach to working. There was a link in his email to an artist's statement on his site. I clicked and read this:

'I am an artist / musician who works in a process-driven way. This frequently manifests itself in the creation of site-specific performances. The sonic content of these performances is improvised, i.e. each sound performance is unique and unrepeatable.'

He goes on to explain how earlier this year he had sent out an email to the 2,000 names on a mailing list of a Brazilian record label, some sort of underground specialist label. He was inviting the recipients of the email to email him back and invite him round to their place to perform his music. But he stipulated that only those who lived on the higher floors of tower blocks should respond and that his performance could only happen at the magic hour just before sunset.

In the email to me he also said that he was about to have an exhibition in a gallery in Derry in Northern Ireland and would like to invite me to write a catalogue essay for the show. The exhibition was to be a record of what he had done in Brazil: sound, video, photos, text, all the usual media of documentation. Now, although this did not fit completely with my hardliner approach on where music should be heading – for a start he was recording it for posterity when, as I have already stated, I don't think we should be giving a shit about posterity – I liked that it was site-specific. I liked that it had to be done in a tower block at a certain time of day when the light was right. I like that he'd gone to Brazil to do it. And I like that he called the show Magic Hour.

So I emailed this Dennis McNulty back. And then we spoke on the phone, arrangements were made and now I'm sitting on a window seat on a Ryanair flight 28,000 feet up somewhere between Stansted and Derry. I can't be any more site-specific because below, as in out of the window, all I can see is cloud.

The term magic hour is something I first came across when Jimmy Cauty and I were attempting to make a film. Henry Braham, the lighting cameraman we were working with, was always going on about magic hour, always trying to get all the filming done in this period of time he called magic hour. As far as he was concerned it wasn't worth filming outside at any other time of day. But according to Henry there were two magic hours. The first is just after sunrise; the second, the one that Dennis McNulty refers to, is just before sunset. It is the time when shadows are at their longest, when physical forms are at their most defined and everything has a golden luminous quality. Once Jimmy Cauty and I saw the rushes of the film we had shot we realised that what Henry had been going on about was a fact. Everything that was shot outside of the early morning or evening magic hours looked flat, dull and unusable.

Ever since then the idea of the magic hour has had a special significance for me: a time when things work, fall into place. The idea of someone making music only to be played at that time and in a setting where it can be fully appreciated has a really strong draw for me. I only wish the idea had come to me first.

It's about 7.30 at the moment. Through the window I can see that the sun has just risen above the eastern rim, casting its rays across the top of the clouds. Everything I can see of creation from this one little window looks stunningly beautiful. 'His wondrous beauties to behold' is the line that comes to mind. It's the magic hour all right. In my head Dennis McNulty's music is providing the soundtrack. It sounds great. I will have to tell him when we meet. The thing is, I've not heard any of his music as yet.

Two and a bit hours later I'm sitting in the Void's foyer / café bit chatting with Dennis McNulty about his ideas and how the trip to Brazil got set up and what his background is and how come he is doing this show in Derry. My first impression on meeting him was that he looked like a younger, better-looking Gerry Adams, but maybe I'm only thinking this because I'm in Northern Ireland. After chatting with him for a bit I go into the gallery space where his show is. It has the usual white walls, the ceiling is low, but it is a good-sized room. Hanging from the ceiling are 116 A6 photographs (I counted them). Each photograph is attached to a red thread. The thread is attached to the ceiling. The photos hang at various heights between crotch and eye level. The air movement caused by me coming into the room causes the photographs to turn and twist gently. A couple of low-level lights in the room positioned about four feet from the floor cast shadows of these turning and twisting photos on the white walls. Music is playing. It's an abstract music that seems itself to turn and twist in time to the hanging photos and the shadows on the wall. The music sounds uncannily like what I was hearing in my head two-and-a-half hours earlier, while 28,000 feet up in the air. Actually it doesn't totally, but it would be great if it did. The main difference between what I imagined and what I heard with my ears is that what I heard was music that had originally been made using a guitar and the music that I heard in my head in the magic hour above the clouds was celestial and was made using instruments as yet unknown to mankind.

In one corner of the room was a red leather sofa. I sat down on it and lost myself in the music while watching the still slowly rotating photos and shifting shadows. On the floor near the sofa was a video monitor. Playing on this was documentation of what l assumed was one of the performances in an apartment in a Brazilian high-rise. I wanted this video documentation to be of the lengthening shadows, high across the cityscape in Rio de Janeiro or São Paulo or somewhere down there. But it wasn't. It was just a bunch of smart-looking arty people lying around an apartment and Dennis McNulty sitting by a window with his laptop open in front of him on a small table. The fingers on his left hand are twiddling the knobs on a little black box. The fingers of his right hand press keys on his iBook. He is wearing a red Fast Food Nation T-shirt.

I stop looking at the video because it is boring. Instead I allow my attention to drift through the music and the sliding shadows on the walls. After a while I realised I had started to sing along to the music. Not so much singing as long-drawn-out aaahhhs. In my head The17 were singing along with the abstract guitar music.

I could see that something had been written or drawn on the back of each of the photos, but from my vantage point on the red leather sofa I could see neither what was written or drawn nor what the photo depicted. I guessed it must have been more documentation of the actual performances.

After about 20 minutes of just sitting there I get up to go. It was then that I noticed a microphone stand with a microphone on it in the far corner of the gallery and on the wall 14 sheets of A4 paper, Blu-Tacked up in a line. Two of these are emails from Dennis McNulty, one in English, the other I assume is a translation in Portuguese. On reading it I realise it is the invitation that he had sent out. The other 12 A4 sheets were printouts of emails he received back, all responding positively to his invitation.

I liked this. It's the sort of stuff I liked to do. I liked the mistakes in their English and their descriptions of their apartments. I must remember what my

English teacher taught us about using the word 'like'.

Outside the gallery space I met up with Dennis again, told him I wanted to go for a walk around the Derry city walls while having a think about what he has done. I asked him if he could read some of the stuff I had written about The17 and on my return from the walk we could have a chat before I got down to the writing.

Outside and heading along Strand Road I can see dark clouds gathering in the west. A very fine rain is already falling.

Back in the late 1950s and early 1960s we had a couple of family holidays in County Donegal. To get there we had to drive through Derry. I have this very clear memory of being up on the city walls looking down across the slums of the Bogside. Up on the walls now I am met by a very different view. Long gone are the Victorian tenement slums, replaced by a whole mix of social housing. The first thing that most visitors would notice is all the Republican gable-end artwork commemorating Bloody Sunday. What I am noticing is the house martins fluttering, diving and swooping above the Bogside homes below. I wondered how many generations of house martins there have been since Bloody Sunday. For that matter, how many generations have there been since the siege of Derry back in 1688-89? And I wonder what birds were outside the blocks of apartments that Dennis McNulty was playing in Rio and São Paulo. I could smell autumn in the air, the faint hint of peat smoke and distant heather moors. The house martins must be thinking of packing in these northern climes for the year and heading back down to Africa for the winter. I wonder what music they will be hearing down there. I carried on my walk around the city wall formulating topics of conversation to have with McNulty when we meet up back at Void.

We boil the kettle. Well, the kettle boils itself. We are both having mugs of camomile and we settle down to have our chat. These sorts of chats with people you have never met before are always difficult; you don't know where the boundaries are. You have to get on familiar terms straight away but you know sod all about each other. The other thing is that you can be in real danger of coming on seriously pretentious in your desire to sound like you know what the fuck you are talking about – what names to reference and which ones to leave out in case they cause offence or make you look stupid.

We start talking. We talk about frustrations with the way music exists. We talk about this being his first exhibition in a gallery. We talk about how he never went to art school but did a degree in engineering and how that has helped him see music. He quotes a line from Spinal Tap, something about music sounding like strands intertwining. Although this line was written and used in the film as a total send-up of the pretensions of musicians, it nevertheless defines how McNulty sees the music he makes. We talk about the guitar, how he still finds it a useful tool, how the love affair with the guitar is never over. I ask him about Vinny Reilly, but I don't think he really knew who he was. He answers by telling me how someone said that his music reminded them of Pink Floyd and this was supposed to be a compliment. He then made it clear that he imagined that what Pink Floyd stood for was everything he was against. I failed to mention that at 17 I thought that Atom Heart Mother by the Floyd was one of the greatest albums ever made.

We talked about burnout and finding new ways to work, about Stockhausen and Cage, about a bloke called Alvin Lucifer, who I'd never heard of. He told me I should visit the site ubu.com to listen to some of Alvin Lucifer's work. We talked about how often it happens that you read about a composer or some experimental music and you love the ideas and the theories but when you hear the recordings you often feel let down. That this type of music should never have been recorded; that hearing it, outside of the context of the time, often renders it useless as a piece of music to listen to and enjoy, even though the idea still stands up. It is those ideas that can continue to inform what you are trying to do in the present. We talked about not really knowing what we are doing or how it should be done and how it is only in the doing of it that we get any idea of how we should be doing it; how, when he first opened up his laptop to start his first performance in Brazil he had no real idea of how it was going to work; and that it is through the process of doing it that you get closer to whatever it is.

I indicated my disappointment with the video documentation I had seen in the gallery space. He explained it was not something that he had planned. It had been shot by a friend of one of the hosts whose apartment he was performing in. He liked the idea that the documentation was something done by others and not mediated by him. I liked this. He then went on to explain that the photos hanging and twirling on the red thread had come about in the same way. They were all photos that people attending the performances had taken of their own accord and sent them to him. I liked this too. I asked him why he had hung them on red thread from the ceiling. He told me he wanted to break up any linear reading of the photos that would exist if they had been affixed to the wail. Being hung from the ceiling and subject to movement of the air in the room broke up all that. I asked about the red thread. He had an answer but I can't remember it. I wondered if I should have taped our conversation so things like that do not get forgotten. I'm wondering now what else might have been forgotten.

He told me how he is going to do it all again but this time in blocks of flats that were put up in Dublin in the 1980s, that the apartments in Brazil were all large and spacious, the homes of the moderately wealthy – what he was doing there didn't touch the underclass masses who lived in the sprawling shantytowns; that the blocks of flats in Dublin were totally different – they were small, cramped and shoddily built for the lower orders; and that they were built without much forethought – the authorities didn't want too many building regs to get in the way of the Celtic Tiger economy as it gathered pace. We stopped talking and ate some nuts from a large packet of assorted nuts. Then I told him I was going to go back into the gallery and sit on the red leather sofa and start writing. And that's what I am doing now and I am just about to stop.

Later. About an hour later. I've checked my email and had a talk with Maoliosa, the director of Void. Dennis McNulty asked me what I thought of the dark room. 'What dark room?' He explained so I went and found it. It was another gallery space but it was in almost complete darkness. There was one small faint light source at the other end of the room. Not enough for me to see if there was anyone else in the room, however much my eyes got accustomed to the darkness. Dennis had explained to me that the microphone on a stand in the main gallery space that I mentioned before was there to pick up the music that was being played in that room, plus the ambient sound of the room, whatever that might be – people chatting or me singing along with it, as I had done earlier – and rebroadcasting it all in the dark gallery. I liked this. I wanted to lie on the floor of this dark room and lose myself in the sound but the concrete floor was too cold and I had only a T-shirt on. So instead I wanted to find out what the source of the very dim light was at the other end of the room. I made my way carefully through the darkness, afraid that I was going to trip over something. The light was coming from a partly open laptop, three books being used to prop it open. Using my mobile as a torch I discover what books have been used for this job: *A Complete Course In Understanding, Speaking and Writing Portuguese; Modern Music (A Concise History From Debussy To Boulez)* and *When Brazil Was Modern (A Guide To Architecture 1928–1960)*.

I thought this was a nice touch. It also reminded me that I had forgotten one whole strand of our earlier conversation. And that was about modern architecture: about Brasilia, the capital city, how he loved it and how it is one of the few places I want to visit in the world. Sod Machu Picchu; give me the city of Brasilia.

I am now on the plane back to Stansted. Things were held up at Derry airport. It is nearly 11.30. It has been a long day. Just before I left we did a short interview on the arts programme for BBC Radio Foyle. Dennis had to get what he was doing down to a soundbite. That is something that I have never been very good at. Dennis had a good go at it. The show's host wanted to know what attracted me to his work and I said something about it being time- and site-specific, but that I had no idea what it was going to sound like until I got here.

Just as I was leaving for the airport I picked up an A5-size glossy comic called *Void Comix*. The strip cartoon in it told the story of McNulty's show using a cartoon character called Arty. Arty is a teenage boy who visits the Void gallery and takes in what Dennis McNulty has been doing and then back home tries to do some sound art himself with disastrous consequences, or at least as far as his family is concerned. This comic was obviously aimed at the younger audience that Void may want to attract. It seems that Void do one of these *Void Comix* starring Arty for each of their shows. I wish I had read the comic before I had written all this; it seemed to get to the heart of Dennis McNulty's work far faster than I have been able to. I've also just remembered a topic of conversation that McNulty and I only touched on but which now seems central. The topic was music and reality. The vast majority of music makers would like their music to be considered real. Dennis McNulty thinks no music is real and never has been real; for him it is music's unreality that is its source of power. People trying to make music real are heading in the wrong direction. Maybe it is just that McNulty's definition of what is real is different from other makers of music.

So back up here again, 28,000 feet above somewhere down there, the magic hour long gone. Should music be real? And if so, what should that reality be like?

Two days later. I emailed the above text to Dennis McNulty to make sure that I had got the facts right. In his return email he pointed out that the Alvin bloke was not called Lucifer but merely Lucier, but Alvin Lucifer would be a cool name for an experimental death metal band. More importantly the project in Brazil was called Anti-tour No. 1 – Magic Hour and the

Rasmus: I don't understand. I'm not sure I'm looking for reality in music.

Robert: It's an impossible abstract question to create reality in a piece of work.

Rasmus: Maybe I'm looking for honesty or what I think is honesty.

198

exhibition in Derry was called dx/dt. He also said that I was not the first person to make the Gerry Adams comparison.

Robert: Even with honesty – you can present something emotional that doesn't have to be honest.

Rasmus: Sometimes you want that illusion.

Robert: And sometimes it's the opposite. Music is an escapist thing for a lot of people.

Rasmus: Like Strawberry Fields.

Robert: Strawberry Fields is a surreal experience but surrealism is a type of reality.

SCORE

11. COMBINE

Take a map of a metropolitan area.
Draw a circle on the map.
Ensure that it encircles five buildings,
each where a different faith is practised.

Go to the first building.
Ask some members of this faith who are
willing to sing
to make non-verbal vocal sounds
on the note of C for five minutes.
Ask them to refrain from using melody
or regular rhythm.
Record their performance.

Go to the second building.
Ask some members of this faith who are
willing to sing
to make non-verbal vocal sounds
on the note of D for five minutes.
Ask them to refrain from using melody
or regular rhythm.
Record their performance.

Go to the third building.
Ask some members of this faith who are
willing to sing
to make non-verbal vocal sounds
on the note of E for five minutes.
Ask them to refrain from using melody
or regular rhythm.
Record their performance.

Go to the fourth building.
Ask some members of this faith who are
willing to sing
to make non-verbal vocal sounds
on the note of G for five minutes.
Ask them to refrain from using melody
or regular rhythm.
Record their performance.

Go to the fifth building.
Ask some members of this faith who are
willing to sing
to make non-verbal vocal sounds
on the note of A for five minutes.
Ask them to refrain from using melody
or regular rhythm.
Record their performance.

Combine and balance the five recordings
so that they can be played simultaneously.

Gather 17 people together.
The17 can include the members of the five
faiths.
Explain what you have done.
Play them the combined and balanced
recordings simultaneously.

Delete all your recordings relating to this
SCORE.

pb Poster 138   2006

PEOPLE DRESSING UP
22 September 2006

Performance art? It's just people dressing up doing silly things, isn't it? For me, it has never been enough for artists to merely shock, amuse or prompt the question 'why?'

I'm in a town called Sete, not far from Montpellier, on the French Mediterranean coast. I am one of 44 artists taking part in a performance art festival called Infr'action.

I arrived yesterday evening. Tonight I am making soup, hoping to instigate a French Soupline. Souplines in general and the French Soupline in particular have nothing whatsoever to do with The17.

The following words appear on **Take A Map Of The British Isles** (Penkiln Burn Poster 54) – *Take a map of the British Isles. Draw a straight line diagonally across the map so that it cuts through Belfast and Nottingham. If your home is on this line, contact soupline@penkiln-burn.com. Arrangements will then be made for Bill Drummond to visit and make soup for you, your family and your close friends.*
This job has been active since 2003. Since 2005 Drummond has been promoting the creation of Souplines in other countries (Souplines International). To learn more visit the Penkiln Burn site.

Tomorrow night I do *An Introduction To The17* performance in a deconsecrated chapel. We visited the chapel this morning. It is perfect. All religious iconography has long since been stripped out of the place. The ceiling is high and the walls are blackened by centuries of candle smoke – or at least I guess that is why they are black.

Sete is a picturesque town of narrow cobbled streets sprawled over a hill. The hill almost feels like an island. Fishing seems to be the main industry. Today is market day. Everything that is good and fresh and French is being sold. While doing my shopping in the market for the soup-making later today I come across a number of the performance artists plying their trade.

The first one was in the process of opening for business. He was standing just outside the market hall dressed in a black tuxedo. To his right-hand side was a five-litre tub of white emulsion paint; to his left, a plastic bin of water. Leaning against the wall behind the tub of paint was a placard. The place was thronged with market day shoppers. He turned the placard round; it read 'Poignées de main fraîches gratis' – I was reliably informed that this read 'Fresh Handshakes For Free'. This man in the tuxedo dipped his flattened but almost quivering right hand into the white paint slowly and purposefully until it was completely submerged. Then he stood slowly and deliberately bolt upright, holding his still-flattened right hand out waiting for a passer-by to shake it. The hand was completely whitened, the paint dripping off on to the flagstones in front of him.

He didn't move. Not a muscle flinched. Except for the almost quivering hand. Most shoppers took no notice. He stood there for some minutes holding his pose. The paint kept dripping from his hand. A bunch of teenage lads strolled past. One noticed. After some deliberation one of the teenagers shook the white hand then washed his own hand in the bucket of water. He used the towel on offer. The sky was blue. More shoppers stopped to stare and wonder. The teenage lads moved on. The man in the tuxedo dipped his hand back in the tub of paint and returned to his position waiting for another passer-by to take him up on his offer of a free, fresh handshake.

The ice was broken. The shoppers started to take notice. The odd one, the more foolhardy, took on the man in the tuxedo's offer and shook his hand. I moved on.

If I had just read what l have just written and you have just read, I would have thought 'A performance artist dressing up and doing a silly thing'. This morning in this town in southern France I was strangely moved.

I walked into the market building. The place was heaving. Stalls of fresh fruit and vegetables, stalls of cheese, stalls of sausages and cured ham, stalls of fresh fish, all of them looked wonderful. I wished we had markets like this in Britain.

Then I spied a man with a brown suit on. He was standing at a stall that was selling fish. He was studiously inspecting the goods on offer. His head was bound up with bandages. You could just see his eyes, nose and mouth. He looked as if he had been in some terrible accident where the top layer of skin on his head had been burned off. I suspected this was not the case, as the bandages were fulfilling another function. They were holding in place at least two dozen rose stalks around his head. Above his head the roses, of various colours, were in full bloom. The image was arresting.

When l arrived yesterday I was given a programme for the festival. On the cover was a head-and-shoulders portrait of this man. He was staring directly from between the bandages into the lens of the camera. On his head was the blooming headdress of roses. This image was also on the fly poster around the town advertising the festival; it was also on the access-all-areas laminate that I was given. My first impression on seeing this image on the programme was

'Man dressing up doing silly things', but now I am here doing my shopping and blending in with the other shoppers I am strangely moved again.

There is no part of me that wants to know why they are doing this or what it is supposed to mean but both the man with the fresh handshakes and the one with the roses communicated directly with my soul. Their actions contained meaning. Yesterday I thought of performance art as something left over from the 1970s. Today it is affecting me in a way I can only be grateful for. Should I learn something from this? Might the same thing happen this evening if I was to walk into a bar in Sete and there was a French singer on a stool with guitar on lap singing songs of loss and regret? Would I be as moved? If so, should I begin to suspect my half-formulated theories about where we should be heading with music?

Last night at the opening do for us 44 artists from all over the world, one of the performance artists came up to speak to me. I vaguely recognised him from somewhere. He spoke to me.
'Hi, my name is Erkki. I met you 14 years ago on a train in Finland. You were on your way to the North Pole with an icon of Elvis. You were with two other men. You told us that you were Zen masters and once you got to the North Pole, you would leave the icon of Elvis there and it would leak good vibes down the longitudes and out across the latitudes, spreading love, peace and happiness.'

It had been a long drunken night on a train bound for the Arctic. My travelling companions were Z (Mark Manning) and Gimpo. The story of the night became a chapter in the book *Bad Wisdom* that Z and I wrote. This man, or the man he was 14 years ago, just so happened to be on the same train as us and started to film the three of us getting drunk and telling our story to anybody who would listen. We had these lengths of wood that I had cut from an elm tree the previous morning. They were our Zen sticks and we kept whacking each other on the head with them to hasten each other's Zen enlightenment. We were leaping from table to table as this train hurtled through the Arctic night. In the morning he was gone. We didn't know who he was and we never saw him or his filming of us again. But now here he is asking me if I remember.

It is now lunchtime in Sete. Lunch is being served on long trestle tables for us 44 artists in the gallery space and festival headquarters. The man wearing the same suit as the man whose head was bandaged with a headdress of roses sits down opposite me. I assume he is the same man.

'Good day, My name is Pekka Kainulainen.'
'Hi. My name is Bill.' We shake hands.
'Bill Drummond?'
'Yes.'
'Every year I show a film to my students of you on a train in Finland. It was filmed by Erkki Pirtola.' He points to the man with the camera that I was talking about. Things seem to be getting stranger and stranger.
'But why?' I ask.
'I use it as an example to show that art does not have to be made to be seen in a gallery or museum but can exist anywhere. Even on a train in the middle of the night when you are drunk. And that art does not have to be something premeditated and thought out. It can happen by accident.'

Well, I don't know if he actually used these words as, of course, I didn't record the conversation and now it is an hour or so later that I am making these notes, but I am hoping that that was the gist of what he was trying to say. So I might have got it completely the wrong way round and he was using this film as an example of exactly what not to be doing while making performance art. The thing is, back in 1992 when we did this journey to the North Pole, I had no idea what performance art was. Not even sure I knew there was such a genre and here I am in September 2006 giving it 'It's all so 1970s' as if I knew all about it.

ON A FRENCH TRAIN
23 September 2006

It was the worst performance of The17 ever. The last thing the French want is some bloke speaking about himself in English to them, for nigh on 40 minutes. When it came to the bit for them to take part in performing *AGE*, it was totally lacklustre. I don't blame them. I'm sure they didn't have a clue what any of it was about. And another thing was we were reliant on the festival to provide us with a PA and the one that was provided had seen better days. Yes, I know: a bad workman blames his tools. The thing is, our hopes were so high. As I mentioned, the chapel we were doing it in was the best place we had ever done it.

John Hirst had the idea of lighting the place with candles. To get to the chapel you had to walk up these winding cobbled streets with high, shuttered buildings on either side. The entrance to the chapel was a nondescript green door, the paint faded and chipped. Walking in from the daylight of the outside into the darkness of the chapel, your eyes could see nothing, even with the 20 or so candles we had dotted around the place. It took some minutes for your eyes to get accustomed to the gloom. I could have spent all day in there by myself just getting into some strange holy place in my head. Instead I had to spoil it all by trying to do The17 with a bunch of French folk who probably had better things to do with their time.

But all that was yesterday. Today I am on a train that is taking me from Montpellier, also on the south coast of France, up to Gare De Lyon in Paris. It's one of these super-speed, ultra-modern trains. Outside, the sun has just risen and the stunning landscape of France flashes by. Shafts of sunlight break through the clouds, hitting the fields. At Paris I have to cross town to get to another station, Gare de L'Est, and from there I catch a train to Nogent Sur Seine where I am to attend a wedding. I have never met the couple getting married. I am to be there as the guest of my friend Ronita Dutta, who is the matron of honour. The journey from Sete to Nogent is to take six hours. The wedding festivities go on until 3 in the morning. I'm told. Tomorrow morning I catch a train at 9.10 to do the return journey to Sete, and another performance of The17. I've got between now and then to somehow come up with a way of making The17 work in the given context. Next week I will be in Moscow and St Petersburg doing the same thing there, so I will still have the language problem. Educated Russians can all read English but have great problems understanding it when spoken.

But all this is an aside to what is going on in my head, over and over again. And it has been going on in my head over and over again since 1968. It's a two-bar melody repeated and repeated and repeated. There is no more to this melody than what goes around my head. It is not part of some longer tune. It is not the hook from some record of my adolescence. And there is no joy to be had out of this melody. Nobody would have penned it to make the world a better place. But over the years it has become a sort of companion and not a welcome one but at least a familiar one. Some days it goes away. Sometimes it's gone for a month or so then it returns, but not with a 'Hi, how's it going' or anything. It just starts up again in my head. Going around and around. The same two bars.

I suspect I am not the only person in the UK who has this very tune in their heads, and this is the reason why. It would have been mid-evening and the radio would have been on, tuned to 247 on the medium wave. That was the wavelength for BBC Radio 1 back then; I would be in my room wanting to listen to whatever was on, maybe the Mike Raven R&B Hour. The signal would start to get weaker, there would be a build-up of static. The signal always got weaker in the evenings. Then, somewhere in the distance, deep in the static and other radio interference I would hear this melody over and over again. Every evening it would be there, fading in and out. Once my attention was caught by it I would lose focus on what the actual record Mike Raven, or whoever it was, was playing. It was not played by a band or an orchestra. It was just an electronic tone. Once, I got my guitar and worked out the notes of the melody. It went B-, B-, BB, AF#, /G-, —, E-.

To begin with I imagined there was someone sitting in a radio station somewhere whose job it was to come in every night and play this dull and dreary tune all evening. But why? As the months went by and the tune was still there I imagined a radio station somewhere with two decks. On each of the decks was a copy of the same long player. These LPs would have nothing on them but this one recurring tune. When one LP came to an end the needle would have already been dropped into the other, so there would be no break in its continuum. But why? Then I heard about tape loop, so I imagined an old-fashioned tape recorder with a loop of a tape going round and round. But still, why?

And then I had an answer, or at least a theory for an answer. When Radio 1 had started up in 1967 there was a lot of bad blood between the pirate radio stations that existed on ships outside the three-mile exclusion zone off the coast of the UK and the authorities in general and Radio 1 in particular. The government had outlawed any companies advertising on these stations so their only source of revenue dried up and Radio 1 pinched all their best DJs. The biggest and best of these stations was Radio Caroline. It was owned by a maverick music business Irishman named Ronan O'Rhally.

Ronan O'Rhally was always looking for ways to gain publicity, attack the laws that prevented his Radio Caroline from staying in business and have a go at Radio 1. My theory was that it was Ronan O'Rhally who was broadcasting this continuous two-bar refrain every night in an attempt to sabotage Radio 1. And in a way it worked. There were numerous evenings when I would be listening to Radio 1 and gradually this repeated tune would almost drown out what I was wanting to listen to. In the end I would just switch off the radio.

Like the mild tinnitus that I suffer from, I have had to accept this dull tune as part of my life. Then, in 1989 or 1990 I heard this programme on Radio 4 about Nicolae Ceausescu, the recently overthrown Romanian dictator. In it was some mention of the Romanian state radio station and their call signal and how it may be familiar to some of us. They played a few bars. And that was it. For all those years it was the Romanian state radio signal that I have been hearing going round in my head. Knowing what it is has not stopped it. At times I try to add some imagined harmonies to it, and lately tried to imagine it being sung by The17 – anything to make it a more interesting thing to have to listen to in my head. But this never works. It stays a dull lifeless tone. Maybe by writing about it now I will get rid of it.

The train is beginning to slow. The outskirts of Paris pass by. I pack my bag and get out my street map so that I can work out a route to walk from Gare de Lyon to Gare de L'Est.

Tomorrow night The17 will be better.

ИЗВЕЩЕНИЕ

ВСЯ СУЩЕСТВУЮЩАЯ МУЗЫКА ИЗЖИЛА СЕБЯ.

ОНА ПОТРЕБЛЯЛАСЬ, ПРОДАВАЛАСЬ, ЗАГРУЖАЛАСЬ, ПОНИМАЛАСЬ, СЛУШАЛАСЬ, СЭМПЛИРОВАЛАСЬ, ИЗУЧАЛАСЬ, ВОЗРОЖДАЛАСЬ, СУДИЛАСЬ И ЛЮБИЛАСЬ.

ОСВОБОДИТЕСЬ ОТ ВСЕЙ СОЗДАННОЙ МУЗЫКИ И ОПЫТА МУЗЫКАЛЬНОГО ТВОРЧЕСТВА — И НАЧНИТЕ ЗАНОВО.

С НУЛЯ.

The 17 - ЭТО ХОР.

ЧЬЯ МУЗЫКА ВНЕ ИСТОРИИ, ОНА НЕ СЛЕДУЕТ ТРАДИЦИЯМ, НЕ ПОХОЖА НА СОВРЕМЕННОСТЬ.

В The 17 - МНОЖЕСТВО ГОЛОСОВ.

ЗДЕСЬ НЕТ ЛИБРЕТТО, ПОЭЗИИ ИЛИ СЛОВ.

НИКАКОГО РИТМА.

НИКАКОГО ЗНАНИЯ МЕЛОДИКИ, КОНТРАПУНКТА ИЛИ ГАРМОНИИ.

The 17 БОРЮТСЯ С ТЕНЬЮ.

И СТРЕМЯТСЯ К СВЕТУ.

pb Poster 126   2006

TELL ME SOMETHING CRAZY
28 September 2006

Stuck in a Moscow traffic jam. Ludmila (Luda) Dmitriev is at the wheel of her battered and ancient Volga. John Hirst is in the back, I'm in the front passenger seat. Our equipment is crammed in with us. We flew into Moscow in the early hours, got a taxi to Luda's apartment, had three hours' sleep and Luda then offered us a huge breakfast in her cramped kitchen where everything that Russia has to offer was on the table for us to eat.

And now Luda is driving us to The Dom in the centre of Moscow where we will be doing another *Introduction To The17* performance this evening as part of the Long Arms Festival. Long Arms is an annual event that has been going for some years, bringing new and experimental music to Moscow.

Luda is the widow of Nickolay Dmitriev, who instigated the setting up of The Dom in 1999. The prime function of The Dom is to promote new and experimental music. They also have exhibitions in the space – I first visited the Dom when I was over in Moscow with Tracey Moberly. Nickolay Dmitriev spent his adult life writing about and promoting the cause of new music. He died two years ago (2004). He was about my age. From what I understand he was a charismatic Moses-type figure. His wife Luda worked with him on all his projects and since his premature death is carrying on with the work.

So that is the background to us sitting in a Moscow traffic jam. The conversation drifts from the state of traffic and Moscow drivers to how there seem to be no parking restrictions anywhere. Luda tells us that if the Moscow city government tried to impose parking fees or, even worse, fines, the Moscovites would refuse to pay en masse. The good people would rather have the current anarchy than have to pay for parking tickets or fines.

She tells us that in the Soviet era there was no problem with traffic because no ordinary people had cars then. Now everybody has a car and everybody thinks it is their right to drive everywhere and anywhere at whatever speed they want and nobody is going to tell them where they can or can't park.

Conversation drifts to what is better and what is worse between now and the Soviet era.
'When Nickolay and I were younger we used to listen to any imported jazz records we could get. They were few and far between but we loved the free jazz – it seemed so dangerous and exciting – but there was this saying that had

existed since Stalin times: "Today you play jazz, tomorrow you sell your Motherland." You were always made to feel guilty for listening to jazz.'
'Did you feel guilty?' I asked.
'Yes. Sometimes very guilty, but still we felt it was important. Just to listen to it was striking a blow for freedom.'
'You know, sometimes I think we in the West are imprisoned, but we just don't know how totally imprisoned we are by the values of the liberal Western free-market economy, where we can listen to what we want when we want, read what we want, say what we want, go where we want, and, if you put in the hours, buy what you want. But somehow it is the perceived freedom that creates the prison we are in. We have all this freedom in exchange for lives without meaning. This lack of meaning in our lives is what imprisons us. We are left in a situation where all ideals and religious or spiritual values look stupid and are ridiculed.'

Of course I didn't say all that while I was in the car in the traffic jam. I just sort of thought it, but thought it too pretentious to say and am only writing it down a few hours later.

'Lots of people miss the Soviet times. Especially the older ones. They miss knowing that tomorrow they knew where they would be, what they will be doing, that they will have something to eat, that there will be work for them to do. But all of that is like being in prison. They would rather be in prison than be free.'

I didn't know what to say so I just looked out of the window at the gridlocked traffic. Then Luda asked me if I knew the work of a certain Russian artist. Whatever the name of this artist was, I can't remember it now and I did not recognise it when she said it. She went on to describe one of his works.

'He had this chair in an exhibition. Just a very ordinary chair. And on the chair was a notice. The notice read: "This is not for you. It is for everyone."'

I didn't say any more, choosing to fall silent and think thoughts.

We got to The Dom in time. Met up with my friend Alexey there. Got things sorted about what we were doing and when. Then I was asked if I would do an interview for a Moscow magazine. I said yes.

There was the journalist and the translator. Both looked like they were in their early 20s. Both were women. The journalist was serious, the translator giggly and flirtatious. They wanted to know all about The17 so I told them all I know about The17.

'But it sounds nothing like The KLF. This sounds so serious.'

'I am a serious person.'

'We were told you were a funny man who does crazy things. That you are a – what is the word? – prankster.'

'Then you were told by the wrong people. I have never done a prank in my life. I only do real things.'

'But all over the internet it says you are a crazy guy, but you look so serious. Everything you tell us sounds like philosophy. The readers of our magazine are young. They want to hear about wild things. Why not tell me something crazy for our readers?'

So I read out to her something I had written on the plane on the way over. Something I thought would replace whatever is the first of The17 scores. This is what I read out to her:

> Imagine waking up tomorrow and all music has disappeared.
> All musical instruments and all forms of recorded music, gone.
> A world without music.
> What is more, you cannot even remember
> what music sounded like or how it was made.
> You can only remember that it had existed and that it
> had been important to you and your civilisation.
> And you long to hear it once more.
> Then imagine people coming together to make music
> with nothing but their voices, and with no knowledge of
> what music should sound like.
>
> The music they would make is that of The17.

'Is that crazy?' she asked.

'That is very crazy,' I replied.

SCORE

1. IMAGINE

Imagine waking up tomorrow morning
and all music has disappeared.
All musical instruments and all forms
of recorded music, gone.
A world without music.
What is more, you cannot even remember
what music sounded like or how it was made.
You can only remember that it had existed and that it
had been important to you and your civilisation.
And you long to hear it once more.
Then imagine people coming together to make music
with nothing but their voices, and with no knowledge of
what music should sound like.

The music they would make is that of The17.

pb Poster 128   2006

NIGHT TRAIN TO ST PETERSBURG
29 September 2006

Wake up bustin' for a piss. Lower myself down from the top bunk in the cramped four-berth cabin. Make my way along the narrow corridor hoping to find the lavatory. Find it. It is vacant. The floor is wet, there is no seat to lift. I take aim. Relieve my bladder. This takes some time as it needed some relieving. Back down the corridor, into the cabin and haul myself up with some difficulty in the dark. Arrange myself under the blanket on my narrow bunk. The other three in the cabin are all asleep, judging by the sounds coming from their bunks. I stare at the ceiling and let my mind wander.

The cabin is one of ten in this carriage. There are 17 carriages being pulled in a north-west direction. I am on the Moscow to St Petersburg night train. Tomorrow night I will be on the night train back again. Between these two journeys I have to do another of my *Introduction To The17* performances as part of a festival of improvised music in an old St Petersburg theatre. I have been looking forward to this train journey from Moscow to St Petersburg for weeks. It is one of the ultimate romantic things to do. And I don't mean in a boy-girl way; I mean in the real way. I have no idea what the landscape is like that we are travelling through but I like to imagine it is the huge and dark Russian forest of myth, legend and nightmare. Most probably it is just an endless equivalent to Slough.

I had planned to download *The Rite Of Spring* onto my iPod to listen to on this journey. I know it is my G year but I had an excuse: *The Rite Of Spring* was the first classical music that I ever got totally into and seeing as Igor Stravinsky was Russian this would have been a great time to listen to it again. Maybe I would hear it in a completely different way. But anyway, I didn't get it together and now I feel glad. It seems better to just lie here in this bunk and let my mind wander as a few feet below me thousands of pine log sleepers are crossed every minute and the rods of steel glint in the moonlight. My mind is now wandering to the subject of the original 17 scores that still need to be reworked before the Huddersfield festival. There are two or three that I may have mentioned before which need to be completely dumped. The one that is in the forefront of my imagination is score 16 (I think), the one about doing all the scores in a foreign land. What is taking shape in my head is that it should be replaced by a score that is basically what I am doing every time I do one of these introductions to The17.

The first few lines of this proposed score keep going round in my head. There is nothing for it. I switch on my bunk light, pull the notebook from my bag, extract a pencil from a pocket and get writing. First I write this – from when I announce I am bustin' for a piss to here – and now I'm going to write the rough of this score before I forget it. It goes like this:

Score
5. PERFORM

Perform Score 1. *IMAGINE*
Then find a suitable venue and announce a time, date and place for a performance by The17. Instigate the allocation and distribution of 17 tickets for this performance.
At time, date and place of performance, introduce yourself to the audience with the following words:
'Good evening* my name is .... and you are The17.'

Ask The17 to perform Score 1. *IMAGINE*.
Then read them Score 4. *AGE*.
Tell them they are going to perform an interpretation of *AGE* even though there is no building with five floors, and there are not five lots of The17 of the required ages, but only The17 that is there of whatever ages they are.

Record The17 performing the five notes – F sharp, G sharp, A sharp, C sharp and D sharp for five minutes each – one after the other.

Provide a pen and sheet of paper for the members of The17 to write down their names and email addresses.
Play back to them all five recordings simultaneously.
Tell them nothing has been added or taken away from the recordings of their voices.
Tell them that they are now lifetime members of The17.
Thank them for taking the risk of performing and not running away.
Delete all recordings so that they can hear the recordings being deleted from your computer's trash bin.
Applaud.
Answer questions if asked and you feel in a position to answer.
Later: email admin@the17.org with list of 17 names.
If you need any technical advice regarding recording The17 contact info@the17.org

17

Good morning or good afternoon, as applicable.

Now that is done, pencil and notebook are put away and I settle back down to the gentle rocking and rumbling of the night train from Moscow to St Petersburg and my future slumbers.

SCORE

5. PERFORM

Perform SCORE 1. *IMAGINE.*

Then find a suitable venue and announce a time, date and place for a performance by The17.
Instigate the allocation and distribution of 17 tickets for this performance.
At time, date and place of performance introduce yourself to audience with the following words:
'Good evening* my name is.......... and you are The17.'

Ask The17 to perform SCORE 1. *IMAGINE.*
Then read to them SCORE 4. *AGE.*
Tell them they are going to perform an interpretation of *AGE* even though there is no building
with five floors, and there are not five lots of The17 of the required ages,
but only The17 that is there of whatever ages they are.

Record The17 performing the five notes F sharp, G sharp, A sharp, C sharp, and D sharp,
for five minutes each, one after the other.

Provide a pen and a sheet of paper for the members of The17 to write down their names
and email addresses.
Play back to them all five recordings simultaneously.
Tell them nothing has been added or taken away from the recording of their voices.
Tell them that they are all now life time members of The17.
Thank them for taking the risk of performing and not running away.
Delete all recordings so that they can hear the recordings being deleted from your trash bin.
Applaud.
Answer questions if asked and you feel in a position to answer.
Later: email admin@the17.org with list of 17 names.
If you need any technical advice regarding recording The17 contact info@the17.org

  * *Good morning* or *Good afternoon* when applicable.

pb Poster 132   2006

I WANT A FRY UP
29 September 2006

We were met outside St Petersburg station, not by the promoter but by a man in a grey beret with a greying ponytail and friendly face. Russian railway stations seem to be the place where the city's alcoholics and life's losers congregate. Many sport threatening-looking scars. I don't think a session in the Priory awaits any of this lot, just cold winters, bitter times and early graves. Was it like this here in the Soviet era? I don't ask.

Maybe I should write a score to be done with 17 street drinkers. I mean, that one I've written for prisoners is all very well in a politically correct way. Every artist who wants to display they have a conscience does something with prisoners. Doing a performance with 17 park bench alkies would really be attempting something. What I would get from it, let alone what they would get from it, I've no fuckin' clue. But it's a thought. One I am afraid I may be returning to.

The man with the grey beret introduces himself as Seva, which is short for something long and, for me, unpronounceable. We load our stuff into the boot of his battered car and climb in. He tells us it is only ten minutes or so to the theatre where the festival is. I make some polite chit-chat with him and then he starts. He tells us how St Petersburg is 100 percent better than Moscow in every way.
'Moscow is all surface, St Petersburg has depth. Moscow is only interested in money, St Petersburg in soul.' He tells us he used to be a musician, played the cello.'There used to be a large underground scene in Russia. I was in a rock band called Aquarium and played cello in the band. It was different to have a cello in a rock band. It made me famous on the underground scene. The man with the cello. It was fun and we enjoyed it and we were interesting. But then perestroika happened and we became heroes. Heroes of the perestroika and from playing underground clubs in the 1980s we were playing stadiums with thousands of screaming girls in the early 1990s. I hated it so I stopped. The singer and main songwriter in the band carried on with the name. He is still very famous. He writes very good words but the music is always the same.'
'So what do you do now?'
'I like to put concerts on. Promote shows. I wanted to open a club for experimental music. Do you know the Knitting Factory in New York?'
'Yes.'
'I wanted it to be like that but it became like CBGB's, just a rock 'n' roll club. I didn't own the bar, only used it some nights a week and nobody wanted the

experimental music, they just wanted rock 'n' roll bands with leather jackets. I wanted it to be better than The Dom in Moscow. But people are so conservative. There is hardly any underground now. The underground used to be deep and connected in every city in the Soviet Union but now it is thin and stretched out. We thought with perestroika we would at least be free to make the music we wanted but it has now been killed by MTV.'

'So don't you play at all now?'

'Well, tonight I have been asked to play cello as part of somebody else's band. I look forward to that, but my fingers are ... how you say?'

'Rusty?'

'Yes. Rusty. Very rusty. I used to practice six hours a day. But now I hardly ever play.'

'I hope you enjoy it.'

'I will but I have to look after you as well today and some of the other musicians and composers at the festival.'

We fall silent. I stare out of the window at the passing buildings of St Petersburg. It looks pretty much as I remembered it from this Welsh language film that I once saw that was set in St Petersburg. Don't ask me why. My mind began wandering back to thoughts of writing a score to be performed by a 17 made up of street drinkers, but before these thoughts took any distinct form Seva was saying, 'Ah, here we are. This is the theatre and here is your hotel for the day. I come in with you. See if your room is OK and sort out breakfast.'

Things are looking up. I never knew there was to be a day room in a hotel. I will leave thoughts of singing ciderheads until later. What I want is a deep bath and whatever the Russians can do that is closest to a full breakfast fry-up.

ПАРТИТУРА

6. ВОЗРАСТ

Найди пятиэтажное здание.

На первом этаже собери 17 человек возрастом 70 лет и выше.
Попроси их взять ноту ля на протяжении пяти минут.
Запиши 17.
Убедись, что исполнение отражает их мудрость.

На втором этаже собери 17 человек возрастом от 45 до 69 лет.
Попроси их взять ноту си на протяжении пяти минут.
Запиши 17.
Убедись, что исполнение отражает их горечь.

На третьем этаже собери 17 человек возрастом от 21 до 44 лет.
Попроси их взять ноту до на протяжении пяти минут.
Запиши 17.
Убедись, что исполнение отражает их самонадеянность.

На четвёртом этаже собери 17 человек возрастом от 13 до 20 лет.
Попроси их взять ноту ми на протяжении пяти минут.
Запиши 17.
Убедись, что исполнение отражает их скуку.

На пятом этаже собери 17 человек возрастом 12 лет и меньше.
Попроси их взять ноту фа на протяжении пяти минут.
Запиши 17.
Убедись, что исполнение отражает их невинность.

Собери все 85 участников 17 в одном месте.
Проиграй все записи одновременно.
Не усиливай и не микшируй записи.

Сотри все записи.

THE NIGHT TRAIN TO MOSCOW
30 September 2006

Back on the night train. The cabin and carriage are identical to the one we were heading north in, less than 24 hours earlier. A middle-aged mother and her 20-something daughter are our fellow-travellers in the cabin for the night. I hope I don't snore.

We were at a festival called Appozicia. I have no idea if that means something or nothing. It all took place in one big old lecture theatre, stretched over the weekend. The promoter of the festival had no real idea what The17 was about, could not believe that no more than 17 people were allowed into the performance. He was a big, tough-looking bloke sporting a Jethro Tull Russia 2002 tour T-shirt.

Paul: To some of my friends, to 'TULL' is to have really bad BO. This phrase was coined in honour of the dusty old blokes who used to buy Jethro Tull CDs in Essential Music in Greenwich, the record shop I used to work in.

'What? You mean people cannot watch The17 perform? This is crazy. People have bought tickets to see all the artists perform and you say you won't perform for them.'
'But didn't the people in Moscow at The Dom explain what The17 was.'
'No, They just said a very famous man from England with his experimental choir.'
'Well, it is experimental and part of the experiment is that there is no audience, just the 17 people who want to take part.'
'How long does your performance take?'
'About two hours.'
'Two hours?! I was told 25 minutes by the people in Moscow. You can never believe people in Moscow. Look, I want your performance to happen as you want to do it, but can you do it in 40 minutes?'
'Yes.'
'Great. We let in the first 17 people who arrive this evening and you can have them for 40 minutes.'
'Thanks. Can we have them all on stage with us and all the lights in the theatre switched off except one, and nobody else watching, not even staff, or you or journalists.'
'Yes. As long as it does not take more than 40 minutes and you start at 6.30 exactly.'

The performance happened as agreed, I didn't bother with all the rambling chit-chat at the beginning. I just read out the proposed score that I had written on the plane on the way over, the one about imagining waking up tomorrow morning and all music had disappeared.

We and all of The17 were on stage gathered around the grand piano. It turned out to be one of the best performances so far.

After it was done I watched another couple of performers, then had a shit meal in a café that had four of those tacky framed electric waterfall light pictures on the wall. I do not know how else to describe them. In London they would be hung for their ultimate kitsch-chic value but here I guess the café owner thought they looked modern and sophisticated. We saw nothing of St Petersburg other than the 100 yards between the hotel and the theatre. The café was between those two destinations.

After the meal and waterfalls and a drink in a bar with pictures on the wall of jazz greats, it was a lift back to the station to get this midnight train to Moscow. I am now back up in my bunk making these notes and thinking about a score for the street drinkers that hang around Russian train stations. Or any street drinkers. Based on some notes I scribbled down earlier, this is my proposed newest score.

    Corral a group of four street drinkers
    willing to hum a note for one minute in
    exchange for four cans of strong lager.
    Indicate the note of D for them to hum in
    unison with.
    Record them humming this note
    for one minute.
    Give them the promised cans
    of strong lager.

    Corral a second group of four street
    drinkers willing to ooh a note
    for one minute in exchange for four cans
    of strong lager.
    Indicate the note of F for them to ooh in
    unison with.
    Record them oohing this note
    for one minute.
    Give them the promised cans
    of strong lager.

Corral a third group of four street
drinkers willing to aah a note
for one minute in exchange for four cans
of strong lager.
Indicate the note of A for them to aah in
unison with.
Record them aahing this note
for one minute.
Give them the promised cans
of strong lager.

Corral a group of five street drinkers
willing to howl a notefor one minute in exchange for five cans
of strong lager.
Indicate the note of D, an octave above
the D hummed by the first group, for
them to howl in unison with.
Record them howling this note
for one minute.
Give them the promised cans
of strong lager.

Combine and balance the recordings so
they can be played simultaneously.

Gather 17 people together.
This may include the various street
drinkers.
Explain what you have done.
Play them the four recordings
simultaneously.

Delete recordings.

SCORE

15. DEBATE

Corral a group of four street drinkers willing to hum a note for one minute in exchange for four cans of strong lager.
Indicate the note of D for them to hum in unison with.
Record them humming this note for one minute.
Give them the promised cans of strong lager.

Corral a second group of four street drinkers willing to ooh a note for one minute in exchange for four cans of strong lager.
Indicate the note of F for them to ooh in unison with.
Record them oohing this note for one minute.
Give them the promised cans of strong lager.

Corral a third group of four street drinkers willing to aah a note for one minute in exchange for four cans of strong lager.
Indicate the note of A for them to aah in unison with.

Record them aahing this note for one minute.
Give them the promised cans of strong lager.

Corral a group of five street drinkers willing to howl a note for one minute in exchange for five cans of strong lager.
Indicate the note of D, an octave above the D hummed by the first group, for them to howl in unison with.
Record them howling this note for one minute.
Give them the promised cans of strong lager.

Combine and balance the recordings so they can be played simultaneously.

Gather 17 people together.
This may include the various street drinkers.
Explain what you have done.
Play them the four recordings simultaneously.

Delete recordings.

pb Poster 142   2006

Bill Drummond

1981 – A FALSE DAWN?
3 October 2006

Global climate change means that the Sahara is growing by so many grains of sand per second; the once-proud Masai warriors are having to sell off their cattle and move to shanty towns; half of Bangladesh is under threat of flooding. Meteorologists are predicting the worst hurricane season yet down in the Gulf of Mexico and I'm sitting out on the ledge enjoying another evening in the Indian summer that the south of England has been basking in yet again.

Some months ago I put together a list of topics that I wanted this book to cover. One thread in this was to consist of a number of stages in my own musical evolution that has brought me to this point, where, as already stated in the book's opening stanza:

> The very urge to make recorded music is a redundant and creative dead end, not even an interesting option, fit only for the makers of advertising jingles and film soundtracks. The sheer availability and ubiquity of recorded music will inspire forward-looking music-makers to explore different ways of creating music, away from something that can be captured on a CD, downloaded from the internet, consumed on an MP3 player; and that the very making of recorded music will seem an entirely two-dimensional 20th-century aspiration to the creative music-makers of the next few decades.

I may want to use an embroidered version of these repeated sentences once again at the end of this book. But this evening I felt the need to restate them before I try and put on paper the next two topics on my list: 1981 and Pete Waterman. But first I should let you know the ginger tom is out on his high wall and the sycamore is standing silent, secure in the knowledge that he knows all that is worth knowing.

When punk happened it was great for all the many reasons well documented by hundreds of writers about music. But by its very nature punk had to be a back-to-basics thing; the downside of this was that all its aspirations were so retro and conservative. Punk wanted to re-establish a conformity of what a band is and does. It wanted to bring rock music and the rock band back to a form that had been defined almost 15 years earlier: a drummer, a bass player, a guitarist or two and a singer trying to tell the world how shitty everything was or how much in love he is, in some vague hope that some part of society will be shocked, or at least stop what they are doing for a few minutes and take notice. When The Who sang *My Generation* and smashed up their equipment live on stage in 1966 nothing had ever sounded or looked like it before. When the Pistols, Clash and Damned took to the highways of the land a decade later it was great fun for all involved at the time and made entertaining copy for the music papers. But with any sort of overview it looked and sounded very dull, and as musically interesting as the trad jazz revival of the 1950s.

What was far more interesting within the sphere of popular music was what Giorgio Moroder, Kraftwerk, The Residents and a few others were doing. I'm not going to describe what these three plus the others were making, it's enough to tell you and remind myself that they started to make records that ditched the whole notion that pop records needed guitar, drums, bass players and all that boring old-fashioned stuff. Pop records could be made using synthesisers, drum machines and computers. Records could be made that didn't hark back to Buddy Holly or have to be rooted in some way in the American R&B traditions of the 1950s. The theory was that with a few bits of cheap gear and a four-track tape recorder great pop records could be made that were far more forward-thinking than any by the punk bands.

But Kraftwerk, Giorgio Moroder and The Residents all came from distant shores. There was no way we felt we had the wherewithal to make records as modern and future sounding as that in Liverpool. Even with our Lori And The Chameleons records we were relying on guitars and real drums and 1960s-sounding keyboards.

I want to clamber back in through the window and check Google to find out exactly when *Being Boiled* by The Human League and *Warm Leatherette* by The Normal came out but I can't be arsed. But those two records were the first I heard by British music-makers after the supposed watershed of punk in 1976–77 that sounded like they were made by people who wanted music to have nothing to do with all the guitar-driven retro pop / rock that had been going on for almost 20 years.

By the time these two records had made their impact in my head, Dave Balfe and I were too committed to the careers of Echo And The Bunnymen and The Teardrop Explodes to be ditching everything to follow some electro dream. And our Lori And The Chameleons thing had failed so on my part any thought of making music myself was shelved forever. Or that's what I thought then. While managing the Teardrops and Bunnymen I tried to ignore how boringly traditional they were in so many ways, and concentrate on what was great about them. In fact, while managing the Bunnymen I was able to convince myself once again that the rock band as a form was still, and maybe would always be, the greatest medium for an artist. But I was doing it as a manager, not as a mere member of the band.

Drummond has written about what he attempted to do with Echo And The Bunnymen in a story called *From The Shores Of Lake Placid.* This was first published on a series of 20 posters that were fly-posted around Liverpool in November 1998. It was then published in a small book of the same title (Penkiln Burn Book One) in an edition of 500 in December 1998. The story was latterly included in *45.*

But all my reinvigorated belief in the rock band came apart at the seams on the night of 4 June 1981 in New York City. I was staying at the Gramercy Park Hotel, so I suppose I was over there trying to make something happen for Echo And The Bunnymen in the States. Also staying in the hotel were The Clash. As I have written earlier; watching and hearing The Clash play in Eric's in Liverpool on the evening of 5 May in 1977 was a pivotal moment in my musical life. Did I say before that it was seeing The Clash that night that had restored my belief that the rock band was possibly the most powerful medium going?

Yeah, I know this runs contrary to what I was saying about how retro and therefore worthless those punk bands were, but if you can't hold at least half-a-dozen contradictory theories at any one time, you are probably not flesh and blood.

Back to The Clash. They were managed by this bloke called Bernie Rhodes. He was almost up there with Malcolm McLaren as an English punk-mentor figure. It was supposedly him who politicised The Clash and got them wearing those clothes with stencilled slogans on them.

It was while down in Rockfield Studios in Wales mixing some track that I first met up with Bernie Rhodes. He was there working on a record by a new protégé of his called Johnny Britain. This lad had a quiff and a young Cliff Richard vibe about him; it all seemed a bit Larry Parnes to me. At the time Bernie was temporarily in retirement as The Clash's manager. He had pissed them off or something. Bernie was a motormouth and at the Gramercy he was back in his position as The Clash's manager. He was full of plans for how they were going to tear America apart and start a revolution. Or at least that was the implication. His room in the Gramercy was an open forum for debate. The walls and floor were covered in roughs of ideas for posters, all heavily borrowing on Latin American revolutionary chic.

The Clash were playing a series of dates at this massive old ballroom called Bonds in Manhattan. The place held 3,000 but because of fire regulations they could only sell 1,300 tickets a night. They did at least a dozen shows there, all of them sold out. The Clash were about to go stadium.

I didn't get to know The Clash themselves in any particular depth. They always seemed to be totally stoned on grass while Bernie was going on about revolution. They did little more than nod their heads to whatever he was going on about while lounging about in Clash-like poses. My take on it was they seemed to be more interested in behaving like traditional rock stars, more than happy to pull the clichéd rock 'n' roll rebel poses than ever entertaining any real revolutionary thinking or action.

I know this was all four years after the height of the anti-hippy punk puritanism of 1977, but on a surface level The Clash just seemed like a bunch of dope-smoking Ladbroke Grove hippies, but with short haircuts. Not that I felt particularly let down by them in this sense, just surprised.

Bernie gave me tickets for the show on 4 June. I went not knowing what to expect. What I got was the dullest, most rambling rock performance I had ever experienced in my life. Much of the audience just lay around on the floor as if they were at a free festival. It was hard to believe this was the same band that had played at Eric's on 5 May 1977.

Later that same evening I was asked to go to a club with a bloke called Roger Aimes who was one of the A&R men at Phonogram records who The Teardrops were signed to. Roger and I were to be the guests of Kid Creole and a couple of his Coconuts. I don't know what the connection between Creole and Aimes was but they seemed to know each other well. Kid Creole was dressed in the full get-up that he was famous for.

The club was down some dingy backstreet by the docks. From the outside it was not what I was expecting. Kid Creole's image was all late 1940s Cuban glamour, cocktails and Latin Rhythms – not this. Nothing could have prepared me for what I was about to witness inside the club. The place was rammed. The clientele were almost all black, and other than the two female Coconuts, all male and very gay. The club was made up of numerous rooms; it was impossible to get any idea of how big the place actually was as it was so chock-full and difficult to get around. There were a number of these fake classical pedestals around the place. On them were huge vases of white lilies. These vases of lilies were picked out by small spotlights. On the bar top was a massive glass bowl of quartered oranges.

This was like no nightclub that I had ever been in before. The energy in the place was everything The Clash at Bonds was not. The unseen sound system was pumping out tune after tune of which I had never heard the like before. Mainly they were stripped-back extended mixes of shuddering electro tracks with soul divas' voices on top; they almost made the Giorgio Moroder records I knew sound like kids' stuff. Track after track, all seamlessly segueing into each other. Never a drop in energy level. If there was a DJ somewhere in this club who was responsible for this he must have been a genius. Up until then I had thought of a DJ as someone who put records on, did a bit of chat in-between and hoped to get a job on local radio. This was something else altogether. It was literally an ocean away from cheesy Euro disco or the soul-boy sounds that dance club would have been playing in the UK.

Then this woman took to a small and cramped stage. She had a cleavage that heaved and a mountain of hair. She was handed a mic, she opened her mouth and out came the most beautiful, scary, sexy, rich, heart-stopping voice. It sounded even better than Betty Wright when I saw her sing at Shades nightclub in Coventry in 1975. I knew immediately it was the voice of Chaka Khan of Rufus fame. She only did three songs but the place went wild. But what I couldn't understand was why she was just singing to a backing track. There was no band. This was something I had never seen before. Theoretically I thought I should have felt cheated – only three songs and no live band – but it felt like one of the best performances I had been to in my life

I left the club immediately, not even bothering to find Aimes, Kid Creole or his Coconuts to say thanks and bye. On leaving the place I noticed it was called The Paradise Garage and have since learnt it was touted as one of the seminal dance clubs that many since have tried to copy. (Since I have rarely been to any sort of clubs, I wouldn't know.)

It was a mile or so back to the Gramercy Hotel. On that walk back people could have been shot and mugged all around me, planes could have been flying into the World Trade Centre and King Kong could have been climbing the Empire State building, I would not have noticed a thing. Inside my head it was all going off, all being worked out. A summary of it was that rock music, in whatever subgenre it preferred to wallow in, was over. Dead. The whole thing was a charade. A worthless one at that. Peopled by pathetic white boys and men pretending to be what they weren't. And what is worse, it was dull, boring, backward-looking, smug and used up. All electric guitars, bass guitars, drum kits, Marshall stacks, Fender twin reverbs, wah-wah pedals, effects pedals of any kind, plectrums, spare strings, Vox AC30s and especially any 1959 Gibson Les Paul Gold Top Deluxe should all be gathered together and burnt and their ashes dumped unceremoniously in the Hudson River.

Then a line of thinking developed. Not so much a theory, more just some questions – and maybe the answer is obvious to you, or if not you, to some academic who knows about these things. This is it: how come the makers of modern Western popular music of the past few decades who are white are always looking back to a golden age? Even in my Birth of Rock 'n' Roll chapter it was a skiffle band. The skiffle craze in Britain of the mid-1950s was trying to mimic something from prewar America, as was the trad jazz boom of the same era.

In the 1960s the vast majority of British rock bands, and subsequently American rock bands, looked back to the black bluesmen of the 1950s or earlier as the greats or the rock 'n' roll 'founding fathers'. Then there were all the various folk revivals. By the time we get to punk we get bands drawing their influences from bands who 10 or 15 years earlier had in turn looked back to the aforementioned bluesmen.

Every corner of modern popular music-making done by white people seems to suffer from this. But none of this is the case with American black music-makers. They seem to abhor the past. The 1920s jazz of Louis Armstrong was the most modern thing on the planet. Come the 1930s it was replaced by the big bands, Basie and Ellington defining what was modern; Louis Armstrong was left for white folks. Then the birth of 'cool' in 1948 and Charlie Parker and the bebop revolution made Basie and Ellington old-fashioned and irrelevant. And on through the decades with soul, funk, hip hop, modern R&B. Always and forever it seems the black music- makers of the USA are never interested in looking back, only in looking forward to what is next. For them there never was a golden age. Or if there is one it is always yet to come.

You would never have got young black musicians in the 1950s wanting to form trad jazz bands like the young white musicians in 1950s Britain were doing. They would have all been too busy discovering what noises you could get out of the electric guitar or exploring the furthest reaches of bebop. We got Aker Bilk and Kenny Ball; they got Miles Davis and Sun Ra.

Once the electric guitar was invented how many black musicians would have bothered with the acoustic guitar? As for the banjo, I bet a black American musician hasn't touched one since 1929. Every time since 1970 I have seen black American musicians play they have always used the latest equipment. None of that searching out pre-CBS Fender Stratocasters when you can be playing the latest Japanese import guitars. Each genre of black music that evolves completely eclipses and makes redundant what has gone before. The only black men who sing the blues today are very old and the only people who pay to watch them are white.

The only creators of black music to take an interest in the past music are hip hop DJs, on the lookout for breaks, beats and samples to use in the music they are making now. And they would be totally insulted if anyone thought that the music they were making was trying in any way to mimic or honour or revive music from past decades. White music-makers look to the past or to black music to give integrity to what they do. Black music-makers only ever look to the future for integrity and no black musician has ever looked to white-made music for any sort of inspiration.

Why? Maybe it's about slavery. The black man has very little he wants to look back at. The best is always yet to come. But that is another whole thing and I would be way out of my depth to comment on it. The only black man you would see with an afro in this day and age (2006) I would wager hangs out with a lot of white liberals. It is impossible for a black man to be postmodern. He just keeps being more modem than those who thought themselves modern yesterday.

Look, I know there is a lot of bollocks in what I am spouting but in the early hours of 5 June 1981 as I lurched along the sidewalks of New York between the Paradise Garage and the Gramercy Park Hotel, it all made sense.

Paul: I guess he's talking about a specific part of black culture related to black pop music – hip hop or R&B for example. The fact that he's using this term 'the black man' made me laugh because it's one of those classic awkward things where he's trying to be upfront and unapologetic in his use of language, but to me it sounds a bit weird and outdated. For one, it's a bit sexist seeing as he's really talking about black culture.

On arriving back at the hotel a couple of members of The Clash were turning up with their entourage. I wanted to beat the shit out of them for being such fakers. Of course I didn't. I went to bed and had a wank instead. It was Chaka Khan's cleavage that did it for me.

The next morning I remembered I was still the manager of Echo And The Bunnymen and whatever theories I may have about music had to be kept in

The bit about afros and postmodernism is plain wrong. You DO see kids with afros worn in a 'postmodern' way –

check while I got on with the job in hand.

Back in Britain I got the sense that what I was feeling was a bit of a zeitgeist thing, that I was not the only person with these thoughts about the redundancy of the rock band. More and more music-makers seemed to be rising up across the country, getting signed to record labels, having hits – *Just Can't Get Enough* by Depeche Mode, *Tainted Love* by Soft Cell, not a guitar or sweaty drummer in sight. But it was the makers of 1978's *Being Boiled* who delivered what I believe was the defining moment of the revolution that was beginning to happen all around – *Don't You Want Me Baby* by The Human League and every other song on their album, Dare, for me was the clarion call that was needed.

like OutKast did or whatever – and they don't hang around with white liberals.

Rasmus: I like the idea that they are not able to be postmodern, because what are they then? Are they modern, or are they something else completely? If they are, then can I be that as well?

Dare by The Human League was future-looking in every way. It didn't borrow from black American culture or the past; it was totally confident in what it was about. It was a celebration of now. And it was incredibly successful around the world. It was everything I thought modern music should be.

Of course The Human League, or any of the others, couldn't keep it up. The year 1981 was a false dawn. Rock 'n' roll did not die the death I wanted it to die, and on a personal level, my own love for rock 'n' roll would still flare up from time to time like some recurring medical disorder.

PETE WATERMAN – THE GENIUS
4 October 2006

Last night I was sitting out there on the ledge to way past one o'clock getting my 1981 chapter done. That whole black versus white theory – I had no idea it was coming. Only after I started to try and recall each street I walked between The Paradise Garage and the Gramercy Park Hotel did I remember how it was on that walk that my whole theory on the difference between black and white attitudes to making music started to evolve.

Reading it this morning, back out on the ledge, I realise there are a couple of things I missed. The Specials had just had their number one hit with *Ghost Town*. I loved *Ghost Town*. You may remember that The Specials were part of the Two Tone ska revival. The Specials and the rest of them dressed up in pork pie hats and sharp and tight tonic suits that I had remembered young cool black guys would have worn in the mid-1960s. The Specials had a couple of black guys in the band. They used to look totally uncomfortable in this get-up. I used to think there was no way they would choose to wear those clothes outside of the band. No way would they want to ape the style of their dads' generation. Just as today no young black lad would be seen doing the whole Rasta pose. The Specials was a totally white concept; having a couple of black lads in the band just gave it a look of authenticity for all the white kids who bought the records.

The trouble is, me being white, British and an unreconstructed postmodern man, I cannot help but do all that looking back, mix and match, borrowing from whatever hasn't been borrowed from for a while. It's in the genes or it's in some part of me and I can't cut it out.

Later in 1981 I saw The Ramones play Hammersmith Palais. Everything about The Ramones was retro. Their whole thing seemed to be about celebrating a time that never existed. We all knew they were complete fakes. Even if they wore those black leather jackets, T-shirts, ripped jeans and Converse sneakers every day of their lives and they slept in them as well, we knew it was just a costume. An act. But that night at the Hammersmith Palais I thought they were brilliant. I could see through it all but that did not dim their genius in my eyes.

Even worse, the following May (1982) The Clash brought out their album Combat Rock. I thought it was fantastic, one of the best albums ever made. It wasn't the case that my faith in rock was restored, it is just that I am riddled with inconsistencies. I may want to be as modern as the black man but my genes won't let me.

But that is all a long time ago and maybe things are changing. In defining what gang you bear your allegiance to, among the gangs of teenagers around where I live in north-east London, the colour of your skin or where your grandparents came from means far less than the estate you live on or your postcode. Although we may deplore modern gang culture it seems refreshing that it is based on something that cannot be exploited by the nationalist parties of previous decades.

This chapter is supposed to be about Pete Waterman and I have spent the last couple of pages attempting to wrap up the previous chapter.

Spring 1985. I am sitting in my office at WEA Records in Broadwick Street, Soho, staring out the window and wondering if I was now a corporate arsehole or whether I genuinely looked cool in my new Paul Smith suit, when this bloke walks in unannounced. A bloke that I have never seen before and he starts talking to me like he has known me all his life. He starts telling me how he used to manage The Specials, that he had spent Christmas with Michael Jackson and he is about to be the biggest thing in pop music in the 1980s and then he started going on about steam trains and why The Beatles were still the greatest pop band ever ('until they went weird') and Tamla Motown was the greatest label ever and he was the new Berry Gordy.

What I was looking at was a white middle-aged man with grey hair and a demented stare and an accent from somewhere north of Watford and bad dress sense (he wasn't wearing a Paul Smith suit).

I asked him if he wanted a cup of tea and what his name was. He said yes to the first question and Pete Waterman to the second. He then told me that he had produced *You Spin Me Right Round (Like A Record Baby)* for Dead Or Alive. I've mentioned Pete Burns before, how I was not the sort of person he wanted to be seen speaking to. What I didn't say was that I thought *You Spin Me Right Round* was one of the best records ever made. I decided that either this strange man was lying or I should be listening to him. I listened. He told me that if I had any bands in need of a hit, he and the two lads he'd got working with him could deliver the goods.

I told him there was this band that I had just signed to the label and we were looking for a producer and that they were called Brilliant and they were playing that night at the Wag Club, just around the corner. He told me that he would be there, that he knew Paul McCartney and that he used to DJ in the club in Coventry where I used to go in 1974/5 where I saw Betty Wright. He told me it was him who put her on and we both agreed that TK Records was the best record label of the 1970s and Hamilton Bohannon was a genius. He drank his tea and left.

That night at The Wag Club this band called Brilliant sounded shit. They had been formed by Youth, the bass player from Killing Joke. I had only signed them because my friend and sometime working partner Dave Balfe was managing them and Youth could talk a good band. The band had two bass players for some reason that only Youth could defend. They had a guitarist who wanted to be Jimmy Page, a drummer who drummed and a keyboard player who made keyboard sounds. The songs were a dreary mush of white-boy funk but they had this singer who was this striking black girl with a husky but fragile voice.

Pete Waterman turned up halfway through their set. He immediately came up to me and before he had heard one complete song said that they were shit but if I would sack the band but keep the singer and give him £3,000 next week, he knew just the song she could sing and we would have a top 10 hit in a matter of weeks. Then he left.

Next morning he was back in my office. 'Have you sacked the band yet?'

We then had some convoluted conversation that took in discussing the Flying Scotsman versus the Mallard (trains), Chaka Khan versus Aretha Franklin and why U2 were shite. At some point David Balfe joined us and a compromise was arrived at. The compromise was this: we would sack everybody in the band but Youth 'cause it was his band in the first place and the guitarist who wanted to be Jimmy Page because he did really good artwork and of course the girl singer, whose name was June Montana.

Dave Balfe and I wanted to know what the song was that would deliver the top 10 hit. Pete Waterman said he couldn't tell us until he got half the £3,000 in his bank account. The other half he wanted before he handed over the tapes.

We shook hands on the deal. Then he told us another thing. He wouldn't be wanting Youth or the guitarist who wanted to be Jimmy Page playing on the record.

Two weeks later I'm down on this building site in Borough (south London). The building site is some backstreet Victorian workshops that are being converted into a recording studio. I'm with Dave Balfe, Youth, June Montana and the guitarist whose name was Jimi [sic] Cauty. The session was supposed to have started that morning. There is not even a mixing desk in the place, let alone microphones and tape machine. Pete Waterman is there showing his bank manager around, introducing us to his bank manager as record company moguls and the band as the future superstars he is going to be producing. He was talking complete bullshit that the bank manager could surely see through. Youth, Jimi and June certainly could. We left wondering why we had ever handed over £1,500 to this mouthy madman. If it wasn't for the proven fact that he had produced *You Spin Me Around*, I think we would have cut our losses and never had any more to do with him.

A week later I got a call from him. 'Where are you? All the backing tracks are nearly done and we need that girl singer of yours in here tonight to get the song finished.' And we still didn't know what song he believed would give Brilliant a top 10 record.

I made a couple of calls and Youth, Jimi, June, Balfe and I headed down to Borough. Part of the building site was now shuttered off. Inside was a makeshift studio, no recording booth, just a mixing desk and a pair of NS 10 speakers and a couple of keyboards.

We were met by Waterman who introduced us to his boys, Matt and Mike, and told us the track was sounding brilliant and only needed the vocals to complete it, and could he get his other £1,500 in the morning? We still didn't know what the song was and Youth and Jimi were having an understandable artistic crisis about the fact that a record was being made that was to be released under their group name that they had not written or played a note on and that they didn't as yet have any no idea what the song was.

Matt and Mike were a couple of friendly soul boys and they instantly put us at ease. Pete Waterman got them to play the backing track back to us. It sounded completely different to anything I might have expected. For a start it was in 12 / 4 time. It was moody and spacey and seductive. All the sounds were keyboard generated, all very modern but like dark chocolate. I wanted to say it sounded like a Jimmy Jam and Terry Lewis production but thought I might offend if I did. In the mid-1980s the Jam and Lewis production team were making the best-sounding records in the world. They were young, black and from somewhere in the States. By 1985 all the British groups that had dared to sound modern in 1981 had either given up, been forgotten or were trying to be rock bands. It was only people like Jam and Lewis who were still daring to make records in a way I'd never heard before. And here I was in a broom cupboard of a studio in south London listening to something that sounded like Jam and Lewis.

After a few bars I started to recognise the chord changes, but not what song they belonged to.
'You guessed it yet? We've used the rhythm from *Change Of Heart* by Change. You know, the Jam and Lewis production.'
June Montana was the first to guess the song. 'It's not *Man's World* by James Brown?'
'In one,' replied Waterman.
'I can't sing *It's A Man's World*. It's the ultimate male chauvinist song.'
'That's where you are wrong and why you singing it will make it a bigger song than James Brown's original ever was.'
'How come?' said June.
'Here are the lyrics. The mike is set up through that door; you just go out there and sing it. Then come back and listen to what you have done and then you will see why it is potentially one of the greatest female anthems ever to be released.'

Jimi and Youth didn't have a chance to say anything. Out went June with the lyrics and after a few tries she found a way of singing the song to the tempo of the backing track. And then she was asked to come back through to listen to what they had done. Pete Waterman was right. Those lyrics justifying the ultimate male-dominated world were completely changed in meaning as soon as they were sung by a woman.

Pete Waterman got his £1,500 the next morning but it didn't go as smoothly as we might all have hoped. For a start, the track needed quite a bit more work. This included using a machine called a Greengate to record Youth playing the bass and Jimi playing the guitar. At that time in 1985 I had not heard of the word sample or sampler but this Greengate machine was a sampler. A very primitive one by today's standards. Matt and Mike were able to take a snatch of Youth's and Jimi's playing and use it in the recording of *Man's World*. This went some way to placate Youth's and Jimi's desire as musicians to have played on their own record without having to go through the messy business of actually having musicians playing real instruments.

Those back at the various departments of the record company thought the track sounded like a future hit. Those whose job it is to plug the record to radio stations thought that Radio 1 would love it. I was pleased that they were all pleased and felt somewhat vindicated in having signed such a stodgy band to the record label. It was agreed that Pete Waterman should be contracted to produce the proposed album by Brilliant. Waterman agreed 'cause he needed the money to finish the studio.

Now for the real reason I wanted to write this chapter.

Over the following nine months or so we spent hundreds of thousands of pounds of the band's future royalties down at Pete Waterman's studio. By the time we were done the studio was built. Mike, Matt and Pete were about to define the sound of British pop music for the latter half of the 1980s and turn their surnames, Stock, Aitken and Waterman, into a global brand name for light and breezy throwaway pop.

But for June, Youth, Jimi, Balfe and me it was a different story. *It's A Man's World* was not a hit. Radio 1 did not love it. Neither did they like the next two singles that were released under the band's name. As for the rest of the album, without a hit there was no point in releasing it. It was not like they were a real band any longer whose career you could build by them going out and playing live. If they didn't have hit singles, nobody would buy the album. So there was no point in going to the expense of pressing up the record and releasing it. Brilliant got dropped by the label and I left before I got sacked.

But – and this for me is the important but – in those months down at Pete Waterman's studio, I learnt something from his approach to doing what he does which has influenced everything I have done since and the way that I see music. And it is not that I have wanted to churn out cheesy production-line pop that can sell by the millions or become an over-opinionated mouthy multimillionaire. What I learnt was how to make records, and I guess Jimmy Cauty [Jimi] and Youth did too.

Although Dave Balfe and I had produced Echo And The Bunnymen and Teardrop Explodes records, that had not involved any great vision. It was just a case of trying to tighten up the arrangements of the songs the bands had already written, to stop the band falling out or getting too wasted while recording, to get everything to sound OK and trying to get something that both the band could feel proud of and the record company could sell. So much of making records that way is about taking into account the fragile egos of individual band members, keeping everybody at least moderately happy.

Bill Drummond

The first thing I learnt from Waterman was to dispense with the idea of musicians having any say in what the record is to sound like. Musicians will only ever be bothered with how good they sound, not the overall sound of the record. Drummers will always want the drums to sound louder; guitarists, the guitars and so on. Musicians, by definition, have chosen a particular instrument and then spent years learning to play. They view and hear the world as a drummer or guitarist or whatever.

Pete Waterman wanted to make modern-sounding records. Records for now. If you used musicians on making records, they always had a tendency to make them sound old-fashioned because all musicians hark back. They – even if they don't know it – want to play something that sounds like something on some other record from the past. If you can get a machine to do that part, then all the better. So no real drums, that is a given. Use a real drummer and they just start going on about their favourite drummers from the past and try to use the recording session as a platform to prove what a great drummer they are.

Matt and Mike were both more than adequate musicians themselves. But they had a rule – never play on a record you are making. If you play on it, your ego as a musician will cloud your judgement of what is right for the record that is being made. Matt and Mike would always have a keyboard player hired in to play all the parts. That way they never had qualms ditching any part that had been recorded in favour of trying something else. This meant that they were never trying to make a record that pandered to the sensibilities of the musicians who might be involved.

Now, up until then it had been Matt and Mike this and Matt and Mike that. That is because it was Matt and Mike who were working in the studio all the time. Pete would only come into the studio once or twice a day, or if specifically asked to come in and listen to something. That way his ears were always fresh. Matt and Mike might have been working away for six hours with a keyboard player or singer on some track and Pete could walk in and say, 'You got it completely wrong, lads. Barking up the wrong tree' and then start describing what he thought it should sound like. Often what they had spent the last six hours on was trying to make real what he had described to them six hours earlier. The problem was that Pete could not play a note on any instrument and had no idea about any music theory, so his descriptions of what he was after or could hear in his head were always completely abstract. This could drive Mike and Matt up the wall.

That was the problem, but why this also worked completely brilliantly was

238

that Pete had a massive love and encyclopaedic knowledge of the hit single. He had gained his musical education as a DJ in clubs around the country playing the Tamla or soul hits of the day. He had learned exactly what made the kids want to get up and dance or sing along to. Although he loved pop music, I don't think he ever listened to it for his own satisfaction. He listened to it for what other people could get out of it. Pete loved whatever made people want to dance, or cry, or smooch, or fall in love. But he didn't only love the old Tamla stuff; he loved the new R&B records from the States as in the Jimmy Jam and Terry Lewis-produced records and I'm sure today it would be Neptune or whoever are the R&B producers of the moment.

Of course he was a slippery customer as well and he knew it. He would phone and book dates to get June, Youth and Jimi down, only for them to turn up at his studio to find Matt and Mike working with Mel & Kim or whoever it was.

The recording of the Brilliant album paid for his studio while he got his empire going. Within 12 months of the Brilliant album being shelved and the band being dropped by WEA, Mike Stock, Matt Aitken and Pete Waterman were the most successful production team in the world and defined what British pop music was to sound like in the late 1980s. And yes, I thought most of what they did sounded like formulaic rubbish that I would never want to listen to even if it was the only piece of music I had. But the man was a genius.

What I got from him, and in their own ways Jimmy and Youth got it too, was the importance of having an overview of what you are doing. Never treat anything you do as precious – be willing to dump everything and start again. Don't get drawn into the technical details. Don't be impressed by musicianship; trust your instincts and be willing to move on if your instincts are proved wrong.

Without being witness to the way Mike and Matt and Pete worked, Jimmy Cauty and I could never have made the KLF records. It informed us in so many ways even though what we did and were about was completely different. It also informs so much of what I'm trying to do with The17, even though there may be a million miles between *I Should Be So Lucky* by Kylie Minogue and The17 climbing a mountain to listen to the wind or whatever. Just don't ask me to define exactly what it is that I have been informed about.

FOR VARIOUS REASONS
8 October 2006

In one of the early chapters near the beginning of the book, where I'm on the ferry heading for Gothenburg and laying out my predicament with music, well, I missed a whole chunk out. As well as evolving my alphabetical listening system for the next 26 years, I also contemplated what it would be like to hear music for the first time after not having heard any for a whole year. Once this idea was in my head I could not shake it off. I indulged in fantasies of being some rustic, from a bygone era, wandering into a city after spending the previous 12 months in my hut in a wood somewhere. And in the city, being drawn to the biggest building around, the cathedral. Walk in from the hustle and bustle of the broad daylight marketplace into the dark and still of the cathedral. Find somewhere to sit down and rest my feet 'cause it feels like I've been tramping for days. Sitting there I start to wonder at the sunlight shafting its way through the massive stainglass window high above the altar when ...

... when from some unseen place the cathedral is filled with the sound of a choir. In my fantasy it doesn't matter what they are singing, it is just that huge sound swirling around the natural reverb of the cathedral. The massive chords made of human voices from the high trebles down to foundation-vibrating bass.

Often I would find myself contemplating what that experience would be like. And this contemplation would be a stronger and more powerful musical experience than just listening to music on a CD. Even if it was a CD I really liked.

Now this going a year without music is no more than a fantasy. There is no way that any of us living anything like a normal life could live without hearing music for a whole year. In modern life music is almost everywhere, seeping out of the buildings we pass as we get on with our daily lives. Even if we never deliberately switch it on or play an instrument.

Then I wondered at the possibilities of not hearing any music for a month. Nah, no way that could work either.

A week? Maybe. So I wrote a score about not listening to any music for a week. I worked on it and worked on it, chiselling away at the words. This became one of the original scores for when the idea of The17 was beginning to evolve into a reality. But even though I loved the idea of it and thought the words looked aesthetically great on the page, I knew it too would be impossible for me to do, if not anyone else. So finally my original vision of 365 days without hearing a note of music shrunk down to a mere one day.

But once I had settled on attempting to go one day without hearing or playing any music for 24 hours the idea started to expand. This one-day could be one day every year. No Music Day – an annual event, like no smoking day or breast cancer awareness day and all those other this-that-and-the-other days. So there's an element of irony, but not enough to put me off. And on my No Music Day, I would use the allotted 24 hours to contemplate what I wanted and what I didn't want from music. Not only to blindly – or should that be deafly – consume what was on offer. A day where I could develop ideas, of how this could be achieved.

But on what day should No Music Day fall? As a teenager I had a friend who was in a band called St Cecilia, I asked him, 'Why the fuck are you called St Cecelia? He replied, 'She's the patron saint of music, thicko.' I have no idea what this Cecelia did to become the patron saint of music, but what I did find out from Google was that her Saint's Day is on 22 November and this is the day we are supposed to celebrate music, to thank God for its existence. I decided that No Music Day should be on the day before St Cecilia's Day. Using the same traditional principles as having Hallowe'en the day before All Saint's Day or Mardi Gras on the day before Lent kicks in.

This was back in early 2005, thus my first No Music Day was to be that coming November. I imagined No Music Day 2005 was going to be a personal affair, but as with a number of the other things I've been doing over the past few years, I found myself turning it around, so it became an invitation for other people as well. These are the words that I wrote in my notebook at the time:

On No Music Day:
No hymns will be sung.
No records will played on the radio.
iPods will be left at home.
Rock bands will not rock.
Conductors will not take the podium.
Decks will not spin.
The needle will not drop.
The piano lid will not be lifted.
Films will have no soundtrack.

Jingles will not jangle.
Milkmen will not whistle.
Choirboys will shut their mouths.
Recording studios will not roll.
MCs will not pass the mic.
Brass band practice will be postponed.
The strings will not serenade.
Plectrums will not pluck.
Record shops will be closed all day.
And you will not take part in any sort of music making or listening whatsoever.

No Music Day exists for various reasons, you may have one.

It being the times we live in, I registered the domain name nomusicday.com and working with colleagues Gavin Bush, John Hirst and Cally, got a very basic website up and online. The No Music Day statement above was used as the declaration at the site. Other than having that to read, all that was required of the visitor to the site was to make their own statement in response to the two following prompts –

I will be observing No Music Day by:
I am observing No Music Day because:

You could also view, in theory, the statements already posted by other visitors to the site. That was it, nothing else.

Some time in spring 2005, the Merseyside-based but Scottish artist Alan Dunn asked me to take part in one of his billboard projects. In this one he was asking a number of different artists to design a billboard poster, for whatever ends they wanted. Alan Dunn had in mind a billboard site by the Liverpool entrance to the Wallasey Tunnel under the Mersey. Each artist would have their poster up for a month; my allotted time was to be mid-October to mid-November 2005. This seemed the perfect opportunity to launch No Music Day. I accepted Alan Dunn's offer.

The poster was designed with Cally. It was printed and, come October 2005, John Hirst and I went up to Liverpool to witness the billboard being pasted up. It looked stark and stunning. Or at least I thought it did, on a gloriously dreary overcast northern day towards the back end of the year. Perfection. All the billboard poster had on it was the word NOTICE in huge red letters on a white background. Underneath that, in smaller black type: 'No Music Day; 21st November'; and then in even smaller type in the bottom left-hand corner: 'PB Billboard One 2005'; and in the bottom right: 'www.NoMusicDay.com'. Alan Dunn took photos of it going up and complete in all its glory; these can be seen at alandunn67.com/piesnomusicday.html.

So this billboard poster was the launch of nomusicday.com; no press release, nothing in the media, no viral campaign on the net, but almost immediately hundreds, then thousands of people were visiting the site. They were leaving their statements in droves as to how and why they were to be observing No Music Day. Of course many of them were in total disagreement with what they perceived the sentiments of the site to be. 'Why the fuck should anybody tell me when and when not I can listen to music?' and 'Who the fuck do you think you are?' being a regular style of response. But most importantly a nerve had been touched, a chord struck.

As for my own No Music Day in 2005, I can't recall any great revelations and I do not think music sounded all fabulous, shiny and new come the following dawn. What I do remember was getting in my Land Rover to drive somewhere and automatically switching on the radio, BBC Radio 3, a classical music station. It was a couple of minutes before I realised what I had done. I was not struck by a thunderbolt, just a twinge of private embarrassment.

This year I've let the idea of No Music Day evolve a little. The 'No hymns will be sung etc.' text now exists as one of the scores to be performed by The17. Resonance FM approached me, the London-based art radio station. They were interested in getting involved. I said 'Good'. They are now planning a day without music content in any of their shows. This means that producers and presenters, who would normally be broadcasting music-based programmes on 21 November, are going to have to think harder about what the content of their show on that particular day is to be. So as well as the usual non-music programming for the day, there will be debates, discussions, phone-ins on the nature of our almost unthinking consumption of music; and the changing nature of our relationship with music, now that we can have it where, when and while doing almost whatever we want. In fact a lot of the things that lie behind much of the thinking that has led to The17. Or at least that is the plan. Maybe all the individual programme-makers at Resonance FM will rise up and rebel and play 24 hours of non-stop music on the day.

The British Sunday paper *The Observer* has a monthly music supplement. They asked me to write 1,500 words about No Music Day. If you were to read that, it may mirror much of what I have written in this chapter. I already know that I want to kick this article off with the line – 'All music is shite. Discuss.'

Today (8 October 2006) is still almost six weeks away from 21 November 2006, time enough for unplanned events to affect the outcome of this year's No Music Day. In years to come it may fizzle out, or it may spread like a rash around the globe to a point where even iTunes shuts up shop for the day. It is now time for me to write those 1,500 words for *The Observer*.

Post Script: *The Guardian* has also asked me to write a piece for their weekly classical music page. A feature to tie in with this year's Huddersfield Contemporary Music Festival and The17's appearance at it.

SCORE

10. OBSERVE

NO MUSIC DAY: 21st NOVEMBER

ON NO MUSIC DAY:
NO HYMNS WILL BE SUNG.
NO RECORDS WILL BE PLAYED ON THE RADIO.
iPODS WILL BE LEFT AT HOME.
ROCK BANDS WILL NOT ROCK.
CONDUCTORS WILL NOT TAKE THE PODIUM.
DECKS WILL NOT SPIN.
THE NEEDLE WILL NOT DROP.
THE PIANO LID WILL NOT BE LIFTED.
FILMS WILL HAVE NO SOUNDTRACK.
JINGLES WILL NOT JANGLE.
MILKMEN WILL NOT WHISTLE.
CHOIRBOYS WILL SHUT THEIR MOUTHS.
RECORDING STUDIOS WILL NOT ROLL.
MCS WILL NOT PASS THE MIC.
BRASS BANDS PRACTICE WILL BE POSTPONED.
THE STRING WILL NOT SERENADE.
PLECTRUMS WILL NOT PLUCK.
RECORD SHOPS WILL BE CLOSED ALL DAY.
AND YOU WILL NOT TAKE PART IN ANY SORT OF MUSIC MAKING OR LISTENING WHATSOEVER.

NO MUSIC DAY EXIST FOR VARIOUS REASONS, YOU MAY HAVE ONE

To be performed on No Music Day; 21st of November, every year.
Visit nomusicday.com and register the fact that you will be performing this SCORE.

pb Poster 137   2006

Bill Drummond

MARMALADE ON TOAST
18 November 2006

The bacon, egg, black pudding, mushrooms and grilled tomatoes have arrived. So have hash browns that I did not ask for. The tablecloth is white linen, as is the napkin. The Royal Swan, where we are staying, does not do breakfast, so I have taken myself out onto the streets of Huddersfield to find a place open that does a full English. I am now sitting in the George Hotel's breakfast room, the George being the posh hotel that we are not staying in. It's 7.32. I've left John Hirst and Gimpo snoring and farting in their single beds. The first of the seven performances by The17 at the Huddersfield Contemporary Music Festival will be this afternoon.

At one of the other tables are four people. I assume they are The Smith Quartet. The Smith Quartet are currently my favourite contemporary string quartet in the world. They piss all over the Brodsky Quartet, who, in my eyes, cheapen themselves by doing all sorts of publicity-seeking collaborations with pop stars and world-music types. There is no messing with The Smiths (which is how, I am afraid, they are rather cringingly referred to in some circles.)

Over the past few years I have often had fantasies of The Smith Quartet doing a version of The KLF's *What Time Is Love*. This version by The Smiths would be a faithful interpretation of the original version that Jimmy Cauty and I did before we started throwing all the pop and rap rubbish into it.

The Smith Quartet, like The17, are performing at the festival all week. There is no way I am going to go over and introduce myself and there is even less chance that I would ever ask them if they would be interested in doing a version of *What Time Is Love*. That is just not the sort of thing they would do. That would be the sort of sell-out thing The Brodsky Quartet would do.

Before the breakfast arrived I was reading the piece that I had written about The17 for yesterday's *Guardian*. Yes, I know the rereading of a piece written by oneself once it is on the published page is an obvious and risible vanity but I can't stop myself. For me, the best thing about it is that it is on the classical music page. It is *The Guardian*'s lead feature on the Huddersfield Festival. From screaming 'Big in Japan, we're big in Japan' into the microphone at Bretton Hall in May 1977 to the classical music page in *The Guardian* via *Doctorin' The Tardis* by The Timelords seems like the perfect arc of a career. My pride is fit for bursting. So if you have a pin at hand, feel free.

The full English has been eaten and it's now time for the toast and marmalade and pot of Assam. And I bet those other two fuckers are still snoring.

There was a reason for bringing the notebook, pencil and yesterday's *Guardian* out with me on my search for breakfast. I was woken in the night by the youth of Huddersfield brawling and screaming in the street outside. While I lay there awake, I was filled with the urge to get up, get dressed, go out to the Land Rover, drive to a long stretch of wall that I had seen earlier, a wall at the side of the Huddersfield inner ring road. Once there I wanted to get out my large tub of white paint and large brush and paint one long line of graffiti. This graffiti would be made up of exactly 90 words The trouble was, the urge had to be thwarted as I remembered we had taken the paint and brush out of the back of the Land Rover when we were loading it up to drive to Huddersfield.

The 90 words that I wanted to disfigure / enhance this wall with were the first 90 words that I used in the piece in *The Guardian*. They are also the main body of text in the newest score written for The17. As a score I have given it pole position: it is Score 1 It is the first you would be presented with if you were to visit the17.org or the exhibition that Gimpo, John Hirst and myself hung yesterday at the North Light Gallery where The17 are to be based for the week. I may also use this text as a frontispiece for this book.

Over the past few months I have written these 90 words numerous times. The wording evolves slightly with each writing. I assumed that now they had made it onto a poster, framed and hanging in a gallery for all the world to see, the urge to keep writing them down would dry up. Not so. The urge has just risen to another level.

The urge to commit graffiti is one that I have had to live with for a long time. Other than a few minor incidents, I have been able to curb this urge since being up in front of the beak in Liverpool in early 2000. Then, I was handed down a moderate fine and made to pay the costs of having the wall cleaned. At that time the boss man on the bench was able to make me feel like a rather pathetic middle-aged man who had maybe suffered from a momentary lapse of sanity that would not happen again. I thanked him and told him it wouldn't happen again. I knew, though, these urges were not that easily thwarted. I imagined it must be the same with those who have Tourette's or a mass-murdering syndrome: you know it's silly and does nobody any good but you just can't stop yourself.

The words I want to paint in large white letters along the wall on the Huddersfield ring road are:

> Imagine waking up tomorrow morning and all music has disappeared. All musical instruments and all forms of recorded music, gone. A world without ...

... well you know the rest seeing as they have appeared at least a couple of times already in this book. But I can't stop thinking how great they would look and about all the people stuck in their cars in the morning rush-hour traffic jam, finding their eyes drawn to it as the only thing for their eyes to be looking at that wasn't there yesterday and every other day that they have been stuck in exactly the same place on their way to do the same job. Would they question the validity of the ASBOs being handed out to teenagers; would they think that something should be done about it? Or would they imagine a world without music? Whatever the source of that urge I had in the middle of the night and still have now as I spread the marmalade onto my third slice of toast, I can't stop the persuasive argument tempting me now. It goes something like this. As a score printed on a poster, framed in a tasteful oak frame, hung on the wall of a well-lit gallery, those 90 words have very little power. It's like they have been neutered. Had their balls cut off. No one gets to read them other than those they are least likely to affect. It is the same with so much art. As soon as it is in an art gallery, it is tamed. Safe. Just there as light entertainment for those who like the idea of being interested in art and ideas.

If the paint and brush had been in the Land Rover, I would have gone and done it. B&Q would soon be open. Maybe I should go down there after breakfast and get supplies. But as I write these words and bite into that third slice of toast and marmalade I remember the verbal agreement that I had made with Graham McKenzie some months ago. Before becoming director of the Huddersfield Festival he had been the director of the Centre for Contemporary Art (CCA) in Glasgow. At some point in the mid-1990s, Jimmy Cauty and I walked into the CCA, set up a 16mm projector and showed the film of us burning the million quid. An instant audience gathered to watch the film. We had not sought permission for this impromptu screening. It caused a kerfuffle and tempers were lost.

Some years later the CCA's new head of new media and performance was interested in me being part of an exhibition about Scotland by Scottish artists. At the time I had a habit of stealing motorway signs. On crossing the border into Scotland at the top end of the M6, just south of Gretna, there is a huge Scotland Welcomes You sign. My proposal was that I would brazenly remove this sign, replace it with a hand-painted one, then take the original Scotland Welcomes You sign in the back of a van up to Glasgow and hang it in the CCA within two hours of having removed it from the roadside.

As a youth I had been much taken by the story of four Scottish students in 1950 who had removed the Stone Of Destiny from under the throne in Westminster Abbey and returned it to Scotland where it belonged. Once the authorities got hold of it, it was taken back to London where it stayed until 1996 when it was finally officially returned to Scotland after having been in captivity for more than 600 years.

Now, nicking a motorway sign is nowhere near as heroic as removing the Stone of Destiny, but somewhere in my head there was a parallel. Especially as I knew the motorway sign would only be left hanging on the CCA walls for a few hours before it would be removed by the authorities and taken back down to the border.

The new head of new media and performance liked my idea but the others in senior positions at the CCA thought otherwise. At my first meeting with Graham McKenzie earlier this year (2006) he reminded me of this proposal and informed me that it was him who had put a stop to it. He also told me that he had not forgotten about the impromptu film-screening. He then went on to tell me that he would be more than pleased to have The 17 at this year's festival but he didn't want any 'high jinx' from me. I had given him my word that there would be none and that in fact any high jinx would undermine what I was trying to do with The17. He accepted my word and we shook hands on a deal.

But the urge is still there. 'Come on, Bill, man or mouse? Do you believe in this thing or not?'

And now, as the fourth slice of toast is spread with marmalade, I can hear John Hirst's voice in my head reminding me that doing something like a major graffiti would be the last thing that I need. It would just confirm all the prejudices held by those who think I am nothing more than a prankster. But the urge to get down to B&Q as soon as this fourth slice of toast has been dealt with and get a tin of white paint and a brush is still strong.

I do a deal with the urge. I will refrain from doing the graffiti on the Huddersfield inner ring road in exchange for doing it at an undisclosed date on a particular stretch of the North Circular in London.

Fourth slice is done with and washed down by the last gulp of Assam. As I put my bits away in my bag I notice that The Smith Quartet have already upped and left. I wonder what urges they have to strike deals with.

NO MUSIC DAY
21 November 2006

Sitting in the greenroom for the BBC Radio 4 Today programme. I'm waiting my turn to be called through to be interrogated by one of this morning's presenters. I'm shitting it. Still, I'm glad John Humphries is not on this morning.

The Today programme is something I have been listening to every weekday morning for at least the last 30 years of my life. Well, maybe not every morning but every one when I have spent the night in my own bed. To listen to the Today programme makes you feel you are part of the democratic process of the country without having to do a thing. Whoever holds the levers of power – the prime minister of the day, the captains of industry, the great, the good and the bad – are all hauled in and called to account. The Today programme is one of the few reasons to feel proud to be British, without feeling guilty at the same time.

I got here just before 8.00. I was told I was to be in the slot just after 8.20 but some international breaking news has pushed my fluff item back to about 8.50. This gives me time to collect my thoughts and make some notes.

Today is No Music Day. The second annual No Music Day. Over the past week the idea of No Music Day seems to have snowballed. Scores of requests for interviews have come in from around the globe, most of them asking the same questions and mostly I give the same answers.

What has surprised me is that no one has challenged me about the validity of today being No Music Day. No authority has come along and told me that I have not asked permission, have not filled out the right forms, not paid the subscriptions to whoever is in charge of allotting the days. I mean, I just made up this No Music Day thing, declared it to be, and now it is. People might disagree with it, think it is a pile of rubbish, a publicity-seeking stunt, but nobody has actually told me to stop it or that I can't do it or ...

And here I am about to go on the Today programme, the To-*fucking*-day programme, to discuss it with James Naughtie. Yes, it's true that this year I did put out a press release about it, but I wasn't expecting to get the response it has been getting. Maybe now there is so much media space to be filled they are all desperate for any content to fill it. But I haven't launched any sort of campaign. No adverts anywhere. No tie-in events. That last statement is not quite true. Resonance FM, the London-based art radio station, has embraced it and all the programme-makers have been instructed to make programmes for today that don't involve any music. So I suppose that is a tie-in event.

This morning, before I got the tube to the BBC, I put 'No Music Day' into Google. There were more than 36,000 entries. This, for some reason, seems to have hit a bigger nerve than the money-burning. I started skimming the thousands of blogs and message boards where it was being discussed. Out there in webland were countless people who seemed to have more idea why there should be a No Music Day, and what it signified, than I did. Fierce debates, jibes, ridicule, appreciation, thoughts, angles, propositions and people getting their facts wrong. No, I was not the lead singer of The KLF. No, I'm not a music-business insider. No, I'm not about to release a CD. There are people out there who seem to be able to argue the case for No Music Day far better than me. They should be in here doing the interview on the Today programme.

Of course I'm flattered by the attention it's getting, that it's being taken seriously by some and also as a bit of fluff – a here-today, gone-tomorrow news item.

Last week I added some text to nomusicday.com. These are some of the words:

> No Music Day is an aspiration, an idea, an impossible dream, a nightmare. There are as many reasons for marking No Music Day as there are people willing to observe it – or reject it.
> No Music Day has nothing to sell.
> There is no mission statement.

As for the thousands of entries on the site, maybe over the next few days I should go through them, pick out some of the ones I like, including some of the ones that lampoon the whole notion of the thing, and add them to the end of this chapter.

Three other people were in the greenroom with me. They were all waiting, like me, to be called through to be interrogated by the nation's defenders of democracy. One was a very high-flying, academic-looking woman. She spent her time in the greenroom reading and rereading her notes so that she would be totally prepared for whatever questions were thrown at her. Then there was the man who I was convinced was a member of the Tory shadow cabinet.

But he is not. He is in being interviewed now. From what I can make out through the glass, he was abandoned as a child, then abused in an orphanage and now is campaigning for the rights of young people who are thrown out of such places at the age of 16 to the mercy of our cruel world, expected to survive and prosper while keeping on the right side of the law.

Suddenly No Music Day seems trivial and silly. And once again I am asking myself why I've not done anything with my life that matters. Something for the common good. But it is too late now as I am being beckoned through to the studio. It is time for me to justify myself to the nation. Or at least to try and put over as succinctly as possible what No Music Day is and why it should exist.

Bill Drummond

WHO IS LUKE HAINES?
22 November 2006

On the earliest train out of King's Cross heading north. Change at Wakefield and I'll be in Huddersfield before 8.00 and then to our lodgings to pick up John Hirst. Then we're off to whatever school we are working with this morning.

But for now I'm on the train. It's not even 6.00. Outside, the flatlands of the Fens are flashing by in a blackness as black as their soil. Is Fenland soil blacker than the Bible-black of Dylan Thomas' Llareggub? Don't answer that.

Yesterday was the second No Music Day. Already my head is teeming with conflicting thoughts. What went wrong? What could be done better next year? What changes need to be made to the website? When can I get breakfast? And who is Luke Haines?

I will attempt to respond to the last question first. Sometime in the last month there was a response to the No Music Day site proclaiming that 'Bill Drummond was just ripping off Luke Haines' Pop Strike of a few years earlier.' Now I had never heard of Luke Haines or his Pop Strike but I wasn't surprised at getting this email. Over the years I have had many emails, letters, phone calls and stuff in the media informing me that I was ripping something off or at least borrowing it, or if not borrowing at least making an ironic nod towards something. In the vast majority of these cases I'm not; and if a crime is being committed, it is out of ignorance. Usually I'm inspired to find out more about whatever it is I've been linked with.

Since getting that first email referring to me ripping off Luke Haines I've had several more in a similar tone. A couple of days ago I put 'Luke Haines' and 'Pop Strike' into Google to see what would come up. I learnt that Luke Haines was the main man in a band called The Auteurs who invented Britpop in the early 1990s and that he was also in a band called Black Box Recorder – I remember once hearing a track by them, and liking it – and that he called his Pop Strike in June 2001, the same week that he was releasing a new album. I read an online interview with him and discovered he was a very bright man with a bittersweet wit. He said a number of things I agreed with but the subtext of it all was that he thought he should be getting a lot more recognition than he was. But maybe that is the subtext of so much of what us creative types get up to. With footballers, it is all very straightforward: there are no excuses. If you are any good, you rise to the top. With artists there are always a million excuses we can give to excuse our non-star status: how we didn't get the breaks, how we were misunderstood, unfairly reviewed.

I also learned that Luke Haines is a friend of Stewart Home. Stewart Home called an art strike in 1990. It lasted almost three years. In 1993 Jimmy Cauty and I launched our Abandon All Art full-page adverts in the national press. At that time, neither of us had ever heard of Stewart Home or his Art Strike. I subsequently met Stewart Home in a club called Disobey in London in the mid-1990s. I think he thought we had ripped his Art Strike off. Stewart Home and I became friends. It's strange how things like that work out.

And now to try and answer my other questions … what went wrong? Not much really. Other than the fact that I'm sure on a global scale there was no dip in the amount of music broadcast, sold, downloaded, listened to or consumed in any other ways that music can be consumed. I even heard music. It's not as if I'm going to hide myself away up on the Yorkshire moors for the day.

What could be done better next year? What I don't want to get into with No Music Day is that it has to be somehow bigger and bigger each year. I don't want to be scrabbling around each November trying to come up with stunts and events to capture the media's attention. I will leave that to the likes of Red Nose Day, an event saddled with the problem that if it cannot be bigger and raise more money than it did the previous year, it is deemed a failure. For me, having one almost symbolic act happen each year is enough. That could be as small a thing as switching off the jukebox in one particular pub for the day. Mind you, if iTunes did offer to shut up shop for 24 hours, I won't deny I'd be cock-a-hoop.

The idea that has been brewing in my mind for next year's No Music Day is to screen a film that is well known for its musical score without the score. I don't mean a musical like The Sound Of Music or Grease. That would be pointless. The songs in these films carry the plot. What I mean is a regular drama with all the dialogue and sound effects but none of the musical soundtrack. There have been plenty of films where I have loved the soundtrack but at some point in the past few years something flipped in me. So often when I watch a film now the soundtrack becomes intrusive. It appears to me as an easy (if not cheap) trick to work on our emotions. Every time I hear those welling strings or that hit from yesteryear used over a scene, I start to imagine the scene without it. I try to imagine how well the camerawork and dialogue could carry things if the music was not there.

Bill Drummond

Last year I saw Hitchcock's The Birds again. It had never been a particular favourite of mine. I had no sympathy with the two lead characters, but what held my attention all the way through the film was the non-existence of any musical score. It is this lack of music that gives the film so much of its tension. It has since been pointed out to me that there are bird sounds used throughout the film created by the electronic composers, Remi Gausmann and Oskar Sala (note: not Hitchcock's usual composer, Bernhard Herrmann) so it could be argued that the film does have a musical score.

Once I had the idea to screen a film famous for its soundtrack without the soundtrack, the film I instantly wanted was Apocalypse Now. Where I get confused is with my motivation. Do I want to show this (or any) film without its soundtrack to show how shit and limp it is without it or because I think it could be an even more intense experience without the comfort provided by the music?

Earlier this year I was approached by David McGuinness who is putting together a 50-episode history of Scottish music for BBC Radio Scotland. It is to cover, rather bravely, the last 5,000 years of Scottish music. I have no idea how anybody could know what people were listening to 1,000 years ago, let alone 5,000. David McGuinness was keen to have me interviewed for the series. When we were talking and he learnt about No Music Day he thought that it would be a good thing for BBC Radio Scotland to embrace on 21 November 2007. He went to the director of the station and he was up for it too. I was pleased, even delighted. But there was a downside. I had already done the radio thing this year, as in yesterday with Resonance FM. I wanted 2007 to be about film but BBC Radio Scotland has thousands and thousands of listeners. Not like Resonance FM that has a few odd bods like me who tune in.

Instead of looking this gift horse in the mouth, I gratefully accepted the offer and decided that I would make Glasgow the centre of operations for No Music Day 2007. Whatever film was to be screened could be screened in Glasgow. I was still imagining using Apocalypse Now but my colleague Cally suggested Trainspotting instead. This seemed perfect. One of the most iconic films of the 1990s, an international hit set in Scotland and a soundtrack considered by most people to be a classic.

Mind you, this is all just talk as I have no idea how easy it is to get hold of a film without the score and, if you could, whether the film-maker would want their film shown naked.

Next question: What changes need to be made to the website? The format of nomusicday.com was pretty much exactly the same in 2006 as it was in 2005.

I like simple and to-the-point websites but maybe this was too dictatorial. It allowed little room for those who thought it was a pile of shite, no platform for people to comment on how they got on with attempting a day without music. Some thought needs to be given to this.

Last question to be answered as the train pulls out of Doncaster is when can I get breakfast? Well, there will be no proper breakfast as there is no dining carriage on this train, so it's a trip to the buffet car for a croissant and tea.

Bill Drummond

THE MANAGER
25 November 2006

Some weeks ago I got an email from a Rob Cotter. He reminded me that I had made soup at his and his partner's home in Sale, Manchester, last year, their house being on the Soupline. I remembered. And I remembered their house is also a recording studio where they took pride in the fact that none of the gear they use is digital. All analogue. Rob and partner Julie McLaren have a record label aptly called Analogue Catalogue. Julie produced and recorded the bands and Rob ran the label. I had no idea what sort of music they put out but I liked the vibe of the place.

In this email Rob Cotter wanted to know if I was still active as The Manager and if so, whether I would be up for dispensing some wisdom for the formerly agreed sum of £100. I received this email almost 20 years to the day when I made a short film called The Manager to which Rob was referring.

So back to 1986. After allowing hundreds of thousands of pounds of WEA Records money to be squandered on building Pete Waterman's studio and the lack of success of Brilliant or any of the other bands that I had signed, I decided it was time for me to retire from the music business. Even at the time I recognised it had corrupted me to a point beyond what I liked to recognise as myself. I wrote the following, knowingly overblown, resignation letter to the industry at large and to me in particular.

> I will be 33 ^{1}/$_3$ years old in September,
> a time for a revolution for my life.
> There is a mountain to climb the hard way,
> and I want to see the World from the top.
> These foothills have been green and pleasant
> but I want to smell the rock,
> touch the ice
> and have the wind tear the shirt from my back.
> I entered this party on May 5th 1977,
> forming a band that had no right to be
> and I leave by leaving two gifts,
> the first Zodiac Mindwarp and the Love Reaction
> the only band that can save us from the future,
> the second is yet to come,
> and in between was the greatest album ever made.
> In the past nine years,

I gave everything I could,
and at times some drops too much,
and to those who wanted more,
I'm sorry, it wasn't for the giving.
The reconnaissance party arrive to pick me up on September 11th
on which date my office will be empty.
Gold Discs will gather dust
and telephones will be left to ring.

Goodbye Rock 'n' Roll let the guitar scream forever.

Comrades & Rivals thanks.
'Good Sherpa lead the way'.

I was going to get on with doing what I had wanted to do ever since jacking in art school at the age of 20: write the great and sprawling American novel. Only not American. But before I started to write I wanted to cleanse my soul of all the plastic pop I'd allowed myself to be embroiled in over the previous 12 months. So I decided to write and record a singer-songwriter-type album. I wrote all the songs in a week, went into a studio in Dagenham, Essex, and recorded the songs the following week, only using real musicians. And in the week after I went to see Alan McGee, who ran the then-hippest indie label in town, Creation Records, to see if he wanted to put it out. He did.

I did a photo session for the sleeve. I wanted to look like one of those also-ran singer-songwriters from New York in the early 1960s, before they grew their hair and never made it because they weren't Bob Dylan. Basically I had Phil Ochs in mind. I had no idea what Phil Ochs sounded like but I loved the covers to his first two albums.

The album I did was called The Man. I chose that because I thought it looked like a Johnny Cash album title. The sound of the record was folk mixed with a bit of country and I sang it in a slightly exaggerated version of my own Scottish accent. This record was total indulgence. It was that need to get something out of your system before you can move on. I had no plans for doing anything to promote it. No live dates. No nothing. It was enough for me to hold the finished album in my hands and look at the cover, even though I will regret for the rest of my life that I was not wearing my walking boots for the photo and that I was wearing a pair of pale cream socks. Unforgivable.

Bill Drummond

Alan McGee seemed to like the record and gave me £1,000 to go away and make a promo clip of one of the tracks so they could use it to promote the album. I took the grand and with long-term friend and film-maker Bill Butt, went off and made The Manager, a ten-minute film of me pushing a dustcart along a country lane and pontificating to camera. The thing is, though, I have not seen the film since Bill Butt and I made it 20 years ago. This Rob Cotter wants to know if the offer I was making in the film still stands. I've no real idea what this offer is and since I've kept hardly any copies of records, books or films I have done, there is no way I can check. 'Why keep anything when it's all on the internet?' is my sort-of latter-day defence. I put 'The Manager' and 'Bill Drummond' into Google and up comes a link to YouTube. I click on it and within 20 seconds I am watching this substantially deteriorated film of myself, walking along a country lane pushing a dustcart, spouting all sorts of pompous stuff. But I am hardly listening to the words. What is holding my attention is how horrifically young I look, how lean I am and how stupidly I am behaving. I hit pause and rushed through to the bathroom to have a look at myself in the mirror. How the fuck did all that ageing happen? Who gave it permission? And the hair! I was never supposed to lose my hair. My 93-year-old father hasn't. My grandfather didn't. So why me?

Back in front of the screen I press play and listen to what I've got to say. I'm going on about having left the music business to get on with the greater things in life and how I would never soil my hands in the grubby world of pop music again. But with the twisted logic of my new vantage point of being above it all. I have elected myself to be the manager of the music business. Of the whole thing. I'm overall in charge of every band, orchestra, record label, radio station, publisher, promoter, the Musicians' Union, the Performing Rights Society, everything. I'm going to let them all get on with it just as they are doing already. But if anybody wants my advice, I will be willing to give it. All they have to do is post their problem or query to me, The Manager, at PO Box whatever, enclosing a cheque for £100, and once the cheque has cleared I will respond with my advice.

The PO Box was a real address that I had already used. I don't know if the film was ever used anywhere. Why would it be? It was shot on 16mm; fuck knows where it is now. And fuck knows how anybody has got a copy of it to put on YouTube. That said, the copy on YouTube looks like a VHS copy of a VHS copy and one that has corroded in quality over the years.

So, to the point. This Rob Cotter wants to know if I'm still in business as The Manager as he needs some advice on the record label he and his partner have. l emailed him back saying that I have long since retired from that role but the pair of them should drive over the Pennines and come to one of the *Introduction To The17* performances that I will be doing in Huddersfield in a few weeks' time. Maybe what I have to say in the performance will answer their questions.

Last night the pair of them turned up, listened to what I had to say, took part in the performance and we chatted afterwards. Although they talked through some of the problems they were having with the record label, the main focus of the discussion was that Julie was seven months pregnant but looked like she was going to drop any day, actually more like any second. We talked about the score that I had done to celebrate the birth of a newborn baby and how I had just been reworking it and it now has to have 17 generations for the performance to be complete. But more importantly I asked them if they would be up for being the first couple to start off a performance of this particular score. They were. So I hope before this book is finished I will have been up to their place and kicked off Score 9. *WELCOME.*

That was last night. This morning I'm writing this and worrying about ageing and loss of hair. But there is a new idea that is clamouring for attention. Maybe I should revisit The Manager idea. Do it online: themanager.com and .net have gone but themanager.tv seems to be still up for grabs. Get the domain name set up, a simple site and a Paypal account and off I go. Could be a money-spinner. I could do with some money-spinning. What do you think?

THREE LEAVES LEFT
1 December 2006

It's December, so in my book it is winter, but with all this climate change going on it's warm enough for me to be back out on the ledge. No ginger tom, but the sycamore is still tall and proud, and now it is standing naked and bare. Pot of tea at side, notebook on lap, pencil in hand and I'm off.

Last week in Huddersfield went almost well. Blake's dark satanic mills looked all warm and golden in their spruced-up and gentrified retirement. The curry house in Market Street was a delight. But there were downsides – mainly in my head – about the direction this book is going and what it is about and what should be the title. On the opening page I proclaimed it to be a book about The17 and as such I imagined it would be called *The17* or maybe just *17*. But now I've got it in my head that this should be a book about the future of music.

A book about The17 seems to limit its vision, as though The17 is my own personal way of exploring where we are at with music or even just where I am at with music. Maybe I should go back and rewrite the opening chapter, make it more open, more thrusting, more challenging and less just about The17. Much of the time I think The17 is irrelevant. I feel more like a John the Baptist – that my role in all of this is to be a signpost. I'm here to signal some great changes in the way we will be thinking about, making and consuming music over the next few decades, but I'm not the one to deliver the new music. If I can speed the process up, I will have done my job.

At the beginning of the 20th century Picasso and Braque took apart all the accepted ways that Western artists saw and depicted the world. During the 19th century Western painters of whatever discipline were trying to depict the world they saw (or imagined they saw) on the two-dimensional plane. Photography had been invented almost 70 years before Picasso and Braque met each other and hatched their plans, and photography, like recording technology, was able to document a two-dimensional representation of reality. In some ways the invention and rapid spread of photography made much of the work of the artist redundant and in many ways gave them freedom. But for those 70 years artists still carried on using their canvases to depict faithfully a three-dimensional world on a two-dimensional plane. In 1907 Picasso and Braque changed all that with the paintings they started to make and it was not long before those who decide these things decided that what Picasso and Braque had been up to would forever more be known as Cubism. They broke through an accepted way of seeing paintings, if not the world.

These paintings were ugly, not aesthetically pleasing, but they were a starting point for us Westerners to see painting and the visual arts in a hugely different way. Their Cubist paintings made so much else possible.

No analogy is perfect and the one that I was almost trying to make about the role of photography and that of recording technology hardly works at all. But the point I want to hammer home yet again is that the invention, rise, spread and proliferation of recording technology has completely and utterly held in a vice-like grip the thinking about, making and consumption of music, and that's all music from whatever part of the world. Much in the same way that photography held the way we thought we saw the world in a vice-like grip.

We are now at a stage when we need to break free of the constraints that recording technology has placed on music. Picasso and Braque started that process for the visual arts in 1907. Now, by no stretch of the imagination am I trying to equate myself with Picasso, who was the great genius of 20th-century Western art. He was only 26 in 1907. I will be turning 54 in 2007. I have no great vision, let alone the talent ... all I am saying is that I seem to have accidentally stumbled through a door where I am now viewing the possibilities of music-making in a completely different way.

Picasso may have stumbled through an equivalent door in 1907 but he had the youth, vigour, vision, drive and genius to make great art out of what he saw. I don't have that. There may be a 26-year-old man or woman somewhere in the world right now who has stumbled through a similar door and who has the genius that it takes to make great music in ways we are yet to hear.

I know that what I have written in the past 20 minutes or so can be read as ultimate pretension, my head firmly up my own arse, but it's what I think. Time to put down the pencil and pour another mug of tea from the pot.

As I do so, I notice the tree is not quite bare. There are three leaves left, two less than Nick Drake had.

Bill Drummond

OUT OF THE CANVAS
2 December 2006

Today thoughts of Picasso, Braque, photography, painting and reality have been filling up my head. I feel unsatisfied with the analogy I was making, feel the need to try and make my point more user-friendly and clear-cut.

This evening I am sitting in a curry house in Brick Lane with Tracey Moberly. Tracey has been going on about a Siberian Film Festival that she has recently been a guest judge at. Then she switches topics of conversation mid-sentence to some feminist issue. Two and a half sentences later, another switch. This time she is talking about her two boys Jacob and Izaac, both in their mid-teens and into music.

'I was trying to explain to them about The17 and how they should come along to one of the performances.'

'Yeah.' I'm not really listening 'cause I'm still trying to work out what she was saying about the Siberian Film Festival. My mind even at its most agile finds it difficult to keep up with Tracey.

'Bill, they tell me there is all this new music out there. You know I'm not into music, never have been. Like dancing though. Always went dancing on Saturday night. But Jacob and Izaac are always talking about music. Used to go to The Queen of Hearts in Nelson with Lynne and Stacey. The boys say that you are just not hearing the right new music. That if you did, your opinions would be different. I was only 15, loved dancing.'

None of us want our opinions proved to be wrong. We would rather spend what energies we have on shoring them up than on coming to terms with the fact that we got things wrong, that times have moved on. We fail to notice that the ideals we have held onto since our youth are now irrelevant.

I pick up the second-to-last king prawn on my plate with my fingers and take a bite from it. Wonder if it lived its life in the Bay of Bengal. Wonder who caught it and what they are doing now. Take another sip from the glass of Cobra, stare out of the window at the passing nightlife. While doing this I imagine the music that Jacob and Izaac have been listening to. It sounds good.

'The thing is, Tracey, I'm sure if I was to hear it, part of me would think it was good. But a bigger part of me would be thinking that it's just the same as what had gone before. Another piece of music made by people wanting to make another record that exists in the same way as music seems to have done all my life.'

'But it might not. Its as if you have made a judgement before hearing it. Which is stupid, but you know I don't understand music. Did I ever tell you about when I had this air rifle and we ...'
She may have done but my mind was now elsewhere. I drain the glass of Cobra and order another couple of bottles.

'Yeah, Tracey, but this is my analogy for the night. It is one that I have been developing through the day. Think of all recorded music as the equivalent to all paintings on canvas. For a few hundred years in the West painting on canvas was considered the highest art form. All other mediums were lower down the pecking order. All debates, movements and art wars were primarily about how paint was used on a rectangle of canvas. Now I am not going to try and rekindle some painting is dead debate but ...' The two new bottles of Cobra arrive. We fill our glasses. I take a sip. 'But it's like for all my life the only music we have had has been made by pushing paint around on a canvas and there has been some great music made that way. All sorts of debates, movements and music wars have entertained me and kept me on my toes. But in the end it is still just music made using paint on canvas. And now I want music made in a different way. No longer so two-dimensional. I want an equivalent to a urinal signed R. Mutt. The canvas has become a prison. It is time to think outside the canvas ...'

Tracey said something, but my attention has been caught by what was going on in the street outside. 'Did you see that girl batter her boyfriend with her handbag?'

The conversation drifts. There was no more talk of The17.

On the bus back home that night I got a text from Tracey.

Paul: This brings to mind Ian MacKaye who was in the bands Minor Threat and Fugazi. I heard him talk recently about live performance, and the standard way they are set up for us as an experience, in terms of the similar nature of the venues and the way they're laid out. He's interested in trying to destroy this framework. His new band plays on the same level as the audience, and the band is surrounded by the audience, trying to make the performance connected to everyone – the

Bill Drummond

'Dont 4get we'r goin 2SIBERIA nxt September SO put it in ur diary NOW & on ur calender... & ur analogy is turning me abstract'.

performance is supposed to be a kind of participatory thing. Maybe it's easier to destroy or shift the parameters in music with live performance.

Rasmus: I'm sure if you look at the history of recorded music in the future, the invention of something like peer-to-peer networks would be seen as a defining moment, changing the way we listened to music.

ONE LEAF LEFT
4 December 2006

Back out on the edge. The day is bright and warm enough. Reread what I wrote in the previous two chapters which has prompted me to rewrite the opening chapter of the book. What I want to try and explore now is the subject of religion and music.

I grew up with a religious background, what with my father being a minister in the Church of Scotland. Religion is something I have never felt the need to either embrace or reject. What I have found myself doing over the years is exploring what religion is, why man is drawn to existing religions or to creating new ones, in the same way as I have found man's relationship to music interesting.

As a teenager so many people I knew rejected religion for the very simplistic reasons that they thought it was all made-up stories used to keep people suppressed and that it didn't stand up to any rational thinking. The fact that it was also the cause of so much of the conflict in the world went against it as well. This always seemed to me to miss the point and I couldn't understand how moderately bright people could not get what religion is for and how it works and that it not being rational is irrelevant. The fact that it may have been responsible for much of the conflict in the world is also irrelevant to why it worked.

As far as I am concerned religion gives life meaning for people. When I heard a passage from the Bible about some miraculous act, I wouldn't be thinking, 'Well that obviously never happened'; for me, the words, the poetry, would exude meaning. For something to contain meaning and give life meaning it does not have to be rational. Like if I go and see a film, I'm not watching it and thinking, 'That's just lights on a screen or it's just actors playing parts, it's all a fraud, none of that actually happened.' I allow myself to get enveloped in the drama. The emotions that it triggers are real emotions and I instinctively find meaning in the film even if I'm not doing that in any intellectual way.

It is part of the human condition to want to find meaning in life. We do not have to be aware that we are continually looking for meaning in life. We just do it, like we breathe. Religion has been one of the most successful ways man has come up with to give life meaning. Different religions have evolved to do it in different ways. If a religion is no longer able to provide our lives with meaning, it has to evolve or we will look for something else that does.

Bill Drummond

Before the 20th century religion had far less competition in the marketplace for giving life meaning. During the 20th century the evolution and spread of mass-spectator sport, politics, film and recorded music have all in their own ways been able to give life meaning. The young man of today who gets so much from listening to the tunes stored on his hard drive or watching his team play may look back with incredulity at those who once took Mass weekly, 'believing' they were consuming the flesh and blood of Christ and 'believing' in a whole lot of made-up stories.

In 100 years' time it is just as likely that the equivalent young man may look back at the man of today and wonder how listening to all those tunes on his hard drive could hold so much meaning for him. How the merely made-up rules of football could have provided his life with so many highs and lows and given it drama, shape and substance. This need for meaning is no different in the man or woman of today than it was 2,000 years ago or will be in 100 years' time. (I was going to say 2,000 years but that may be tempting fate). We have a tendency to assume that what gives our life meaning is a fixed thing, that its power is eternal. Maybe to contemplate that it is not fixed and eternal would start to undermine our belief in it, start to weaken its capability to give our life meaning.

If somebody is into a certain composer or recording artist or type of music, it is because it makes them feel a certain way, triggers certain emotions. If it does this, they believe the music to be of a standard, to be worthwhile, to have value, to be great. The person who listens to a lot of music in this day and age is the same person who would have needed a lot of religion in centuries past. The same belief systems are in place – it's only the packaging that is different. Of course nobody goes to war over what music they think people should be into. To answer why people go to war would take another whole book altogether, one that I am not going to start writing any time soon.

I no longer believe in recorded music because it no longer triggers the right emotions in me, so no longer helps give my life meaning. In the same way as you may no longer believe in Christianity because it no longer triggers the right emotions in you and gives your life meaning.

If you are thinking, hang on a minute, what's Drummond going on about here, because religion is all about telling you what you should and should not do, and listening to music isn't. That's maybe how it seems to you at the moment, but the right and wrong thing is only part of Christianity / Islam / Judaism's window-dressing, a way to entice you in and hold you once you are there. The main deal is what lies beneath our need to give meaning to the mystery of life.

As for Marx and his quote about religion being 'the opium of the people', if Marx was alive today, I think he would exchange the word religion for music, sport, film or the internet. That said, whether religion or music is the opiate of the masses, Marx's understanding of what religion was for was rather shallow and one-dimensional.

Bill Drummond

THE FLAW
8 December 2006

The engine of Motivation knows no more powerful fuel than that of the promise of Fame & Fortune.

The evolution of recorded music in the 20th century enabled the promise of a level of fame and fortune through success in music way beyond anything possible in previous centuries. With nought but the right attitude and innate genius thousands of aspirant teenagers have been propelled to worldwide fame and untold fortune over the second half of the 20th century. From Sinatra to Britney, the story was the same.

By the turn of the millennium there were any number of easy-to-use, easy-to-share, music software packages a teenager with a modicum of talent could use to make tracks that sound slick and professional, and with the internet they have the means of distribution, which in theory provides them with a worldwide platform.

This democratisation has undermined so much of what held the postwar generations in thrall to pop success. The mystery has been debunked, the alchemy delivering nothing but fool's gold. The promise of fame and fortune has been watered and watered down again, year on year. By the time I was 21, I had only ever met one person who had played on a record (the drummer in St Cecilia); nowadays it feels like every second person you meet has made a CD, or at least got tracks up on MySpace. Your average premiership footballer can out-earn, out-pull, out-column-inch whoever is number one in the charts the week I'm writing this and probably the week you are reading it too. Having a number one record no longer means anything. A new album by a major artist is no longer a cultural landmark. Every jobbing cultural commentator has made a similar observation at some time since the beginning of this century. There is nothing new in what I am saying.

But here lies the rub for me, the flaw in all that I have written about in this book and dreamed of these past few years. There is no way that The17, or its like, can ever deliver fame and fortune for anybody. Without that fuel of fame and fortune there is little to motivate the dreams, let alone actions, of would-be music-makers. Beyond a few odd bods and interested parties,

Paul: There is something exciting about the sheer amount of music that is being made available online. You could argue that the developments in production and distribution has made recorded music better and more relevant than ever before.

Robert: Is it now harder to find the interesting music?

what I am proposing will never capture the imagination of the public at large, not even 17 other people you might know.

Rasmus: Well, as Bill said, it's no longer a big cultural event when a record is released. The idea of the superstar is growing massively though. You get the stars like Britney Spears, where they are almost completely divorced from the music, and at the same time you have the democratisation of recorded music, where anybody can produce and distribute it. It's like the music and the stardom are moving in opposite directions.

Rasmus: The17 is a utopian ideal. That it is flawed is something that we have known all along. It's just a way of looking at music, or a point from which we can discuss how to break the 'canvas' or discuss what the 'canvas' is. The17 will never be the next Beatles.

Robert: Do you think secretly he believes it could be?

Paul: I don't think so.

Robert: You have to play up to the utopian ideal for people to become interested and take note.

Paul: I think it's just an interesting idea for a project that has turned into a bigger book because he can use it as a way to wax lyrical on his more general gripes with the music business.

Bill Drummond

The17 IN BETHLEHEM
24 December 2006

Christmas Eve. Stuck in Gatwick. Our flights have been delayed for eight hours all because of the big fog that descended on the bottom half of the country over the past few days. At least things are better than they have been during the past few days when 50 percent of the flights were cancelled.

I'm with members of my family and we are supposed to be on our way to Norway for Christmas.

While waiting, my thoughts are drifting off to the idea of The17 in China. When doing The17 in Huddersfield, one of the performances was attended by a woman from the British Council. The British Council exists to promote British culture abroad. It is considered good PR for UK Plc if Johnny Foreigner is exposed to our culture. The sun may have long set on the British Empire but cultural imperialism is still the best game in town when you want the world to buy what you've got to sell. Popular music and Hollywood have done it for the USA ever since the end of World War I. The Beatles and Shakespeare continue to do it for the UK to a lesser extent. The British Council is there to promote British culture that may not be able to hold its own in the marketplace but is still thought to show the UK in a good light.

So this woman from The British Council in Huddersfield introduces herself to me after the performance. Her name is Leah Zakss, an interesting name I thought. Leah tells me it is Latvian; I tell her I had a number of Latvian friends in Corby; she tells me her auntie used to live there. She then steers the conversation on to what she is supposed to be talking about. She tells me she is in charge of music for North Africa, the Middle East and all the rest of Asia. She asks me if I had ever done anything before with the British Council (BC). I tell her about the BC's involvement with the Soupline in Estonia and how that went well but BC didn't want to know in Sweden when I was going over there with The17, 'cause they thought hard-earned taxpayers' money should not be spent on money-burners like myself. She then told me she was interested in exploring ways of The17 working in some of her territories.

And that was that. I didn't hear back from her – that is, until the day before yesterday. Then we spoke at length on the phone. She wanted to know what was happening when and where and would I be interested in going to China with The17. Who wouldn't be interested in going to China, if somebody else were paying? But what she told me next I found to be the most revealing.

'We are being encouraged to find work to take out to China, work that will appeal specifically to intelligent and thinking 18 to 35-year-olds.' I should not be surprised at the cynicism. We all know that China is to be the mega economy of the 21st century. We, UK Plc, need to get in there with the young and intelligent Chinese now, make our mark on them before they are running the place in a few years' from now. It would be a waste of our tax payers' hard-earned money sending The17 out to win friends and influence people in countries that are going to mean jack shit in 50 years' time.

I have always found this sort of thing hard to square with my puritanical nature. I don't want to be part of the PR arm of our Evil Empire. If I go to China, it will be for my own reasons, not in the hope that they will be buying Aston Martins and drinking Glenfiddich in 50 years' time. But The17 in China. It almost sounds like the title of a TV documentary, bit of a nod to the opera *Nixon in China* by John Adams.

I occasionally get asked by TV production companies if I would be interested in making a TV film about my work or my past or something. I never follow any of this through. I have a pathological fear of TV as a medium. Nearly every time I have been involved in television in the past I feel it has reduced or ended up trivialising what I'm doing.

But here I am trying to kill time at Gatwick Airport, having fantasies about The17 in China and what the documentary would look like. Maybe make up a score specially for the trip. One that involves hundreds of people at the same time singing in Tiananmen Square or on the Great Wall or on a boat sailing up the Yangtze or standing in paddy fields. And how the programme would be screened the week this book comes out in 2008. And how the big challenge in making it would be that it could not contain any of the music of The17 as that is never to be broadcast and so on.

These thoughts were exciting me and I was forgetting all about the drag of sitting around in an airport hour after hour. Then all the excitement imploded 'cause I remembered reading something last week about a reality TV show about a bunch of kids from a London comprehensive school who had never sung in a choir before in their lives before, being turned into a real choir by some charismatic choir master and then being whipped off to China to take part in the Choir Olympics. So as far as TV is concerned, choirs and China have been done.

Then an idea makes its presence felt: it's Christmas Eve – where do one's thoughts turn to on Christmas Eve, if you have had any sort of Christian upbringing? Bethlehem. The teenage Mary and her belly fit for bursting and no room at the inn. I have had a thing about the Holy Land most of my life. Never been there. But I have always seen the valley of Jordan not only as the beginning of the Rift Valley that goes all the way down into central Africa but a fault line on the human soul. Where three tectonic plates of the three great monotheistic religions of the world grind up on each other. Jerusalem may have the Temple Mount – the site of the Israelis' first temple and Mohammed's ascent to heaven and all the conflict that, that has inspired. But Bethlehem holds a stronger pull in my imagination. Somehow, the nativity story, as it is played out in thousands of schools and churches every year around the globe, dovetails neatly into the idea of modern Bethlehem, the home of Palestinian refugees and all their poverty and stateless misery.

So that's it. If I can swing it, I would love to do The17 in Bethlehem with a bunch of Palestinians, both Christian and Muslim. Write a score specifically for the place and occasion. And if the British Council and a TV production company are up for being involved, so much the better.

I would like to round this chapter off by reporting that our flight has just been called. But I know there are still at least two hours to wait.

POP JUSTICE
2 January 2007

Got an email about ten minutes ago. It had a link to the website
popjustice.com. I clicked on the link and read:

> **Something kind a Mu**
> Tuesday 02 January 2007
>
> Precisely 20 years ago TODAY, Bill Drummond
> invented the second-greatest male pop duo of all
> time: The KLF (also know as The Justified Ancients
> of Mu Mu, The Timelords and about a million other
> things).
>
> Here, apparently is how it happened:
>
> 'It was new years day 1987. I was going for a walk in
> the morning and I thought, "I'm going to make a hip
> hop record. Who can I make a hip hop record with?" I
> phoned Jimmy up that day and said "Let's form a
> band called The Justified Ancients Of Mu Mu". Within
> a week we had recorded our first single.'

Knowing popjustice.com like I do, I guessed the first greatest they are
referring to is The Pet Shop Boys. But of course they are way off the mark.
They have obviously forgotten to consider The Everly Brothers, The
Proclaimers, Soft Cell, Jan & Dean, Stealers Wheel, Zager & Evans, The
Righteous Brothers, Sam & Dave, Suicide and, of course, the greatest: Simon
and Garfunkel. But I'll pass on all that, because the bit about me going for a
walk on New Year's Day triggered something else in my mind that I wanted to
get down on paper.

The particular New Year's Day in question was about four months after
making The Manager, the film that I was going on about a few pages back. It
was four months after I completely and utterly retired from the whole messy
world of making pop records of any persuasion. From then on I was going to
dedicate my practice as an artist to writing books. Every day of the autumn of
1986 I took myself off to the local library and got on diligently with writing the
great sprawling masterpiece. The trouble was that while doing this my mind
kept straying off to thinking about pop music instead, and hip hop
in particular.

Hip hop had been evolving for some years, as had its rap element. It is not the sort of music aimed at me, me being white and then in my 30s, and it is not a form of music that I would choose to listen to for mere entertainment. But it did intrigue me; it held my interest. It stimulated thoughts. What I liked most about it was that it was a form of music that dumped so many of the givens of popular music. For a start, it dumped melody almost entirely along with traditional musicianship, song-writing craft, singing ability. It sidestepped dance and romance as its raison d'être. It never felt sorry for itself: it was all about confidence, but not in the super-stud lover-man way of soul singers of the 1970s and 1980s.

I wasn't particularly motivated to trace its roots and motivation, although as an owner of an LP by the Last Poets from the early 1970s and as somebody who had been exposed to too many mid-1970s Jamaican dub records featuring dull-sounding MCs toasting over the top I could cobble together a lightweight theory.

Since the early 1980s there had been the odd novelty record featuring rapping that had made the UK charts, Blondie's *Rapture*, Tom Tom Club's *Wordy Rapping Hood*, Grandmaster Flash's *The Message*, The Fat Boys' *Jail House Rap*, Run DMC's *Walk This Way* for instance. But these didn't interest me. This was just the fodder that was light and fluffy enough for Radio 1. Even Run DMC with all their blackness seemed too cuddly in an MTV-friendly way.

There was a theory that I had going that went something like this: in the early 1950s some black bluesman in Chicago formed the first band whose line-up consisted of a drummer, an electric bass player, one or two electric guitarists and a vocalist. I have no idea who is actually responsible for this but I am sure there are numerous books on the history of blues that could tell you. Whoever put that band together created the blueprint for the vast majority of musical ensembles that have existed ever since. Tens and tens of thousands of bands have followed this formula. Every single neighbourhood in the world has spawned a band that has stuck rigidly to that same blueprint for making music. It has swept all else before it. There have been slight variants to the tried-and-tested: a keyboard player here, a brass section there, the odd novelty instrumentalist added for flavour (fiddle, harmonica, banjo and so on). Billions of records have sold using this line-up.

We are almost into the seventh decade of this blueprint being the standard. As I write, young bands will be forming using the exact same line-up and will undoubtedly go on to become worldwide stars in the next couple of years. To my thinking we have willingly stuck ourselves in a cultural rut with this form.

I wrote in an earlier chapter how black American culture has the great fortune of apparently never feeling the need to look back and always looking to the next thing, the golden age yet to come. By the time the first British invasion hit the shores of America in 1963 using this very blueprint, black American culture had all but dumped the line-up of drums, bass guitar, electric guitar. Since the 1950s there has been no genre of black American music where the electric guitar has been the central instrument. Yes, the guitar was still used for years to come in the making of black music, but only as part of the rhythm section or a little motif here or there, never any more important than any of the other instruments. But white musicians around the world took the electric guitar and turned it into an icon, an icon that represented freedom, rebellion, sexuality.

Of course there was the odd exception that proved the rule. If you are thinking of Hendrix or Prince, the vast majority of their audience was white – an audience to whom they were knowingly marketing themselves. And, come the 1960s, the audience for the old black blues guys who were first with the sound were almost all white liberal types. In the late 1960s when the great innovator Miles Davis wanted to break free of the whole jazz cul-de-sac he imagined himself to be in, he hired John McLaughlin, a white British rock guitarist, for his new band to give it that guitar edge. There were no young black guys who were up for it and who could do the gig.

It amazes and staggers me that us white blokes have stuck with the form through the decades from The Beatles through Zeppelin, the Pistols, Joy Division, Metallica, U2, Nirvana, Korn, The Guillemots to whoever is this week's new thing. They still want to explore what can be conjured out of the tension created between guitar, bass, drums and vocals.

In an earlier chapter I wrote about the false dawn of electro-pop and how it failed to overthrow the continued hold guitar bands had on the white male psyche. It wasn't until the mid-1980s that I began to become aware that hip hop was not just a novelty but a whole new way of thinking about making music, that this could be as big and as global as rock music had become. I loved the fact that, in its elemental form, it did not use any instruments played by musicians, that there was no way that it related to rock 'n' roll. All you needed was a couple of lads, one with a beat box and a couple of decks and some records to spin and the other with a mic, some rhymes to rap and, of course, attitude. Being able to sing or play an instrument were completely irrelevant. It seemed so pure. A new beginning.

It was hearing a cassette of the first Schoolly D album in 1986 that made me realise that this was the future. This was the starting point. To my white ears it sounded as primal as those Muddy Waters or Howlin' Wolf records from the early 1950s. This was the new blueprint. And maybe there is an element of racism in this but I imagined that generations of white musicians would take this basic form and stretch it and bend it, explore it and exploit it just like they had done before and I wanted to be a part of that stretching and bending, exploring and exploiting. But I was already 33 and a third. I wasn't going to be getting myself a pair of decks and starting to learn to scratch. I wasn't going to start rapping about the Bronx in some fake American accent.

Then, while sitting in Aylesbury library on 5 November 1986, a fully formed idea landed in the notebook where I was trying to write the great and sprawling novel. I would attempt to make a hip hop record. This idea took into account that Jimmy – he had dropped the Jimi – Cauty had bought himself a Greengate DS3 sound sampler while a member of the now-defunct Brilliant. It was the same as the one Stock, Aitken & Waterman had. On this admittedly very primitive Greengate you could sample up to three seconds of sound on its hard drive. This sample could be edited and looped. It could not time-stretch or alter the pitch of the sample – it was some years before samplers could do that.

The fully formed idea went like this: if I was to work out and make a note of the musical key of every tune on every record I owned and then work out and make a note of the beats per minute (bpm) on every tune of every record I owned, then theoretically a bar of music from The Sound Of Music in the key of A# with a bpm of 104 could run seamlessly into a bar of music from The Sex Pistols that is in the key of A# with a bpm of 104 could run seamlessly into a bar of music from Hamilton Bohannon that is also in A# and 104 bpm. Thus, theoretically, a whole new way of creating and putting together music could be stitched together and the entire history of recorded music was at our disposal to create, mix and match and conjure up new music from old.

I spent the next five days not writing the great and sprawling book but instead going through my whole record collection working out what keys every song was in and, using the second hand of our kitchen clock, what bpm they ran at. This amounted to thousands of songs. I then cross-referenced all these songs to find which ones matched up, having the same key and bpm. If I had never taken the project any further, this would have been a rewarding exercise in itself.

Most of the hip hop / rap tunes at that time were around the 90 to 104 bpm speed. And as I was interested in making hip hop I dismissed all of the tunes in my list that did not exist between these two beats. This reduced considerably the possible choice of tracks.

What interested me about the possibility of making a hip hop / rap record wasn't about attempting to make one that could pass as the real thing. I knew that was a total impossibility. Everything about me is white, not just my skin colour: I think like a white man, dress like a white man and move like a white man. I was not going to start pretending otherwise. What interested me was what a couple of white blokes drenched in the history of rock and pop from a very British perspective would come up with if they started using the approach to music that underground American hip hop artists were using.

Knowing that Jimmy Cauty had one of these Greengate things and knowing he, like me, had a broad and rather skewed interest in music, I contacted him to ask if he wanted to make a hip hop record. Cressida, his girlfriend, answered the phone. She told me it was his birthday, his 30th, and he was depressed. He came on the phone, I wished him a happy birthday and he told me to fuck off, so I asked him if he wanted to make a hip hop record and he said yes.

After Christmas and New Year we made our hip hop track and called it *All You Need Is Love?* – the question mark differentiating it from the song by The Beatles. We called ourselves The Justified Ancients of Mu Mu after a secret organisation that existed in the pages of *The Illuminatus! Trilogy*. I could write a trilogy of books myself explaining the background of why we chose this name and what Jimmy Cauty and I did working together over the next few years. I won't because now is not the time. And anyway, the internet has enough information on that already. All that needs to be said is that we were never really able to explore the making of hip hop records before we got sidetracked into a hundred different directions at the same time.

Back in December 1986 I imagined that hip hop / rap would be a starting point in the same way the electric blues bands of early 1950s Chicago had been a starting point. And that white culture would run with this music and take it to every corner of the world like white culture did with the guitar, bass and drums format. That never happened. What happened is that the black man went and did it himself. As you may already know and I may have already stated in that café in Moscow, rap – and its cousin, modem R&B – are the biggest money-earning genres of music in the world today. No longer used and abused by the whitey music industry. They *are* the industry. Modern R&B, dragging along rap in tow, defines what modern popular music sounds like.

I have just had to cross out a page or so that I started to write about how we got from the Greengate DS3 sound sampler of the mid-1980s to where we are now; how the laptop is the icon of the modern world and how it defines the making of contemporary music – but I will leave that to a chapter of its own.

I will finish off this chapter by telling you that earlier today I took every vinyl 45 and LP, every CD and cassette I own down to the local Oxfam and left them there. The feeling is fantastic, as though a massive weight has been lifted that I have been literally carrying around with me for the last 35 years. Tomorrow I plan to take all my books.

ON THE SOFA
4 January 2007

Sitting on the sofa watching TV, it is the beginning of Celebrity Big Brother 2007. I can't wait for it all to unfold. To find out who this series' contestants are going to be.

Eighteen months ago I had no interest in Celebrity Big Brother in the slightest. There had been times when I would watch I'm A Celebrity Get Me Out Of Here but that was more because I warmed to Ant and Dec's light and friendly banter than any interest I had in the celebrities.

But the 2006 Celebrity Big Brother – the one with Pete Burns and George Galloway – started to pull me in. That was mainly because my younger children were watching it and I was becoming fascinated by how they related to it and the various contestants far more than they ever related to any of the characters in soap operas. Why were they captivated by the daily chit-chat and vague bullying of has-been pop stars, maverick politicians and other assorted minor players from the world of sport, showbiz and infamy, none of whom they had ever heard of before?

In the 2006 Big Brother, the non-celebrity one, I got drawn in even more by my then 11- and ten-year-old daughters talking incessantly about the ongoing shenanigans of Glynn, Grace, Pete and Nikki. For them it was like there was nothing else going on in the world that needed commenting on. These four young people – who had achieved nothing in their lives as yet and who had no particular talents – entered the Big Brother house with no one having heard of them except friends and family, to leave it a few weeks later – still appearing to have achieved nothing and having no particular talents – being about the most photographed and talked-about people in the country. Then, within what seemed like days, they were all but forgotten.

The concentrated tabloid media attention focused on these young housemates was far greater than ever was focused on the pop stars of the previous four decades. The weekly print media dedicated to pop music has dwindled to just the *NME*, which I've heard rumoured is soon to be retired in its print form, while there now seems to be dozens of weekly celebrity magazines. My now 12-year-old daughter needs her weekly fix of *Heat*.

During the past 12 months that Big Brother has begun to pull me in I also became aware that Paul Morley, the journalist, was regularly turning up in different situations giving his cultural commentator bit on the Big Brother Phenomenon. Paul Morley was the first music journalist that I ever met. He interviewed Big In Japan for the *NME* in the summer of 1977. Reading the interview when it was published a week or so later was the first time that I became aware that the reality as portrayed by a journalist may differ from how I saw it. Paul Morley seemed to be describing a different band to the one I thought I was in. Up until then I had taken everything I had read in newspapers as fact. You must be thinking how naïve I was, especially as I must have been 24 by then. It's not that Paul Morley was telling any lies, it was just that he had his own take on things. His own agenda.

Over the next few years Paul Morley became the music journalist who defined what young would-be music journalists aspired to. He always had the intellectual overview at the same time as letting you think he understood the populist angle. He brought postmodernism into pop journalism and I always enjoyed what he had to say even if I didn't agree with it or thought he was more interested in his own turn of phrase than the supposed subject he was writing about.

Last October (2006) I got sent a CD called North By Northwest. It was a compilation album recorded by bands from Liverpool and Manchester between 1976 and 1984. The CD had been 'compiled, curated and constructed' by Paul Morley. It contained tracks by all the bands you would expect it to include except The Wild Swans, who should have been on it. The package contained a booklet that included an essay by Paul Morley. I skimmed it to see what he had to say about Big In Japan. This is what he wrote:

> Big In Japan formed early in May 1977, possibly directly after a Clash gig at Eric's, and were immediately a trashy punk metaphor for how difficult young Liverpudlian musicians found it to follow on from The Beatles, who had made the city of Liverpool world famous, but also destroyed it as anything other than a kind of theme park for pop nostalgia. Early Liverpool punk bands formed by post-Bowie/Roxy style kids charged up by punk did more talking and posing than playing music. It was as if they were worried that their music would either create a new Liverpool Merseybeat scene that would never be as vital as the one inspired by The Beatles, or be a new thing that would never live up to the 1960s. Big In Japan were like a deranged cartoon version of a really great punk group, a theoretical theatrical estimate of what a new post-Pistols Liverpool group would look and sound like if the

biggest groups of all time had been The Velvet Underground, The Monkees and The Scaffold. It was all idea and no soundtrack, all build up and no punch-line. The group screamed that they were big in Japan, read out that week's chart positions over some feedback, acted like they had been dressed by Dali and styled by Warhol. They contained Ian Broudie, who would later form The Lightning Seeds, Holly Johnston, later the lead singer of Frankie Goes To Hollywood, Bill Drummond, who would eventually be the mastermind behind all sorts of projects, scams, labels, freak outs and promises including The KLF, Budgie, the drummer who would later be in The Slits, Siouxsie and the Banshees and The Creatures, and Jayne Casey, who went on to form Pink Military Stand Alone and Pink Industry, lost in time but in some universe as loved as The Cocteaus and as famous as Eurythmics. Jayne would also become the spokesperson for Cream nightclub and an avant-garde art impresario. Bill Drummond and David Balfe formed The Zoo label in part to release records by these raving no-hopers. Drummond counts the day that Big In Japan formed as the day he entered the music business. Big In Japan barely hinted at the influence and impact that their members were eventually to have and were put out of show business – some said put out of misery – by a petition signed by 2,000 locals concerned that the city that had gone inside 10 years from The Beatles to Big In Japan would never recover its musical reputation. In fact, the punch-line to Big In Japan might be that thirty years after they split up in 1978, Liverpool is the European Capital of Culture. If they return for the occasion, they will be the great Liverpool super group that never was in the first place.

In these nearly 30 years since Paul Morley first wrote a piece about Big in Japan I've got more than used to reading about events that I've been involved in being reported in considerably different ways to how I had observed and experienced them. In the same way that when I write about things I accept others may read and think, 'Well that's not what fuckin' happened.' So after reading the above quote about Big in Japan I had to suppress the urge to track down Paul Morley to tell him we were the tightest and best rehearsed band in all of the north-west circa early 1978 and that as far as musicianship went, Budgie was probably the best new wave drummer in the country and Ian Broudie could play every guitar lick going. Then I thought, fuck you and your 'all idea and no soundtrack, all build-up and no punch-line'.

I read it again and I liked what I read and thought it sounded like a great band to have been in, even though it didn't sound like the one I had been in. Then

I read the whole of his essay from beginning to end and noticed he had entitled it 'Memory Versus Oblivion' which I thought was good. In his fourth paragraph he hits a riff where he starts name-checking all concerned and how they all led to something contemporary – and I quote 'how The Buzzcocks led to the Arctic Monkeys ...' 'How Echo And The Bunnymen led to Nirvana ...' 'How Joy Division led to The Editors ...' In among all this riffing I read 'How Big In Japan led to Big Brother' and I stopped and made myself a pot of tea. What did he mean? 'How Big In Japan led to Big Brother'? What could he possibly mean? 'All attitude and no talent' came the reply from some dark corner. I sort of liked his comment, even though it was beyond nailing in any logical way.

I poured myself a mug of tea and decided I should get on with the day's work so I clicked on 'send and receive' on my Mac to see what emails I needed to be dealing with. Among them was an email that had been forwarded to me from Mick Houghton. Mick has been the PR for things I have been involved with since 1980.

Paul: He's banging on with that classic argument about the virtuoso musician vs the punk attitude again. But really he contradicts himself here because here he is talking about how Budgie was the best new wave drummer. So this just shows that one doesn't work without a bit of the other. I suppose it all depends on your criteria for defining good musicianship.

Rasmus: Wasn't there some bands that could barely play their instruments?

Paul: There were a few I guess – but that was never what was interesting about them. This argument always gets boiled down to the black and white of what punk was supposed to be about, but it's not a straightforward thing.

From: Charlotte Blackmore <blah.blahblah@endemoluk.com>
Date: Fri, 13 Oct 2006 15:58:32 +0100
To: <blahblahblah@aol.com>
Conversation: Bill Drummond
Subject: Bill Drummond

Dear Mick,

After the huge success of this year's 'Celebrity Big Brother', the next series will transmit in early January 2007. The exact dates are still to be confirmed, but the series will run for approximately 25 days.

'Celebrity Big Brother 2006' had an audience share peaking at 40 percent; received massive media coverage in both the broadsheets and the tabloids; and participants raised around £480,000 in total for the charities of their choosing.

We would like to invite Bill Drummond to take part in the show, and I would be grateful if you could pass on my request to him.

If Bill is interested, we would like to set up a meeting in the very near future, at a mutually convenient time and venue, to discuss the proposal in more detail. As always, there will be a substantial fee available, should he wish to appear on the programme.

Owing to the nature of the show and the fact that contestants' identities are kept secret until they actually enter the Big Brother house on launch night, we would be grateful if you treated our request in the strictest confidence.

Please do not hesitate to contact me for any further information and I look forward to speaking to you shortly.

Best regards,

Charlotte

Celebrity Producer
Celebrity Big Brother 5
Tel: 0208 6666666 / 07808 666 666
Blah.blahblah@endemoluk.com

I was dumbfounded. Floored.

How do things like this happen? How has the universe been so ordered? How does Big in Japan lead to Big Brother? Yeah, I know it's just coincidence and it's just what we read into the coincidences that somehow seems to give them meaning.

I never responded to the offer. I didn't even want to know what I could get paid in case I might be tempted. But when I showed it to my younger children hoping they would be impressed, they went berserk with me. They were not impressed at all, just angry that I was not going to take up the offer.

'But do you want to go into the playground in the morning knowing that all your friends will have seen me snoring and farting as I lay asleep in the Big Brother bedroom the night before?'

I didn't bother trying to explain to them about how it is only has-beens who go on the show, that they are there for the nation to ridicule and laugh at, that by going on Big Brother I would undermine everything that I am working on. My youngest, who was then six, was the most angry with me, telling me he would now not love me, ever give me a Christmas present or go fishing with me again.

Bill Drummond

It is time for me to get back to sitting on the sofa waiting for Celebrity Big Brother 5 to begin. And it does. We watch as this year's celebrities tell us who they are and what they have done that should be celebrated. We watch as they stroll, cavort, saunter along the catwalk, through the baying mob, to make their entrance into the Big Brother house.

And all the time I am thinking, 'That could have been me.' And if I was there, who would they not have had? And far more importantly, if I was there, what would that have meant for The17?

Robert: The idea of Big Brother and The17 clashing is really interesting because in many respects they are complete opposites. One is a dystopian view of the world and the other puts behind it the failures of the music world as we know it and looks for new forms for music to exist in. Dystopia meets Utopia.

Paul: I am surprised that Bill is actually famous enough to be on Big Brother.

Rasmus: Most of the celebrities in Celebrity Big Brother were not that famous.

Robert: That is true. They have a semi-public history that people can talk about. And obviously Bill has lots of stories up his sleeve.

SCORE

317. REPEAT

Choose a city.

Travel through the city recording 100 groups of 17 people. These 100 groups of 17 could be:

17 Prisoners, 17 Anglers, 17 Dancers, 17 Boy Scouts, 17 Hairdressers, 17 Rugby Players, 17 Choir Boys, 17 Chimney Sweeps, 17 Big Issue Sellers, 17 Dinner Ladies, 17 Turf Accountants, 17 Park Keepers, 17 Head Teachers, 17 Barbers, 17 Ramblers, 17 Girl Guides, 17 Bowlers, 17 Market Stall Holders, 17 Footballers, 17 Fish Mongers, 17 Fitters, 17 Policewomen, 17 Sex Workers, 17 Asylum Seekers, 17 Councillors, 17 Visitors, 17 Traffic Wardens, 17 Mothers, 17 Small Time Crooks, 17 Pigeon Fanciers, 17 Funeral Directors, 17 Priests, 17 Vets, 17 Uncles, 17 Carpenters, 17 Drug Dealers, 17 Chiropodists, 17 Newsagents, 17 Cricket Players, 17 Waiters, 17 Key Cutters, 17 Well Dressers, 17 Accountants, 17 Nurses, 17 Joggers, 17 Dentists, 17 Grandfathers, 17 Chefs, 17 Clubbers, 17 Cyclists, 17 Artists, 17 Gardeners, 17 DJs, 17 Road Sweepers, 17 Swimming Pool Attendants, 17 Critics, 17 World War Two Veterans, 17 Children, 17 Caretakers, 17 Solicitors, 17 Teenagers, 17 Pharmacists, 17 Journalists, 17 Bakers, 17 Fathers, 17 Dog Walkers, 17 Primary School Teachers, 17 Barmaids, 17 Surgeons, 17 Lorry Drivers, 17 Soldiers, 17 Odd Job Men, 17 Florists, 17 Farmers, 17 Warehouse Workers, 17 Vicars, 17 Corner Shop Owners, 17 Bricklayers, 17 Bus Drivers, 17 Lovers, 17 Mechanics, 17 Librarians, 17 Aunties, 17 Butchers, 17 Grandmothers, 17 Cousins, 17 Patients, 17 Swimmers, 17 Doctors, 17 Brass Band Players, 17 Taxi Drivers, 17 Imams, 17 Dustmen, 17 Receptionists, 17 Train Drivers, 17 Labourers, 17 Jewellers, 17 Dress Makers, 17 Drummers, 17 Train Spotters, 17 Bouncers.

Record the first 20 groups of 17 making non-verbal sounds with their mouths on the note of F sharp for five minutes.
Record the second 20 groups of 17 making non-verbal sounds with their mouths on the note of G sharp for five minutes.
Record the third 20 groups of 17 making non-verbal sounds with their mouths on the note of A sharp for five minutes.
Record the fourth 20 groups of 17 making non-verbal sounds with their mouths on the note of C sharp for five minutes.
Record the fifth 20 groups of 17 making non-verbal sounds with their mouths on the note of D sharp for five minutes.

Combine and balance all of the recordings so they can be played simultaneously.

Gather these 1,700 members of The17 together at a given time and place in the city centre.
Using a substantial public address system play them back the combined and balanced recordings simultaneously.

Delete all recordings.

Repeat the whole process of this performance in the same city, on the tenth anniversary of the first performance, with 100 different groups of 17.

Repeat again on every 10th anniversary.

Until you die.

pb Poster 157   2007

Bill Drummond

THE LAPTOP
16 January 2007

Did an interview with a bloke from a German newspaper this morning. He suggested we meet in a café bar in Shoreditch called Prague. We met, exchanged pleasantries and then he got down to the business of interrogating me.

'So, do you do the laptop thing?'

'What?'

'Like here in this café.'

And with a sweeping gesture of his arm he indicated the five other mid-morning patrons of this café bar, all sitting at separate tables, all gazing into the screens of their laptops, tapping away on the keyboards. Some tapping more delicately than others.

'Do you go into a café and tap on a laptop?'

'Well no. I write longhand into a book like this one.' I show him my current Black n' Red.

'But I often write in cafés or on buses or anywhere.'

'Berlin is full of fashionable cafés and in all of them are young men and women sitting alone and gazing into their laptops. They could do whatever they do at home but it makes them feel better if they go out to a fashionable café or bar and do it. They like to think that all the others who are doing the same thing will be thinking they are writing a novel, editing a movie or mixing a techno track. It is how we display to our would-be peers and rivals that we are part of the modern creative economy. We are not part of the 9 to 5 world. We may be somebody. Or might be, some day.'

'I like to be as anonymous as possible. I don't like going to these sorts of cafés in case people might know who I am and somebody wants me to explain myself or something.'

Then he got down to that serious business of asking me questions like, well, I can't remember what he asked. The usual ones I suppose.

Interview done, and on the bus back – it's the 149, a bendy one; I like them – I started to think about the laptop. When I was in Moscow last September at the Long Arm Festival, one of the other acts that night was Manorexia, which I was to learn was Jim (J.G.) Thirwell in one of his many guises. I have been a vague fan of Thirwell's since I read a review of the first Scraping Foetus Off The Wheel LP back in 1984.

Listening to the actual records was irrelevant to me. I just liked the way this

Thirwell bloke seemed to conduct his career and the names and titles he chose. But this was the first time I had seen him play. On stage were a classical pianist, a string quartet and Slim Jim standing moodily behind his laptop. He spent the whole set staring into its screen and occasionally tapping a few keys or clicking on his mouse. He was the star turn and the less he did the brighter his star shone. You could tell that that was what the audience wanted from him. The pianist and string quartet provided rhythm and structure; Still Jim provided prerecorded abstract sounds from the laptop. It was heavy. And I liked it.

Two months later at the Huddersfield festival I went along to see Pan Sonic, the Finnish techno boys. On stage with them was a string quartet. The two lads from Pan Sonic stood almost motionless, gazing into the screens of their laptops, occasionally tapping their keyboards. The quartet provided the rhythm and the structure; from their laptops they provided the abstract sounds. They also provided the charisma. I liked what I heard. I was transfixed. I am obviously forcing the similarities between what Thirwell and Pan Sonic have to offer.

For some time now I've considered the laptop as a prime style icon of our age, going way beyond what the electric guitar has been for previous decades. With a laptop you can be engaging with or creating all the important cultural traffic of modern times. The way we're seen by others to relate physically to our laptop is every bit as important as how rock stars in those previous decades were seen to relate physically to their electric guitars. The physical relationship may in one sense be a thousand times more subtle than anything Jimi Hendrix or Pete Townsend might have had with their 'axe' but those subtle moves and non-moves can still be read by all people who are there to read it. It seems that all cultural activity that we deem to be modern and not backward-looking is created and consumed with the use of the laptop. I'm exaggerating to make my point but you know what I mean. I am also aware that not everybody had an electric guitar and even fewer people could play one but now almost every young person in the developed world has a laptop and can use it, so the parallels I am making are not perfect.

I've always (since I was 20, anyway) been of the opinion that the available tools, technology and media have defined the cultural artefacts of any era, far more than any visions that troubled the geniuses of the day. As artists we always follow the tools. We may abuse them, stretch their possibilities, ignore the instructions that come with the packaging; but at the end of the night we, us artists, are never the ones to come up with the new technology, tools or media that in some way enable us to make our visions real.

Now I'm getting to my point. By the time I got off the 149 at the other end of Kingsland Road and was starting the ten-minute walk to my flat I had come to the conclusion that the laptop completely and utterly ruled what I was attempting to do with The17. You take the laptop out of the equation and you are left with almost nothing.

Here I am wanting a year zero, a blank page, but I'm just making another version of laptop music. Here's me thinking I'm ahead of the game, pointing the way to a new horizon and I am, in reality, stuck well and truly in the zeitgeist doing what all the others posing with their laptops are doing. I'm fooling myself just 'cause I'm never actually seen gazing into its screen or tapping the keys.

I will return to this theme later when I can think of a way of wriggling out of the trap I have set myself.

ON THE SOFA (Part Two)
28 January 2007

Back on the sofa 25 days later, watching the final of Celebrity Big Brother 5. By the time you are reading this, you may have forgotten all the furore that surrounded this particular series of Big Brother: the return of Jade Goody; our introduction to Shilpa Shetty; South London girl versus Bollywood star; the racism; questions in The House; burning effigies of Channel 4 controllers on the streets of Mumbai.

Over these 25 days I've become hooked, not only with watching the programme each night but with going out and reading what the tabloids have to say on it all the next morning.

There is nothing I have to add that some cultural commentator on the broadsheets will not have said already and I have no real excuse for allowing myself to be sucked into spending so many hours over the last month watching this meaningless tosh. I have been trying to convince myself that I would not have done so if I had not been asked to be a contestant on the programme. As I watched it I tried to imagine how I could have used it as a vehicle for The17. But in the end I'm glad I only had to face the wrath of my six-year-old son for not doing it and not the ignominy of having done it.

RAKE'S PROGRESS
14 February 2007

Heading down the M1 in the Land Rover. Radio 3 on, blasting out Igor Stravinsky's opera *The Rake's Progress* which is a bit coincidental as I saw Hogarth's original on Sunday at Tate Britain and had been wondering, had I been in the young Rakewell's silk britches, whether my progress would have been similar. Anyway, that heading down the motorway has been suspended because I've pulled into the Watford Gap services for some refreshment and time to catch up with getting thoughts on paper. This has meant I have had to forgo listening to the Stravinsky before the Rake got that far down his spiral.

The Watford Gap service station has never been one of my favourites. But it does hold some sort of place in my imagination and in the nation's musical heritage. As a teenager it was almost legendary as the service station of choice for bands to stop off at for a midnight face-filler on their way back to London from wherever they were doing their gigs in the Midlands or the north.

Somebody who I used to work with when I lived in Coventry had a sister who met Jimi Hendrix at 3 in the morning at the Watford Gap. I cannot hear a Jimi Hendrix track without thinking of the Watford Gap or drive past the Watford Gap without thinking of Jimi Hendrix and The Experience sitting there having a small-hours fry-up. This has seared itself so strongly into my own memory banks that I have even found myself telling people that it was me who saw Jimi Hendrix there.

Today has been a good day. Woke early and drove up the motorway to Leicester. It was pissing down all the way. Wipers on. Fast and furious. Met up with Kev Reverb at his place and went through the latest version of the *OPEN* score with him. This is the text:

> Go to prison.
> Find 17 inmates willing to sing.
> Find a place within the prison walls
> Where The17 can gather.
> Perform score 4 with The17.
> Go back home.
>
> Go back to prison.
> Find the 17 inmates willing to sing.
> Find the place within the prison walls

Where The17 can gather.
Evolve another score with The17.
Perform this score with The17.
Go back home.

I would not have wanted to write this score if it had not been for working with Kev Reverb at Woodhill nick in Milton Keynes some years back. I did the *How To Be An Artist* performance with some of the regular prisoners and again on the nonce wing. The regular cons hate the nonces and would beat the shit out of them given the opportunity. The nonces look down on the regular cons for being thick. On my very limited experience the nonces seemed the brighter lot. I also did a one-to-one with a lad called Robert Stewart who was in Woodhill's close supervision wing. Not many prisons have close supervision wings. They are for the most difficult and disruptive inmates in the prison system. The one in Woodhill was purpose-built. None of the prisoners in there ever get to spend any time with any of the others. The infamous Charles Bronson – the violent criminal as opposed to the actor – is one of the inmates.

Robert Stewart was in his early 20s when I met him. He was slight of build, had the pallor you would expect of a prisoner, and I'm sure plenty of girls would think him cute. From his physical presence the only thing you might find disturbing about him is the tattoo he has on his forehead. It is one of those self-inflicted ones made using a needle and ink. It is the three letters R I P, but because he did it himself while looking in a mirror for guidance they are back to front.

Robert's case gained a certain amount of notoriety in the British press which branded him a psychopathic racist thug. This was understandable considering the crime he committed. We, the consumers of the press, were left with the image of him as the stereotypical psycho skinhead numbskull. Now I don't know if that cliché of the psycho skinhead numbskull has ever really existed outside the cartoons in newspapers but the Robert Stewart that I met was a sensitive young man who wanted to talk about music. His great passion is music, of all genres and from all periods in musical history. The two artists in particular that he wanted to talk about with me were Nick Drake and Marvin Gaye. But these two and the other artists he talked of were mainly in relationship to his own music, the music he composes.

He would love to record his music but this is an impossibility, an indulgence that I can't imagine he will ever be allowed. Stewart is in 24 / 7 solitary. He is considered too dangerous to ever be allowed to share a cell. It is also probable that he will spend the rest of his life inside. Not only will he never get to record his music, he is not allowed to have any kind of instrument to play it on either in case he turns it into a weapon. Nor is he allowed a radio or anything to play CDs or cassettes on. So he never gets to hear any music other than the music in his head. What he is allowed is a notebook where he can write down his compositions.

He had this with him. He showed me a couple of the compositions. He has never learnt to score music on staves; instead he has evolved his own method of notating music and he also used text to describe the sounds – the build-ups, the quiet patches, the orchestration. All of these pieces were instrumental. Not songs as such. No lyrics. More like tone poems, to borrow a term from the classical tradition.

So as I am sitting here in the Watford Gap services remembering how Robert Stewart was talking about Jimi Hendrix's guitar on *Little Wing*, I'm thinking about Jimi Hendrix sitting here eating his fry-up at three in the morning with Mitch and Noel some time back in 1966. And I start to marvel at Robert's capacity to imagine music and wonder if there is anybody else in the country who can do it in the same way. Is it what many of us would do if we were deprived of access to either instruments to play or tools to listen to music on? If Robert had been born into different circumstances and not some deprived Manchester background, would he now be in his third year at the Guildhall School of Music?

My mind jumps to Beethoven writing his Ninth, the choral one. Did he write that one when he was deaf? And when my mind wasn't really concentrating on anything and flitting about I noticed my Land Rover sitting outside in the car park and seeing it parked there brought my mind back to Benjamin Britten's *Rake's Progress*. I'm wondering if the opera has come to an end yet. If I stuff my mouth with what's left on my plate, will I still make the last act? But before I actually start cramming the last of the steak and kidney pie and chips and peas into my mouth, I start thinking about Benjamin Britten in general and how Robert Stewart's situation would make a great story for a Benjamin Britten opera: It's a very defined and claustrophobic situation as a setting for the opera, suppressed sexuality, misunderstood motives, self-serving thick and bitter prison officers, maybe a female education officer who recognises Robert's hidden depths and talents, the background threat and shadow of the other solitary lifers such as Charles Bronson. The opera could start the morning after Robert's cellmate Zahid Mubarek had been beaten to death and end with him ... well, it should end in obvious tragedy. Like Peter

Grimes or Billy Budd or Death In Venice.

So I try to stop thinking about the obvious tragedy and get back to stuffing my mouth and thinking that it would be good to get Robert Stewart to write a score to be performed by The17.

On my way back to the Land Rover I remembered again that Benjamin Britten had nothing to do with *The Rake's Progress*. It is an Igor Stravinsky opera. I wonder where my progress will lead.

Robert: There is a strange coincidence here. Stravinsky was living in America and having work done on his home. The carpenter that was working for him asked not to be paid with money but to be paid in the form of a musical composition. Stravinsky agreed to his request and wrote the carpenter a piece titled Lullaby. Stravinsky later incorporated Lullaby into his score for The Rake's Progress.

This exchange of labour between Stravinsky and his carpenter mirrors the exchange that has taken place between us and Bill. We invited Bill into the Royal College of Art to hold some form of event, in return we offered Bill some work. Bill held The17 at the college and we're writing these notes as our part of the exchange. We call it 'Work for Work'.

After doing The17, the next person we asked to exchange work with us was David Hockney. He too has done an illustrated version of Hogarth's The Rake's Progress, which hangs in the senior common room at the Royal College of Art. This room is out of bounds to the students at the college. David came in and, as a member of senior common room, invited us up to see his Rake's Progress.

SCORE

14. OPEN

GO TO PRISON.
FIND 17 INMATES WILLING TO SING.
FIND A PLACE WITHIN THE PRISON WALLS
WHERE The17 CAN GATHER.
PERFORM SCORE 4 WITH The17.
GO BACK HOME.

GO BACK TO PRISON.
FIND THE 17 INMATES WILLING TO SING.
FIND THE PLACE WITHIN THE PRISON WALLS
WHERE The17 CAN GATHER.
EVOLVE ANOTHER SCORE WITH The17.
PERFORM THIS SCORE WITH The17.
GO BACK HOME.

pb Poster 141   2006

WELCOME FRANCES
21 February 2007

Dawn. Lying in bed in a strange room in a strange house in a town called Mossley. It's Wednesday. On Sunday I drove up to Liverpool with my three youngest children who are on half term. In the back of the Land Rover was an edition of 100 posters. Going to Liverpool and the 100 posters has nothing to do with The17 but may have something to do with the future of music. The text on these posters reads:

LIVERPOOL
In your 'Year Of Culture' I challenge you to deliver

Something
That has not been shipped in from the outside world.

Something
That has not been mediated by experts bought in from the outside world.

Something
That has not been financed by the Arts Council, the Department for Culture, Media and Sport or even the A Foundation.

Something
That is not retro sounding.

Something
That avoids blueprints that were drafted years ago.

Something
That is not just sticking two fingers up to the establishment
In the hope that it will grab media attention.

If you succeed
You will win nothing but the respect of all those who doubted you

Something
That only Liverpool could do.

Bill Drummond

Fifty of these posters have now been fly-posted on the regular fly-posting sites around Liverpool. The other 50 were folded into paper boats and launched onto the swirling current of the ebb tide on the mighty Mersey. My poetic hope is that, like the many thousands of ships that have set sail from the Mersey before them over the past 200 years, they would take their cargo to far shores and distant lands.

I have written elsewhere and at length why I was doing this, but not in this book. There is no point in repeating those words here. All that needs to be added is that only 27 of the 50 paper boats were launched into the middle of the Mersey before the river police arrived in their launch and stopped me from launching any more. If you live on a far shore or distant land and did not get one of these posters sailing to you, that may be the reason why.

Drummond had been invited to write an essay for a catalogue for the exhibition *Centre Of The Creative Universe: Liverpool and the Avant-Garde* at the Liverpool Tate (20 February–9 September 2007). His essay was entitled *Liverpool Will Never Let You Down*. The writing of this essay inspired the edition of 100 posters. The poster was titled **I Challenge You** (Penkiln Burn Poster 125). The essay can be read and the poster can be viewed at the Penkiln Burn site.

Before leaving Liverpool yesterday, and heading for the Pennines, I made a visit to where Temple Court, Rainford Gardens and Mathew Street converge. To the spot where Peter O'Halligan decided that Carl Gustav Jung's dream of the city was centred. This too I have written about at length elsewhere (*45*, Little Brown, 2000). It is the spot where I stood on a manhole cover in May 1984 hoping to harness the power of the intergalactic ley lines and did.

The plan was to measure the dimensions of the manhole cover, which would then dictate the dimensions of the first manhole cover that I am going to have cast in my performance of Score 12, *CAST*.

What I discovered – to my initial dismay and then relief – was that in the pedestrianisation and touristification of Mathew Street and surrounds, the original manhole cover has gone and there is no trace of a replacement. Just ersatz cobbles where the Victorian red-granite cobbles once were.

The dismay bit was that I felt the first manhole cover in the performance of this score should be placed in the exact spot of my first major manhole cover experience. It only seemed right and proper. The relief was the knowledge that if the first manhole cover had been placed there, it would have become just another part of the shoddy tourist trade that Liverpool now deals in.

So that was Liverpool. The reason for driving over to Mossley was to meet up with Rob Cotter and Julie McLarnon. Mossley is a small mill town to the east of Manchester and when the sun begins to rise it finds itself in the shadow of Saddleworth Moor. The dark myth of Saddleworth Moor is deeply etched into our common psyche and will be long after Ian Brady is dead and buried. Remember Julie and Rob from The Manager chapter? Julie gave birth to a wee baby girl called Frances back in January and last night 17 of us gathered together with Frances in one of the larger rooms downstairs. It's a big old rambling house, and Julie recorded us humming a note for 3 minutes 27 seconds (the classic length for a 7" single). This was the first stage in making a performance that is going to take 16 more generations of direct descendants to complete. The chance of this happening are very slim. That is one of this score's major attractions for me; I also like the idea that there will probably be far more than 17 generations of ways that sound is both recorded and kept as a recording before this score is complete. I like the way it makes me think about what music will be like in however many years into the future that will be (320 at the very least) and what, if we have any, our descendents' relationship with music will be like then. What role will it play in their lives and will there be anything left of the recorded music of the early-21st century for them to reference or will it all have been lost on that fateful day when somebody switched the internet off and all the files got deleted?

I take some sort of satisfaction that there is nothing that has been used to store recorded music on to date that does not deteriorate and corrode with time, whether that's analogue tape, digital CDs or even trusty old vinyl. In 320 years' time no one will hear *Strawberry Fields Forever* like I heard it but there will still be the manuscript scores that Beethoven wrote his Ninth on. We may now be living in a time where more culture is being produced than at any other time in the history of man on earth but hardly any of it will exist in future centuries.

I can hear baby Frances making her presence known somewhere else in the house and decide this is the time to get up and get going with the day.

SCORE

9. WELCOME

A baby must be born.
Contact 17 people asking them to meet the
newborn baby.
Ask The17 to gather around the newborn
baby and hum a chosen note in unison
for a given time.
Record this humming.
Try not to upset the baby.
Put the kettle on.
Keep the recording safe.

The child has grown and now has a
baby of their own.
Contact 17 people asking them to meet the
newborn baby.
Ask The17 to gather around the
newborn baby.
Play the original recording.
Indicate a note a fifth above the original
note and ask the17 to hum the new note.
Record this humming.
Try not to upset the baby,
Put the kettle on.
Keep the two recordings safe.

The child has grown and now has a
baby of their own.
Contact 17 people asking them to meet the
newborn baby.
Ask The17 to gather around the
newborn baby.

Play the previous recording.
Indicate a note a fifth above the original
note and ask the17 to hum the new note.
Record this humming.
Try not to upset the baby,
Put the kettle on.
Keep the three recordings safe.

Life is short.

Request that this process is continued for
17 generations in all.

With each newborn baby the note to be
hummed is to be the fifth,
above or below the last.

If you were the 17th baby and now have
grown up, carefully combine and balance all
of the recordings.

Gather friends and family.

Play them the combined and balanced
recordings simultaneously.

Delete all recordings.

Start the process again.

pb Poster 136   2006

BRING ON THE UNKNOWN
23 February 2007

Global warming or climate change, as I understand we should be calling it, is turning her tricks again. The sun is out, I can feel her warm rays on my cheek. I pull up the sash window and climb out onto the ledge for the first time in 2007. The deckchair is still in the same position it was when I sat on it in early December.

I get myself a pot of tea, my Black n' Red notebook and a copy of a Finnish magazine I got in the post this morning. The sycamore is still in place and already I can detect small buds swelling at the tips of each and every branch. A blackbird is singing loud and clear from some unseen vantage point. A blue tit busies himself with his daily chores and a magpie lands on a high branch with a twig in her beak. The beginnings of a nest can be seen clearly. I loathe magpies. They bring death and destruction on the bird world without seemingly bringing anything to the table for the rest of creation. Much like Homo sapiens, you may comment.

On the cover of *Soundi*, which is the name of the Finnish magazine, is a head-and-shoulders shot of the singer from the band Lordi that won the Eurovision Song Contest in 2006. I turn the first page, a double-page advert for electric guitars. Modern heavy-metal guitars. To my eyes they all look silly. There are also pictures of guitarists from bands I've never heard of lending their endorsement to these guitars. Bands like Children Of Bodom, The Rasmus, 69 Eyes, Amorphus, God's Plague, Suburban Tribe, Stamina, Thunderstone, Mirror Of Madness. I've written that list of names down for no other reason than I've always liked lists of band names, especially when I don't know who the bands are. I like to imagine what the bands sound like, what their history is, what their hopes for the future are, who their fans are and why they are into them. I know that actually listening to their music would bore me but all the other stuff interests me. Now that we have heavy metal, will there always be a demand from lads in their early-to mid-teens to consume it?

I flick through further pages of the magazine. Heavy metal seems to be the main thing. There is a reason for me being sent this magazine. I did an interview with them a couple of months back and this is the issue containing the interview. It was done to tie in with No Music Day but they wanted to cover some of the other stuff I have been up to since The KLF. Mainly they wanted to ask about the series of recordings Mark Manning and I made in Helsinki between 1996 and 97.

Bill Drummond

To make sure I don't repeat exactly what I wrote about these records in the book *45* I've just clambered back through the window, found the one copy of *45* that I have, read the relevant chapter and have now got a mini case of writer's block. Re-reading what I wrote almost ten years ago has made me feel whatever I write now will be old and tired and lacking and … fuck it and fuck that. Writer's block ain't going to get me that easily.

These recordings that Mark Manning and I made over ten years ago were supposed to be the soundtrack to our book *Bad Wisdom* (Penguin, 1996). The book was the story of our attempt to get to the North Pole where we were to place an icon (in the Greek Orthodox sense) of Elvis in the belief it would leak love and good vibes down the longitudes and out across the latitudes of the globe and world peace would break out. We knew this to be rubbish in a literal sense but the poetry in at least attempting it had a huge amount of power for us. Much of the journey we documented in the book was us travelling up through Finland, heading north and further north. Mark Manning, at a later stage, reinterpreted the meaning of the journey as a symbolic attempt to place the spirit of rock 'n' roll as far away from us as possible, a spirit that had caused so much self-destruction in our own lives. He may be right.

The soundtrack album to accompany the book was originally going to be made of tracks we had heard on Finnish radio and in bars on our journey. When we went back to Finland to track them down and attempt to licence them we discovered that they all sounded shit compared to how we remembered them. So instead we invented a whole load of Finnish bands and singers. We imagined their histories, their highs and lows, their dreams and their real names. Then we wrote their songs, went back to Helsinki, found a bunch of musicians, booked ourselves into a studio and got to work.

We loved every last detail of the bands and I will list them here and now for you to wonder at: The Daytonnas, Dracula's Daughter, Gormenghast, Kristina Bruuk, Molten Rock, The Blizzard King and The Fuckers. The Daytonnas had been going since the early 1960s. Seven brothers managed by their mother, they played instrumental hot-rod rock 'n' roll. Their music had not changed over the passing decades, just got faster. Dracula's Daughter were four Andy-Warhol-meets-indie art-school girls and one of them wore glasses. We fancied them. Especially the keyboard player who wore woollen skirts and woollen tights. Gormenghast were progressive. In a very Nordic way. They were led by Peter Darklord, the ultimate rock recluse. Darklord thought of himself as more Beethoven or Bartok than Pink Floyd or Yes. His pretensions were his greatest strength. Kristina Bruuk was a 40-something failed singer-songwriter, one-time lover of Peter Darklord, sometime user of heroin, suicide attemptee and near genius. Her songs deal with love and loss. If Nick Drake had lived and been female, he might have recognised Kristina Bruuk as a serious rival to his crown. I was both scared of her and in love with her. Molten Rock was a metal band who played covers of metal anthems. Except they did not think of them as covers. They thought of them as how the songs should have been recorded originally. Their version of the *Immigrant Song* is the heaviest rock I have ever heard. The Blizzard King is a solo male singer. He lives a semi-nomadic life in the frozen north of Finland, a life that in some ways has been unchanged for centuries. He occasionally stumbles into a recording studio to lay down his weird and fucked-up versions of crooner standards and rock classics. His version of *Strangers In The Night* pisses all over Sinatra's and is almost as good as the one by Sid Vicious.

But our favourites were The Fuckers. Billy Fuck on vocals, Nasty Fuck on guitar, J.J. Fuck on bass and Sick Fuck on drums. Brothers in every way but parentage. The eternal punk losers, pissed and pissed off. Angry at everything as well as each other. Every song they wrote a blur of three-chord rage. To change is to sell out. Forever the outsiders. And that's the way they like it.

So we recorded this album and much more besides. We passed on releasing through a major label for reasons discussed in *45*. Instead we pressed up 500 7" vinyl singles by each of the bands on our made-up Kalevala label and exported them into the UK from Finland. Every one of these songs dripped love and devotion from those who had so carefully crafted them. Attention to detail was total.

I hoped that their obvious exquisiteness would find champions, their praises would be sung and an audience, if only a cult one, would be found. But almost immediately the whole thing was rumbled as an attempted scam by those past-their-sell-by-date hoaxers, The KLF. I was crestfallen and broken-hearted. All that love and craft and attention to detail and it's written off as a prank. If that's the way they are going to play, I'm going to take my ball home. So I prevented the records from having any further distribution and scuppered all plans for the soundtrack LP. I decreed the same fate for the albums by Kristina Bruuk and The Fuckers that had also been recorded. Mark Manning was understandably pissed off with me.

The way I justified it at the time was that as an artist I got a lot out of co-creating the fiction of those bands, writing the songs, recording them, having

Bill Drummond

them pressed up as 7" singles. Why spoil it all by having them put out into the marketplace where they will be misunderstood and misrepresented?

Ten years later I still have boxes of them in my workshop. And not a week goes by without me thinking about the careers that Mark Manning and I dreamed up and wondering what The Fuckers or Kristina Bruuk or The Daytonnas are up to now. But I have learnt something from this – any time an artist stops trying to make music or art or words in a way they have never been done before, they are dead. As soon as they start to look back and want to make music, or allow themselves to be overtly influenced by music, art or words from the safety of an earlier era, they are creatively dead. That is what Mark Manning and I were doing: wanting to recreate, even though it was with all the love and devotion we could muster, music in genres that were already defined by history using tried-and-tested methods.

I will take it even further. As soon as an artist knows what they are doing and how to do it and why, they are dead. They are little more than a cabaret act doing a turn. They may as well be a candidate on Pop Idol or X Factor or whatever. The thing is, I've instinctively known this since I was in my late teens. So I've got no excuse.

It is time for me to wheel in The Beatles again to use as my analogy. So. The Beatles broke up in 1970. In 1972 McCartney was getting his Wings band together and I remember reading an interview with him where he was going on about wanting to get back to his rock 'n' roll roots, wanting to be in a band that went out and played gigs. And how he and Wings were embarking on a tour of the country all together with their gear in a transit van. To me as a 19-year-old it seemed commendable in one sense but in another it seemed such a dereliction of duty. After all the exploration and redefining and movement forward that happened in the 1960s, McCartney wanted nothing more than the nostalgia and security provided by being in a beat group, turning up to play at a Friday night college dance. As far as I was concerned, Lennon was a spent force as soon as he released the Imagine album in 1971. But when he did his album of rock 'n' roll covers I lost interest in him altogether. I instinctively felt that as soon as any artist working in any media wants to return to the supposed comfort and certainty offered by the past, they are dead. Or at least dead from a creative point of view.

Yeah, I know we all need to recharge and reassess where we are going. We need to make mistakes and sometimes we need the comfort that only a Rich

Tea biscuit or baked beans on toast can give. But bring on the unknown and risk all on the art yet to come.

The unseen blackbird still sings. The blue tit still busies himself. The magpie is back with another twig for her nest and the buds on the sycamore are that much closer to bursting open. I flick through the rest of the magazine and wonder again why such an outmoded form as rock 'n' roll still exists.

UNTITLED
9 March 2007

Today is the day I should have finished writing this book. I should be up at that hotel at Scotch Corner going through the whole thing, chopping and changing, dumping, correcting and getting some sort of order into all the stories to date. But I'm not there. I'm in my flat and I've still got a load of things not yet written; still want to get the manhole cover done; the prison score done, the one that takes in five different places of faith; and I still want to do a graffiti version of Score 1, *IMAGINE*, on a wall alongside some major road.

I'm stuck in my flat, curtains closed. Staring into the computer screen. I click 'send and receive' just to see if there is anybody out there wanting to make contact. There was an email from my friend Tracey Moberly. She wanted to know if I knew 'today's featured article' on the Wikipedia main page was about The KLF. I didn't know that Wikipedia had a main page. There was a link on her email. I clicked on it, got through to the main page and read:

> The KLF (also known as The Justified Ancients Of Mu Mu (The JAMs), The Timelords and other names) were one of the seminal bands of the British acid house movement during the late 1980s and early 1990s.

> Beginning in 1987, Bill Drummond (alias King Boy D) and Jimmy Cauty (alias Rockman Rock) released hip hop-inspired and sample-heavy records as The Justified Ancients Of Mu Mu, and on one occasion (the British number one hit single 'Doctorin' the Tardis') as The Timelords. As The KLF, Drummond and Cauty pioneered the genres 'stadium house' (rave music with a pop rock production and sampled crowd noise) and 'ambient house'. The KLF released a series of international top-ten hits on their own KLF Communications record label, and became the biggest selling singles act in the world for 1991. The duo also published a book, *The Manual*, and worked on a road movie called The White Room.

> From the outset, they adopted the philosophy espoused by the esoteric *Illuminatus! Trilogy*, gaining notoriety for various anarchic Situationist manifestations, including the defacement of billboard adverts, the posting of prominent cryptic advertisements in *NME* magazine and the mainstream press, and highly distinctive and unusual performances on Top Of The Pops. Their most notorious performance was at the February 1992 Brit Awards, where they fired machine gun blanks into

the audience and dumped a dead sheep at the aftershow party. This performance announced The KLF's departure from the music business, and in May 1992 the duo deleted their entire back catalogue.

With The KLF's profits, Drummond and Cauty established the K Foundation and sought to subvert the art world, staging an alternative art award for the worst artist of the year and burning a million pounds sterling in The K Foundation Burn A Million Quid. Although Drummond and Cauty remained true to their word of May 1992 – the KLF Communications catalogue remains deleted – they have released a small number of new tracks since then as the K Foundation, The One World Orchestra and most recently, in 1997, as 2K.

(More...)

I then clicked on the (More...) which was a link through to the KLF page on Wikipedia. Although over the past few months, and especially since I got rid of all my books, I have begun to use Wikipedia a lot for reference purposes, I have never read the KLF page. That was until I clicked the (More...) link about an hour ago. What I read shocked, excited, disgusted, angered me, gave me a hard-on, made me cry out 'I am not worthy, I am not worthy'. Except I didn't actually get a hard-on or proclaim that I was not worthy. I poured myself a cup of tea, opened the curtains and stared out at the street below.

What I read made what Jimmy Cauty and I did together, under our various guises, sound like the greatest thing ever. It made me feel like I should have gone and lived in a hut somewhere up the Andes and never done anything again other than tend my vegetable plot or at least commit suicide. If that had happened, The KLF would have been a complete and stunning piece, something that could never be beat or tarnished. All this 17 stuff seems so small and insignificant compared to the myth I've just read.

Is it too late to destroy everything I've done over the past few years and head for South America? Live the rest of my life as a recluse like Captain Beefheart or Scott Walker and let the myth do the talking? Fuck it. It's too late for that. And anyway, I need to do The17 – can't stop myself, or it. Best thing is to make sure I never read anything again like this Wikipedia stuff about The KLF. Then I start wondering who writes all this stuff about The KLF on Wikipedia. Where do they get their information from? Should I email them to correct them on some of the mistakes they have made?

Bill Drummond

Pour myself another cup of tea and decide to get this book done as fast as I can and get on with getting The17 out there. Then I hear that song in my head

> Out on the road today I saw a Dead Head sticker on a Cadillac, a little voice inside my head said don't look back. You can never look back.

You know the song. Can't remember what it was called. It was sung by some bloke who was in The Eagles.

Maybe tonight I should go out with the pot of paint and the brush and get the graffiti done and call it a day.

'IT'S NOT TRUE UNLESS IT MAKES YOU LAUGH'
18 March 2007

The day didn't get called as I didn't do the graffiti and I have found myself doing the looking-back thing as well. But there is a reason, if not a justification.

Last December (2006) I got an email telling me that Robert Anton Wilson was dying and he was skint and they were hoping that some of those who appreciated his work would contribute to a fund set up to pay his hospice bills until Robert passed away. Robert Anton Wilson is the co-author of *The Illuminatus! Trilogy* and, as the Wikipedia entry for The KLF says, *The Illuminatus!* had a big influence over the way that Jimmy Cauty and I worked. Another thing about Robert Anton Wilson is that he is American, and my reaction to the email was 'Fuck it. If the Yanks can't get it together to have a national health service, why should we help out?' If I'm going to dip my hand in my pocket, there are at least a few million other causes more deserving than a burnt-out West-Coast hippy who probably smoked too much dope and had a messiah complex.

Three weeks later, on 11 January, he died. A few days after that I got a call from a man at the South Bank Centre (a large arts complex in London) telling me that they were staging an evening of events to celebrate the life and work of Robert Anton Wilson and that they would like me to be involved. Do a reading or something. I asked if anybody else was doing a reading. The man said Alan Moore was. I am a fan of Alan Moore and thought if Alan Moore is doing it, so should I. Then, some days after that I got an email from them offering me £500 for doing 15 minutes.

I had no idea what I would do with the 15 minutes so I thought I should read *The Illuminatus! Trilogy* again. As I had got rid of my copies of the book, along with all the other books (well, nearly all) in the great purge, I went onto Amazon to order them but discovered they are only available to buy now as one combined edition.

Two days later it arrived, all 805 pages. I remembered how turgid most of it is and how I never finished the trilogy when I got the books in the first place in 1976. Back then I had to read every page at least twice to get what was going on and I'm not that fast a reader at the best of times.

I thought, if I'm going to have to read this book, it's got to be worth my while. So the next day I emailed the bloke at the South Bank saying I would do it for £1,000. He was pissed off 'cause he thought we had already agreed on the £500. We settled on £750. I liked the perversion that I was haggling over the fee when I had sent nothing for his hospice fund. I knew that this would have to form part of my talk at the South Bank. Maybe I would even ask the audience what I should do with the £750, pick the best suggestion and follow through with it.

That was just over a week ago. This evening I have to do my 15 minutes and I still haven't got a clue what the words that come out of my mouth will be about. Over the past week I have been trying to get the book read. I got to page 805, let's say, about 23 minutes ago. Reading the book after so many years has been a revelation to me. When I first tried to read the trilogy in 1976, the books were not published in the UK. They were given to me by the director, actor and playwright Ken Campbell. He and Chris Langham were going to turn them into a stage play. I was then working as a stage-set builder at the Everyman Theatre in Liverpool. Ken Campbell had asked me to design the sets for his adaptation of *The Illuminatus!*. It was to be staged in Liverpool at Peter and Sean O'Halligan's Liverpool School of Language, Music, Dream and Pun in Mathew Street. Ken Campbell decided our company would be called The Science Fiction Theatre of Liverpool.

Back then I did not get much further than reading the first part of the trilogy. Most of the action in the mammoth eight-and-a-half-hour play was taken from this first book. At the time it did not strike me as one of the great books of our time. Jack Kerouac, Henry Miller, Jack London, Ken Kesey, Hunter S. Thompson: these were the people I had been reading. 'Spontaneous and confessional prose style' – to quote somebody – was my thing. I wanted the first-person narrative to be the thoughts of the writer. The first-person narrative in *The Illuminatus!* kept shifting without warning. You had no idea whom you were supposed to be identifying with or what the authors thought. And of the numerous first-person narratives, there was not one I took a liking to.

I also did not like the cynicism. But it did inspire me to question the surface interpretation of whatever is going on. What I learnt back then, I learnt from Ken Campbell. What Ken had to teach was pretty simple. If you want to do something, do it. Everything is possible or at least entertaining the idea that everything is possible is a start. I learnt more from working with Ken Campbell than I had from any teacher, tutor or lecturer before.

Ten years later in 1986 when I jacked in doing music to get on with writing, I was wanting to write about the Liverpool I had lived in between 1973 and 1976, or at least the narrative of my time in Liverpool and use that narrative to hang all my thoughts and opinions on. So I decided to reread *The Illuminatus!* books or at least attempt to get further than I did the first time. Reading it then, at the age of 33, it seemed like a completely different book. I was no longer after the 'spontaneous and confessional prose style' rush that Kerouac et al. had provided for me in my late teens and early 20s – this book was working on me on a whole other level. Although I was never one for conspiracy theories (and that is a big part of the book), I was into the contradictions it presented: how something may appear to be one thing but then turn out to be the opposite, or how something could be what it is and its opposite at the same time.

This chimed with a contradiction I had long felt to be at the heart of human existence: that we are totally trapped and totally free at the same time. This thought had landed when I was 20, sitting in the library at Liverpool Art School, when it dawned on me that if you viewed the world and everything else from a totally material point of view, if you knew everything that had ever happened, absolutely everything, and you put it into a massive equation, then you could work out everything that was ever going to happen. This I found profoundly depressing. Some years later someone told me this was called causality. I stayed profoundly depressed for less than a minute. Luckily for me, another completely contradictory idea landed inside my head. It went something like this: I was completely free to do whatever I wanted and in accepting my freedom I had to accept its consequences – the brick walls, the hidden pitfalls, the (un)certainty of death and that of course everyone else is just as free as me even if they do not accept it. So from that moment in June 1973 I decided to accept the total contradiction that everything from the Big Bang through to the end of time is preordained in every sense and that we are totally free to do whatever the fuck we want.

I've condensed this to just three words – 'accept the contradictions' – and used that as a motto ever since. It has helped me to go with the urges even if the rationality does not stack up. Mind you, I can't vouch for it always paying off.

As I have already documented in the Pop Justice chapter, it was while attempting to reread *The Illuminatus! Trilogy* for the second time in autumn 1986 that the whole urge to make music kicked off. The thing is, on attempting to read *The Illuminatus!* for the third time over the past couple of weeks I realise I only ever got to page 138 when I was trying to read it for a second time in 1986. So all the influence it supposedly had on Jimmy and me came from the first 138 pages of a trilogy of books that has more than 800 pages in it. Jimmy Cauty had not read the books either although he had seen the play when it transferred to the Roundhouse in London.

The first thing I learnt in starting to read it again was that we had got our name wrong. We had called ourselves The Justified Ancients Of Mu Mu, whom I had assumed to be an organisation that had been going for thousands of years, always at war with the power of order and control. On page 127 I discovered they were called The Justified Ancients Of Mummu. Somehow an 'm' had got lost and what had been one word got split into two. But more importantly, I began to realise what a great book it is; how it works on many levels; how well it is written from a purely literary point of view; and how it took huge liberties with what we understand as fiction and made it work. Of course it is dated in so many ways, very much of an era, but it's still a fantastic read. And still worth the read, even if somebody is not paying you a grand to do it.

Only 20 or so pages in, it started to be obvious what an influence, in a literary sense, *The Illuminatus!* had on the way I wanted the *Bad Wisdom* trilogy of books that I have been working on with Mark Manning to be. The continual and unannounced shifting of the first-person narrative, the mixing of fact and fiction, the interruption of the timeline, the apparent lack of coherent plot, the need to save the planet and the soul of mankind, the trivial mixed with the big themes of life; it was as if Mark Manning and I had set out to write out our own version of *The Illuminatus!* I spoke to him earlier today to ask him about this. He told me he had never read it, but he thought the third and final book of our *Bad Wisdom* trilogy should be called Fall Down And Worship Me. It's a line from the gospel of St Matthew, where Jesus has spent his 40 days and 40 nights in the wilderness and Satan is attempting to tempt him with all that the world has to offer in exchange for falling down and worshipping him.

But as I read on things got stranger. The figure of the rabbit is a recurring image in the book, whether Bugs Bunny or a more mythical rabbit. I first started reading *The Illuminatus!* some two years before the band Echo And The Bunnymen was formed and named. A band, although I worked with them almost from their beginning, I had no say in naming. If you have read my story *From The Shores of Lake Placid,* you may remember how their name, The Bunnymen, took on a mythical meaning for me and I felt the presence of this rabbit like an other-worldly figure. And now I find the same presence leaking from the pages of this book.

(A bit of an aside, but sort of relevant – you can imagine how freaked out I was when I first saw that film Donnie Darko which starts with Echo And The Bunnymen's classic *Killing Moon* as the soundtrack over the opening scenes and how this scary rabbit figure haunted the film and in a sense is the protagonist, if not the leading man.)

Then I got to page 502. Way into virgin territory compared to my previous attempts to read the trilogy in full. If there is a central character, it is Hagbard Celine. Prior to the following quote, Hagbard has just accepted a bribe.

> Hagbard put the money in his clam-shell ashtray and struck a match. There was a brief merry blaze, and Hagbard asked calmly
> 'Do you have any other inducements to offer?'
> 'I'll tell you anything you want to know about the Illuminati!' Harry shrieked really frightened now, realising he was in the hands of a madman to whom money meant nothing.

So this *Illuminatus! Trilogy* even contains money-burning. I was getting paranoid, not a condition I am normally prone to. Was this book in some way in control of all my creative life over the last 30 years? No wonder whoever had posted The KLF entry on Wikipedia had written 'From the outset, they adopted the philosophy espoused by esoteric novels, *The Illuminatus! Trilogy*'.

I read on. A further money-burning reference on page 510. More rabbits appearing. The events in the book started on a 23 April and took place over the following few days. When I got to page 590 all the subplots were coming together. It was going to be now or never. The Illuminati were either going to destroy the world or Hagbard Celine and his gang were going to save it. And what day is this all going to happen on? On 29 April. And that particular day is not just any day – it is my birthday. I couldn't give a fuck for astrology or synchronicity or numerology or any of that quasi-bollocks, and yes I know that every 365th person on earth will have been born on 29 April but it is me reading the book right now, or it was me last night trying to get it finished. It was me seeing all this other stuff in it that seemed to have either predicted or preordained in some way what I was going to be getting up to over the years. If I was to read it again in another 20 years' time, when I am 73, would it in some way be full of stuff that predicted how I'm about to spend the next 20 years? As it happens, it didn't all happen on 29 April. My birthday was the day before it all came to a climax in the book, and 30 April is Hitler's birthday.

Bill Drummond

You may be wondering what the fuck all this has got to do with The17 and the future of music and how meaning evolves. Maybe not much, but there is another seam that runs through the whole book. From page 15 to 802, anyway.

But first I want to remind you about how I usually respond to the question 'So why is it called The17?' and how I usually trot out that same answer by first telling whoever is asking the question that I have no idea, I just know that ever since I became aware of the big dark sprawling sound of The17 singing in my head it has been called The17. How, when I was ten years old standing in our kitchen in Scotland, the wireless presenter on the BBC Light programme made an announcement. There was no one else in the kitchen at the time so I felt he was talking directly to me. And this is what he said – roughly:

'I want you to stop whatever it is that you are doing and listen. I have just been handed a copy of a long-playing record by that new singing sensation, The Beatles. It is the first long player by the fab four from Liverpool. This will be the first time anywhere in the world, a song from this LP has been played on the wireless. The tune you will hear is track one of side one, a song called *I Saw Her Standing There*'.

I don't know if it was the radio presenter's official BBC English tones or what, but I instinctively felt this was a special occasion like the first live transatlantic television broadcast the year before or Yuri Gagarin being the first man to go into space the year before that. Up to that point I had not heard either of the two Beatles hit singles. In fact I had never heard anything by The Beatles. But I was aware that they were this new sensation that all the girls in my class were talking about. Even my mum was.

My eyes were fixed on the wireless. The music started. I knew I must concentrate. The singing started. The first line went, 'She was just seventeen, you know what I mean …' and whatever else was said in the song did not matter. By the time I learnt what it meant I had already started collecting in my head all these song lyrics that had the number 17 in them. And then there was that stuff about the importance of the age of 17 and that choir called The Sixteen that I like and maybe I just wanted to go one better. Anyway, now that I have just read *The Illuminatus! Trilogy* from cover to cover for the first time in my life I think there may be another reason. And I really wish it wasn't the reason because I'm quite happy with the half-baked ones I have already.

Most people are aware that the number 23 comes with a lot of baggage, hocus-pocus and interesting facts; and to a lesser extent so does the number 5. In *The Illuminatus! Trilogy* both the number 23 and 5 feature heavily. Jimmy Cauty and I used the numbers 23 and 5 in our joint work at almost every turn. Not because we were into numerology or even knew what that was about; we just liked it, were drawn to it. What I didn't know was that there was a third number in this book that makes its presence felt throughout. The number 17. It first surfaces on page 15 and does not bow out until page 802. It is featured at least 40 times while The Justified Ancients Of Mummu (The Jams) are only name-checked 27 times.

After I became aware of the regularity of the number appearing in the book I started underlining some of its more obvious appearances. Flicking through the book in the past few minutes I've chosen 17 examples at random.

1) ... Professor J.N. Marsh was delivered in 17 minutes (p.299)
2) 'I've killed men, I've sent them to the electric chair. Seventeen times ...' (p.291)
3) Need I add that the page was 17 and the line was of course, line 23? (p.304)
4) The sun beat down on the town of Daleville on July 17 ... (p.129)
5) In the centre of the room was a pyramid of seventeen steps ... (p.205)
6) 17 people had died of heart prostration the day before (p.237)
7) ... but there it was again 23 and 17 (p.237)
8) 23 hours and 17 minutes ago, a flying saucer landed in Iowa ... (p.238)
9) One hundred and fifty seven women, one wife, and seventeen boys. (p.352)
10) Spot the hidden 17 in there? (p.251)
11) 'Number Seventeen,' read Professor Curve... (p.274)
12) 17 being a number with virtually no interesting geometric, arithmetic or mystic properties (p.279)
13) ... passed an olive garden and saw the Seventeen ... (p.324)
14) ... it was a sunny afternoon in October and the drapes in the living room on the apartment on the seventeenth floor ... (p.334)
15) If the seventeen original apostles – five of them have been purged from the records – had been left on their own, they would have passed horror and terror. (p.337)
16) The seventeen Illuminati representatives vanished in the dark. (p.353)
17) ... and the beverage was a blend of the Japanese seventeenth – herb Mu tea ... (p.427)

So what do I do? Just accept this book has had some sort of profound influence on what I've done over the past 30 years and will probably continue to do so? Or do I just take it down the Oxfam shop and forget it? Or read it again to find if there are any more hidden signs in it that I should take note of when it comes to steering the direction of The17? It all seems so childish. All that *Illuminatus!* stuff was OK as part of the trappings of a postmodern pop group back in the late 1980s. But I'm fucking 53 now, 54 next month. I'm trying to explore where we are with music, where it may be going and what is its meaning.

Best leave it there for the time being. I've got this 15 minutes to sort out for this evening. Maybe I should demand 17 minutes or refuse to do the show. After tonight I will want to get rid of this copy of *The Illuminatus!*. I can feel the urge to burn it coming on. Maybe go up to the roof on my flat and tear every page of it out, page by single page, light the first with a match and then light each new freshly ripped-out page from the last flicker of flame from the previous one. Wonder how long it will take?

40 YEARS AGO TODAY
30 March 2007

While stirring the porridge an hour or so ago I heard an interview on the Today programme on Radio 4. It was with Peter Blake the artist. He was being interviewed about his design for the cover of The Beatles album Sgt. Pepper's Lonely Hearts Club Band. It was 40 years ago today since the photo for the cover was taken. I am aware that a Beatles thread is running through this book. This was not by design and I will refrain from spending the next few pages going on about this album cover and the way it changed, if not the universe, the inside of my head. Instead I will confront the number 40. In the previous chapter on *The Illuminatus!* I touched on the numbers 5 and 23 and went on about the number 17. I had to resist getting dragged into talking about the number 40 as well. This has got to me over the past dozen days and when I heard it on the radio this morning I knew I would be helpless to resist its pull once the notebook was open.

For me the number 40 has been a big one ever since I can remember numbers having any pull on my subconscious; this, by the way, was years before I even knew there was such a thing as a subconscious. I've always put it down to my exposure to the power of the Bible from an early age. The number 40 recurs regularly in the biblical stories. The story of Noah and his ark in Genesis is the first time the number 40 crops up.

I have just gone to get the Bible off the shelf, to check that fact and was a bit disturbed, but in some ways not surprised, to find the appearance of another familiar number.

> On the seventeenth day of the month all the fountains of the great deep broke up and the windows of heaven were opened. And the rain was upon the earth for forty days and forty nights.

Later we learn that once Moses had led the Israelites out of Egypt they spent 40 years wandering the wilderness before crossing the River Jordan into the Promised Land. And then, much later, we learn that Jesus spent 40 days and 40 nights sorting his head out before he set about his mission.

Somewhere in my young head the number 40 had taken on a significance, especially when it came to measuring the passage of time. Some years back I learnt that the number 40 in Hebrew or Aramaic or whatever was not only meant to mean literally 40, but also to mean 'a lot'. Maybe not 100s but a lot all the same. I guess in the way we can use the word 'couple' as in 'a couple of minutes' and we do not have to mean literally two minutes.

This took a bit of the specialness of the number 40 away for me but there was also a part of me that was relieved. This has not stopped Mark Manning and I wanting to use the phrase '40 Days & 40 Nights', as the subtitle for the last in our trilogy of Bad Wisdom books.

So a couple of weeks back when I was ploughing through *The Illuminatus!*, underlining any interesting mentions of the number 17, on page 239 I came across stuff about 'The 40 Enigma' and – more interestingly – 'without invoking the mystic 5 we still arrive at 40 by adding 23 and 17. What then is the significance of 40? – Jesus had his forty days and forty nights, Ali Baba had his 40 thieves, Buddhists, their 40 meditations, the solar system is almost exactly 40 astronomical units in radius ...'

That was the last bit of cod information I wanted to cloud my thinking with. So to try and empty my head of the numbers and the meanings we give them I click on 'send and receive' to see what mail the night has brought in. There was one from a bloke called Phil Hargreaves. He was sending in a score. This is what he wrote:

> The unit of life is breath.
> The choir is divided into two groups. The first group are sustainers.
> If you are in the first group you will:
> Take a breath.
> Choose a note that no-one else seems to be singing.
> Sing that note for as long as the breath lasts.
> Continue, choosing fresh notes if necessary, or if you feel like it.
> The second group are Declaimers. If you are in the second group you will:
> Take a breath.
> Sing as many syllables on as many notes as fast as possible. Do not attempt recognisable language; speed and density are of the essence here. Listen to the other members of your group while singing. Keep going until the end of your breath. Then join the Sustainers.
> There are three members of the Declaimers; no more and no less. Your membership lasts for one breath, and is not renewable. The three people should not be predetermined – the group should negotiate this membership as the piece progresses. As soon as someone runs out of breath and joins the Sustainers, someone must replace them. But only one person. It is a balance the group must maintain.

The piece ends when there are no more people to join the Declaimers. At this point, every member of the choir finishes the breath they are singing with and the piece comes to a halt – unless any member of the choir wishes to begin again, at which point they draw breath, and begin singing. The other sixteen then have a duty to repeat the entire process, bring the Declaimers up to quorum and maintain them there until everyone has left the Declaimers again. In this manner, the piece lasts until everyone is satisfied that it has lasted long enough.

By Phil Hargreaves 29 March 2007

Notes:
I noticed that a fair few of your scores involve people singing chords of one sort or another, and I can see an argument that if you were going to use harmony in a situation where music hadn't been invented, the most attractive interval would be a perfect fifth. In fact, the first time we invented music, this sort of harmony was a bit of a late development, and people started with monophonic music (i.e. one note at a time), and then moved on to polyphony (i.e. still one note at a time, but kind of interweaving). Out of this, people started to notice how some notes sat better with other notes. Maybe a thought for future scores. Also, there are people who simply can't sing you back a note you've just played them. I read once that archaeologists can examine old skulls and tell what the previous owners did with them from the grooves that the muscles have worn into the bone. From this they have concluded that we sang before we developed language, and that language was in fact an extension of singing. This is why I have included the 'Declaimer' group, doing a kind of glossolalia. The 'Sustainers' idea is a load of people trying to invent harmony the day after it has been abolished. I think you'd find some lovely chords swelling up out of nowhere, and then being lost again almost as quickly. The whole structure of the piece demands that the participants listen closely to the rest of the group.

I look forward to trying out this score and as he has not given it a title, I will name it *BREATHE*. As for Phil Hargreaves' note, it addresses some obvious contradictions that run throughout the whole of The17. The history of music is a vast subject – you could fill a whole library with the books that have been written about it. I have not read a single one. Although I do not want to bask in or boast of my ignorance, I can't see myself visiting that particular library any time soon. That said, three weeks back I flew to Glasgow, took the train from there to Mallaig on the Argyle coast. The last stretch of that line is one of the great train journeys on this earth, now made famous in the Harry Potter films. At Mallaig we caught the ferry across to the Isle of Skye where we were met by John Purser.

John Purser, a man in his 60s and Glaswegian by birth, is a composer, musicologist, historian, poet and crofter. His most major work to date, a book entitled *Scotland's Music*, has had a profound influence on the way those who think about these sort of things think about Scotland's musical heritage – and led to a renaissance of interest in Scottish classical composers from previous centuries. And I thought it was all about Andy Stewart and Moira Anderson. He is currently working on a 50-part series of programmes for BBC Radio Scotland, covering the history of Scottish music over the past 5,000 years. The producer of the series, David McGuinness, asked me to be interviewed for the series. McGuinness had taken part in a performance of The17 in Newcastle and had also shown interest in No Music Day. Have I already told you some of this in a previous chapter?

John Purser lives on his croft on the Isle of Skye, with his wife, the cellist, Barbara Purser. Earlier this year (March 2007), I was invited up to his croft for the interview. My contribution was to be used in the final of the 50 programmes. If The17 can be described as Scottish music because I have a Scottish background, I do not know, but I'm pleased The17 is to be included anyway.

On my visit to his croft I found John Purser an entertaining but challenging man. He was also tough, hardy, self-sufficient. His croft was no mere affectation. Him and Barbara were welcoming and generous hosts. Their table groaned with produce shot, picked, caught, slaughtered or grown on their croft.

If you want to know what music was being made in Scotland 5,000 years ago, and how and why it was being made, he is the man to ask. The trouble is I forgot to ask him while I was there. David McGuiness and I were too busy carrying out the tasks we had been put to around the croft, and then with all the eating, answering John Purser's questions and drinking bog-myrtle beer that had to be done, there was no time for me to be asking questions.

So as I have no facts to base my thoughts on, I have based them on fantasy. The fantasy goes like this: many thousands of years ago, let's say 5,000, a bunch of people were sitting around their fire making what they thought to be pleasing sounds with their mouths and throats and lungs. And then one of them made a sound that was not the same note as any other person was making, but it complemented it. It was a harmony of it. To my 21st-century Western ears the most obvious harmony would be a fifth, a note five tones up from the note the other person is making. And when this happened, harmony was born. And in my fantasy that was one of the greatest moments in the cultural development of mankind. Up there with developing the wheel, learning to harness the power of the wind to drive a boat, and vastly surpassing putting a man on the moon. This harmony would have seemed like magic. It *is* magic. It would have been revered and added to the list of things that gave life meaning to these people.

The word 'meaning' seems to be slipping into this book more and more, although I have never been bothered about what things mean before I set out to make them. That has always seemed irrelevant. The basic urge to do it is all the meaning I've needed. And I rarely ask of a work of art that I'm consuming – be it visual, music or text – what it means. But I do know that a huge part of the human condition is our need for meaning. Sometimes it feels like our need for meaning is bigger and more important than our perceived need for that trinity of late Western culture: health, wealth and happiness, and of course that old fraudster, freedom.

But this seems like it is too big a topic for now and maybe I will return to it in the last chapter of the book. Maybe the book should be called Meaning. Just that one word.

MEANING
BY
BILL DRUMMOND

So instead of thinking about that, I will get out of the house, cross the road and have a look at my current favourite manhole cover. Now that I know I am not going to make one for the bottom of Mathew Street in Liverpool I've decided the first one is to be almost identical to the one across the road.

Except that instead of it reading 'Amhurst Iron Foundry Co Hackney E8' in raised cast words around its inner circle it will read 'Stand On This Manhole Cover And Listen. The17 2007'. And when I've had it cast, I will replace it under the cover of broad daylight.

Bill Drummond

TIPS FROM TONY
2 April 2007

This morning I had a meeting with Leah Zakss at the British Council. This evening I will be watching The Rebel starring Tony Hancock. But right now the notebook is open and the words are forcing themselves out of the pencil.

The idea of the Bethlehem film was discussed. Leah Zakss informed me that although the British Council does have an office in the Palestinian territories it is very difficult to plan things there in advance as the situation is in such a state of flux. At the time of writing the BBC radio correspondent has been kidnapped and nothing has been heard from him or his kidnappers. Also at the time of writing I have been reading *Palestine*, the graphic memoir by Joe Sacco about his time in the Palestinian territories in the early 1990s. It is a brilliant work on many levels but one of the things that it alludes to is the number of Western journalists who are there, all trying to get their frontline stories. And how the Palestinians will welcome them and be open but once they have their story, these same journalist are off back to the safety of wherever it is they have come from. Their story gets published, they get another notch in their belt, but nothing changes for the Palestinians. I am not a journalist but reading Joe Sacco's book has made me change my plans. Although I always suspect my motives and often try to turn those suspicions into part of whatever it is that I am doing, this time I'm giving into my suspicions about my motives in wanting to do something in the Palestinian territories. Do you follow my drift?

Leah Zakss told me she was going to be having meetings with some folks from the Indian British Council tomorrow and she would like to bring up the topic of The17 with them. She also told me how difficult it is to explain The17. Although it had been an incredibly powerful thing for her to take part in and felt it would be so for anybody else taking part, trying to describe it is almost impossible, she said, there were no reference points for people to get or hold onto. This concerns me. This is information I've been given before. This has altered something in my head and, thus, my plans.

Some years ago I went to Calcutta. I was supposed to be writing a film script. Instead I wrote a story called *Kali Versus Ted*. Later in this chapter I will come back to the subject of Calcutta, the British Council and a film about The17. But first I want to go in a different direction.

The story Kali Versus Ted tells the tale of launching 98 paper planes from the window of the Mumbai to Calcutta train as it makes its way across India. Each of the paper planes were made from pages torn out of Ted Hughes's then recently published book *The Birthday Letters*. At another level the story deals with 'trouble in the mind and war in the head'. The Ted referred to in the title is Ted Hughes, the Kali is the Hindu goddess who is often depicted with multiple arms each clutching the severed head of a man. Kali Versus Ted was published as the main text in the small book *Annual Report* (Penkiln Burn Book Two), published 1998 in an edition of 500.

Also, at the time of writing, The Proclaimers are at number one in the UK singles chart with their song *I'm Gonna Be (500 miles)*. The song was originally recorded in 1988 and only got to number 11 in the UK charts in August of that year. The reason why they are at number one almost 20 years later is that the song was picked to be used for the Red Nose Day charity record for this year's Red Nose Day. As such, it was re-recorded featuring Matt Lucas in character as wheelchair-bound Andy from Little Britain, and Peter Kay as his wheelchair-bound character from Phoenix Nights. I am very pleased that The Proclaimers are at number one, not because I'm a great Red Nose Day supporter but because of events that occured back in 1979 when David Balfe and I are trying to make records in Liverpool. Trying to put them out, trying to manage two bands, but mostly we are having this vision about a thing called The Zoo that is far more than a provincial record company. We wanted to change the world, not just make cute records that people in decades to come could feel nostalgic about. We wanted to revolutionise what culture was and how it worked and how people would respond to and consume it.

We failed. But there was a lasting by-product of our failure and that was, and still is, Zoo Music Ltd, a company that we are still 50–50 shareholders in. Zoo Music is a music publishing company. A music publishing company's job is to get the copyright to music and then exploit it. This copyright is not in the recording of the music but in its compositions, the songs or the music itself. A music publishing company will contract songwriters or composers for a certain amount of time and all songs or music that they write in that time becomes the property of the company. Every time a piece of music is used in a film or on TV or on radio anywhere around the world the music publishing company's job is to make sure that the agreed sum paid by the film-maker or broadcaster for the use of the music is collected and paid over to the songwriter or composer. For doing this, the music publisher keeps a slice of the action. Also, any time a record, cassette, video, CD, DVD or download is sold, the music publisher's job is to collect the agreed percentage from the record or film company for the composers or songwriters, again keeping a slice of the action.

Back in 1979 Dave Balfe and I knew next to nothing about music publishing. At most I knew that on all the Beatles records I owned there was this mysterious credit to something called Northern Songs. Who or what Northern Songs were I had no idea.

Dave Balfe and I were approached by one Rob Dickins, then the boss of Warner Brothers Music (now Warner Chappell). He offered us a deal to set up our own music publishing company that Warner Brothers would administrate. We told him we knew nothing about music publishing. He told us all we had to do was sign songwriters who we thought had talent to our publishing company and Warner Brothers would do the rest. They would get their cut, we would get ours and the lion's share would go to the songwriters. This seemed a good idea so Dave Balfe and I set up Zoo Music Ltd, did our deal with Warner Brothers and initially signed the individual members of The Teardrop Explodes and Echo And The Bunnymen and ourselves. And over the next ten years we signed a number of others, but not that many. You could buy a round for all the songwriters we signed and still get change out of a fifty quid note. You'd better make that £100. If we're paying, they will all want doubles.

So Zoo Records fizzled out and we gave up on management, and whatever joint vision Dave Balfe and I shared lost its focus, but Zoo Music Ltd carried on. Twice a year we get a cheque from Warner Chappell. Although that money has never been enough to support an enviable lifestyle ('depends who is doing the envying'), let alone retire on, it is a steady flow, enough at times to provide the initial funding for KLF Communications and a number of things I have done over the years, including The17.

And this is where it starts getting dark and the contradictions start to make their appearances. First, in 1969 the ailing and ageing Hollywood film company Warner Brothers Pictures was bought out by the Kinney Corporation. The Kinney Corporation had nothing to do with the West Coast entertainment business. They ran parking lots and funeral parlours in New York. There was big money in parking lots in Manhattan where land was at a premium. And all that money was coming in, in grubby, used low-denomination notes, if not nickels and dimes. More importantly, this parking lot and funeral parlour business was a front for the Mafia. As well as good revenue, it was a business that was perfect for money-laundering.

The Kinney Corporation had the methods to turn the glamorous but failing Warner Brothers around. All I knew about the Mafia was what I had learned from watching the Godfather films. If you have watched them, you may remember that one of the themes of those films was about the Mafia wanting to go legit and get involved with the seemingly glamorous world of the West Coast entertainment industry.

It was not long before Dave Balfe and I realised we were in the pay of the Mafia. And although Warner merged with Time in 1990 and the Mafia connections have long since faded into the background there is still that sense that follows me to this day that it was serving my time as a small-time flunky for the New York Mafia, bringing in the cash from wherever it can get it, that means I can do what I am doing now.

So what does this have to do with The Proclaimers or the British Council, let alone The17 and the future of music or even meaning?

As documented earlier I once recorded a solo album called The Man. Before it was released Dave Balfe warned me not to embarrass myself. He had heard a couple of tracks from the record and thought that any credibility I had would be utterly compromised by the release of this joke record. I did not heed his warnings. A couple of months later he called me to tell me he had just seen a couple of blokes on The Tube, the then hip and happening TV music programme presented by Paula Yates and Jools Holland, singing a couple of songs that reminded him of my album. I was curious to find out why anybody would want to sing in their natural Scottish accent and attempt to make it in pop music at the same time. Nobody in the histories of Scottish pop or of rock music had ever attempted this before.

We tracked down a video recording of the show. The two of us thought these two blokes – twins, it was obvious – had a rare talent. So we got into the business of trying to sign them to Zoo Music. And we did. They were The Proclaimers. They went on to make some great records and sell several million of them around the world, the income of which continues to more than trickle, if not exactly flow. A couple of months back Dave Balfe contacted me, telling me he had heard that a Proclaimers song was going to be used for this year's Red Nose Day and we should contact someone in order to waive our cut and have it donated to the charity. However worthy the cause, the forced jollity of Red Nose Day has never appealed to me. If I am going to give to a charity, it will be one of, and at a time of, my choosing. I suggest to Dave that we should wait to see if anyone approached us with a request to waive our cut. This has not happened. The money coming to me from Zoo Music Ltd through this record will be hitting my bank account in early April 2008. It will not be as much as some would like to think but however much the amount is, it will not be going to the various charities I may or may not support. Instead, it will be spent on furthering the exploration of the future of music and the part The17 may play in it. 'Pompous or what?'

To celebrate this I have just taken a break from writing and gone onto iTunes and downloaded *I'm Gonna Be (500 miles)* and played it at full volume and leapt around the room while singing along. This has broken my self-imposed rule about what I'm supposed to be listening to this year. It is the year of all bands, groups, ensembles, singers, soloists, composers or orchestras beginning with C.

As I said, plans have been changing. The plan was that this book would cover carrying out of all scores but so far the prison one, the religious one, the wedding one, the death one, the manhole cover one have not been done. The manhole one will be done, as discussed, in the next few weeks. But I want to get the book finished and if I don't bring it to a close pretty soon, there will not be enough time to sort out the publishing and get it scheduled in time for spring 2008 when plans for attempting to take The17 to another level are already in place.

Dave Balfe and I were on the phone to each other earlier today. The conversation was ranging far and wide but it kept on coming back to all this stuff I've been going on about. How meaning is in a constant state of flux, the future of music, what The17 is, and then he brought up the word 'meta-narrative'.

In the late 1970s and early 1980s Dave Balfe and I would often have to drive down from Liverpool to London, picking up records from pressing plants, delivering them to distributors, having meetings with record companies and agents and whoever. On these drives we would have massive eight-hour conversations. These conversations would cover everything. Well, not everything, but loads of stuff: politics, world affairs, books, religion, art, what we were doing wrong, why The Beatles were still the greatest, disco and which girls he thought worth shagging.

Since then we have invented spurious reasons at various times to go on long drives together so we can have similar discussions and debates. So when we were on the phone earlier today I asked him if he was up for a drive to the Isle of Skye where we would climb one of the Cuillin Hills, maybe with this John Purser, if his new hip replacement is in good working order. On our return I would write up whatever I considered pertinent and that would be the book done. Maybe we could even tie in me visiting the Scotch Corner Hotel on the way back down.

As for the other scores not yet done, I will use my cut from The Proclaimers record to get a flight over to Calcutta – thus not going cap in hand to the British Council – and instigate the performance of these scores. Maybe a couple of the other ones too. I definitely fancy doing a manhole cover over there, hire a local cameraman and sound guy and make a film of their staging, knowingly (if not cynically) using the colourful backdrop of Calcutta to make a film. A film that will not feature any of the music made by The17.

Back in the UK, the film will be edited together and hopefully be broadcast to tie in with the publication of this book, or as a DVD packaged with the book. Mind you, by the time you read this and I have got the film made someone will have put it up on YouTube for all to see.

The day has past, the laundry is done and it has been the first day of the year that I have been able to hang it on the outside line to dry in the fresh air.

Now is the time to slip in the DVD The Rebel and pick up some tips from Tony.

HALFWAY UP SNOWDON
11 April 2007

Halfway up Snowdon. My youngest son, Flint (7), is my climbing companion. His birthday gift from me was a view from the top of a mountain. Within the next two hours I hope he will get his present. Of course he would rather have a Sony PlayStation 3 at the very least, but he seems to live a life where he gets what he wants every other day of the year so I thought I would try to invert the traditional order of things and give him something that was 'good' for him on his birthday. Even if he doesn't want it.

It has taken us a good two hours to get this far and every 100 yards or so he tries to make a stand. Complaining that he has climbed far enough, that we should have taken the train, that he never wanted to come in the first place and that grown-ups should not be allowed to tell children what to do. Then, among all this are his incessant questions. And I am loath to report this but most of his questions are about wealth and fame – James Bond, how much footballers earn, Aston Martins, the best way to kill somebody and how much I would pay him to climb the rest of Snowdon.

The Queen's crown is made from Welsh gold – or so I think I was told once. And if my memory serves me well, Snowdonia was a source of that gold.
'Flint, did you know that the stones at the top of Snowdon contain gold?'
'What, real gold? Gold that you can buy things with?'
'Yes, real gold. But you have to get to the top to get the stones that contain the gold.'
'Will there be enough for me to buy an Aston Martin?'
The shit we tell our children. Maybe you don't. Maybe you don't have any. Maybe it serves me right for being so pompous and holier than thou to pass off a view from the top of a mountain as a birthday present. And one day all this deceit and vanity on my part will return to more than haunt me when at some stage in his development he remembers how I lied to him and got him to climb a mountain with the promise of a crock of gold as reward.

On our way there have been numerous skylarks climbing to the skies and singing their hearts out. This alone has made the climb so far worthwhile. There would be no point in indicating them to Flint; just more boring information from his old dad.

So we are halfway up. And halfway up Snowdon these days is a café called the Halfway Up Café. That is how I know we are halfway up. We have stopped here for a proper rest and some refreshment. There have been a number of times in the past that I've climbed Snowdon. The climb has taken on a somewhat symbolic meaning for me, becoming part of the myth of my own life. The first time was in December 1974 when I was 21.

Yesterday Flint and I got the train up from Euston, changed at Crewe and arrived at Bangor. From there we got the bus to Llanberris where we got ourselves a B&B and started our climb this morning. On the train up I started reading *Memphis Underground* by Stewart Home. Stewart Home and I send each other our books and we recognise some sort of kindred spirit in both of us being autodidacts, him more than me, in that he knows more than me. Stewart is burdened with a piercing intellect that I can only be jealous of one day and grateful I don't have the next. Books could be written about the way Home's mind works, and seeing as he already does it I won't bother to start doing so here. Enough to say I always find his books challenging in all sorts of positive ways. *Memphis Underground* more than most. More important than what it's all about is the recurrence of the number 17 in its text. Now there is nothing in this book that makes any nod to numerology – that kind of bogus thinking has nothing to do with what interests Stewart Home. The fact that the number 17 seems to be making repeated appearances in this book is purely accidental.

On page 36 I started underlining all numbers that appeared in the text and keep count of them. This includes numbers written as words or numerals. By page 208, where I am now, there are twice as many 17s as there are of any other number. Now I know you must be thinking that this says far more about me than about the significance of the number 17 but I can't stop myself now. Whatever Stewart Home is going on about pales into insignificance compared to the number count.

Stewart Home's books are usually filled with lots and lots of words. Yeah I know, but there seem to be more words in his books even if there aren't. The words play games with hardcore dialectics and not-so-thinly disguised autobiography. The hardcore dialectics centre on art, literature and politics. Other than cold cynical sex, Home rarely deals with human relationships. As human relationships are what sells the vast majority of books, Stewart's books never make the best-seller lists. On the subject of autobiography, he often splices untruths, if not outrageous lies, into what he is writing about himself. And in his fiction he has himself turning up as a character. This is done to make points about the nature of truth, lies and literature and is done to great effect. At a couple of points in *Memphis Underground* he concludes that autobiography is a fictional genre.

The implication is that we can't help but choose to leave far more out about ourselves than we put in. That process of selection is what creates the fiction and, by implication, a vanity-strewn fiction at that. It's as though putting in the obvious lies about himself in some way vindicates him from the accusation of vanity in his autobiographical writing. This is something I am unable to do. Even though I am very aware that what I write is a fictional genre for the very reason that Stewart Home makes clear and my vanities are there for all to see, I can never take that step of making stuff up that never happened to make a point or just make a better read. Well, OK, maybe once or twice.

And now, sadly, I have to report a truth. By page 209 in *Memphis Underground*, the number of appearances of the number 3 had overtaken those of 17. And also – and strangely on that page, 209 – Flint and I make an appearance. It seems that the character in the book that Stewart Home has playing himself phones me up to get some information but before I give it to him I hang up 'because his baby son, Flint, needed attention'.

On the subject of Flint and myself, thirsts are now quenched, limbs rested, it's time to put away the notebook and return to the climb.

HALFWAY DOWN SNOWDON
11 April 2007

Well it serves me right. We made it to the top of Snowdon. The view was as uplifting as you could want. And I promised myself to get more mountain-climbing back into my life. Although one of the scores for The17 was written to be performed while climbing a mountain, I specifically did not bring a copy of it with me. I wanted this climb with Flint to be a 17-free zone. Just him and me and none of that other stuff. I suppose that was too much to expect.

At the top of Snowdon I could distinctly hear The17 singing in my head in harmony with the sense of wonder that I was feeling. This wonder was promptly broken when the mobile rang and a whole new train of thought kicked in.

But before I get into that I will make plain in what way I was served right. Once we actually got to the top of the mountain and I tried to instil in Flint how, at that point in time, not a boy in the whole of England or Wales was higher up than him.
'What about the boy on that aeroplane?' as he points to a jet that must be about 30,000 feet higher than us.
'But that doesn't count.'
'Why?'
'He didn't climb up there himself.'
'But he is higher and can see further. You said I would be able to see further than I had ever seen before. When we went to Kos on holiday last summer, I could see further than this on the plane.'
There was no point in pushing the subject any more. And anyway, he was more interested in finding the rocks and stones that contained gold. And he found plenty and now my haversack is filled with them. The weight of these rocks has been my constant companion on the way down. A reminder not to make up tall stories in an attempt to get your kids into doing something. Especially crock-of-gold stories.

So now we are back at the Halfway Café, but this time halfway down and not halfway up. Flint is playing and I have got the notebook open, wanting to catch some of the thoughts that have gone through my head since getting the call on the mobile when we were at the top.

The phone call was from Adam Peters who is a musician and composer. I haven't talked to him, let alone met him, since the mid-1980s. Back then he was an arrogantly confident 19-year-old. He somehow had become part of the Echo And The Bunnymen entourage. But he proved himself to be far more than just another one of the hangers-on that gravitate towards successful rock bands. He was there when Echo And The Bunnymen recorded their album Ocean Rain in Paris. The Bunnymen and me thought it would be good to have some strings on some of the songs in a Jacques Brel sort of way. I was up for us finding a French string arranger to do the parts. This Adam Peters insisted he could do it. All I had to do was get him some music manuscript paper and book an orchestra for the next morning to play the parts. I got the musicians booked for the next morning. We were to use an old studio where many classic French film soundtracks had been recorded. Adam Peters spent all day and night writing the parts for the songs. Then copied them all out for each of the members of the orchestra.

At 10 the next morning all these seasoned French session musicians were there, waiting for the maestro to turn up and wave his baton. Instead they got this dishevelled-looking lad who had not slept a wink. They tried to take the piss in that sort of snooty Parisian way but Adam took no shit from them and within one three-hour session we got all the parts done. And it sounded brilliant. Adam Peters' string arrangements were the icing on the cake of the greatest album I have ever been involved with. His talent was truly precocious.

Look, maybe Adam was 21 or even 22 at the time. Me saying he was 19 was partly for teenage effect.

But back to the phone call. It seemed that Adam was now living in Joshua Tree in the Californian desert and had been given the job as musical director of, and I quote, 'Syd Barrett – Madcap's Last Laugh', an evening in homage to the eccentric genius of Pink Floyd's founding member, which was to be staged at the Barbican in London. His job was to get the band together and contact suitable featured artists. It seems Lemmy was wanting to do an acoustic version of See Emily Play. The event was going to take place on 10 May, less than a month away. Adam was contacting me to see if I wanted to be involved. There is no way I can remember if we had even spoken about Syd back in the mid–1980s; one thing for sure was that Adam would have been way too young for The Pink Floyd in the 1960s and probably even too young for the 1970s stadium version of Pink Floyd. There is also no way that Adam would have known about what I've already written about Syd Barrett for this book. I told him I would not want to be involved as a musician – 'Bill Drummond (ex-KLF) sings The Gnome from Piper At The Gates Of Dawn' sort of thing.

But I'd give it some thought.

So on the way down from the top of Snowdon to here at the Halfway Café while carrying my rucksack full of rocks and trying to make sure Flint does not go flying off one of the escarpments my mind is going all Syd. This is what I think I would like to do: publish one of the pamphlets that I have done in the past few years. These pamphlets are usually published for time- or site-specific events. It would only be available to those attending this Syd event. The pamphlet would contain the text I've already written, the *Syd Is Dead* one. And then there would be some other text that I've not yet written, asking everybody who had a copy of the pamphlet to perform a massed version of Score 16, *COMPLEMENT*. This score, as it stands at the moment, reads:

> Someone must die.
> Contact 17 of the deceased's family and friends.
>
> Ask The17, that at a given time on a given day,
> to stop what they are doing and think about one
> incident in the dead person's life that had a
> positive influence on their life.
>
> Ask them to start making a sound with their
> mouth, while they're doing the thinking, a sound
> that in some way complements their feelings
> about the incident.
>
> This performance should last no more than a
> minute.

I would want the performance to take place at noon on 7 July 2007 – the anniversary of Syd's death. Obviously I would hope that scattered all over the place would be considerably more than 17 people taking part in this performance and, as the vast majority of them would not be family and friends of Syd Barrett, we would have to be thinking about some way in which Syd's songs have had a positive influence on our life.

Flint is wanting me to stop writing so we can get down off the mountain, so we can get some football in at the garden of the B&B before nightfall. He also wants to know if we can turn the rocks into gold in the oven back at my flat.

SCORE

16. COMPLEMENT

Someone must die.

Contact 17 of the deceased's family and friends.

Ask The 17, that at a given time on a given day, to stop what they are doing and think about one incident in the dead person's life that had a positive influence on their life.

Ask them to start making a sound with their mouth, while they're doing the thinking, a sound that in some way complements their feelings about the incident.

This performance should last no more than a minute.

pb Poster 143   2006

BUGS BUNNY AND HIS FOURTEEN CARROTS
16 April 2007

It's gone 11. The evening has been dry and warm. Too warm for this time of year. I've been out on the ledge book-burning. Well, not book-burning plural, just *The Illuminatus! Trilogy* as I proposed flippantly at the end of that other chapter.

It didn't quite work out as proposed there. The first page was ripped out, the match was struck, the page held out to touch the flame, but before the paper caught fire the match blew out. A second match was struck. This time the page was lit, but by the time the second page was ripped from the book and ready to light the first page had burnt itself out. Although not a windy night, what breeze there was ... A third match was struck but it was soon clear that my plan was not going to work and that to burn the book page by page would take at least as many matches as there were pages.

I climbed back through the window and got my soup pan. The big one. Took it out to the ledge, tore the next page from the book, crumpled it, dropped it in the pan, struck a match within the shelter of the pan, lit the page, ripped the next one from the book, lit it from the dying flames of the last one as I placed it in the pan. And on and on I went, ripping page after page out of the book, letting each one catch light from the flames of the last, each page taking no time to flare up then burn itself out. There was no time to take it slow, just keep going.

While I was doing this I let my mind wander over the events of the day. But before those are reported I would like to tell you, that as part of my 17 minutes at the Queen Elizabeth Hall, I asked the audience if they could come up with an idea for what I could do with the £750 fee that I was getting. And if they had one, I told them they could let me know after the show, and where and when I would be sitting out in the foyer, waiting to receive their suggestions.

The trouble was, none of the suggestions took my fancy. So maybe I should just squander it on the usual things I squander money on – feeding and clothing for the kids, that sort of thing. That evening I was also told that Jarvis Cocker was going to be curating this year's Meltdown festival at the South Bank Centre (SBC) and that he was interested in talking to me.

This morning Jarvis Cocker called me. He was about to board a plane to New York to promote his solo album. I was about to put the kettle on to make a pot of tea. I told him if I was to do something at this year's Meltdown, I would want to do it as The17. He seemed to be up for this, even if it was in a way that would not be accessible to the general public. He told me I should deal with Glenn Max at the South Bank Centre to sort out practicalities.

This afternoon I went down for a meeting with this Glenn Max bloke and a look around the place. I told him I need a room with a piano in it which could hold 17 people comfortably and told him how *An Introduction To The17* works. But as I was tearing the words from *The Illuminatus!* and watching them burn page by page the idea evolved. Instead of doing the one-off performance in the South Bank Centre I would rather go into five schools in the surrounding area, a different school each morning, from Monday to Friday between 18 and 22 June. Do a version of *AGE* with the students and then get them to do their own score like I did up and around Sunderland and Huddersfield. In the afternoon I would have each of their scores art-worked up and printed as one-off posters. These posters I would then fly-post around the South Bank area.

Right now I'm sitting on my bed making these notes. By my side is the cover of *The Illuminatus! Trilogy*. I refrained from torching the cover. I loathe the fact that I love the look of the cover the way it is now: with the long list in my scrawl of all the page numbers where the number 17 appears; opposite that, with all the pages that The Justified Ancients of Mummu / The Jams appear. Both these columns are scribbled on the inside cover. The inside spine of the cover is all a flurry of what is left of each page after they were torn out.

I have made myself a promise. I did not want to let any physical objects into my life that I don't mind losing. No works of art, no books, records, carpets, clothes, furniture. Nothing. A life where I won't be arsed if all my worldly goods disappeared tomorrow. Everything I own can be carried in my memory, or at least on my hard drive. The tattered remains of this book lying on the bed beside me seems to be getting in the way of my aspiration.

Good night. Sleep tight.

Post Script:
I'm a fucking tosser.

It's the next morning. I've just been out on the ledge to get the soup pan that I left out there last night. It wouldn't budge. The heat from the book-burning had heated its base to such an extent that it had melted the tarred roofing below. Then when the tar cooled and hardened again, it held the pan fast to the roof. I've just had to use a hammer and chisel to get it off. In doing so I've fucked the pan and made a crater on the roof where the rain will get in.

Bill Drummond

'I DID WHAT I THOUGHT WAS RIGHT'
11 May 2007

Dawn is creeping through my uncurtained windows, and I as I lie awake at this early hour, knowing what little sleep I've had is all I'm going to get, my whole being is gripped with what must be anger, even rage.

I've never had much time for being angry with politicians: if one doesn't like what those in power are doing, set about changing it, don't just seethe. Getting angry in your armchair just seems like a waste of your all-too-precious energy. But right now I am in a rage.

In 1997 I wrote a piece that was included in the *45* book. This piece documented me going to the Labour Party conference in Brighton. It was the first one they'd had after winning the general election a few months previously. When the whole New Labour brand was being rammed down our collective throat and Tony Blair was inviting the Gallaghers round for tea and Cool Britannia was being launched. The big deal for me was that Tony Blair was my generation exactly. In fact he was and still is seven days younger than me. He would have been into the same bands as I was at the same time, bought the same issues of the *NME* and *Melody Maker*, watched Robert Dougall read the news – Biafra, Vietnam, the Six Day War. Yeah I know he went to public school and had all the education that money could buy and my four 'O' levels pale in comparison to whatever he got, but if we had bumped into each other at a gig when we were both 17, we would have had more in common than not. Or that's what I thought.

Whatever negativity I felt towards New Labour's brazen PR tactics back then (1997) simmered down and I was pleased with many of the things that Tony Blair seemed to be achieving but then the Twin Towers collapsed and before you knew it our boys were in Iraq and I could feel my anger brewing up again. But other than go on one march in London I did nothing to try and stop the war. Did not write one letter to the Queen, or go around to Number 10 for a chat, try and make Tony see sense, didn't even throw a brick though his windows. Instead I let it all be done in my name.

So here I am lying in bed seething and what's got me going is one particular line in his farewell speech, that I have just heard broadcast on the World Service. And this was it: 'I ask you accept one thing. Hand on heart. I did what I thought was right.'

Well every fucker does what they think is right. I'm sure Hitler, Stalin and Pol Pot all thought what they were doing was right. To do what you think is right is a given – it is nothing to brag about, nothing to be applauded. Every failed and sacked football manager did what they thought was right, but they still had to be held accountable as their team drifted into the relegation zone. And just as my seething cannot seethe any higher, it shifts into a whole new gear. What does this is one of the closing lines to his speech. 'The British people are special, the world knows it, in our innermost thoughts, we know it. This is the *fuck!* greatest nation on earth.'

With those lines he sinks as low as a politician can go and attempts to appeal to our nationalism. He knows it, we all know it, that quote from Samuel Johnson – 'Patriotism is the last refuge of a scoundrel.'

I switched off the radio, got out of bed to go for a piss. Lying on the floor is one of my pamphlets and all thoughts of Blair, his farewell speech and Doctor Johnson and his wisdom are forgotten. I pick up the pamphlet. This is the real reason for my anger, rage and seething. It's got nothing to do with Blair – that was just an excuse. It is my vanity, my bruised ego, my over-inflated ... that has made me angry.

The pamphlet is entitled *Syd Is Dead*. Last night was the Syd Barrett – Madcap's Last Laugh concert at the Barbican Centre in London. The one that I was asked to perform at. The one that I said no, that I would do one of my pamphlets containing the *Syd Is Dead* story and the one called *Halfway Up Snowdon*. And I was going to distribute these 1,000 pamphlets to the first 1,000 folk who turned up to remember and celebrate Syd. And as far as I knew the promoters of the concert were more than happy for me to do it.

So I turn up late yesterday afternoon, with a cardboard box containing 1,000 pamphlets under my arm. I stroll past the scruff of stage-door Johnnys waiting to get the autographs of the passing rock legends (the Floyd are rock legends to me), past security, down some corridors and out into the main hall where Damon Albarn is on stage soundchecking. The song he is singing is *Baby Lemonade*. Adam Peters is accompanying him on his cello, as is Kate St John on her cor anglais, as well as a couple of other musicians. It is sounding good in a ramshackle way. Chrissie Hynde is waiting her turn to soundcheck. Nick Mason from the Floyd is strolling about. I'm feeling good in a way that maybe I shouldn't.

Bill Drummond

After Damon has done his bit, Adam Peters and I shake hands and do that thing that you do after you meet someone you haven't met for 20 years. The trouble is Adam looks as youthful as he did when I last saw him in the mid-1980s: trim figure, full head of hair. He takes one of the pamphlets and heads off to find Joe Boyd, who is the overall producer of the event. Joe Boyd is one on my heroes. He produced some of the records that shaped my tastes and appreciation of music in the late 1960s – The Hang Man's Beautiful Daughter by The Incredible String Band, What We Did On Our Holidays and Unhalfbricking by Fairport Convention. Maybe not a Phil Spector, but he defined the sound of an era – the Britannica Pastoral with hints of psychodelia.

A couple of minutes later Joe Boyd and I are shaking hands. I'm fully expecting him to tell me how glad he is that I am contributing to the evening's events and how cool he thought the pamphlet looked. Instead he tells me there's been a mistake, that my pamphlet is not wanted, and he talked to me like he didn't know who the fuck I was. 'Of course you can hand them out to people outside, we can't stop you from doing that. And hey, you can stay and watch the show if you want.'

Without saying a word I picked up my box of *Syd Is Dead* pamphlets and like Elvis before me left the building to sit in a pub and brood.

So now it is the morning and I've been doing what we all do from time to time, something I loathe. Instead of addressing my own vanities and failings I'm letting my emotions give Tony Blair a good kicking. Patriotism may be the last refuge of the scoundrel, but having a go at the prime minister of the day from the safety of my armchair is the first refuge of the weak and useless middle-aged man. I may as well go to the match and scream abuse at the ref and demand the resignation of my team's manager.

I put the kettle on, lift up the box of 1,000 now-pointless pamphlets and read one more time the blurb on the back: 'This pamphlet has been specifically published for those attending *Syd Barrett – Madcap's Last Laugh* at the Barbican Centre, London 10 May 2007.'

Rasmus: Maybe we could have these pamphlets; we could do something with them. Maybe put a sticker over that Barbican bit.

Paul: Wouldn't it be nice to print this story on the pamphlet, as a big sticker. That would be really good, to have the object and the story of the object together. You could even print the chapter on the sticker with the comments including this one, if you really want to build up the meta-levels.

GUATEMALA
22 May 2007

This morning this short email was in my mailbox:

Subject: The17

I want to become a member, I live in Guatemala, Central America, I love everything about ancient Music.

Adios,

Roger Marro

So I get the atlas out to check that Guatemala is where I think it is. It is. And then I send this email:

Subject: The17

Dear Roger,

Great to get your email.
Some questions:
How did you come across The17?
Where in Guatemala do you live?
Are you already involved with music?

Yours,

Bill Drummond

And then I got the following:

Subject: The17 Contact FROM GUATEMALA!

Dear William

First of all MUUUCHAS GRACIAS, for writing me back, i will answer you questions, but first i have a moral duty to share with you.

I'm a struggling musician in this square minded country, I was in a band with my best friend, we were a TRIO, an dedicated to do experimental music for 11 years, never had a chance to make a decent record, every place we played we were adored by European people but not for the locals, 1 month ago my best friend left this country, so the band had to come to an end, im still sad, the day he told me that he was leaving we went for some CERVEZAS!! And on my way back i was crying in my car! And i had to stop driving around 3 am, and looked to the sky and asked the great ancient universe manipulator to give me some kind of sign that my musical life was not supposed to be paused or finished, that was on a Saturday, April 21th to be precise.

On Monday, at the office, i receive an email from a very good friend that lives in Peru, Lima, it was a link to an interesting blog, so jumping from blog to blog, i stopped in one that has some information about how ONE person can start an inteligent project to get into musical business, it was your manual, William, you practically save my life, and gave my sooo much to conspire, so much to think, so much to idealize, and so many reasons to get my life full of projects, musical projects by myself, so im starting to get as much vibe to charge my spirit batteries!! Ha-ha to face this interesting adventure im about to take.

I live in a beautiful town called ANTIGUA GUATEMALA, im also a Photographer an have a mega passion for music, so when a read about your revolutionary way of fooling the music industry and how clever you were to get the right elements to possess the mases psiques! i started looking for information about you, i wanted to know you, so now i got the most direct way to ......

HASTA PRONTO

Roger Marroquin

So that is a bit disappointing. Not quite what I was hoping for. But I check out Antigua Guatemala on the internet. It looks fantastic – two volcanoes and everything. This is enough for my response to Senor Marroquin's email, to take a spin of 180 degrees and more.

Subject: Re: *The17 Contact FROM GUATEMALA!*

Dear Roger

Thank you for your email that answered my three questions.
I have been considering making a film about The17.
First I thought of doing it in Bethlehem.
Then I thought of doing it in Calcutta.
Now I want to make it in Antigua Guatemala.

I have looked on the web and read a number of things about your city and Guatemala and feel it would be the right place to make this film. I had already been planning on translating some of The17 website into Latin American Spanish (as well as Russian, Chinese and Arabic). This is a link to another website that I do that is in the process of being translated into those languages: openmanifesto.com/

Regarding *The Manual*, it was written almost 20 years ago, thus most of it is out of date in a practical sense and was only ever pertinent to working in the UK. What I hope is not out of date and not just limited to the UK, is its underlying message. What I hope is: if you want to do something do not wait to be asked and start on Monday. As for fooling the music industry that was never my intention and I do not think it can ever be fooled anyway. Do not make music to try and fool anybody, just make the music that you want to make.

I hope your musical project develops and are any of your photographs on line?
You may not hear back from me for some time.
But you will do.
And I will come over to Antigua Guatemala for The17 to perform there.

Yours,

Bill Drummond

So I get an email back from him later in the day:

Dear Bill

what a great surprise that you are thinking of coming and work something in this country, if there's anything i can do to collaborate in your project, dont hesitate in contact me, my native language is spanish, but a can write and speak english very good, and can do some of the translating work also, and i offer myself as your private tour guide ha-ha i really mean it, OK?

best regards

Roger Marro

p.s. thank you very much for your good advice, I know this is just the begginig, its a period that things get set in, like cause and effect.
THANK YOU!

Bill Drummond

So now I'm planning on heading over to Guatemala to make the film. I've forgotten all about Tony Blair and Joe Boyd and Syd – 'Move on baby, Move on.'

I've not yet done the five religious centres score or the prison one or even the manhole cover score. Maybe I should do these all and more over there. Maybe stretch the deadline for this book even further, so I can fit in the Guatemala trip. End the book at the top of a volcano in Central America instead of in the Scotch Corner Hotel.

PERFORMANCE FOR CRITIQUE
23 May 2007

And while we are on the subject of emails, a few weeks back I got this one.

> Hello Bill,
>
> We are students on the Communication Art & Design course at the Royal
> College of Art. We would like to invite you to give a lecture or
> conduct an event for the students at the college. We were given your
> email address by Ryan Gander who we have worked for as graphic
> designers.
>
> We thought that it would be interesting for us if you gave a
> lecture about your work in relation to Penkiln Burn, but if you have
> other ideas you want to do that would be fine too. In payment for the lecture
> we will each offer you a day of our time for you to use (we are four and have
> many skills including those often described as graphic design).
> We call it Work for Work.
>
> Best wishes,
>
> Robert, Rasmus, Paul & Mia

I took them up on their offer, agreeing to do an *Introduction To The17*
performance at the Royal College of Art, London. This is part of the email that
I sent back to them.

> ... I am currently in the last furlong of writing a book about a lot of the topics
> that The17 throws up. I would like each of the four of you to read what I have
> already written and give me a written critique. This would then form part of
> the text that would be included in the book. This critique of yours could be
> just the odd sentence at different points through the book or a lump of text
> towards the end. That would be down to how each of the four of you would
> want your text to appear. You would all be individually credited.
>
> I, of course, would retain editorial control. This would be not to try and
> control what you want to say but because I have to allow for the fact that as an
> experiment it might not work.
>
> Yours,
>
> Bill Drummond

Bill Drummond

Earlier this evening the performance took place. It was shit. One of the worst. I was crap and our gear gave up and we had to cobble some equipment together from what they had in the college. If they do this critique, I do hope that the shoddiness of the evening's performance does not influence their impression of the book or the overall aims of The17.

CONCLUSION
7 June 2007

> Birds were the first musicians. There are those who say their song is
> purely functional, designed like human speech to convey information;
> but that does not stop bird song or speech from giving pleasure, to birds
> and to humans. The calls of a raven to his consort-for-life are no doubt
> more appealing to her than those of his brothers. There is a happy
> reassurance in such recognition. What aesthetic value she puts upon his
> croaks is not for us to determine any more than we can dictate musical
> taste to each other.

The above is the first paragraph in *Scotland's Music* by John Purser, first
published in 1992.

In the chapter 40 Years Ago Today I mention how I had spent a couple of days
on John Purser's croft on the Isle of Skye being interviewed for his series for
BBC Radio Scotland about the history of Scottish music over the past 5,000
years. As well as his large and weighty *Scotland's Music,* he has written a
more compact book on Jack B. Yeats, the Irish artist with a more famous
brother. This book has a two-page conclusion. These are the opening
sentences of this conclusion: 'Conclusions are foolish things. One begins a
work with bold assertions and it is enough that one does not justify half of
them without being obliged to admit it.'

When I read that it made me feel better about how I could conclude this book.
It also made me think I should return to Skye and climb one of the mountains
with John Purser in an attempt to kick off this score:

> CLIMB
> Chose a mountain to climb.
> At the top of the mountain
> listen to the sound of The17 in your head.
> Describe that sound in words.
> Email your description to climb@the17.org
>
> When 17 descriptions have arrived
> from 17 different climbers
> of 17 different mountains
> these descriptions will be combined
> to create one score.

Bill Drummond

This score will be performed at a given time
and location.

It will also be published for others to perform.

The trouble was that John Purser, for all his toughness and hardiness, had recently had both his hips replaced. Thus mountain climbing was not on the doctor's list of things to do. But Purser said his hips would be fine and dandy come June and he would be well up for a climb up Ben Meabost, the small but perfectly formed mountain that rises up at the back of their croft.

The day before yesterday I started the drive north to Skye in the Land Rover, picking up Dave Balfe from his place in Bedfordshire. We went via Liverpool where I was to open an art school end-of-year show. We spent the evening in Liverpool bumping into people from our joint past.

After a night in the Adelphi Hotel, we were out on the motorway by 6.30. We had to make the ferry across to Skye by 5.30. It was the last one of the day. Dave drove. We made it with time to spare.

This morning the three of us set off on foot from the croft to climb Ben Meabost. At the foot of the mountain John announced he was going to climb it barefoot. He removed his boots and socks. We thought this was madness. A few hundred feet up and he is insisting we are missing out on one of the great sensual delights of life, by not climbing the mountain barefoot. Dave Balfe begins to remove his boots. There is no way I was going to be out-toughed by Balfe. We left socks and boots where we took them off in the hope they would not be nicked by a passing sheep. The sward beneath our feet was an undeniable sensual delight.

The top of Ben Meabost is flat with a modest cairn to mark its peak. The 360-degree view is more than modest – it is stunning. Dave Balfe has this tendency for talking. John Purser announced we should stop talking. After 17 or so minutes of not talking, surveying the view and resisting describing it in written words, I started to write these notes. Meanwhile John Purser and Dave Balfe, using stubs of pencils and scraps of paper scavenged from me, responded in writing to the score *CLIMB*.

It is now 12 hours after being at the top of Ben Meabost and writing the above. I'm now tucked up in bed. The sounds of the Skye night slip though the

348

window of the small room that John and Barbara have me sleeping in. I read
what Purser and Balfe wrote at the top of the mountain.

John Purser first:

> There was no number in the air.
> The human silence was only broken by a gentle whistle.
> The whistle was made to hold the attention
> Of a distant stag pausing also to listen,
> But without giving an answer.
> But there was an answer through the filigree of lark song
> A few gentle whistles on a single note
> The call of a Golden Plover
> Pitch perfect in the sweet loneliness
> Of the first unwritten score.

Then Balfe's:

> I try to hear The17, all I hear is my mind. It says –
>
> The great masses of the mountains are a music of their own, not the
> mathematical harmonies of the music of the spheres, but synaesthetic
> – those sheer blocks of stones are their own unheard sound.
>
> Then I think of the Wagnerian Romantics that sought to capture these
> brooding magnificent presences, but I don't want to go there, to other
> music.
>
> I try to get back to a fresh, empty mind to see what music might
> emerge into that silence. I quiet myself and listen. I hear the low
> rushing whistle of the wind through the grass and the stone cairn, I
> hear the distant pealing of birdsong, but nothing of The17.
>
> And then I become aware of my arrogance, and the sheer
> impertinence of man's pitiful creativity that could imagine his own
> music worthy of even idle contemplation when all he should be doing
> is worshipping the infinitely superior products of the original great
> creator.
>
> Though many have used music to worship.

Bill Drummond

Maybe music by The17 should be music so humble as to question its own worthiness to exist?

No I'm wrong – a great song is the equal of a mountain range; a great songwriter the equal of any god.

Music may have been born out of man's attempt to recreate – in lowly places and dark hours - some mystical connection with the grandeur of all this. To recreate some morsel of nature's beauty when it has been cruelly removed by the night, or the oppression of crude and mundane civilisation.

Is music something sucked out of us by the vacuum of beauty's absence?

Or maybe music, for all its supposed virtue, actually is merely a product of man's pride. Born out of our insolent urge to compete with nature, or merely to impress our fellow man, or potential mates.

Or is it magic?

Or just what happens?

Or ...?

But The17 is many people – ask a group of people what happens when they act together, not a single man what he thinks alone. This sublimely magnificent landscape forces me to contemplate myself as an insignificant individual. The17 is social.

In the end the mountains, the blue sea, the lochs, the bright sky, the awesome clarity of so much undigestible beauty is all too much. I can't think about anything else. Put me in the dark and ask again.

I tried to hear The17, all I heard was my mind dribbling as usual. Wait, is that The17?

So two down and 15 to go. Maybe I'll do one from the top of one of those volcanoes in Guatemala.

There was another reason, other than climbing a mountain, for making this long drive up to the Isle of Skye. This reason was to ask a question of John Purser. But first my preamble before I lay out my question and document his reply.

John Purser's book *Scotland's Music* is the first book on the history of music that I've even flicked through, let alone digested. What flicking of it that I have done I've used to confirm my prejudices that our relationship with music constantly evolves, as our capacity and technology for making music evolves.

The position held by music in the world of my early school days is so different to the position it holds in our culture now. And that's in less than one lifetime. What music was, how it was created and what it was used for 5,000 years ago would be almost unrecognisable to us now. Or so it seems from flicking through John Purser's book.

This was my question:

'So John, you have made it your business to learn about the music of 5,000 years ago, how it was made and what part it played in the culture. I would like to ask you what do you think the music of 5,000 years in the future will be like, but I won't. Instead I want to know what you think the music in a mere 50 years will be like?'

He doesn't even stop to take a sip from his tumbler of an Islay single malt before he responds.

'Bill, ours is not to be concerned about the music of the future. There will be plenty of folk with time enough to deal with it then. What we have is all the music of the past. That is enough to be going on with.'

Well that put me in my place, and there was little more to be said on the matter. But as I lie in bed with notebook out, his answer no longer satisfies and I'm itching to stray from 'my place'.

The music of the past was for other people in other times. I want the music of tomorrow, but I want it today. I'm not content with the now, let alone the past that is on offer.

SCORE

6. CLIMB

Chose a mountain to climb.
At the top of that mountain
listen to the sound of The17 in your head.
Describe that sound in words.
Email your description to climb@the17.org

When 17 descriptions have arrived
from 17 different climbers
of 17 different mountains
these descriptions will be combined
to create one SCORE.

This SCORE will be performed at a given time
and location.

It will also be published for others to perform.

pb Poster 133   2006

TEAR IT ALL TO SHREDS
8 June 2007

In the previous chapter I mentioned in passing that Dave Balfe has a tendency for talking. It is precisely because of this tendency that I have invited him along on this drive to the north.

Nothing holds Dave back from saying whatever he thinks and what he thinks is always backed up with a rationale. If you want some brutal truth, ask Dave Balfe.

Balfe entered my life on a sunny spring day in 1978 when I was 24. Someone was banging on the door of Eric's – Eric's being a club in Liverpool where I worked as an odd-job man and where Big In Japan rehearsed. I opened the door. There was this eager face, with intense eyes and mop of dyed blonde hair. He looked like a bushbaby on speed.

'I will be your new bass player,' said the face.

Big In Japan had put it about that we were looking for a new bass player as we had sacked our previous one, Holly Johnson, for being consistently late for rehearsals. We had already tried a couple of replacements but they had not worked out and we had a gig the next day. Whoever this would-be bass player was he suffered from having an accent from over the water, meaning the Wirral. In Liverpool, the worst thing you can have is an accent from the Wirral. And if you don't know the Wirral, it is just the other side of the Mersey from Liverpool, less than a mile away.

Introductions were made and this Dave Balfe became our bass player – by default, without us hearing him play one note, as in we needed someone, anyone, for the gig the next day. But during the rehearsal that afternoon he began making a play for our lead singer Jayne and trying to rearrange all our songs.

We were the biggest band in Liverpool and this bushbaby from the Wirral with a lisp was trying to take over the band. He was not quite the catalyst for the band breaking up a few weeks later but his confrontational presence did not help. But this was also the beginning of a working partnership and friendship that has lasted the intervening 29 years and counting.

Together we learnt how not to manage bands, how to produce classic records, how music publishing is where the money is, how to run a record label badly, how to mess up people's lives, how to make a success of things and then still go and blow it all.

I was the best man at his wedding and I would probably ask him to be mine, if ever I was to get married again. We must have spent hundreds of hours in each other's company speeding up and down motorways. He was then a Thatcherite, I was woolly liberal; he was Catholic, I was Protestant; he was for taking as many drugs as you could, I was not; he was anti-marriage, I was married at 23; he thought he had the biggest cock in the world, mine was bigger.

Without Balfe's input and inspiration I would not have been able to do most of the things that I have done. But this input and inspiration has often come in a perverse way. At various points over the past three decades, I will tell Dave about something I am thinking of doing or a direction I may be heading in. He will then completely and systematically take apart whatever I was eagerly and lovingly planning. He will explain all the faults and inconsistencies in my new direction. And then go and top all that by telling me that I will be an embarrassment to myself. My reaction to his criticism is usually first to sink into a deep well of zero-confidence. In time I climb out of the well screaming the words, 'I'll show the bastard'. And that becomes my motivation.

It is for these reasons that I wanted Dave Balfe to come on this journey, via Liverpool to the Isle of Skye and back. Balfe had never been to one of the performances of The17, has not read any of the words in this book, and knows only vaguely what the whole thing is about. But I know that before I drag The17 out into the full glare of media debate and get ripped apart by those armed with dialectics, I needed to take The17 through Balfe's hedge backwards.

BYE-BYE SOOTY
8 June 2007

We caught the 8.30 ferry back to Mallaig on the mainland then hit the long (and winding) road south via Fort William, Glencoe and Loch Lomond. Some hours later while bypassing Dumbarton, just north of Glasgow, we were trying to pull away from a set of traffic lights, and there was a loud grinding, followed by a louder CRUNK from under the rear quarter of the Land Rover. And that was that. The gearbox had appeared to have given up. We pushed several tons of scrap metal to the side of the road. This I thought was the death of the machine that had been my travelling companion for the last 200,000 miles of my life. This, I also thought, was a fitting place to end the book.

Phoned the AA. The AA arrived. It was not the gearbox but the crankshaft. The AA man explained that being a 4x4, it could be driven off the front two wheels.

We got going again, but we had lost a couple of hours so had to cancel a meeting in Glasgow. The noises being made by the Land Rover were different, thus my ever-present internal version of The17 was singing parts that I had not heard before. I enjoyed these differences.

After Glasgow we headed down to Peebles to visit a couple of friends, Stella and Keith. We sat in their garden having afternoon tea. I listened to the sounds of the near-by rookery. When I was a kid in Newton Stewart, there was a rookery in a wood across the road outside my bedroom window. Every evening in the summer months, when I was supposed to be in bed, I would push the sash window up as far as it would go and sit on the sill in my pyjamas, my legs dangling over the edge. And every evening as the sky was turning golden all the rooks would gather and then make this great sweeping flight together across our small town. A huge circle of a flight, always in a clockwork direction. It was as if they were riding the boundaries, inspecting all was well and secure in their take on creation before returning to the rookery and settling down for the night. It was while they were doing that whole settling down that I loved their collective chorus the best.

If I was ever asked to do Desert Island Discs, I would say, 'Sod the discs, Mr Plumley, just give me the luxury item of a wood with a rookery in it. And for it to not be more than 50 yards from where my hammock is slung.'

So after saying 'Bye now' to Stella, Keith and their new baby Noah, we headed over the Cheviots across the border into Northumberland and down past Newcastle and onto the A1.

Bill Drummond

The evening was glorious. Over these past three days, of driving of which Dave has done the lot (he didn't trust mine), I have been the one doing most of the talking. Going on and on about where we are at with music, how the primacy of the recorded work is now fading into the musical history of the 20th century; how whole new ways of music-making and experiencing it are going to open up; how musicians will no longer be measured by the albums they have made; how the whole canon of recorded music of the last 100 years will fade from significance – Miles, Dylan, Zappa, Ellington, Glenn Gould, The Beatles, Nirvana, Jacqueline du Pré, Motown, Arthur Rubinstein, Elvis, James Brown, Nick Drake, Stravinsky, Stax, Coltrane, Spector, The Pistols, Shadow Morton, even the Sugababes, will all begin to gather dust-like sheets of music-hall songs from the previous century. Relevant to no one but the perverse.

The more tunes we have on our MP3 players the less there is there that we want to listen to, and the more that we will want to be part of music and music-making in a totally different way. Of course we will always want to dance and for dance we need a music that gets the hips swaying ... and on and on I went into the darkness until finally Dave Balfe responds.

'Bill, I've kept my mouth shut and at times it has been difficult. I know that you asked me on this trip to respond to whatever it was you were going to want to tell me about. You say you have spent the last year or so writing an expansive book about The17. Exploring all the ideas it throws up. From what you have been telling me, if you had been using a modicum of discipline you could have got it all down to a 2,000-word essay. And once you had got that written and someone with a sharp mind had gone through it and pointed out all your inconsistencies, you could have forgotten all about this and moved on.'

'But Dave, it's the inconsistencies that make great art. As I always say, "Accept the contradictions".'

'Well I don't. Why should I? Why should anyone? You can't just stomp around all over the place with your proclamations about the end of recorded music and how The17 is going to save music and when somebody points out some obvious flaws you tell them to "Accept the contradictions".'

'Yeah but ...'

'I mean, I thought it was all about the experience of music while you were making it, but from what you have been telling me about The17 so far, it has been totally reliant on you going out with a laptop, software, mics, a PA system and that the highlight of each performance is that the punters get to hear a playback of something they have recorded, as if it was a real recording they were making. This is no different to what's going on in music departments of secondary schools up and down the country right now. It may be a cute trick but it ain't Elvis or even Stravinsky ...'

'Yeah but it's not meant to be.'

'But Bill, every time I say something, point out a flaw, you try to make out I'm missing the point or that ... Look, if what you were doing was any good you wouldn't have to write a whole book about it first. You would just go out and do it. And if it were any good, it would catch on. James Brown, The Beatles or Bartok never wrote a book about it first. They just did what they did and it was good.'

'Yeah, but I bet you Cage and Glenn Gould did.'

'And you are not them. They were great thinkers as well as great musicians. You can strum a few chords and know how to help make a pop record and that's about it.'

'Well I think that if Jimmy and I had not written and published *The Manual* first we couldn't have focused our minds on how to make The KLF singles.'

'But *The Manual* was a step-by-step manual. It made sense. It was something that people could follow. From what you have been saying this book is going to be a sprawling mass of words.'

''Yeah, so?'

'Fuck off, Bill. You want me to give my thoughts and all you can respond with is a "Yeah, so?", I may as well not bother.'

'Sorry.'

'It seems that you want what you are doing to have gravitas and kudos. You want it to exist in the same world as serious contemporary music, or whatever they call it now. But you can't be bothered to apply the discipline that sort of music demands. You slip from pseudo-tautological rigour to a would-be intuitive holistic approach whenever it suits you. You need to have a greater grasp of the rationale behind your concepts to defend them, and not just you saying something like "Well that's the way I feel it". Your woolly ideas and artistic feelings are not good enough.'

'Yeah. OK, Dave.'

And silence descends as the light drains from the sky. We pull up at the Scotch Corner Hotel. Check in. Get a beer and play best of three at pool. Dave wins.

We retire to our twin room. Sitting in our parallel beds, me 54, Dave 49, staring blankly at the TV. It's some crap sitcom about two young blokes who decide to start a record label.

Say bye-bye, Sooty.
Say bye-bye, Sweep.

Rasmus: Dave really does the job he's hired to do.

Robert: Although he doesn't say what's interesting about The17, only what's wrong with it. You can agree with all these faults and still find the project interesting.

Paul: This passage is included in the book for a reason. Maybe this isn't even what Dave said. This bit works as Bill's device that shows us he's aware of all these flaws. but he doesn't reach a great conclusion, does he?

APPENDIX 1

THE FOLLOWING PEOPLE BECAME LIFE TIME MEMBERS OF The17 BETWEEN 1 JANUARY 2004 and 31 DECEMBER 2007. The various schools involved requested that their students would only have their first names appearing on the membership list.

Leila Abbas, Clare Abbatt, Abbie, Abbie, Abdul, Abigail, Simeon Ackroyd, Adam, Adam, Richard Adderley, Adrian, Ulrika Af Scmidt, Akins Agbeni, Agnew, Johan Aguren, Ahlam, Marcus Ahlsted, Peyman Ahmadzade, Aimee, Aimee-Louise, Akeeme, Ylva Åkesson, Akiethan, Akim, Alan, Alannah, Ophélie Alegre, Alex, Alex, Alex, Alexander, Vassiuos Alexou, Alice, Alisha, Alisha, Jonathan Allen, Jeanette Amberndtsson, Amelia, Amelia, Ammuni, Amy, Amy, Amy, Anna Andersson, Sabina Andersson, Stina Andersson, Jamie Anderton, Andrew, Andrew, Andrew, Thomas Andro, Åsa Anesäter, Anisa, Anita, Anna, Annie, Anthony, Anthony, Antonia, Antonia, Steve Appleton, Aqib, Philippe Arellano, Arin, Niclas Arndt, Flemming Arnott, Sebastian Aronsson, Arpit, Edander Love Arvefjord, Ashley, Ashley, Figge Askergren, Maria Asplund, Lars Åstrand, Dylan Atkins, Günther Auer, Lindgren Sally Avdelius, Fanny Axelsson, Sengey Axenov, Linder Anna Axerup, Susanne Ayoub, Anneli Bäckman, Jonathon Bake-Bates, Jessica Baker, Jon Baker, Emily Baldock, James Baldock, Joshua Baldock, Richard Baldwin, Dave Balfe, Andrew Barker, Lahsen Barnouche, Sue Barr, Sharon Barrett, Jay Barsby, Ada Basgül, Kat Beautiful, Becky, Becky, Erik Bejmar, Lisi für 2 Bekannte, Sarah Bell, Malik Bendjellonl, Mette Bendtsen, Benedict, Robin Bengtsson, Benjamin, Claire Bennett, Julia Benon, Alexander Benz, Ylva Bergqvist, Joanna Bergström, Jonas Bergström, Beth, Bethany, Owen Bevan, Sibel Beymen, Robert Bialy, John Bickerdike, Astrid Bin, Nicola Birch, Steve Bird, Maria Bjurestam, Blake, Beatrice Blomberg, Tom Blyth, Bobbie, Angela Boggiano, Kathrin Bohm, Claes Boklund, Josh Bolchover, Samira Bouabana, Alan Boulton, Nick Bourne, James Box, Grigoriy Boyarsky, Bradley, Bradley, Louise Bradley, Maria Brandén, Roger Brent, Brittany, Dan Britton, Matthew Broadhead, Eva Broberg, Brogan, Karl Broman, Julian Brooks, Aron Brown, Megan Brown, Bryany, Patricia Buck, Magnus Bunnskog, Jonathon Burns, Bill Burreu, Richard Bushnell, Adam Buss, Julian Butter, James Byng, Sheri Cafer, Callum, Callum, Callum, Cally, Cameron, Djemila Capucine, Caran, Grinde Carl, Carly, Donna Carter, Josefin Cederholm, Elina Cerderberg, Fiona Chamberlain, Hannah Chamberlain, Sarah Chamberlain, Chandler, Chanel, Sanaz Charbaf, Charlie, Charlotte, Charlotte, Charlotte, Charlotte, Chelsea, Chelsie, Eleanor Cherry, Chey, Patricia Chi, Chineden, Chiwew, Patryk Dawid Chlastawa, Chloe, Chloe, Chloe, Chloe, Christie, Adam Christner, Christopher, Guillaume Chuplot, Pascal Ciapp, Alice Cicolini, Dan Civico, Claire, Bella Clark, Sam Clark, Robert Claspe, Louise Clements, Angie Cockren, Wendy Cocks, Jonny Cole, Harvey Coleman, Laurence Coleman, Rosalind Coleman, Lisa Colton, Paul Comley, Victoria Conlan, Connie, Connor, Connor, Connor, Charlotte Convey, Neil Cooper, Stuart Copeland, David Corbett, Kevin Cormack, Cornell, Frances Cotter, Rob Cotter, John Court, Courtney, Courtney, Henry Covey, Rob Cowen, Marian Crabtree, Craig, Marcus Cramer, Callum Crawford, Peter Creed, Clara Crivellaro, Curtis, Sylvia Czarnocka, Joe Dagnierre, Daisy, Jeff Dale, Daniel, Daniel, Daniel, Daniel, Daniel, Danielle, Johanna Danielsen, Steinar Daniezsen, Danny, Emma Davenport, Simon Davenport, Fiona Davies, Haydn Davies, James Davies, Carl Dawson, Sam Dean, Debbie, Ekaterina Dementieva, Jennifer Denitto, Daniela DePaulis, Devan, Devante, Devel, Geraldine Dewing, Diego, Monica Dikanski, Ludmila Dmitrieva, Tanya Dmitrieva, Jon Doe, Dominic, Michael Donnison, Dountae, Andy Doyle, Paul Drake, Alexander Drangd, Drew, Bill Drummond, Bluebell Drummond, Flint Drummond, James Drummond, Kate Drummond, Tiger Drummond, Alan Duffy, Nisha Duggal, Frederic Dumand, Jon Duncan-Rees, Ronita Dutta, Dylan, Dylan, Toby Dyter, Cristóbal E. Duran, John Eadon, Karin Edlund, Gwilly Edmondez, Anna Efraimsson, Niklas Eisen, Bert Eke, Eleanor, Fredrik Eliasson, Elios, Elizabeth, Ellen, Ellen, Paula Ellwood, Eloise,

Bill Drummond

Alexandra Elvesund, Emily, Emma, Emma, Emma, Wilma Enberg, Laurie Endeaw, Erik
Engström, Linn Enhage, Jennifer Eriksson, Ksenia Ermoshina, Chris Essen, Erik Essén, Ethan,
Peter Evans, Ezgi, Fabian, Amanda Fade, Fahima, Faisul, Faith, Anthony Farthing, Aurea Florio
Fava, Faye-Marie, Fergus, Joakim Figveiredo, Rich Fisher, Rasmus Fleischer, Duncan Fleming,
Katie Fletcher, Bob Floyd, Tamina Fogelberg, Barry Follett, Alison Foote, Dennis Foster-Jones,
Dave Fotherringhame, Benji Fox, Tim Fox, Nick Francis, Ben Freeman, Freya, Mia Frostner,
Gabriel, Gabrielle, Pasha Galloween, Catherine Gasson, Mike Gatrell, Dan Gay, Johan Gehlin,
Gemma, Genevieve, Michael George, Georgia, Nicky Getgood, Jason Gibbons, Sylvia Gibbs,
Joseph Giffard, Je Gilbe, Richard Ginns, Josefin Gladh, Malin Glanzmann, Herbert Gnauer,
Monica Goodrick, Fabian Göransson, Sarah Gottlieb, Ant Gould, Jackie Grace, Magnus Granberg,
Linda Granfors, Mal Gray, Warren Gray, Greenman, Matthew Gregory, Sam Griffin, Sally Griffith,
Dave Groak, Grumps, Chris Guy, Loolie Habgood, Markus 'Marx' Hafner, Jenny Hägglund, Maria
Hägglund, Lukas Hagman, Dagmar Haid, Martina Hall, James Hands, Suzie Hanna, Hannah,
Hannah, Hannah, Pauline Hanson, Lisa Hansson, Suzanne Hardy, Martin Härjemo, Lee Harman,
Fredrik Harmjanz, Stephen Harris, Harrison, Harry, Peter Hart, Mike Harte, Brian Hartley,
Harvey, Paul Harvey, Graeme Hawkins, Rob Hayler, Hayley, Julia Head, Roger Heathcote,
Heather, Sara Hedberg, Helena, Katy Hellen, Rosi Hellquist, Torbjörn Hellsten, Bryony
Henderson, Karla Henderson, Elias Henning, Andrew Henty, Russell Herron, Ben Heslop, Dan
Hewitt, Jennifer Hewitt, Tom Higgs, Becci Hill, Desmond Hill, Carolina Hindsio, Shan Hira, Hiral,
John Hirst, Alexandra Hoffman, Julia Hofmann, Michael Holliet, Holly, Holly, Holly, Anna Holm,
Adina Holmertz, Anders Holtman, Steve Homer, Peter Hörmanseder, Andre Höschele, Dawn
Hoskin, James Hoskins, Laura Hough, James Howe, Rob Howe, Darren Hubbard, Ronee Hui,
Johan Hultgren, Emma Humphrey, Ted Humphreys, Robbie Humphries, Lauren Hyde, Richard
Hyde, Cleo Ibberson, Ryan Icing, Dmitri Iliushin, Marja/Liisa Ingler, Iona, Iris Ionita, Ben Isaacs,
Isabella, Michelle Ishak, Isshiah, Jack, Jack, Jack, Jack, Jackson, Chris Jackson, Melissa
Jacobsson, Jade, Jade, Jake, Jake, Jake, James, James, James, James, Eugene James, Jamie,
Astner Sofie Jansson, Valera Louise Jansson, Jarit, Andrew Jarvis, Emma Jarvis, Jasmine, Anne
Javenzon, Jazmin, Keith Jeffrey, Jenade, Jenneil, Jermaine, Elizabeth Jesse, Jessica, Jessica,
Jessica, Andreas Jismark, Jiwoobe, Joanna, Denis Jobling, Jodi, Joe, Camilla Johansson, Katarina
Johansson, John, John, Heidi Johnson, Jon, Jonathan, Jonathan, Jonathon, Alan Jones, Chris
Jones, Lyndon Jones, Tommie Jönsson, James Jonston, Jordan, Jordan, Jordan, Jordon, Louise
Josefsson, Joshua, Joshua, Josie, Joy, Julia, Mo Julian, Julieanne, Bettina Julin, Junaid, Kaitlyn,
Nicklas Kappelin, Kareem, Karen, Jonathan Karkut, Karl, Thomas Karlsson, Andreas Karperyd,
Ivan Kashin, Kate, Kathryn, Katie, Katie, Katie, Kayne, Sam Keating-Fry, Keeley, Keely, Keesje,
Keiran, Keiron, Keith, Simon Kelly, Kelly-Ann, Kelsey, Kemill, Age Kempe, Charlie Kerr, Kerry,
Johanna Ketola, Kevan, Khoa, Karl Kilian, Sarah Kim, Kimberly, Nigel King, Jo Kirby, Becci
Kirkham, Kolmodin Emma Kjellqvist, Klaudle, Johannes Klenell, Olaf Kneer, Frida Koci, Jens
Kockvitz, Alice Kok, Galia Kollectiv, Pil Kollectiv, Joesph Kratjewski, Maxim Kuemen, Olga
Kulikova, Sofia Kumlin, Eugeniya Kurteva, Kurtis, Julia Kuzmina, Zak Kyes, Kyler, Kym, Patrick
Lacey, Lawrence Laden, Niklas Landberg, Matilda Landsberg, Andreas Lang, Kristian Lang,
Natalia Larina, Larissa, Emil Larsson, Latoya, Laura, Lauren, Lauren, Lauren, David Lawrence,
Leah, Leandro, Jim Leaviss, Lee, Colin Lee, Gaz Lee Park, Sophie Lee, Leeanne, Russel Leeming,
David Leicester, Brit Leissler, Anna/Sofia Lejman, Leo, Leon, Nick Letchford, Joel Levack,
Samuel Levack, Nathalie Levi, Jennifer Lewandowska, Lewis, Erwan Lhuissier, Edwin Li, Liam,
Liam, Lileth, Fredrik Lindberg, Sanna Lindberg, Rikard Linde, Andrew Lindenmayer, Kenny
Linder, Sonja Lindgren, Elliot Lindquist, Lindsey, Stefan Lindström, Dean Loach, Anna Lord,
Richard Lord, Louis, Louis, Louisa, Harriet Lovelock-Gaunt, Jonathon Lovett, Jon Lowe, Sophie
Lowe, Hamilton Lublin, Lucile, Lucy, Lucy, Luke, Luke, Luke, Jess Lumley, Kelly Lumley, Nicola
Lumley, Wood Emily Lundberg, Mats Lundell, Ida Lundén, Parmer Baltzar Lundgren, Luri, Joe
Luscombe, Olga Lyatifova, Lydia, Carol Lynn, Ant Macari, Will Mace, Sally Madge, David
Magnusson, Per Magnusson, Pavel Makhaev, Gary Malkin, Alian Man, Louise Mangeot, Mansi,

Tom Mansi, Maranfee, Moa Mård, Maria, Mark, Adam Marsh, Aled Marsham, Sofia Marteleur, Pedro Martinez, Amy Marvill, Mary, Lawerance Marzouk, Jack Mason, Stephanie Masters, Matthew, Matthew, Matthew, Matthew, Dolly May, John McCabe, Andrew McDonnell, Andy McIntosh, Teresa McIntosh, John McKechnie, Amanda McLaren, Julie McLarron-Cotter, Sheena McWhirter, Helen Meads, Megan, Megan, Megan, Megan, Jones Melander, Nisse Mellberg, Jöns Mellgren, Robil Mengheisteah, Meritta, Jason Merritt, Peter Messner, Nils Mexin, Michala, Micheal, Micheal, Michelle, Aimee Middleton, Mikayha, Nikki Milavec, Andrea Miletic, Milly, Karl Minns, Yumiko Miyawaki, Tracey Moberly, Mohammed, Mollie, Jane Moloney, Sarah Montegu, Anna Montelius, Nick Montgomery, Aaron Moore, Moraye, Anna Moreva, Tony Morley, Rob Morris, Jane Morriss, Ben Moss, Nick Mott, Moussa, Louise Mowbray, Rowena Moyle, Marianne Mueller, Roger Muffin, Nick Mullen, Alisdair Munroe, Murad, Nigel Murgatroyd, James Murray, Muthonl, Stefan Mutvig, Minna Mwakisopile, Myah, Mauritz Myhre, Tania Mylnikova, Nacera, Zucua Nasha, Nathan, Nathan, Billy Neath, Catherine Ness, Ned Netherwood, Emma Neville, Niall, Liz Nicholas, Nicole, Nika, Tuvalisa Nilsson, Amie Noble, Raman Noori, Martin Nordgren, Lise/Lotte Norelius, Mirjam Norinder, Jennifer Norman, Mikaela Norman, Vanessa Norwood, Elin Nyblom, Katherine O'Carroll, Kevin O'Connor, Sofia Ödborn, Cirillo Isabelle Öhman, Peter Öhman, Olivia, Carlsson Lisa Olofsson, Anna Olsson, Calle Olsson, Carl Olsson, Sara Omari, Deirdre O'Neill, Oscar, Ole Österberg, Bessie Östergren, Tanja Ostojic, Carita Ottosson, Daniel Padden, Padmadaka, Saffron Paffron, Paige, Paige, Helena Palm, Mattias Palm, Kristin Palme, Paris, Taz Parish, Keith Parker, Julie Patterson, Paul, Paul, Johanna Paulsson, Helen Pearson, Mrs Peatfield, Vinny Peculiar, David Pennington, Perry, Emil Persson, Karin Persson, Mattias Persson, Megan Petersen, Simon Petherick, Philip, Hannele Philpson, Ian Pichard, Paul Pieroni, Kris Pohl, John Powell, Kristian Powell, Joshua Price-Roberts, Sergey Ptchelintseu, Anne Pujanen, Racheal, Rachel, Rachel, Bruce Rafeek, Ståhle Mathilda Rahmqvist, Rainne, Chris Ramsey, Peter Rantasa, Ric Rawlins, Reanne, Rebecca, Rebecca, Rebecca, Rebecca, Rebecca, Ian Redhead, James Rees, Charlotte Reilly, Karen Reilly, Eva Reinbacher, Kev Reverb, Alexandra Reyes, Emelie Reyes, Jan Reynolds, Rhianna, Mattias Ribbing, Ribeiro, Richard, Adam Richards, Colin Richardson-Webb, Deborah Richardson-Webb, Scott Richardson, Boris Riley, Maggie Rimassa, Melanie Robb, Robbie, Robert, Robert, Gaz Roberts, Jocelyn Roberts, Craig Robertson, Holly Robinson, Jason Robinson, Mark Robinson, Robyn, Anton Rodionov, Isobel Rodrigues, Rohail Arif, Rohan, Lilia Romanevitch, Romario, Evelina Roos, Joakim Roséen, Antoine Rouselle, Yassen Rousser, Rufus, Sören Runolf, Ryan, Ryan, Ryan, Ryan, Ryan, Deborah Ryan, Ksenia Ryobeva, Elodie Sabardeil, Pelle Sacklén, Tom Sadd, Safa, Saffron, Gerrard Sagar, Mårten Sahlén, Erik Sällström, Johan Sällström, Paul Salt, Sami, Natalia Samkova, Samuel, Sanchez, Robert Sandall, Jonna Sandell, Emmy Sanger, Sarah, Sarah, Sarah, Sarah-May, Sarah Sarkar, Alex Sarll, Chris Saunders, James Saunders, Martin Saunders, Savannah, Savannah, Andrei Sazeonov, Christoffer Schieche, Hannah Schildt, Veronique Schinelli, Peggy Scholte, Beate Schrank, Robin Schroder, Bettina Schultz, Helga Schwarzwald, Jan T. Scott, Naomi Scott, Andrew Searson, Seb, Sebastian, Sebastian, Christine Selander, Serena, Erkan Sezer, Elena Sfendoni, Shabaz, Rothwell Shackleton, David Shah, Shahnur, Shalise, Shamso, Shancu, Shane, Shannan, Shannon, Shannon, Susan Shaw, She-neil, Elaine Shepherd, Sherice, Calum Shone, Sue Shone, Anna Shvets, Catriona Siddall, Harriet Siddall, Pepper Siddall, Tom Siddall, Max Silin, Andrei Silvesfruu, Dominique Silvestre, Tom Simmons, James Sinfield, Calle Sjonell, Emma Skeldon, John Skinner, Susanne Skog, Ylva Skog, Mike Skrgatic, Teresa Skrgatic, Dan Smiles, Sarah Smith, Sanna Soderholm, Erik Södersten, Loraine Softly, Martin Softly, Sohail, Vivienne Solayrol, Robert Sollis, Sonny, Sophie, Sophie, Sophie, Sophie, Danielle Spittle, Robin Spurrier, Rebecca Staf, Kajsa Ståhl, Josef Stankiewicz, Peter Stebbings, Alexander Stenbeck, Stephanie, Stephanie, Stephanie, Stephen, Stephen, Louise Stephenson, Steven, Warren Steven, Claudia Stockhausen, Jakob Stolpe, Hilary Stone, Liv Strand, Davey Strange, Rachel Stringer, Cecilia Strömbeck, Phil Suddaby, Sumayya, Johan Sundell, Wenche Sundsrud, Jussi Suvanto, Kim Svensson, David Swain, Grainne Sweeney, T.J., Tabitha, Lukas/fm4 Tagwerker, Tamara, Kent Tankred, Matthias Tarasiewicz,

Bill Drummond

Tayler, Deb Taylor, Joe Taylor, Teah, Angela Terris, Tevin, Dirk Thegwarth, Thomas, Thomas, Thomas, Judy Thomas, Douglas Thorburn, Tiana, Tiana, Veronique Tiberghein, Sperandio Angela Tillman, Hugo Timm, David Timmons, Paul Tisdell, Anna Tisserat-Rasle, T.J., Tracey Tofield, Tom, Tom, Dan Tombs, Chris Tomlinson, Toni, Ake Tornkrist, Petra Tornmalm, Hayden Torr, Dominic Tracey, Trey, Tristan, Rasmus Troelsen, Sum Tse, Damien Tuffnell, John Turesson, Amy Turner, Ben Tweedel, Lydia Tweedel, Jane Twigg, Tycho, Filip Tyden, Tyler, Tyrell, Ubald, Lisa Ullén, Unknown Member, Vanessa, Vanessa, Adina Van Klooster, Salla Vapaavuori, Adrian Verroca, Jacob Vesterlund, Vian, Victor, Victoria, Morris Vikman, Oliverias Gabriel Vilches, Kaija Vogel, Roland Von Der Emden, Vera von Platen, Dmitry Vorohov, Andreas Wahlberg, Katarina Wahlund, Ema Walken, Petronella Wallensteen, Anna Walsh, Stefan Walters, Ossian Ward, Graham Wardman, Jane Wardman, Anthony Warpole, Rob Watson, Roxy Watson, Sue Watson, Tara Watson, Jake Wayne-O'Neill, Perry Webster, Conny Wedam, Celia Wee, Rebecca Welby, Michael Louis Wells, Marie Wennersten, Adrian Westaway, Louise Westberg, Brian Wharton, Louis Wheatley, Claire Wheeldon, Clive Wheeler, Josh Whitaker, Iain White, Paul White, Andrew Whittaker, Frida Wiberg, Roman Widholm, Rasmus Wieselgren, Jon Willett, William, William, William, Mark Williams, Plum Williams, Tara Williamson, Sally Wilson, Lina Wirén, Jim Wodall, John Wood, Michelle Woodall, Andy Woods, Dave Woolf, Jennifer Woroniak, Jon Wozencroft, Anton Wretling, Robert Wright, Georgina Wu, Laura Wynne, Xavia, Xavier, Slim Yarwood, Ariella Yedgar, Yohanna, Miranda Yung, Yusuf, Ilia Zaharov, Leah Zakss, Oleg Zardorozhniy, Lovisa Zaunders, Zeenat, Zoe, Sasha Zubanova.

PERFORMANCES, EXHIBITIONS and EVENTS
By, for or about The17 between November 2003 and the end of 2007.

2003

17 November	Event	The making of Many Voices (Penkiln Burn Poster 59)

2004

01 September	Performance	Memphis, Stay Free, Leicester, UK
17 September	Performance	Memphis, Stay Free, Leicester, UK
06 October	Performance	Artsdepot, Finchley, London
11 November	Performance	Artsdepot, Finchley, London

2005

8–21 November	Billboard	Entrance to the Mersey Tunnel, Liverpool
21 November	No Music Day	Worldwide

2006

16 February	Performance	Friends Meeting House, Upper Goat Lane, Norwich, UK
13–25 March	Exhibition	Fylkingen, Stockholm, Sweden
14 March	Performance	Mariaskolan, Stockholm, Sweden
15 March	Performance	Engelbrektsskolan, Stockholm, Sweden
15 March	Performance	Fylkingen, Stockholm, Sweden
16 March	Performance	Hagerstens Asens Skola, Stockholm, Sweden
16 March	Performance	Sodra Latin, Stockholm, Sweden
16 March	Performance	Fylkingen, Stockholm, Sweden
17 March	Performance	Asogrundskola, Stockholm, Sweden
17 March	Performance	Ostra Real, Stockholm, Sweden
17 March	Performance	Fylkingen, Stockholm, Sweden
20 March	Performance	Fylkingen, Stockholm, Sweden
21 March	Performance	Fylkingen, Stockholm, Sweden
22 March	Performance	Fylkingen, Stockholm, Sweden
23 March	Performance	Fylkingen, Stockholm, Sweden
24 March	Performance	Fylkingen, Stockholm, Sweden
24 April – 21 May	Exhibition	Hatton Gallery, Newcastle, UK
26 April	Performance	Broadway Juniors, Sunderland, UK
26 April	Performance	Hatton Gallery, Newcastle, UK
27 April	Performance	Belmont School, Belmont, UK
27 April	Performance	Hatton Gallery, Newcastle, UK
02 May	Performance	Easington Colliery Primary, Co. Durham, UK
04 May	Performance	Wearhead Primary School, Co. Durham, UK
05 May	Performance	Bexhill Primary, Sunderland, UK
05 May	Performance	Southwick Primary School, Sunderland, UK
10 May	Performance	Hatton Gallery, Newcastle, UK
11 May	Performance	Belmont School, Belmont, UK
11 May	Performance	Hatton Gallery, Newcastle, UK

15 May	Performance	Easington Colliery Primary, Co. Durham, UK
15 May	Performance	Broadway Juniors, Sunderland, UK
16 May	Performance	Bexhill Primary, Sunderland, UK
17 May	Performance	Southwick Primary School, Sunderland, UK
17 May	Performance	Shotton Hall School, Peterlee, UK
17 May	Performance	Hatton Gallery, Newcastle, UK
18 May	Performance	Wearhead Primary School, Co. Durham, UK
18 May	Performance	Hatton Gallery, Newcastle, UK
19 May	Performance	Shotton Hall School, Peterlee, UK
19 May	Performance	Hatton Gallery, Newcastle, UK
10 June	Performance	Lynton & Lynmouth Festival, Devon, UK
15 July	Performance	Radio Orange, Vienna, Austria
25 August	Performance	Greenbelt Festival, Cheltenham, UK
26 August	Performance	Greenbelt Festival, Cheltenham, UK
21 September	Performance	Infraction, Sete, France
24 September	Performance	Infraction, Sete, France
28 September	Performance	The Long Arm Festival, DOM, Moscow, Russia
29 September	Performance	Appozicia Festival, Saint Petersburg, Russia
17 October	Performance	Academy of Fine Arts, Oslo, Norway
19 October	Performance	Academy of Fine Arts, Oslo, Norway
17 – 26 November,	Performances	Huddersfield Contemporary Music Festival (HCMF), Huddersfield, UK
17 November	Performance	HCMF, Honley High School, Huddersfield, UK
17 November	Performance	HCMF, All Saints High School, Huddersfield, UK
18 November	Performance	HCMF, North Light Gallery, Huddersfield, UK
19 – 26 November	Exhibition	North Light Gallery, Huddersfield, UK
19 November	Performance	HCMF, North Light Gallery, Huddersfield, UK
20 November	Performance	HCMF, Ashbrow Junior School, Sheepridge, UK
20 November	Performance	HCMF, Birkenshaw Middle School, Cleckheaton, UK
20 November	Performance	HCMF, North Light Gallery, Huddersfield, UK
21 November	No Music Day	Worldwide
22 November	Performance	HCMF, Whitechapel Middle School, Cleckheaton, UK
22 November	Performance	HCMF, West End Middle School, Cleckheaton, UK
22 November	Performance	HCMF, North Light Gallery, Huddersfield, UK
23 November	Performance	HCMF, Gomersal Middle School, Cleckheaton, UK
23 November	Performance	HCMF, North Light Gallery, Huddersfield, UK
25 November	Performance	HCMF, North Light Gallery, Huddersfield, UK
26 November	Performance	HCMF, North Light Gallery, Huddersfield, UK

2007

20 February	Performance	Analogue Catalogue, Mossley, UK
21 March	Performance	One Year Gallery, Luton, UK
11 May	Publication	*Syd Is Dead*. Pamphlet. Edition of 1000.
23 May	Performance	Work For Work, Royal College of Art, London
24 May	Performance	Fine Art Department, University of Northampton, UK
25 May	Performance	Public Works Group, London

14 June	Publication	*Scores 18 – 76*, a small book by members of The17 with text by Bill Drummond. Edition of 500.
17–24 June	Exhibition	Meltdown, Spirit Level, Royal Festival Hall, London
18 June	Performance	Meltdown, Lillian Baylis School, Kennington Lane, London
19 June	Performance	Meltdown, Woodmansterne Primary, London
20 June	Performance	Meltdown, Clapham Manor Community Primary School, Belmont Rd, London
21 June	Performance	Meltdown, Archbishop Sumner C of E Primary, Reedworth St, London
22 June	Performance	Meltdown, Ashmole Primary School, Ashmole St, London
June	Performance	Meltdown, Violet Room on the Spirit Level, Royal Festival Hall, London
03 July	Recording	Wearhead Primary School, Wearhead, County Durham, UK
04 July	Recording	Broadway Junior School, Sunderland, UK
19 September	Presentation	BBC Scotland, Glasgow, UK
20 September	Performance	Q Gallery, Derby, UK
01 October	Publication	*The Open Window*. Pamphlet. Edition of 2000.
12 November	Performance	Seventeen Gallery, 17 Kingsland Road, London
19 November	Performance	Seventeen Gallery, 17 Kingsland Road, London
21 November	No Music Day	Worldwide
26 November	Performance	Seventeen Gallery, 17 Kingsland Road, London
06 December	Performance	Norwich School of Art & Design, Norwich, UK
03 December	Performance	Seventeen Gallery, 17 Kingsland Road, London

BILL DRUMMOND by year
Last updated 31 December 2007

1953
Born in the Transkei, South Africa,
on 29 April.
Father a Church of Scotland (Presbyterian)
missionary.
One older sister.
Mother teaches in mission school.
One month later (29 May), Tenzing Norgay
(Sherpa Tenzing) conquers Everest.

1954
Learns to speak Xhosa from the schoolgirls
looking after him.
Eats mealies.
Meets a snake in the grass.

1955
Family sail back to British Isles on the
Edinburgh Castle.
Settle in Newton Stewart, Galloway, in rural
south-west Scotland.
Father minister at local Church of Scotland.
They live in the manse.
Does not understand this other language.
Wonders why everybody is white and where
all the black girls have gone. Stops speaking
for six months.
Starts to draw pictures.
Starts to learn this other language.

1956
Lies under the apple tree in the garden and
watches the dappled light dance. Gets taken
to a small river near Newton Stewart called
the Penkiln Burn.
There are bluebells on the bank.
Family adopt stray cat; they call it Tenzing.
Watches his father paint watercolours.

1957
Told he cannot climb on mother's lap because
she is going to have a baby. Brother is born.
Sails to Belfast for first time.
Learns the legend of the Red Hand of Ulster.
Father takes him fishing in the Penkiln Burn;
he falls in.
Climbs the apple tree and takes a bite from an
apple. (It does not taste good. It's a cooker.)
Is discovered dancing naked in front of
wardrobe mirror in his bedroom.
The mirror is removed.

1958
Starts at Penningham Primary.
Learns that Scotland is God's own country.
Father also chaplain at local prison.
At Christmas party for the children of prison
staff, experiences the performance of a skiffle
group whose members are inmates.
Draws pictures.
Climbs other trees.

1959
Sees a Kingfisher fly up the Penkiln Burn.
Teacher wonders if he is disturbed.
Accused of stealing a toy from a classmate;
confronted by teacher; parents called in,
admits to the crime even though he had not
committed it.
Is ill and off school for whole term.
Enjoys the stories in *Struwwelpeter*.
Draws more pictures.
Watches pipe band march past.
Waves at Winston Churchill.
Goes to the fairground and hears rock 'n' roll
music.
Rides the dodgems.

1960
Told he could not have piano lessons until he
learns to read properly.
Climbs Cairnsmore with sister.
Maternal grandfather takes him to the
museum in Norwich Castle; loves the
dioramas of natural history and prehistory
scenes; loves the paintings by the Norwich
School (circa 1803–33).
Lifts log of wood to discover adder coiled
beneath it.
Is caught stealing sweets from Hinton's.

Bill Drummond

Is told by Mrs Hinton – 'That is no way for the son of the manse to behave.'
Listens to his father read *Treasure Island* every night for two weeks.
Hears *Only The Lonely* by Roy Orbison at the fairground.

1961
Listens, watches and falls in love with Elvis Presley at the local picture house.
Climbs lots of trees.
Is put in the backward class.
Goes fishing in the Penkiln Burn as often as possible.
Picks bunch of bluebells from its banks.
Stares into its waters and wonders.
Catches, cooks and eats trout and eels.
Steals apples from other people's gardens.
His father takes him to a small stone circle in the countryside near their home.
His mother tells him about his great-great-uncle, Oliver Tomkins, who went to New Guinea as a missionary and was eaten by cannibals.
Finds New Guinea on map.
Visits Mr McQuirter's workshop. Mr McQuirter is a joiner and his workshop is dark and mysterious place. Drummond loves the swishing sound made as Mr McQuirter planes the wood. He also loves the smell of the wood shavings.
Hears *Halfway To Paradise* by Billy Fury at the fairground.

1962
Finds human skull in graveyard beside the Penkiln Burn.
Marches up the main street of Newton Stewart with the skull on top of a pole.
Hitchhikes to Wigtown.
Returns to Mr McQuirter's workshop on numerous occasions.
Daydreams of fighting alongside Robert the Bruce at Bannockburn.
Is given a pile of old *National Geographic* magazines in which are photographs of tribesmen in New Guinea with strange masks and painted bodies.
Wonders if these are the same tribesmen that ate his great-great-uncle.
Saws wood, hammers nails, and tries to make things.
Finds poems written by his father.
Listens to the sound of the rain on the tin roof of their shed.
Throws his pocket money away in the hedge to see what it feels like to throw money away. Told by his mum to go back and find it. Finds it. Told by his mum to put the money in the missionary box.
Builds tree house.
Sits in tree house smoking a Xhosa pipe, wrapped in his Basuto blanket.
Hears *Telstar* by The Tornados in the ice rink at Ayr.

1963
Climbs Merrick with sister; they get lost in the snow.
Spends week in Belfast. Loves the bright lights and big city.
Father does three month job exchange with minister of First Presbyterian Church, Lexington, North Carolina, USA.
Family sail to New York on the *Queen Elizabeth*.
Drinks Coca Cola for first time.
Takes lift to top of Empire State Building.
Disappointed to not see Marilyn Monroe.
Family takes the train from Grand Central Station down to North Carolina.
Sees black faces again.
Family Buick has radio that plays pop music.
Mum and Dad like *Hello Muddah, Hello Fadduh* by Allan Sherman; he likes *Cinnamon Cinder* by The Pastel Six.
Family visits Washington.
Watches Bobby Kennedy give speech in House of Representatives.
Is disappointed that it is not his brother Jack Kennedy, the President.
Family sail back to British Isles on the *Queen Mary*.
Back at school in Newton Stewart he is no longer backward but still odd.
Climbs a tree hanging over the Penkiln Burn.
Stares down into the water at a large brown trout.
Thinks it is the most beautiful and mysterious

thing in the world.
Wishes he was that brown trout.
Makes things out of wood and metal.
Kills a crow with air rifle.
Climbs Cairnsmore by himself.
Listen to the cry of the Curlew.
Stares out at the far blue yonder and wonders.

Sings in the church choir.
Listens to *Don't Let Me Be Misunderstood* by
The Animals in Mr Grimm's classroom.
Gets first pair of walking boots.
Visits Avebury stone circle for first time
Collects bird's eggs.
Learns to fish in English rivers.

1964
Runs on pitch after match between Queen of
the South and Rangers, where his hero Jim
Baxter pats him on the top of his head.
Passes Cub Scout swimming badge in the
Penkiln Burn.
Family move to Corby in the English East
Midlands.
Corby is a one-industry town. The industry
is steel.
The population of Corby is 85 percent Scots.
There are reasons for this.
A pylon stands at the back of their
council house.
Loves the humming sound the pylon makes
on misty mornings.
Attends Beanfield Secondary Modern. The
teachers are English.
They do not know about Robert the Bruce or
God's own country.
Everybody's mum is listening to Jim Reeves.
Decides not to be a mod or a rocker.
Listens to the rattle of the bottles on the milk
float early in the morning.
Listens to *You Really Got Me* by The Kinks at
friend's house.

1965
Is taught not just to hear but how to listen
to music by Mr Grimm, the school music
teacher.
Mr Grimm makes him sing the first verse
of *Silent Night* solo at school Christmas
carol concert.
Mr Grimm tells them stories about the great
composers; learns how Paganini sold his soul
to the devil in exchange for being the greatest
violinist in the world.
Drummond wonders what he could get in
exchange for his soul.
Is top of the art class.

1966
Is transferred to Kingswood Grammar School
(later a comprehensive school).
Likes maps.
Wants to be a geologist.
Dougie King introduces him to pirate
radio stations.
Dougie King also supports Rangers.
Hears Bob Dylan.
Watches grass snake swim across river.
Bakes his first cake.
Catches a pike.
Becomes friends with Peter McMahon – he
supports Celtic.
Drummond had never got to know a Celtic
supporter before.
Watches clip of Ike and Tina Turner perform
River Deep – Mountain High on BBC TV
programme Top Of The Pops.

1967
Buys his first record, *Strawberry Fields
Forever* by The Beatles.
Listens to it over and over again.
Watches Scotland beat England's World Cup
winning squad, on TV.
Watches Celtic be the first British club to win
the European Cup, on TV.
Dougie King beats him up because
Drummond is pleased that a Scottish team has
won the European Cup.
Believes that The Beatles are the greatest
thing in the world.
Still goes fishing.
Listens to *Good Vibrations* by
The Beach Boys.
Watches Jimi Hendrix on Top Of The Pops
perform *Purple Haze*.

Bill Drummond

1968

Hears Stockhausen on school exchange visit to Germany.

Picks up record sleeve of Live At The Apollo by James Brown and his Famous Flames and wonders what it sounds like.

Forms his first imaginary band.

Considers joining the merchant navy, training as a ships engineer, like his paternal grandfather and great-grandfather.

Buys copy of *The International Times* in Carnaby Street.

Would like to grow his hair long.

Starts to learn to play his sister's acoustic guitar.

Listens to Muddy Waters, Howlin Wolf and Elmore James on Mike Raven's Rhythm & Blues BBC radio show.

Buys his first pair of red tab, button-fly, shrink to fit, Levi 501s.

Goes to folk clubs.

1969

Passes four 'O' Level exams, in Mathematics, Geography, Technical Drawing and Metalwork.

Hears Switched On Bach by Walter Carlos.

Sister sends him 7" white labels from Kingston Jamaica.

Sees The Rolling Stones in Hyde Park.

Is now in four imaginary bands.

Watches Johnny Cash live at San Quentin on the television

Listens to Unhalfbricking by Fairport Convention.

Career advisor advises that he should get an apprenticeship at local steel works.

Goes to Isle of White Pop Festival; watches Bob Dylan perform.

Enthralled by what John Lennon is doing with Yoko Ono.

Thinks The Beatles should announce their end on 31 December.

1970

Asked to leave school by headmaster.

Turns 17 and is into Van Der Graf Generator.

Conversation with another careers advisor:

'What do you like?'

'Music'.

'What do you think you are good at?'

'Making things.'

He is advised to become a musical instrument maker.

To do this, he is told, you first have to do a course in furniture-making, but before you do that you first have to do a foundation course at an art school. He draws some pictures and goes along to the local art school in Northampton. Is accepted but will not start until September.

Visits the Callanish stone circle on Isle of Lewis, for the first time.

Has first tweed suit made in Stornoway.

Gets job in Corby steel works.

Saves £130.

Uses money to buy second-hand Gibson ES-330 guitar from shop in London's Denmark Street.

Gets lift to Iceland on a trawler out of Grimsby with his sister.

Attempts to walk across Iceland from top to bottom.

Fails in the attempt.

Goes to Isle of White Pop Festival; watches Miles Davis, The Doors, Jimi Hendrix and Leonard Cohen. Leonard Cohen was the best.

Goes to art school. Meets Bill Butt and Jim Gregory. Jim Gregory is a greaser and a royalist; he teaches Drummond why art is important and why it is not.

Grows his hair long.

1971

Listens to *Rite Of Spring* by Igor Stravinsky.

Falls in love with the work of Rembrandt, Turner and Degas.

Decides to dedicate his life to painting.

Reads lots of art history books.

Goes to Andy Warhol retrospective at the Tate Gallery (Britain).

Watches Led Zeppelin, Pink Floyd, The Grateful Dead, Frank Zappa.

Thinks David Bowie is boring and decides that rock music is dead.

Bill Butt's parents have a fruit and veg stall on Northampton market.

Learns from Bill Butt that it is presentation that sells.

Jim Gregory plays him and Horace Panter Prince Buster's Greatest Hits.

1972
Commences a three-year fine art course at Liverpool School of Art.
Peter Prendergast, his tutor, tries to teach him to see and not just look.
Peter Prendergast insists Drummond spends eight hours a day, five days a week, doing life drawing.
Decides, after nine weeks, he can no longer cope with the regime so gives up life drawing.
Meets Kev Ward. Kev Ward talks about Andy Warhol.
Visits Jim Gregory at Nottingham Art School where Gregory plays Prince Buster's Greatest Hits to Jerry Dammers.
Buys leather coat from the flea market in Amsterdam.
Listens to A Love Supreme by John Coltrane.
Also listens to Roland Kirk, Pharoah Sanders and others. Does not listen to Miles.
Watches La Vallee, a French film set in New Guinea about a bunch of hippies that go in search of a lost valley. These hippies meet tribesmen that look like those in the *National Geographic*.
Thinks Roxy Music are just art school posers dressing up for the Christmas dance.
Falls ill with pneumonia and pleurisy.
Is in a state of delirium for a number of days.
Thinks he is dying.
Still in love with Elvis.
But in his head he is listening to *Distant Drums* by Jim Reeves.

1973
Health gets better.
But life gets complicated and scary.
Cuts hair for court case.
Is threatened with four years.
Case gets dropped.
But then ...
To explain what got complicated and scary and what the court case was will be explored at a later stage.
Everything changes.
Wanders aimlessly around Liverpool.
Decides that painting is a redundant form.

Decides that Art should use everything.
Decides that Art should be *out there*.
Decides that Art should be unknown, random, incidental, everywhere.
Decides that an Artist should not make status symbols for the rich, that Art should be available for all.
Attends one-day workshop given by Gavin Bryars about the Portsmouth Sinfonia.
Discovers the idea of making music without first being a proficient musician. Goes to the Somali Club too many times.
Dances to *Sex Machine* by James Brown.
Listens to *Clean Up Woman* by Betty Wright.
Reads hundreds of books. Then reads *On The Road* by Jack Kerouac. Hammers in nails, saws wood.
Asked to leave art school by principal.
Reads poetry.
Decides to experience the real world, and as an artist to use whatever medium is to hand.
Realises that pencil and notebook are cheap and easy to have with you at all times.
Realises that paperbacks are cheap to buy and easy to have with you at all times.
Discovers that the means of production between notebook and paperback is a problem.
Meets Bill Harpe; works at the Blackie.
The Blackie is the first artist-led community centre in the world.
It was set up by Bill and Wendy Harpe.
Is taught how to play creative games by Bill Harpe.
Grandfather dies; unable to attend funeral.
Learns that The Wicker Man was filmed in and around Newton Stewart.
Gets job with the Liverpool Corporation as an assistant gardener.
Enjoys the work of Chinn & Chapman.
Listens to *I Love You Love* by Gary Glitter on the radio while digging shrub beds.
Threatens to burn unopened pay packet in front of work colleagues but bottles out.
Runs away from Liverpool.
Climbs mountain.
Starts writing.

Bill Drummond

1974
Works as milkman.
Works as nursing assistant in mental hospital.
Works in steel works (again).
Reads *As I Walked Out One Midsummer Morning* by Laurie Lee.
Goes off to join the revolution in Portugal; hears gunshots in the distance, gets frightened. Runs away.
Works as apprentice trawler man out of Aberdeen during the 'Cod War'; his trawler gets chased by Icelandic gunboat.
Gets frightened. Quits apprenticeship.
Continues writing.
Bill Butt gets him a job in Belgrade Theatre, Coventry, as carpenter.
Learns how to scene paint.
Discovers the work of George Jones.
Listens to Kraftwerk and Toots & The Maytals.

1975
Moves to Devon.
Works as shuttering joiner on the Exeter bypass.
Listens to Hamilton Bohannon.
Watches KC & The Sunshine Band in club in Exeter.
Buys copy of *Stand By Your Man* by Tammy Wynette.
Continues writing.
Leaves Devon.
Tenzing the cat dies. Decides that if he ever feels the need to use a pseudonym he will use Tenzing Scott-Brown in honour of the cat and his paternal grandmother.
Offered job at Everyman Theatre, Liverpool, as master carpenter.
Returns to Liverpool under cover of darkness.
Learns how to design stage sets.
Works with Bill Nighy, Julie Walters, George Costigan, Bernard Hill, Pete Postlethwaite and others.
Watches Dr Feelgood at the Liverpool Stadium.

1976
Meets Peter O'Halligan in Mathew Street who tells him to read *Memories, Dreams, and Reflections* by C. G. Jung.
Is taught by Peter O'Halligan that poetry is not just words on paper but can exist in everything you do.
Becomes lifetime member of the Liverpool School of Language, Music, Dream and Pun.
Gets married. Signs on the dole.
Meets Ken Campbell in Mathew Street who tells him to read *The Illuminatus! Trilogy*.
Gets job as stage set designer with Ken Campbell's Science Fiction Theatre of Liverpool.
Works with Chris Langham, David Rappaport, Jim Broadbent and others.
Is taught how to entertain the idea that anything is possible and how to make that anything happen by Ken Campbell.
Listening to *It Should Have Been Me* by Yvonne Fair.
Sees photo of Johnny Rotten in music paper.
Experiences Lindsay Kemp performing *Salome* at the Roundhouse.
Stops writing.
Rereads the Sermon On The Mount.
Meets Clive Langer, Jayne Casey, Ian Broudie, Paul Rutherford and Holly Johnson in Mathew Street.
Watches The Sex Pistols at new Liverpool club called Eric's run by Roger Eagle in Mathew Street.

1977
Designs stage set for the National Theatre.
Listens to *Love Goes To Building On Fire* by Talking Heads.
Has conversation with Sir John Gielgud about dying.
Designs stage sets for touring theatre companies.
Learns that a bright and successful career lies ahead.
Meets Clive Langer in the Grapes pub, in Mathew St, Liverpool (on 5 May), and is told to dump the bright and successful career that lies ahead and form a band.
Watches The Damned, The Clash, The Stranglers, The Slits, X Ray Spex, The Ramones, The Saints, The Talking Heads and others at Eric's.
Stops designing stage sets for theatre companies.

Still listens to Jim Reeves singing *Distant Drums* in his head.
Forms Big In Japan with Kev Ward.
Writes songs on ES-Gibson 330.
Roger Eagle decides to be the manager of Big In Japan.
Play scores of gigs.
Becomes member of the Ramblers Association.
Reads *A to B and Back Again.*
Everybody talks about Andy Warhol.
Buys Bringing It All Back Home by Bob Dylan.
Elvis dies.
Cries.
Meets Rob Dickins, boss of Warner Brothers Music UK.
Budgie joins Big In Japan.
Kev Ward leaves.
Listens to *I Feel Love* by Donna Summer and Marquee Moon by Television.

1978
Meets Dave Balfe who joins Big In Japan.
Splits Big In Japan.
Forms The Zoo with Dave Balfe.
Discusses art and disco music with Balfe.
Reads *Hawk In The Rain* by Ted Hughes.
Releases records by bands made up of friends and rivals on The Zoo label, including The Teardrop Explodes and Echo & The Bunnymen.
Listens to *You Make Me Feel (Mighty Real)* by Sylvester.

1979
With Dave Balfe, becomes the managers, producers and publishers of these bands.
With Dave Balfe, shares love of girl pop and appreciation of the work of Shadow Morton.
They make girl pop record with Lori Lartey.
Touch by Lori & The Chameleons is record of the week on BBC Radio 1, but only very minor hit.
Tony Wilson of Manchester's Factory Records asks The Zoo to take part in joint venture.
Zoo Meets Factory Halfway – A Music Festival at Leigh.
Nobody comes.
Watches Joy Division as the light drains from the sky.
Needs specs.
Tony Wilson advises them not to sign bands to major record labels down in London.
Sign bands to major record labels down in London, as they are skint and do not have well-paid-day job as TV presenter.
Signs off the dole.
Pete de Freitas joins The Bunnymen.
Gets specs.
Reads *Crow* by Ted Hughes.
Corby, no longer a 'new town', loses its steel industry
Listens to Dusty Springfield's Greatest Hits.

1980
Bill Butt is enlisted to design light shows and direct pop videos for bands.
The Bunnymen teach Drummond about mystery.
Bill Butt reminds Drummond the pair of them are artists and always will be and there is no way out. Feels that he does not need reminding.
Lori & The Chameleons' follow-up, *The Lonely Spy*, is not even a very minor hit.
Is taught how the music industry works by Rob Dickins.
Is taught how to make money out of the music business without selling any records by Seymour Stein. Forgets what he is taught.
Experiences Merce Cunningham dancing to music being made by John Cage at the Everyman Theatre.
Meets Mick Houghton and is taught what PR is and how it works
The bands become successful. Bunnymen debut album reaches 17 in the UK charts.
Matters get complicated.

1981
Gets out of his depth as the bands get even more successful.
Falls in love with the work of the artist Richard Long, who makes his work by walking and doing things on his walks.
Buys maps, and wishes he did what Richard Long did.
Reads more and more poems by Ted Hughes.

Bill Drummond

Identifies with the subject matter of
these poems.
On being asked by a journalist why so much
creativity comes out of Liverpool answers:
> Because there is this interstellar ley line that
> comes in from outer space and hits the earth
> where the Atlantic rift begins in Iceland; its next
> fixed point is Mathew Street in Liverpool; it then
> leaves earth and heads back into outer space from
> New Guinea. Down this interstellar ley line
> surges a creative energy that effects all that get in
> its way

Laughs.
The journalist laughs.
But matters get even more complicated.

1982
Life gets dark and twisted.
Sends Echo & The Bunnymen off to Iceland
for photo-shoot for next album. Releases
album of various recordings titled To The
Shores Of Lake Placid. Claims the music
on this album is taken from a play of the
same name.
The play exists in his head.
Revisits the Callanish stone circle in the
Outer Hebrides.
Wants The Teardrop Explodes to do photo-
shoot for their next album cover in
New Guinea.
First child is born. The mother is not
Drummond's wife.

1983
Billy Fury dies.
Can't pay rent.
Takes up offer from Rob Dickins of three-year
contract to become A&R consultant for WEA
Records in London.
With Dave Balfe signs Strawberry Switchblade
to Zoo Music.
Moves to Buckinghamshire with wife.
Tries to persuade Echo & the Bunnymen that
their forthcoming fourth album, Ocean Rain,
should be their last.
And from now on they should only ever
play live.
And never record again.
Thus, their status as the greatest cult band the
world has ever known will be sealed.

They do not heed his advice.
Stops managing bands.
Inspects the collection at the National Gallery.
Rock music appears to have died.
Matters fall apart and focus is lost.

1984
Has expense account.

1985
Meets artist and musician Mark Manning
(also known as Zodiac Mindwarp), Meets
artist and musician Jimmy Cauty.
Meets artist and designer Cally.
Meets Pete Waterman – he has a machine
called a sampler and an ego.
Mark Manning teaches him about magic.
Peter Waterman teaches him and Jimmy
Cauty how to approach making records in a
completely different way and how a sampler
can help in this.
Jimmy Cauty buys a sampler.
Travels to New Orleans to try and persuade
Pete de Freitas to come home, stop taking
drugs and that the duck is not the most
significant creature in the universe. Fails.
Pete de Freitas has breakdown.
Reads his father's poetry.
With Dave Balfe, signs Zodiac Mindwarp to
Zoo Music Publishing.
Starts thinking about hip hop.
Collects watercolours by the Norwich School.
Second child is born, this time to wife.

1986
Tenzing Norgay dies.
Decides to leave music business to get on
with art, life, writing and climbing mountains.
But first decides to write and record solo
album.
The Man by Bill Drummond released on
Creation Records.
His Gibson ES-330 featured on cover of album
and used to write all songs.
Makes film with Bill Butt – The Manager.
Leaves music business.
Still in love with Elvis.
Starts writing book *Why Andy Warhol Is Shite*.

Listens to Schooly D.
Decides that hip hop is the only music that is
fit for these modern times.
Decides to see if a British version of hip hop
can be created.
Balfe and Drummond sign The Proclaimers to
Zoo Music.
Contacts Jimmy Cauty to make a hip hop
record using his sampler.

1987
On 1 January they start working together as
The Justified Ancients of Mu Mu in order to
make a British hip hop record.
Drummond and Cauty discuss music, art, life
and the way things could be. They decide that
their records and everything else they do
should be released through their made-up
organisation, KLF Communications. People
think that KLF stands for Kopyright Liberation
Front; it doesn't.
They do things.
Lots of things.
The music papers start writing about them.
Drummond co-produces, with Dave Balfe, the
Zodiac Mindwarp & The Love Reactions,
album Tattooed Beat Messiah and the
accompanying hit singles. This is a heavy
rock record and has nothing to do with
hip hop.
Drummond is taught by Jimmy Cauty to
accept the contradictions.
Goes for long walks in the country.
Picks blackberries.
A third child is born.

1988
Stops listening to hip hop and starts listening
to Chicago House music.
Jimmy Cauty and Bill Drummond meet radio
promotions man Scott Piering who teaches
them what music daytime BBC Radio One will
play and what they will not.
Cauty and Drummond decide to use this
knowledge to make a novelty record and to
become one-hit wonders.
Which they do.
Doctorin' the Tardis by The Timelords goes to
number one in the UK.

They write a book – *The Manual (How To
Have A Number One The Easy Way)*.
Acid house dawns.
As The KLF, Cauty and Drummond record
and release the first of their series of five
Pure Trance 12" singles. This is the first time
the word trance is used to define a genre
of modern music.
They play at raves.
Listens to a nightingale singing in a bush just
before dawn.
Roy Orbison dies.
Pete de Freitas is killed in motorcycle
accident.
Drummond attends funeral and cries.

1989
They decide to use the money made from the
novelty hit to make a road movie like Wim
Wenders might.
Bill Butt is enlisted to be the director.
They begin work on the film The White Room
in the Sierra Nevada.
Discover that they are not Wim Wenders.
Bakes cakes. Picks wild damsons to
make jam.
Attends Dave Balfe's wedding in the role of
best man.

1990
Drummond brings together the words 'chill'
and 'out' to be used as the title of the first
album by The KLF.
Chill Out is released.
They describe the music on Chill Out as
ambient house.
Tens of thousands of words describing Chill
Out and its influence are written. Included in
the words are *seminal* and *self-indulgent*.
Sometime after the release of the album he
notices that the words 'chill' and 'out' are
being brought together with a hyphen to form
one word – 'chill-out'.
And the use of this word chill-out is spreading
through culture like a virus.
Cauty and Drummond decide to make a series
of records called the Stadium House Trilogy
which includes version of songs they have
already written called *What Time Is Love, 3AM*

Bill Drummond

Eternal and *Last Train To Trancentral*.
He uses the Gibson ES-330 to co-write all these songs.

1991

The Stadium House Trilogy become worldwide hits. Number ones in dozens of countries.
He is still in an imaginary band that he has been in since 1968. He rips off ideas from this imaginary band to use in The KLF.
They decide to have a Christmas number one, and so enlist the 'First Lady of Country', Miss Tammy Wynette, to provide the lead vocals on a remake of one of the first songs they wrote together, *Justified and Ancient*.
Queen's Freddy Mercury dies.
Justified and Ancient featuring Tammy Wynette only makes it to the number two slot on Christmas Day.
The re-released *Bohemian Rhapsody* by Queen is number one.
But *Justified and Ancient* does go to number one in 18 other countries.
The KLF are officially the biggest-selling band in the world for 1991.
Their album The White Room is a multimillion seller.
Drummond is listening to Bach's The Goldberg Variations as performed by Glenn Gould.

1992

Starts recording The Black Room.
Stops recording The Black Room.
The KLF are nominated in four categories in the UK 'BRIT' awards, and are asked to perform at the awards ceremony.
Drummond is talked out of chopping off his right hand on stage and throwing it into the audience, a reference to the legend behind the Red Hand of Ulster. Instead the KLF slaughter a sheep and do a thrash metal version of their hit *3AM Eternal*, with the help of the band Extreme Noise Terror.
Honoured guest George Solti walks out of the venue in protest at the noise. Solti is the only musician in the audience that Drummond has respect for. Cauty and Drummond use the occasion to announce their retirement from

the music industry.
They leave.
They are given the award for the best British band of the year in their absence.
Drummond is listening to the music of Arvo Pärt.
Life grows dark and twisted again.
He splits up his last remaining imaginary band.
Drummond runs away to Mexico, then heads north and crosses the border at Brownsville.
That night he witnesses a snake swish through the grass away from him. He imagines that it has just left his body.
He returns to the UK.
His marriage disintegrates.
He is listening to George Jones.
Listens to his father preach a sermon.
Drummond lives alone in a two-up, two-down railway cottage in the middle of nowhere, with no telephone, TV, radio or record player.
Starts writing letters to Mark Manning that discuss art, murder, poetry and rape, but not suicide.
Spends too much time on his own.
Buys pickup truck. Picks blackberries.
Manning, Drummond and friend Gimpo set off to the North Pole via Finland, taking with them an icon of Elvis Presley with a plan to place the icon of Elvis at the North Pole in the belief that it will radiate love and happiness down the longitudes and out across the latitudes, thus enabling world peace to break out.
Fail to get to the North Pole. The icon now hangs in the most northerly lighthouse in the world, off the north coast of Norway.
Drummond listens to a blackbird singing from the top of the hedge across the road.

1993

On the night that Cauty and Drummond are burying their BRIT award at Stonehenge they decide to instigate the K Foundation. They have no idea what the K Foundation is for.
The two cloaked and top hatted figures that can be seen lurking in the background of the *Scream* by Munch are to be its trustees, and the bulk of the money earned from The KLF is used as capital.
They believe that the art being produced in

the UK is not dangerous enough.

The first work carried out by the K Foundation is the *1994 K Foundation Award* designed to hold up a dark mirror to the Turner Prize award.

The K Foundation are catapulted onto front pages, achieve art world infamy and are hailed as the champions of those that know fuck all or too much about art.

They try to buy the Rollright stone circle but can't.

Has third tweed suit made in Edinburgh.

Chill-out enters the Oxford English dictionary. As does a new definition of the word Trance – as a musical genre.

Select magazine lists the 100 coolest people in pop. From Elvis Presley to Kurt Cobain, from Johnny Rotten to Robert Plant. From the 100th to the 1st. And in this list they name Bill Drummond as number one, top of the heap, the coolest man in pop.

Drummond listens to the wind.

1994

The K Foundation's second work is the burning of £1,000,000 in fifty-quid notes of their own money, intended to be done in the full blaze of the world's media. The latter part is rejected in favour of a derelict boathouse on the Isle of Jura off the west coast of Scotland.

The act is filmed by Gimpo and witnessed by one journalist, Jim Reid.

They then felt it their duty to their families to come up with a very good reason for doing such a thing.

Discover that there is never a good enough reason and a colleague suggests that they should not try and explain or defend the event but just leave it there for people to make of it what they will:

Witness how some people consider the work to be a con;

Witness how some people consider the work to be a publicity stunt;

Witness how some people consider the work to be a tax dodge;

Witness how some people consider the work to be a lie.

Realises that this one event will continue to cast a dark and long shadow over everything else that he ever does in the future and how all his other work will be judged in its context.

Richard Long walks across Iceland from top to bottom and on the walk he makes a stone circle.

The K Foundation's third work – the only musical piece – is the making of a record that would only be released once world peace had broken out. For this they enlist the Red Army Choir and Orchestra and record them performing a medley of Doris Day's *Que Sera Sera* and John and Yoko's *Happy Christmas (War Is Over)*. The track is entitled K Cera Cera.

Drummond decides that it is the best thing they ever recorded together.

1995

Buys a tower in Cushendall, Northern Ireland. It is called the Curfew Tower. Cushendall is a small town on the Antrim coast. He buys it because he believes that the internet is going to change everything.

And this change is for the good.

Fourth child is born to third mother.

Buys, for $20,000, photography and text work by Richard Long called *A Smell Of Sulphur In The Wind*. And hangs it on bedroom wall. The work depicts the stone circle constructed by the artist while walking across Iceland in 1994. Coincidently it also depicts the spot in Iceland where Drummond and his sister had given up walking across Iceland in 1970.

Goes to watch George Jones perform.

The fourth and final work of the K Foundation was the donating of several thousand cans of Tennent's Super lager to the homeless in London on Christmas Eve.

Drummond is still listening to the work of Arvo Pärt.

1996

Drummond, and Manning's account of them attempting to take their icon of Elvis to the North Pole is published by Penguin Books. Manning expressed that the underlying impulse for their journey was probably not

Bill Drummond

world peace but an attempt to rid them selves
of the lure of rock 'n' roll by dumping Elvis as
far away as possible in the artic wastes, in the
hope that the king would freeze and die.
The book was to be entitled Lighthouse At
The Top Of The World (Book One in the Bad
Wisdom Trilogy).
Penguin publishes it as *Bad Wisdom*.
Drummond & Manning tour a spoken-word
performance of *Bad Wisdom* in the United
States and UK.
Drummond drives through red lights and
writes-off pick-up truck; he is physically
unscathed.
Manning and Drummond believe that they
have sold their souls to the Devil. But cannot
recall when.
Or what they got in return.
They make plans to get their souls back.
With Gimpo, they travel to the heart of the
Dark Continent.
Sail up the River Congo on a barge.
This much is fact.
But on reaching the river's source they
believe they will find the Tree of Knowledge
still standing.
And in its branches, the Serpent still up to
his beguiling tricks, offering bites of apples to
the innocent.
And while Gimpo entertains His Satanic
Majesty, Drummond and Manning will slip
around the back of the tree.
And find where he stashes the souls.
And find theirs.
And nick them back.
They carry out this plan.
Sort of.
They do not know if they actually got their
souls back.
Fifth child is born.
Buys a Land Rover.

1997
Discovers Mark Manning also has imaginary
bands in his head.
Drummond and Manning go to Helsinki and
write and record songs with Finnish groups
and artists. The names of these groups and
artists are The Daytonas, Kristina Bruuk,
Molten Rock, The Blizzard King, Aurora

Borealis, Dracula's Daughter, Gormenghast
and, their favourite, The Fuckers. These
groups and artists only exist in Drummond's
and Manning's collective imagination. But the
songs and recordings are real and are created
with a bunch of Finnish musicians. This is to
be the soundtrack to the book *Bad Wisdom*.
Uses Gibson ES-330 to co-write all songs.
Cally designs record sleeves for these
recordings.
Kalevala Records releases recordings as a
series of 45s.
Each in an edition of 500.
They are also only available on export
from Finland.
Reads the Book Of Psalms.
Drummond is listening to Sibelius.

1998
Returns to the Penkiln Burn; shows two of
his older children where he would like his
ashes scattered.
Reads *Birthday Letters* by Ted Hughes while
on a train between Bombay and Calcutta.
After reading each page he tears it from the
book, folds it into a paper plane and launches
it from the window.
Decides to evolve a way of working that
sidesteps the long shadow cast by previous
works. The main thrust of this plan is to
produce and release work anonymously,
outside of the contexts that music, art and
literature normally rely on, away from
London, at distance from the media.
This proves difficult.
Discovers that the shadow has ways of
turning corners and that his vanity seeks
applause.
Decides that all his future work is to be
released, published, made public, distributed
under the unifying banner of The Penkiln
Burn. This is not the river but something else.
Continues to work with Cally in all aspects of
The Penkiln Burn.
Publishes the first Penkiln Burn Pamphlet.
Tammy Wynette dies.
Drummond is invited to take part in an
exhibition in a house in Belfast.
He responds to the invite by making soup for
40-odd folk who turn up at the house.

Considers the soup-making to be a success. Publishes small book, *From The Shores Of Lake Placid* (Penkiln Burn Book One). The story in this book is also printed on a series of posters that are pasted around Liverpool. These turn out to be the first of dozens of Penkiln Burn Posters to be printed and pasted on walls around Europe.

Realises he no longer has a satisfactory relationship with *A Smell Of Sulphur In The Wind* by Richard Long.

Decides to sell it for the original $20,000.

And take the cash in one-dollar bills to Iceland.

And then to start walking across Iceland from top to bottom.

And bury the cash in the centre of the stone circle.

And take a photo of the now enriched stone circle.

And complete the walk across Iceland.

And hang this new photo on the wall of his bedroom.

All in the hope that his relationship with the work would be reinvigorated.

Drummond turns down an invitation from the Scottish Football Association to write and record the official song for Scotland's World Cup squad.

The Curfew Tower becomes an artist's residency.

Ted Hughes dies.

Drummond starts work on a larger book to be called *45*.

Starts drinking coffee.

Is listening to Creedence Clearwater Revival very loudly.

1999

Continues to write *45*.

Creates his first website: penkilnburn.com. It exists to document the jobs that he has begun working on.

Roger Eagles dies.

Stops reading poetry.

Is persuaded to designs first stage set in over 22 years. The play is called *Cruel Britannia*, written by Johny Brown and stars Tam Dean Burn. He uses the pseudonym Tenzing Scott-Brown in the programme credits. The stage set is made from neon lighting.

Matters appear to be getting dark and twisted again. Starts suffering from strange mental glitches. These recur when the dark and twisted bits start to overload. One of these glitches causes him to have another car accident on Christmas Eve. The other car is a write-off. Both parties are physically unscathed.

2000

45 is published by Little Brown. The blurb on the back – written by Mick Houghton – contains the two following sentences:

He avoids and confronts issues, infuriates and inspires those around him, muses and confuses, creates and destroys. He has maintained a penchant for reckless schemes.

45 reaches number 17 in the *Sunday Times* best-seller list.

Scott Piering dies. Gives address at funeral.

Discovers that the city of Belfast is not twinned with any other foreign city so Drummond twins it with *Your Wildest Dreams* and this is welcomed by the people of Belfast. Instigates the Intercontinental Twinning Association (ITA).

Loathes nostalgia.

Sixth child born.

2001

Drummond has not walked across Iceland or even sold work by Richard Long for $20,000. Decides to cut the work up into 20,000 equal-sized fractions and sell them at a dollar a go. Cally encourages him to consider things.

Jim Baxter dies.

Refers to the work carried out under the name of The Penkiln Burn as *jobs* and not as *works*.

Publishes poems written by his father.

Artist's residency at Curfew Tower continues. Artists from all over the world apply.

Is surprised to learn that his great-great-uncle, Oliver Tomkins, was actually eaten by cannibals in New Guinea on 4 April 1901. Attends centenary memorial service in his honour.

Reads account of Tomkins in book about

Bill Drummond

fellow missionary James Chalmers, who was eaten at the same meal.

Meets artist Tracey Sanders-Wood.

Finds his musical palette jaded.

Refuses to accept that the music of his youth was better than that of today. Wonders what it would be like to hear no music for an entire year.

And then hear it again.

Decides this would not only be impractical but impossible.

Vows to only listen to music that has been recorded in the previous 12 months by bands, soloists, ensembles or composers who have never made or released a recording before.

2002.

God Is Not A Cunt is the proposed title of an exhibition that Drummond is invited to take part in. He considers the title of the exhibition inappropriate as some may consider God to be a cunt.

Influenced by watching Pop Idol on television, sets up two phone lines.

One to phone if you think God is a cunt, the other if you think he isn't.

This job evolves in numerous directions.

One direction is to give away 40 bunches of daffodils to complete strangers. He does this.

He then makes a commitment to give away 40 bunches of daffodils to complete strangers every year for the rest of his life.

How to Be An Artist (Penkiln Burn Book Six) published.

In this book Drummond explores ideas surrounding our relationship with art and the process he has embarked upon with the Richard Long work.

Drummond can no longer resist the urge to start painting again, but first he lays down certain stipulations.

The stipulations are:

No more than 25 paintings – all canvases the same size – 1,910mm X 1,350mm.

Only use acrylic paint.

Palette limited to black, white and the three primary colours.

No mixing.

The subject – text.

The typeface – Trade Gothic Bold Condensed.

These paintings must act as markers signposts or

adverts for his other Penkiln Burn jobs.

Gives *How To Be An Artist* performance / sales pitches at various places around the UK.

Meets John Hirst.

These include drop-in centres, schools, art galleries, prisons and other places. Between 2002 and 2005 he gives 83 of these performance / sales pitches, selling more than 9,000 of the fractions.

Starts to work with John Hirst and takes his consel on how to construct performances and other things.

How To Be An Artist evolves into an exhibition; which later goes on to be exhibited in ten major regional public galleries between 2002 and 2005.

Drummond decides to resume this process at a later date, when all 20,000 fractions will be sold.

Tracey Sanders-Wood shows him some chicken wire and teaches him that all things are connected.

Considers the funerals he has attended over the past years do not work. Responds to this consideration by launching mydeath.net.

In response to the threatened invasion of Iraq, creates card game Silent Protest.

They do not prevent the invasion of Iraq.

Wonders if he could go a month without listening to any music.

Decides this would be impractical and impossible.

Stops drinking coffee.

Considers going on the game for one month at the next Liverpool Biennial at £1,000 a trick. Publishes pamphlet – *You Whore*.

Becomes aware of a weird strange primeval choir of voices that sing in his head when he drives the Land Rover.

Names this choir The17.

Beanfield School Secondary Modern is demolished.

2003

Decides to make The17 a reality.

But.

Does a deal with himself that he will not make The17 a reality until he is 60.

Makes soup in a packed house in Nottingham, a strangely successful event. Instigates the

382

Soupline and writes the following text for a poster:

Take a map of the British Isles. Draw a straight line diagonally across the map so that it cuts through Belfast and Nottingham. If your home is on this line, contact Soupline@penkilnburn.com Arrangements will then be made for Bill Drummond to visit and make one vat of soup for you, your family, and your close friends.

Gives away 40 bunches of daffodils to complete strangers in Milton Keynes. Tries to go a week without hearing any music – he fails.
Has conversation with Seamus Heaney about the Antrim coast in general and The Curfew Tower in particular.
Mark Manning sends him illustrated copy of *The Sermon On The Mount* with a recommendation that he should read it at least once a year.
Twins Hull with Your Darkest Thought.
Creates a poster – it reads:

The Intercontinental Twinning Association (ITA) exists
To twin cities, towns or thoughts.
These twinnings can be random, premeditated or instantaneous.
These twinnings can take the outward appearance of traditional town twinning or not.

Makes film of drive in Land Rover from one end of the M62 (Hull) to the other end of M62 (Liverpool).
Breaks vow to only listen to music released in the past 12 months by artists who have never released an album before by listening to Pet Sounds by The Beach Boys immediately followed by The Byrds Greatest Hits.
Decides that over the next year will only listen to bands, soloists, ensembles or composers whose name or surname begins with B.
And over the next 26 years work his way through the alphabet.

2004
Dougie King dies.
Gives away 40 bunches of daffodils to complete strangers in Lincoln.
Thinks that nobody should make a work of art bigger than themselves.
Inspired by this thought and a ball of blue tack stuck to the dashboard of his Land Rover

launches *The Open Manifesto* at www.openmanifesto.com
Prints new poster, it reads:

The Open Manifesto Exists.
It exists to define what art is and what art is not.
And how art should be made.
And what art is to be used for.
And how it can be discussed.
And what there is to be learnt.
And whom it is for.
It accepts.
Whatever is said today makes redundant what was said yesterday.
What was said ten years ago might be suddenly as fresh as what will be said tomorrow morning.
The Open Manifesto is ongoing, never-ending.
The Open Manifesto needs more.
All new doctrines, dogmas or principles are welcomed for consideration to be added to the Open Manifesto.
Please visit www.openmanifesto.com and make your submission.
WARNING: No jokers, time wasters. Mean what you say even if you fall short of what you proclaim.

Reneges on deal with himself and decides to make The17 real and now.
Enlists 17 men to sing what he hears in his head.
Records them.
Uses the recording to be soundtrack for M62 film.
Twins Kensington, Liverpool with Kensington, London, using the medium of kettles.
Drinks Red Bull.
Launches youwhores.com
Wishes he hadn't.
Tracey Sanders-Wood gets married.
He makes her and groom three-tiered wedding cake.
She is now Tracey Moberly.
Discovers he has painted 25 paintings but still feels the urge to paint more.
Starts painting over already painted canvases.
Is very excited about the The17.
But dumps the M62 film.
Writes the following statement:

All recorded music has run its course. It has all been consumed, traded, downloaded, understood, heard before, sampled, learned, revived, judged and found wanting. Dispense with all previous forms of music and music making and start again. Year zero now.
The17 is a choir. Their music has no history,

follows no traditions, recognises no contemporaries. The17 has many voices. They use no libretto, lyrics or words; no time signatures, rhythm or beats; and have no knowledge of melody, counterpoint or harmony. The17 struggle with the dark and respond to the light.
Is arrested.
Spends night in cell.
Is summoned to court on charge or driving while banned.
Barrister tells him to bring pyjamas, toothbrush and a change of clothes, just in case.
Does not go to prison.
Is given 60 hours' community service.
Goes a day hearing no music.
Moves to Norwich with three youngest children and partner.
Reads *Chronicles* by Bob Dylan.

2005
Does community service digging ditches on the Norfolk Broads.
Thinks long and hard about music while digging ditches.
Decides that now we have arrived at a time where all recorded music from the entire history of recorded music over the past 100 years can be listened to wherever, whenever, while doing whatever we want; our relationship with music is changing in a very fundamental way.
Realises that recorded music will be seen as a medium of the 20th century.
Decides that The17 exists where any group of 17 people gather to make music using their mouths, throats, lungs, ears and mind.
Decides the music of The17 will never be recorded for posterity, never be broadcast on radio, TV or internet, never be commodified for the market place, never be performed for an audience.
Decides that it exists only for the experience of those performing it.
Community service comes to an end.
He enjoyed digging ditches.
Long-term relationship disintegrates.
Heart breaks.
Does not listen to George Jones.
Has vasectomy.
Gives away 40 bunches of daffodils to

complete strangers in Lambeth. Instigates Souplines International in Estonia.
First Curfew Tower Award presented to the artist who has created the 'best' work of art in the previous 12 months.
The 'best' work was voted for by the residents of Cushendall.
Listens to *Push The Button* by the Sugababes.
Constructs first Cake Circle.
The Intercontinental Twinning Association continues, but sees its efforts flag. Goes public with No Music Day on 21 November.
The 22 November is Saint Cecelia's day.
Saint Cecilia is the patron saint of music.
And nomusicday.com is launched.
The Wild Highway by Drummond & Manning published.
The Wild Highway is book two of the *Bad Wisdom Trilogy*.
It is based on their journey up the Congo in 1996.

2006
Russian language version of mydeath.net is launched in Moscow as part of *Death & Desire*, a joint exhibition with Tracey Moberly.
Gives away 40 bunches of daffodils to complete strangers somewhere in Sweden.
Moves to London to be near his younger children.
Website the17.org launched.
The17 perform in Moscow, Oslo, Saint Petersburg, Newcastle, Stockholm, Sete, Huddersfield, Vienna and other places.
Fifty-nine performances in all.
The second Curfew Tower Award is held, voted for and given.
BBC's Most 20 Punk people list Drummond at number 18, one below Quentin Tarantino and one above Tracey Emin.
Spends too much time in the city.
Starts work on a book with working title *17*.
On 21 November, Resonance FM observes No Music Day 2006.
Turns down offer to be housemate on TV series Celebrity Big Brother.
Time heals.

2007
Fails to give away 40 bunches of daffodils to complete strangers anywhere in spring time.
Tony Wilson dies.
Thinks.
Continues work on book to be called *17*.
Cally continues to encourage him to consider things.
Kingfisher flashes past.
Has inspected the collection at the National Gallery every year since 1983.
Third Curfew Tower Award held, voted for and given.
The Open Manifesto remains open and is now available in Arabic, Chinese and Spanish.
Adder crosses his path on the Isle of Wight.
On 21 November, BBC Radio Scotland observes No Music Day 2007.
Still does not smoke and still only drinks in moderation.
Peter Prendergast dies.
Tracey Moberly sends him text messages he can't understand.
Considers what he learnt from Peter Prendergast about seeing and not just looking to be a lifelong learning thing.
Still works with Gimpo and John Hirst.
Decides he would like to stop drinking Red Bull.
Is in regular contact with Jimmy Cauty.
The Gibson ES-330 is still ready and waiting for the call of duty.
Climbs Table Mountain.
Commences writing the final book in the *Bad Wisdom* trilogy with Mark Manning.
His relationship with God is founded on something far more solid than the whimsy of faith.
Has unsettling dreams about managing Echo & The Bunnymen at least once a week.
These dreams are mainly bad and often concern the death of Pete De Freitas.
Is no longer in love with Elvis.
Finds he has long lost the ability to support Rangers.
Would rather Queen of The South had won on that day back in '64.

Consults Dave Balfe regularly.
Admits that other than *the Bible* and the *Guinness Book of British Hit Singles*, *On The Road* by Jack Kerouac is the book that has had more influence on his life than any other.
George Jones is still alive but Drummond has no need of his services at present.
Finishes book called *17*.
Decides to compile a year-by-year biography for media use.
Stockhausen dies.
Attempts to give away 40 bunches of daffodils to complete strangers in Corby, UK, on 20 December.

NOTES
Inventory as at December 2007:

Since the inception of The Penkiln Burn there have to date been:
Three major twinnings,
Four international soup lines built,
11 books published,
20 solo exhibitions mounted,
25 paintings painted,
28 pamphlets published,
29 soup makings,
166 different posters printed,
318 performance / events performed,
322 scores written for The17,
And lots of time taken.

Drummond is concerned there may not be enough time to get everything done before he dies

Post Script.
The above text was based on random notes and snippets of recorded conversation. These were ordered and edited by Cally and should be considered purely subjective in nature.
Drummond hopes that no lies were told, except the one about listening to Glenn Gould's Goldberg Variations in 1991. He has never listened to them in their entirety but wishes he had.
He has wanted to keep the children and women in his life out of this to save them further ...

Bill Drummond

Further Reading to appendix 3:

1953

Transkei
http://en.wikipedia.org/wiki/Transkei

Church of Scotland
http://en.wikipedia.org/wiki/Church_of_Scotla
nd

Tenzing Norgay
http://en.wikipedia.org/wiki/Tenzing_Norgay

1954

Xhosa
http://en.wikipedia.org/wiki/Xhosa

1955

The *Edinburgh Castle*
http://en.wikipedia.org/wiki/Union-
Castle_Line

Newton Stewart
http://en.wikipedia.org/wiki/Newton_Stewart

Manse
http://en.wikipedia.org/wiki/Manse

1957

Belfast
http://en.wikipedia.org/wiki/Belfast

Red Hand of Ulster
http://en.wikipedia.org/wiki/Red_Hand_of_
Ulster

Norwich School
http://en.wikipedia.org/wiki/Norwich_school

1959

Stuwwelpeter
http://en.wikipedia.org/wiki/Struwwelpeter

1960

Cairnsmore
http://en.wikipedia.org/wiki/Cairnsmore_of_F
leet

Adder coiled
http://www.bbc.co.uk/arts/apictureofbritain/g
allery/shortlist/single/england_north_rural_3.
shtml

Son of the manse
http://news.bbc.co.uk/1/hi/programmes/the_
westminster_hour/3471191.stm

Treasure Island
http://en.wikipedia.org/wiki/Treasure_Island

Only The Lonely
http://en.wikipedia.org/wiki/Only_The_
Lonely

1961

Half Way To Paradise
http://en.wikipedia.org/wiki/Billy_Fury

1962

Robert the Bruce
http://en.wikipedia.org/wiki/Robert_I_of_Scotl
and

Basuto
http://en.wikipedia.org/wiki/Basotho

The Tornados
http://en.wikipedia.org/wiki/The_Tornados

1963

Merrick
http://en.wikipedia.org/wiki/Merrick,_Gallow
ay

Lexington
http://en.wikipedia.org/wiki/Lexington,_Nort
h_Carolina

The *Queen Elizabeth*
http://en.wikipedia.org/wiki/RMS_Queen_Eliz
abeth

Grand Central Station
http://en.wikipedia.org/wiki/Grand_Central_T
erminal

Hello Muddah, Hello Fadduh
http://en.wikipedia.org/wiki/Hello_Muddah,_
Hello_Fadduh

The *Queen Mary*
http://en.wikipedia.org/wiki/RMS_Queen_Mar
y

Curlew
http://www.birdsofbritain.co.uk/bird-
guide/curlew.asp+Curlew+bird+british&hl=en
&ct=clnk&cd=2&gl=uk

1964

Queen of the South
http://en.wikipedia.org/wiki/Queen_of_the_So
uth_F.C.

Rangers
http://en.wikipedia.org/wiki/Rangers_F.C.

Jim Baxter
http://en.wikipedia.org/wiki/Jim_Baxter

Corby
http://en.wikipedia.org/wiki/Corby

Jim Reeves
http://en.wikipedia.org/wiki/Jim_Reeves

You Really Got Me
http://en.wikipedia.org/wiki/You_Really_Got_
Me

1965

Paganini
http://en.wikipedia.org/wiki/Niccolò_Paganini

Don't Let Me Be Misunderstood
http://en.wikipedia.org/wiki/Don't_Let_Me_B
e_Misunderstood

Avebury
http://en.wikipedia.org/wiki/Avebury

1966

Celtic
http://en.wikipedia.org/wiki/Celtic_F.C.

grass snake swim
http://www.treknature.com/gallery/Europe/U
nited_Kingdom/photo19237.htm

River Deep Mountain High
http://en.wikipedia.org/wiki/River_Deep_-
_Mountain_High

Top Of The Pops
http://en.wikipedia.org/wiki/Top_of_the_Pops

1967

Strawberry Fields Forever
http://en.wikipedia.org/wiki/Strawberry_Field
s_Forever

Good Vibrations
http://en.wikipedia.org/wiki/Good_Vibrations

Purple Haze
http://en.wikipedia.org/wiki/Purple_Haze

1968

Stockhausen
http://en.wikipedia.org/wiki/Karlheinz_Stock
hausen

Live At The Apollo
http://en.wikipedia.org/wiki/Live_at_the_Apol
lo_%281963_album%29

The *International Times*
http://en.wikipedia.org/wiki/International_Ti
mes

Mike Raven
http://www.imdb.com/name/nm0265631/bio

Folk clubs
http://en.wikipedia.org/wiki/Folk_clubs+%22f
olk+clubs%22+britain+wikipedia&hl=en&ct=c
lnk&cd=1&gl=uk

1969

Switched-On Bach
http://en.wikipedia.org/wiki/Switched-
On_Bach

Stones in the Park
http://www.bbc.co.uk/bbcfour/features/rock-
docs/stones-in-the-
park.shtml+%22Stones+in+the+park%22&hl=
en&ct=clnk&cd=2&gl=uk

Live at San Quentin
http://en.wikipedia.org/wiki/At_San_Quentin

Unhalfbricking
http://en.wikipedia.org/wiki/Unhalfbricking

Isle of Wight Festival 1969
http://en.wikipedia.org/wiki/Isle_of_Wight_Fe
stival_1969

1970

Van Der Graf Generator
http://en.wikipedia.org/wiki/Van_der_Graaf_
Generator

Callanish Stones
http://en.wikipedia.org/wiki/Callanish_stone_
circle
Gibson ES-330
http://en.wikipedia.org/wiki/Gibson_ES-330

Isle of Wight Festival 1970
http://en.wikipedia.org/wiki/Isle_of_Wight_Fe
stival_1970

1971

Rite Of Spring
http://en.wikipedia.org/wiki/The_Rite_of_Spri
ng

Prince Buster
http://en.wikipedia.org/wiki/Prince_Buster

Horace Panter
http://en.wikipedia.org/wiki/Horace_Panter

1972

Peter Prendergast
http://en.wikipedia.org/wiki/Peter_Prenderga
st_%28artist%29
http://www.welshartsarchive.org.uk/galleries/
peter_prendergast.htm

Jerry Dammers
http://en.wikipedia.org/wiki/Jerry_Dammers

A Love Supreme by John Coltrane
http://en.wikipedia.org/wiki/A_Love_Supreme

La Vallee
http://en.wikipedia.org/wiki/La_Vallée_(film)

1973

Gavin Bryars
http://en.wikipedia.org/wiki/Gavin_Bryars

Portsmouth Sinfonia
http://en.wikipedia.org/wiki/Portsmouth_Sinf
onia

Betty Wright
http://en.wikipedia.org/wiki/Betty_Wright

On The Road
http://en.wikipedia.org/wiki/On_the_Road

Bill Harpe
http://www.theblackie.org.uk/biography.htm+
%22Bill+Harpe%22&hl=en&ct=clnk&cd=1&gl
=uk

The Wicker Man
http://en.wikipedia.org/wiki/The_Wicker_Ma
n

1974

As I Walked Out One Midsummer Morning
http://en.wikipedia.org/wiki/As_I_Walked_Out
_One_Midsummer_Morning

Portuguese Revolution
http://en.wikipedia.org/wiki/Carnation_Revol
ution+portugal+revolution+wikipedia&hl=en&
ct=clnk&cd=1&gl=uk

The Cod War
http://www.kwintessential.co.uk/articles/artic
le/Iceland/Cod-War-in-Iceland/527

George Jones
http://en.wikipedia.org/wiki/George_Jones

Toots & The Maytals
http://en.wikipedia.org/wiki/Toots_&_the_Ma
ytals

1975

Hamilton Bohannon
http://en.wikipedia.org/wiki/Hamilton_Bohan
non

KC & The Sunshine Band
http://en.wikipedia.org/wiki/KC_and_the_Sun
shine_Band

Stand By Your Man
http://en.wikipedia.org/wiki/Stand_by_Your_
Man

Everyman Theatre, Liverpool
http://en.wikipedia.org/wiki/Everyman_Theat
re

Dr Feelgood
http://en.wikipedia.org/wiki/Dr._Feelgood_(b
and)

1976

Memories, Dreams and Reflections
http://en.wikipedia.org/wiki/Memories,_Drea
ms,_Reflections

Liverpool School of Language, Music, Dream
& Pun
&
Peter O'Halligan
http://www.guardian.co.uk/g2/story/0,,201764
7,00.html#article_continue

Ken Campbell
http://en.wikipedia.org/wiki/Ken_Campbell_(
actor)

David Rappaport
http://en.wikipedia.org/wiki/David_Rappaport

Lindsay Kemp
http://en.wikipedia.org/wiki/Lindsay_Kemp

Clive Langer
http://en.wikipedia.org/wiki/Clive_Langer

Eric's
http://www.bbc.co.uk/liverpool/content/articl
es/2004/08/31/culture_music_erics_feature.sh
tml+%22Eric's%22+liverpool&hl=en&ct=clnk
&cd=4&gl=uk

1977

Big In Japan
http://en.wikipedia.org/wiki/Big_in_Japan

Rob Dickins
http://www.lboro.ac.uk/service/publicity/degr
ee_days/degree_2002/dickens.html+%22Rob+
dickins%22&hl=en&ct=clnk&cd=1&gl=uk

1978

Dave Balfe
http://en.wikipedia.org/wiki/David_Balfe

Ted Hughes
http://en.wikipedia.org/wiki/Ted_Hughes

The Teardrop Explodes
http://en.wikipedia.org/wiki/The_Teardrop_E
xplodes

Echo & The Bunnymen
http://en.wikipedia.org/wiki/Echo_and_the_B
unnymen

1979

Shadow Morton
http://en.wikipedia.org/wiki/Shadow_Morton

Zoo Meets Factory Halfway
http://www.cerysmaticfactory.info/fac15.html+
.+Zoo+Meets+Factory+Halfway+-+A+Music+F
estival+at+Leigh&hl=en&ct=clnk&cd=1&gl=uk

Joy Division
http://en.wikipedia.org/wiki/Joy_Division

1980

Seymour Stein
http://en.wikipedia.org/wiki/Seymour_Stein

Merce Cunningham
http://en.wikipedia.org/wiki/Merce_Cunningh
am

John Cage
http://en.wikipedia.org/wiki/John_Cage

1981

Richard Long
http://en.wikipedia.org/wiki/Richard_Long_%
28artist%29

1983

Strawberry Switchblade
http://en.wikipedia.org/wiki/Strawberry_Switc
hblade

Ocean Rain
http://en.wikipedia.org/wiki/Ocean_Rain

1985

Zodiac Mindwarp
http://en.wikipedia.org/wiki/Mark_Manning

Jimmy Cauty
http://en.wikipedia.org/wiki/Jimmy_Cauty

Cally
http://www.nickdrake.com/Cally_Q_and_A.ht
ml

Pete Waterman
http://en.wikipedia.org/wiki/Pete_Waterman

1986

The Man
http://en.wikipedia.org/wiki/The_Man_(albu
m)

The Proclaimers
http://en.wikipedia.org/wiki/The_Proclaimers

1987

Justified Ancients of Mu Mu & The KLF
http://en.wikipedia.org/wiki/The_KLF

1988

Doctorin' the Tardis
http://en.wikipedia.org/wiki/Doctorin'_the_Ta
rdis

*The Manual (How to have a number one the
easy way)*
http://en.wikipedia.org/wiki/The_Manual

Trance music
http://en.wikipedia.org/wiki/Trance_music
1990

Chill Out
http://en.wikipedia.org/wiki/Chill_Out

chill-out
http://en.wikipedia.org/wiki/Chill_out_music

1991

The White Room
http://en.wikipedia.org/wiki/The_White_Roo
m

Tammy Wynette
http://en.wikipedia.org/wiki/Tammy_Wynette

Justified and Ancient
http://en.wikipedia.org/wiki/Justified_and_An
cient

Glenn Gould
http://en.wikipedia.org/wiki/Glenn_Gould

1992

The Black Room
http://en.wikipedia.org/wiki/The_Black_Room
+%22Bad+Wisdom%22+wikipedia&hl=en&ct=
clnk&cd=1&gl=uk

BRIT Awards
http://en.wikipedia.org/wiki/BRIT_Awards#19
92

Extreme Noise Terror
http://en.wikipedia.org/wiki/Extreme_Noise_
Terror

George Solti
http://en.wikipedia.org/wiki/Georg_Solti

Gimpo
http://en.wikipedia.org/wiki/Alan_Goodrick_(
Gimpo)

1993

Stonehenge
http://en.wikipedia.org/wiki/Stonehenge

The K Foundation
http://en.wikipedia.org/wiki/K_Foundation

The Scream
http://en.wikipedia.org/wiki/The_Scream

The Turner Prize
http://en.wikipedia.org/wiki/Turner_Prize

Rollright Stones
http://en.wikipedia.org/wiki/Rollright_Stones

1994

Watch the K Foundation Burn a Million Quid
http://en.wikipedia.org/wiki/The_K_Foundati
on_burn_a_million_quid

K Cera Cera
http://en.wikipedia.org/wiki/K_Cera_Cera

Arvo Part
http://en.wikipedia.org/wiki/Arvo_Pärt

1995

The Curfew Tower
http://freespace.virgin.net/hearth.nireland/To
wer.html+%22The+Curfew+Tower%22&hl=en
&ct=clnk&cd=6&gl=uk

1996

Bad Wisdom
http://www.amazon.co.uk/Bad-Wisdom-
Lighthouse-Top-World/dp/customer-
reviews/184068108X

1997

Kalevala Records
http://www.probe-
records.com/KALEVALA/page.html

Bill Drummond

1998

Birthday Letters
http://en.wikipedia.org/wiki/Birthday_Letters

The Penkiln Burn
http://www.penkiln-burn.com/

In You We Trust
http://www.penkiln-burn.com/highlights/stay_there/stay_there.html

1999

Roger Eagles dies (obit)
http://www.guardian.co.uk/obituaries/story/0,,296703,00.html

2000

45
http://en.wikipedia.org/wiki/45_(book)

2001

James Chalmers/Oliver Tomkins
http://www.wholesomewords.org/missions/bchalmer2.html

Jim Baxter dies (obit)
http://news.independent.co.uk/people/obituaries/article35189.ece

Vows to only listen to music that has been recorded in the previous 12 months by bands, soloists, ensembles or composers who have never made or released a recording before.
http://www.the17.org/score.php?score=319

2002

Is God A Cunt?
http://www.penkiln-burn.com/highlights/is_god/is_god.html

40 Bunches Of Daffodils
http://www.penkiln-burn.com/highlights/daffodils/daffodils.html

Tracey Sanders-Wood
http://www.sanderswood.com/index.html

How To Be An Artist
http://www.penkiln-burn.com/highlights/fs_smellof/fs_smellof.html

25 Paintings
http://www.penkiln-burn.com/highlights/twentyfive/twentyfive.html
You Whore
http://www.penkiln-burn.com/highlights/whore/whore.html

Soup
http://www.penkiln-burn.com/highlights/soup/soup.html

2003

http://www.the17.org/score.php?score=320

2004

Dougie King dies (obit)
http://www.northantset.co.uk/evening-telegraph/Radio-stars-pay-tribute-to.776376.jp+%22Dougie+King%22+DJ+Corby&hl=en&ct=clnk&cd=1&gl=uk

Chronicles by Bob Dylan
http://en.wikipedia.org/wiki/Chronicles,_Vol._1

2005

Norfolk Broads
http://en.wikipedia.org/wiki/The_Broads

Soup Lines International
http://www.penkiln-burn.com/highlights/construct/construct.html

No Music Day
http://www.the17.org/words/44.htm

Saint Cecilia
http://en.wikipedia.org/wiki/Saint_Cecilia

The Wild Highway
http://www.amazon.co.uk/Wild-Highway-Bill-
Drummond/dp/customer-reviews/1840681160

2006

The17
http://www.the17.org/words/45.htm

2007

Peter Prendergast dies (obit)
http://www.guardian.co.uk/obituaries/story/0,
,1995745,00.html

BBC Radio Scotland observes No Music Day
http://www.bbc.co.uk/scotland/music/events/
no_music_day/index.shtml

Stockhausen dies (obit)
http://music.guardian.co.uk/obituaries/story/0
,,2224081,00.html

Bill Drummond

ACKNOWLEDGEMENTS

All of the following people helped to make the
PERFORMANCES, EXHIBITIONS and EVENTS
by, for or about The17 between November 2003 and the end of 2007 happen.

Kev Reverb, Rob Vom, Gimpo, Cat Ledger, John Baker, Karen Reilly,
Jay Barsby, Owen Bevan, Andrew McDonnell, David Lloyd, Rob Howe,
Dave Balfe, Aaron Moore, Robin McGinley, Carita Boklund, Nik Rose,
Clive Keable, Lucy Whetstone, Bluebell Drummond, Gwilly Edmondez, Dan
Hewitt, Stuart Copeland, Ben Ponton, Lee Callaghan, Grainne Sweeney,
David Fry, Lorna Fulton, Simon Cullen, Fiona Lockwood, John McCabe, Liz
Gill, Kathryn at Weirhead, Graham McKenzie, Heidi Johnson, Will Mace,
James Saunders, Alexey Glukhov, Lyudmila Dmitieva, Nadya Bakuradze,
Frode Markhus, Nadia Capitaine, Jonas Stampe, Tom Hodgkinson, John
Davies, Sarah Dean, Ronita Dutta, Robert Jelinek, Eva Kuntschner, Louise
Clements, Jane Twigg, Mick Houghton, James Drummond, Robert Barry,
Eric from Stockholm, David Hoyland, Glenn Max, Jarvis Cocker, Julia
Lawrence, Stella MacPherson, Jane Twigg, Jack Jackson, Maija Handover,
Robert Sollis, Rasmus Spanggaard Troelsen, Mia Frostner, Paul Tisdell, Flint
Drummond, Andreas Lang, Stein Rønning, Tracey Moberly, Gordon Ross,
David McGuinness, Jackie Lancaster, Rob Cotter, Julie McLarnon, Frances
Cotter, John Harper, John Purser, Bar Purser, Susan Stenger, Dennis
McNulty, Maoliosa Boyle, Tiger Drummond, Simon Petherick, Charlie Myall,
Melanie Robb, Ed Baxter, Muslim Alim, Sushil Dade, Jeff Zycinski, Alan
Dunn, Marie Wennersten, Yuri Suzuki, Daniel Padden, Laurence Coleman,
Seva Gakkel, Andy Eastwood, Neil Cooper, Claudia Marzendrfer, Nik
Mummer, Stewart Home, Adam Peters, Paul Smith, Paul Pieroni, Mike
Chavez-Dawson, Phil Hargreaves, Simon Mills, Lyndon Jones, Ian Siegal,
Akins Agbeni.

Paul Morley's text appears with kind permission in the chapter On The Sofa, and was taken
from his sleeve notes for the album NORTH BY NORTH WEST: Liverpool & Manchester from
Punk to Post-Punk & Beyond 1976 – 1983. The album was released on Korova Records in 2006
and was also compiled by Paul Morley.

For
Will, Mac, Les & Pete

CREDITS

Rosa Ainley – Editor
Cally – Designer (www.antar.cc)
John Hirst – Guidance
Gavin Bush – Webmaster
Beautiful Books - Publishers

Mia Frostner, Robert Sollis, Paul Tisdell and Rasmus Troelsen who provided the ongoing critique, graduated from the Royal College of Art, London in 2007 and now jointly run Europa
http://www.europaeuropa.co.uk/

Penkiln Burn Book Nine 2008

www.penkilnburn.com

BEAUTIFULBOOKS

www.beautiful-books.co.uk

Beautiful Books Limited
36-38 Glasshouse Street
London W1B 5DL

ISBN 9781905636266

9 8 7 6 5 4 3 2 1

Afterword

BOLLOCK NAKED
9 March 2008

> Even youths grow tired and weary
> And young men stumble and fall
> But those who hope in the Lord
> Will renew their strength
> They will soar on wings like eagles
> They will run and not grow weary
> They will walk and not be feint.
>
> Isaiah 40:28 – 31

Nearly midnight. Sitting crossed-legged and bollock-naked on the double-bed of a bland, could-be-anywhere hotel room. The bed and the floor are strewn with 483 sheets of A4 paper. The sheets of paper have print on one side and blankness on the other. On the print side are hundreds of scrawled notes in red ink.

Inbetween my legs is an open copy of the Gideon's Bible. The quote above is on the page open in front of me. A storm is brewing outside. The wind is causing a branch to worry the windowpanes. Last night's news warned of storms heading across the Atlantic; we were to batten down the hatches in readiness for it hitting our shores some time tonight.

The 483 sheets of A4 is the manuscript of this book as printed out this morning.

I'm knackered, done in, confused, but alive. The effect of the three now-empty cans of Red Bull is wearing off. That said, I am tempted to change that quote above to read 'But those who drink three cans of Red Bull ...' but I won't. For much of the past day I was convinced I would be dead by now. Not 'cause the punishment was capital or the disease terminal or even that Johnny Suicide had come a-calling, but because I was overcome with a sensation that on my drive north my part in a fatal accident would render me one of the statistics for the day, The fatal accident, wherever it was, didn't involve me, so I'm sitting here, weary and tired, and looking in the pages of the Gideon's Bible for some words of uplift. Over the years, when staying alone in hotel rooms, reading the Gideon's Bible has been a habit of mine. Me and Rocky Raccoon.

Last night, back at my place, I was sitting on the sofa with my two youngest,

397

Bill Drummond

Flint and Tiger, watching The Harder They Come, the early 1970s Jamaican cult film. I'd never seen it before. Flint fell asleep; Tiger got bored and went on her MySpace. It may not be the greatest of films, but I was transfixed. Watching the progress of Jimmy Cliff – starring as Ivanhoe Martin – from poor naïve country boy to Jamaica's most wanted with a soundtrack of some of that island's greatest music was well worth the two hours of life invested. From first hearing *007* by Desmond Dekker back in June 1967 to the day before the release of Bob Marley's Catch A Fire album in 1973, reggae had a special place in my heart and in my record collection. Once it was decided that Bob Marley could be marketed to a worldwide album-buying audience it was over, the golden age was gone, but that's another story.

It was while sitting on the sofa listening to Jimmy Cliff singing *Many Rivers to Cross* that I suddenly remembered it was 8 March, as in the day before today, 9 March, as in two years to the day of this book starting. A year late but the right date.

So I made a decision. Tomorrow (as in today, the day that I wrote this) after taking Flint to his football match, watching him play, cheering his side on, taking him back home, I will head up the Great North Road (remember, the A1) one more time to the Scotch Corner Hotel and do what I had originally planned to do, but a year later. Go through the whole lot and see if it can be wrestled into any sort of shape.

Sod knows what started it. Maybe watching The Harder They Come, but it was while lying in bed last night that this whole sense of imminent death started taking over. This morning all these thoughts were suppressed as I got on with parental responsibilities, but as soon as they were done and I was heading up the Holloway Road in a northerly direction they swept over me again. The perfect ending to the book – my death. It would be like Otis Redding dying just before the release of *Sittin' On The Dock Of The Bay*. Instead of doing the responsible thing of turning around and heading back home, I texted John Hirst – 'if I die could you ask John Davies in Liverpool to take my funeral' – nothing else, no explanation. He knew nothing of my planned journey up the A1 to Scotch Corner.

There was / is / will be a small bird skimming across fields and over hedgerows heading north and further north, and he has been for several days now. No stopping, no rest, no crisis of confidence. He has been travelling from southern Africa all the way up, skirting the Kalahari, over the mighty Congo, traversing the Sahara in one night, across the Straits of Gibraltar, up the

Iberian peninsula, then France, the Channel, up and over the White Cliffs of Dover, the Downs and on. And for the past 20 years I've seen him on the same day, 15 March. Of course it is not the same Swallow that I see each time. But for me when I catch a glimpse of that Swallow, as fleeting as the moment is, something leaps with joy inside me. He is back, the circle is complete. Life continues, all is not lost. The chance of it always falling on 15 March must be slim, but it always has been. Mind you, all his brothers and sisters and distant cousins will be arriving within a few days of each other. With climate change and global warming I understand they've been getting to Blighty a bit earlier each year. But for me it has always been the same mid-March day.

The text for the rest of this trip up the A1 insists on the present tense.

The sky is clearing while the sun sinks as I head out of London and up through the fields of Hertfordshire. Daffodils are out in force. They wave at me so I wave back. Make mental note to get my annual daffodil-giving done in the next week if I survive this drive.

Since 2003 Drummond has been giving away 40 bunches of daffodils to complete strangers each spring. The following text appears on **Make A Commitment** (Penkiln Burn Poster 80) - *Make A Commitment to give away 40 bunches of daffodils to 40 total strangers every spring for the rest of your life. If you discover a reason for making this commitment, please send it to daffodils@penkiln-burn.com* WARNING: *Offering bunches of daffodils to total strangers may prompt them to be suspicious of you. Ignore their suspicions.*

My attention wanders from the road in front and the traffic around me to those fields and hedgerows of Herts. I hope the stranglehold of the 15th will be broken this year, that things will be different and I catch a glimpse of that Swallow six days early. The sun is sinking, its last rays turn the virgin white of the Blackthorn blossom a pinky gold. Darkness falls. No chance to see the Swallow now.

Pull in at the Baldock service station to fill up with diesel. Flick through the limited CD rack, hoping to find a Dylan or Miles Davies album. I'm listening to Ds this year. If I'm going to die tonight, it may as well happen while listening to a couple of the undisputed.

No Dylan or Miles. Fuck it. Who the fuck cares what I listen to? I leave clutching a Best of James Brown, a Best of Johnny Cash and the Beach Boys' Pet Sounds. Each for under a fiver. I load these three CDs along with one by John Coltrane, an Avro Pärt and a Moondog collection that have been littering up the Land Rover for some years. The CD cartridge holds six.

Back into the traffic. I flick the switch and bang – full volume, the might of the opening horn riff from *Papa's Got A Brand New Bag* sends a bolt of life force through every vein and nerve in my body. Instantly I am charged to the max, alive. James Brown is dead but I'm still fucking alive and if ever there is a moment to die, it is now while listening to James Brown exalting us all to 'get up off of that thang'. And just as the truck that is overtaking me does not glance my wing mirror causing me to lose control and bring everything to a crashing end things align. I notice a slither-thin new moon low in the north-west portion of the clear sky. I love a new moon. As much as a fat full moon commands our attention with its majesty and power, you know it is already beginning to wane as you watch, its power draining. But a new moon has all its life ahead.

And up ahead there is a bend to the left in the road. From my vantage point in the inside lane I can see the side of the Tempsford Bridge me and James will be crossing. It is an old one, built from limestone. It has three arches. The central arch has a prominent keystone. The bridge is crossing the Great Ouse a mile or so south of the Black Cat roundabout. Instantly there are three voices inside my head. The first is James Brown who is exalting me this time to 'take it to the bridge'. Second is the voice of Robert Burns reciting lines from his most celebrated of narrative poems – Tam O'Shanter. And I am Tam on my poor mare Meg, desperately trying to make the keystone of the bridge over the River Doon before the witches and warlocks get me. And if you're like Tam and me, you will know that witches and warlocks cannot cross over a river. Make the keystone and you are free. And I quote from the words in my head:

> Now, do thy speedy-utmost, Meg,
> And win the key-stone o' the brig,
> There, at them thou thy tail may toss,
> A running stream they dare na cross.

And just as I make the keystone of the Tempsford Bridge over the Great Ouse in the Land Rover and James Brown makes it to the bridge of *Papa's Got A Brand New Bag*, I'm suddenly Jimmy Cliff in character as the hapless Ivanhoe Martin singing *Many Rivers To Cross*.

And before I even ask how many more rivers to cross, before I make Scotch Corner, I know. The answer is nine – the Nene, the Welland, the Trent, the Don, the Aire, the Warfe, the Nidd, the Ure and the Swale. And yes, I know about the other smaller brooks and streams, but for the telling of this story I will leave them out. If the Pennines form the backbone of this land, those rivers are its ribs. And I have to cross them all before I make the Corner. Each of those rivers holds a story or at least a moment in my life. Way before the

Israelites crossed the Jordan or Hindus bathed in the Ganges man will have been projecting powers and properties onto rivers, way beyond the rational.

For me it must have begun at the age of three or four when my parents took us for walks along the banks of the Penkiln Burn above Minnigaff in Galloway. I was eight years old before I first started to stare from a vantage point on the bank or from an ovehanging branch down into the clear waters of the Penkiln. For me, another universe was within those waters, a mystical and magical one. One I have never tired of and it has continued to feed my imagination down through the decades. I'm surprised that Jimmy and I never did a river song. Using the Congo as the main motif in *The Wild Highway* that Mark Manning and I wrote, went no way to sate this urge. My life can be measured with my relationships with different brooks, steams, burns and rivers. No wonder I want my ashes scattered on one.

But back to those rivers that are being crossed on this new moon night and the stories they hold for me. I will not be able to stop myself from telling some of them here and now. I will start with the Ouse, the Great one, not to be confused with the one that runs into the Humber.

Forget the Carp – as far as I am concerned the Chub is the king of the coarse fish; the Dace may be the dashing prince but the Chub is regal and strong, not lazy and fat like the Carp.

It was on the banks of the Ouse near Huntington, on an early summer's day, that I watched my homemade float bob once, twice, thrice and then sink. I struck. It took a few minutes to land but what I had on the grass was the finest-looking and undoubtedly largest Chub I had ever seen, let alone caught. The hook removed, I immediately returned him to the water. He disappeared into the murky depths of his kingdom. That was one of the most perfect days of my life, utter communion with that other world.

James Brown is now singing *Try Me*. This dates from before he had invented funk and was still singing with his Famous Flames. No man before or since has been able to beseech in song with as much conviction and longing as James Brown. His yearning in this short song with minimal lyrics is boundless.

The Great North crosses the River Nene at Wansford. On a winter's day in early 1966 I caught the bus from Corby to Oundle, a few miles upriver from Wansford, for a day's Pike fishing. The live bait was caught and hooked up to entice those sharks of the fresh water, the ultimate predator. The wait was not long before I saw that fat red float being dragged upstream against the current. On striking, my quarry took off and it took some time before I had him on the land. He was my first Pike, not that big for a Pike, no more than 30 inches long. But every one of those inches pure and beautiful killing machine. I knew Pike flesh to be sweet and succulent; I left him to die on the bank so I could take him home and cut him into steaks and fry.

The day wore on. Nothing else was caught. The Pike was too big to fit in my fishing basket, so for the one-hour bus ride home I kept him hidden under my coat. Didn't want to disturb any fellow passengers.

Back at home I filled the washroom sink with cold water; it was a big sink for washing clothes in. I placed him in the sink to clean him before cutting him up. My mother came through to see what I had caught for tea. What she saw and I saw was a Pike beginning to move; its gills were breathing and within seconds he was attempting to swim. This fish had been out of the water for over nine hours but here he was alive in the sink of our washroom. Were we witnessing the Resurrection? Had the Word been made fish? If any creature deserved to live, it was this one, but we lived miles from any river. My mother decided we should fill the galvanised baby bath we still had, put the Pike in it and she would drive it and me back to the Nene. We drove the 14 miles to Oundle. We crossed the field to the riverbank and in the blackness I returned Him to his waters. With a flash and a splash he was gone.

But it's the opening strings of *It's A Man's Man's Man's World* – the unsurpassed original, nothing like the version I described in the Pete Waterman chapter. How does music get this good?

> Man made the trains to carry heavy loads
> Man made electric light to take us out of the dark
> Man made the boat for the water, like Noah made the ark.

Eight rivers to go. Cross the border from the old Soke of Peterborough into Lincolnshire by Stamford. And it's over the bridge across the Welland. It is a moderate river compared to the Ouse and the Nene but in my own myth it is as dark and dangerous as the Congo. And this is for one reason alone. And yet again it was fishing, my boyhood method of communing with the other world, that brought it on. I can't recall what year it was but it must have been autumn as I remember collecting a big bag of mushrooms from the field, and not those so-called magic kind.

Not much was biting, nothing for an hour or so. Then the float sunk without a trace. I struck and I was against the fiercest fight I had ever had. After ten minutes I was all for cutting the line and being done with it. Let it be the one that got away. I wish I had. Another seven minutes passed before the monster was on the bank. An Eel over four feet long and as thick as my wrist. I had it by the neck in my left hand while I was using my right to try and remove the hook from its mouth. Its teeth were sharp and he was soon drawing blood from my fingers. His body was writhing and twisting around my left arm. He was getting the better of me but the hook was not free. In the basket there was a small camping axe. I took the axe and still holding the Eel by its neck in my left hand I held it to the ground and took a swing of the axe. His head came clean off but still its body writhed and contorted.

Now anybody who has killed an Eel will know that the nerves in its body will continue to cause it to flick and twitch for up to an hour after it has been killed, however brutal its death has been. But this monster seemed possessed. From the grassy bank it made its headless way back into the Welland and was gone. Of course it was just accident that caused it to tumble back into the river but I can never cross the Welland without thinking of it teeming with headless Eels.

The life cycle of the Eel remained a mystery for thousands of years. Nobody knew where they came from or where they went, let alone how they bred. Only in the past 100 years have we learnt that it is in the becalmed waters of the Sargasso Sea that they return to mate, give birth and die. The new baby Eels (elvers) take three years to cross the Atlantic to get to the rivers and streams of Europe.

And as we heave on by the Ram-Jam Inn with its tales of highwaymen and robbers, James Brown is all done, his mission complete. It is now the singular vision of Johnny Cash that fills the Land Rover cab at maximum volume.

> I keep a close watch on this heart of mine
> I keep my eyes wide open all the time

Johnny entered my life in the early summer of 1969. It was the Live at San Quentin film on Granada TV that got me and he has never let go since.

> How high's the water Mama?
> 'Three feet high and rising ...'

The Trent is a mighty river, but it's a river I have never developed a relationship with. As for its tributary the Dove, I have returned to it time and time again over the years. I first fell for the Dove via the pages of that other bible - Izaak Walton's *Complete Angler* (1653). While walking its banks one spring morning I found myself standing and staring into its waters, hoping to spy a Grayling. What I saw was a strange bird walking along the river bottom, some three feet from the surface. Birds don't walk the bottom of rivers, so was this another miracle I was witnessing? I later learnt it was a Dipper and they make a habit of such behaviour.

But I shot a man in Reno just to watch him die ...

By now I can feel all my senses mingling and my mind beginning to open. A perfect day with the king of coarse fish: a Pike that resurrects; witches and warlocks on my tail; headless Eels; autumn fields full of mushrooms; and a slither of a new moon pulling the tide of life. The rail-track rhythm of *Folsom Prison Blues*. Dick Turpin riding past on Black Bess. Trucks ploughing by with Polish number plates. And then:

> BANG
> Wouldn't it be nice if we were older?

And as we cut through Sherwood Forest, Will Scarlet and Little John jump on board and start singing along with The Beach Boys and me.

> If You should ever leave me
> Though life would still go on, believe me
> The world could show nothing to me
> So what good would living do me?
> God only knows what I'd be without You.

And over the border into Yorkshire. Make the bridge across the Don just in time for Coltrane's A Love Supreme, the greatest modern jazz album ever recorded. Jimmy Garrison on bass, Elvin Jones on drums and Coltrane blowing his horn out front. Sod everything I have said in this book to date, how could music this good ever be redundant? 'The whole canon of recorded music that has been stockpiled over these past 110 years is going rotten, rapidly losing any meaning for anybody.' What rubbish, what was I thinking? This is the way to listen to music.

I can still hear The Beach Boys singing and the moon is sharp and pure. Hang on, how can The Beach Boys still be singing? Maybe they have joined The17 in my head along with James Brown and Johnny Cash and Robert Burns, all of them singing together with John Coltrane. Higher and higher we take it. And we cross in turn the Aire, the Warfe, the Nidd and the Ure. Each keystone taken, each river crossed, we beat one coven of witches and warlocks hot on our tail only to find others gathering to give chase. Will Scarlet and Little John are up on the roof rack of the Land Rover, clutching their long bows and firing arrows in the direction of eldritch cries behind. But none can catch The17 as we keep heading north to the next bridge and that bit closer to the Corner. And even Desmond Dekker and his Aces have joined in singing *007*, over the top of everything else.

From Coltrane to Arvo Pärt's *Berliner Messe*. I don't know what the fuck they are singing and don't care, but we are all singing along except Coltrane who is still blowing his horn. The Avro Pärt CD is breaking up after about 15 minutes just as Timmy Thomas joins us with *Why Can't We Live Together?* And over the Swale, the last of the rivers, where I once saw a dead lamb being swept down on the spring flood.

The sixth of the CDs in the cartridge is Moondog – the Viking of Sixth Avenue. Not much time left, so I skip to the closing track on the album; it is the epic *Invocation*. If you don't know Moondog, life would be so much richer if you did. The massed ranks of The17 are with Moondog all the way on this track. A recording you never want to end. A tune that has inspired me to write a score for The17, to be performed in any land that has an east coast and a west coast. The track pumps and pushes and pumps again. The JBs brass section joining in, Elvin Jones on drums, me banging the steering wheel of the Land Rover. Even Jacqueline Du Pré is in there somewhere with her cello. And in the rear-view mirror I can see the headless Eels gaining on us.

But just as Moondog's *Invocation* is reaching its climax, we make Scotch Corner roundabout. We pull into the hotel car park and the Land Rover comes to a grinding and shuddering halt. The engine is switched off. All falls quiet. The last of the voices I can hear is that of Robert Burns reciting his own lines:

> But pleasures are like poppies spread
> You seize the flower and its bloom is shed,
> Or like the snow falls in the river
> A moment white then melts forever.

I climb out, somewhat unsteady on my feet, but not dead. Wander into the hotel. Check in. Find my room. Make a pot of tea and get down to work.

So sitting here naked and knackered I've read most of the book. Not in any particular order and much of it I've just skimmed. I begin to question the motives behind everything I have written. For a start I know that recorded music is not about to fizzle out, become a creative dead end, just as folk didn't get bored with the printed word after a century or so of printing presses churning out books. We will want the printed word as long as we want to make sense of the mystery of life. We will use recorded music for just as long or maybe even longer. Like one of the students said, 'He uses his own naïve idealism as an engine to create work.' And just for the record, the voices of the Robert, Rasmus and Paul – other than the removal of one line for reasons of third-party sensitivities – have not been edited. Mia read the book too but decided not to make her thoughts known.

The above admissions do not mean I will not explore the idea of The17 for the rest of my life (now that I'm not already dead). The manhole cover score is scheduled to be done in Birmingham before this book is published; a new score called *REPEAT* is to be performed this summer with 100 groups of 17s across Derby; and then the score about five different places of worship is to be performed in Derry, N. Ireland; then it's off to Berlin to do one there; and then the big one, the one inspired by Moondog, the coast-to-coast one is going to start from Kitty Hawk in North Carolina and go all the way to the Pacific Ocean.

As for the gauntlet that I flung at your feet in the opening chapter, pick it up and prove me right or wrong. The choice is yours.

The End.

SCORE

318. CONSIDER

Chose a country with an east coast and a west coast.
Take a map of that country and draw a horizontal line across the map.

Go to the point on the east coast of the country where the line begins.
Stand on the shoreline beating out a steady beat on a big bass drum.
Record yourself beating this beat for 17 minutes.

Travel across the country keeping as close to the line as possible.
Document the crossing as you stop at 15 points on the line and
gather 17 people together who are willing to perform a sound in unison for 17 minutes.

A sound made using voices, implements or found objects,
A sound that compliments and can be combined with those already recorded on the crossing.
A sound that may not be constant and may evolve.
A sound you record.

At the point where the line reaches the sea on the west coast of the country,
Stand on the shoreline beating out the same steady beat on a big bass drum.
Record yourself beating this beat for the 17 minutes.

Combine and balance all 17 of the recordings so they can be played simultaneously.

Send out invitations to all of those members of The17 who took part in the performances across
the country, asking them to meet at a given time and location on the line.
Play them back the combined and balanced recordings,
using a substantial public address system.

Delete all recordings.
Consider which country you might chose next.

pb Poster 158   2007

ALTERNATIVE ENDING
10 March 2008

Job done. Having that shit took somewhat longer than I thought. I feel unblocked, refreshed, cleaned out. Time to head for home. The weather is miserable. Pissing down. Climb back in the Land Rover. Notice an unopened envelope on the back seat; it had arrived sometime in the last couple of weeks. I open it, a CD. It's a Volcano The Bear album. I put it on. Turn the engine over and get in gear. Pull around the roundabout and head out into the southbound carriageway of the A1. From the corner of my left eye I notice a Swallow skim over the hedge. All I need now is to hear in my head the creak of a door opening into a room where I've never been before.

Accept
The contradictions
Inherent in much of this book
And all you imagine The17 to be about
By instigating a performance of one of the scores.

Or

Instigate
The creation of
An entirely different form of music
That the world is yet to hear.
This music may be diametrically opposed
To everything you imagine The17 to be about

The Beginning